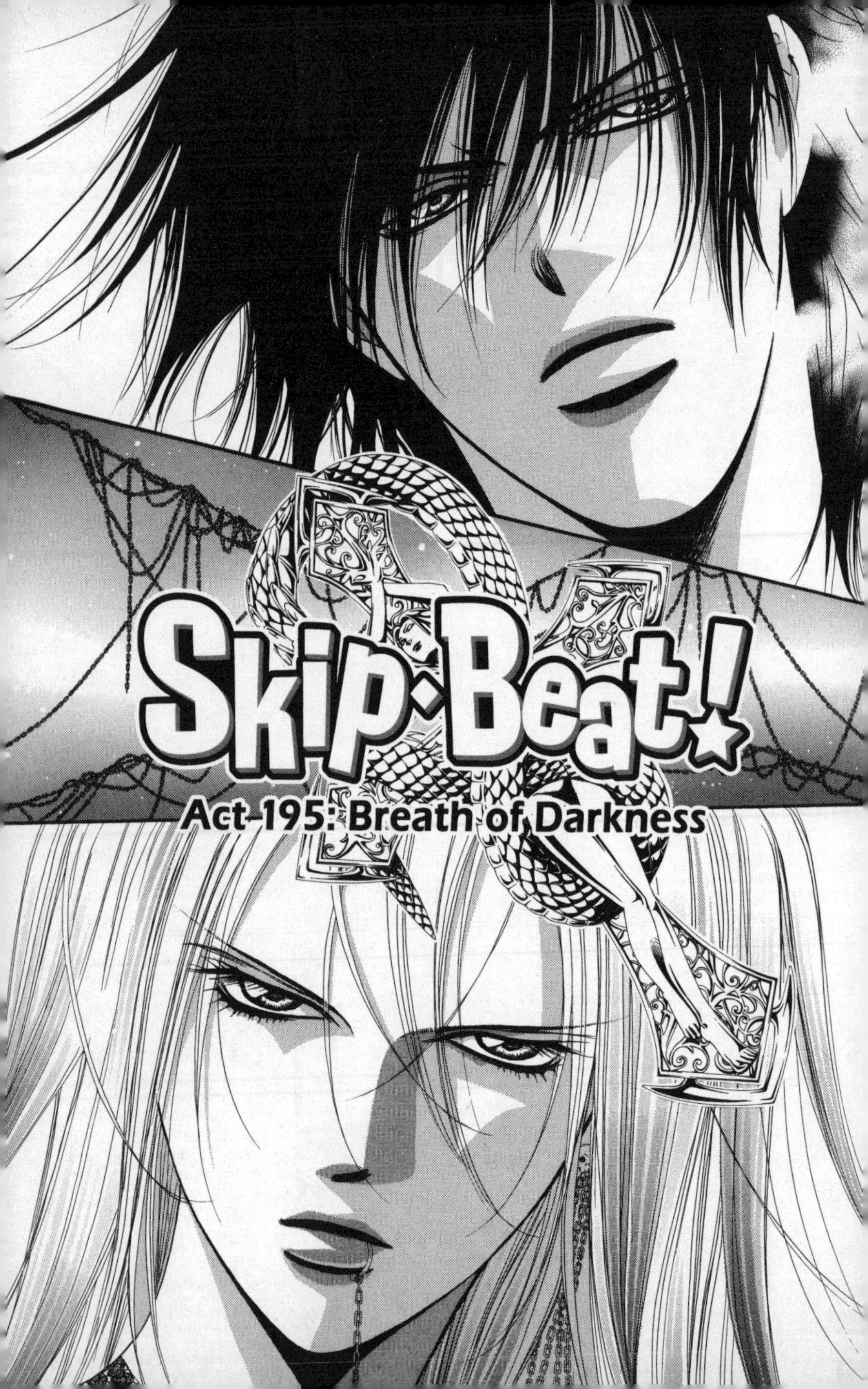
Skip·Beat!
Act 195: Breath of Darkness

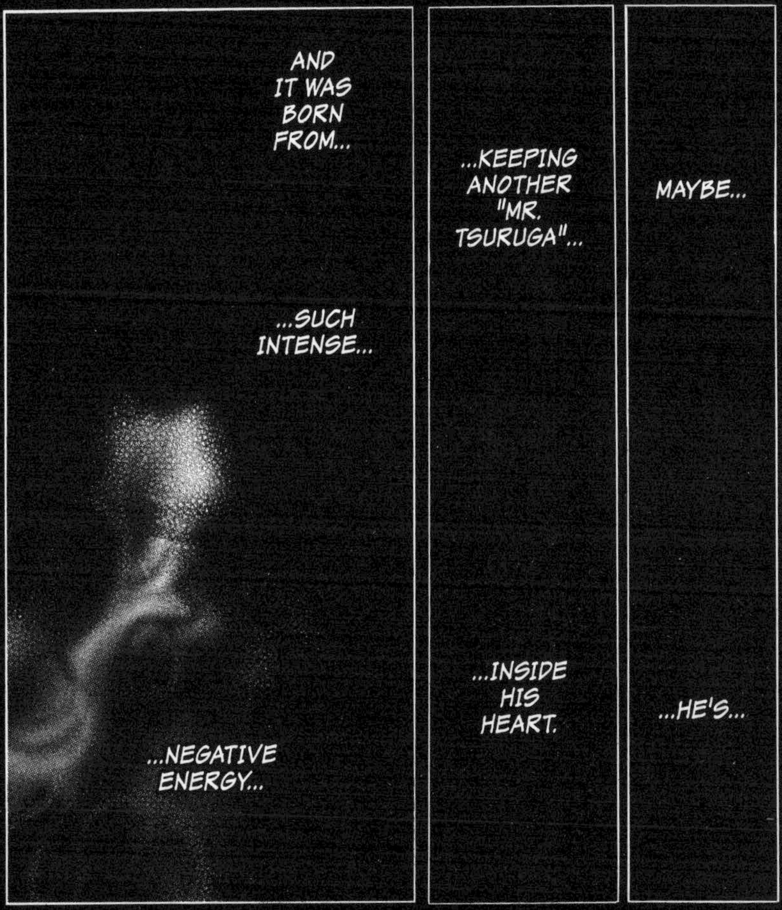
MAYBE...
...HE'S...
...KEEPING ANOTHER "MR. TSURUGA"...
...INSIDE HIS HEART.
AND IT WAS BORN FROM...
...SUCH INTENSE...
...NEGATIVE ENERGY...

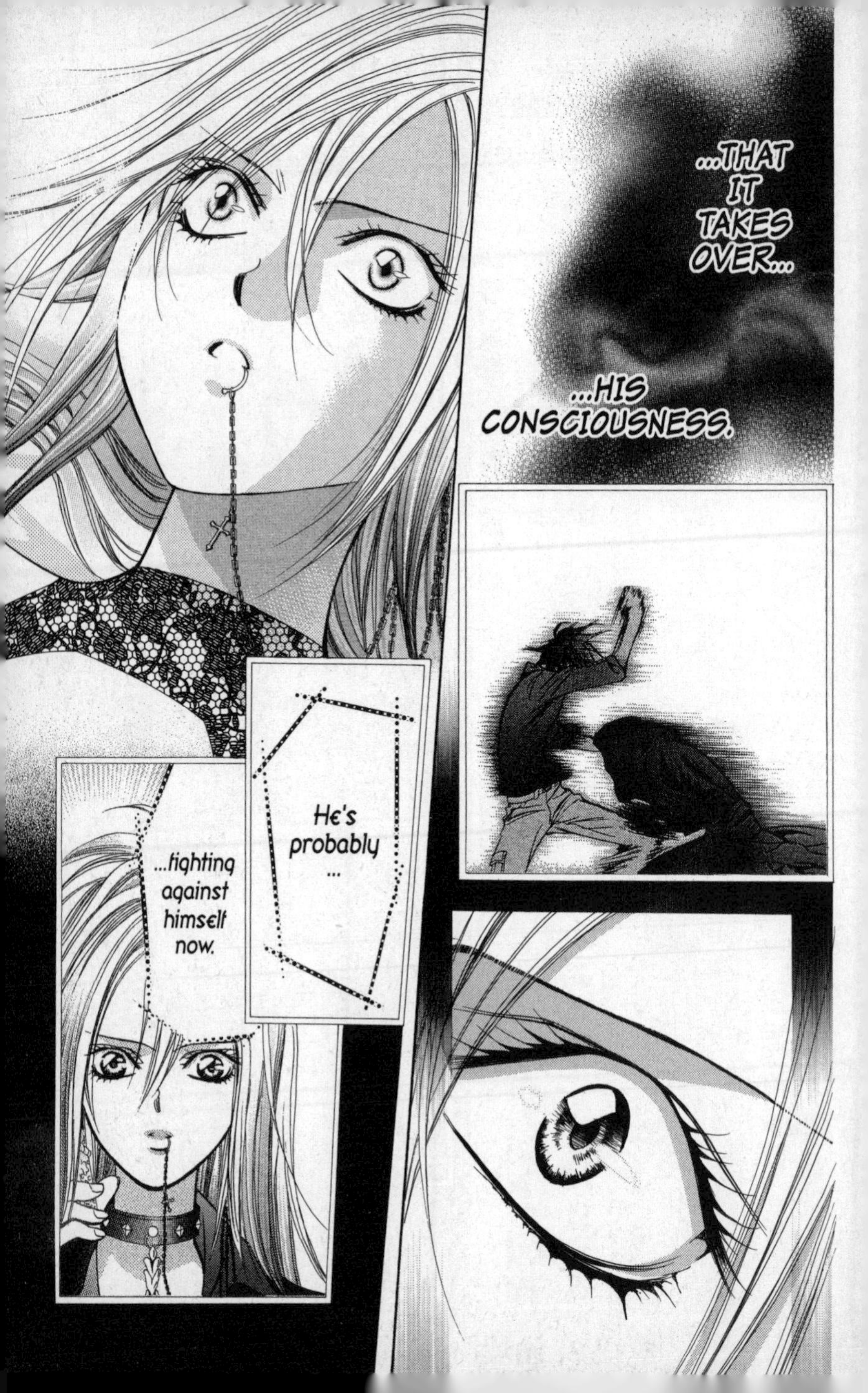
...THAT IT TAKES OVER...
...HIS CONSCIOUSNESS.
He's probably ...
...fighting against himself now.

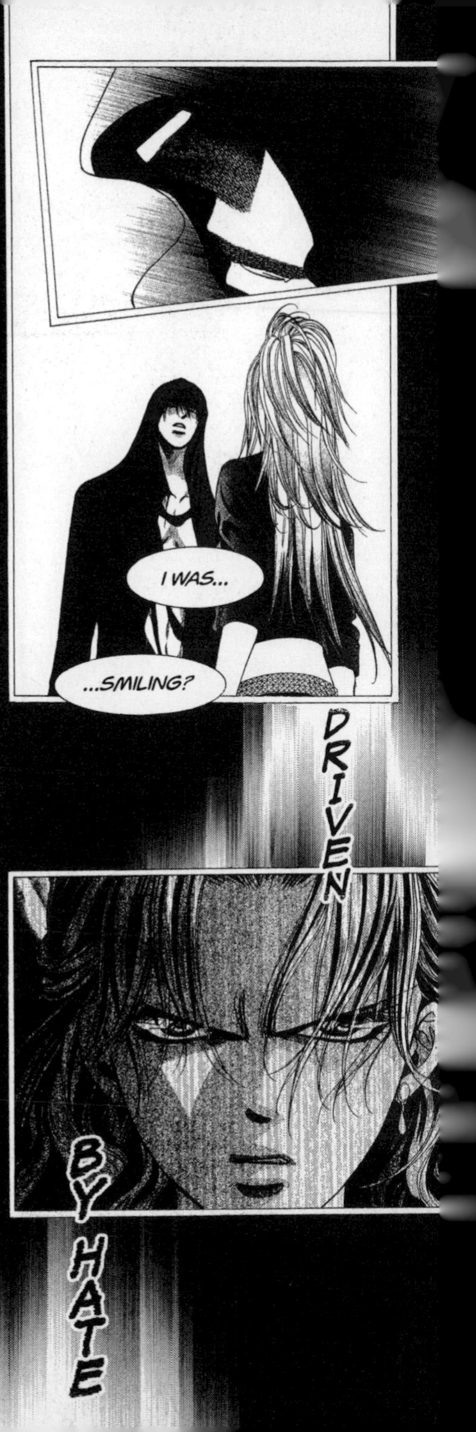
I WAS...
...SMILING?
DRIVEN
BY HATE

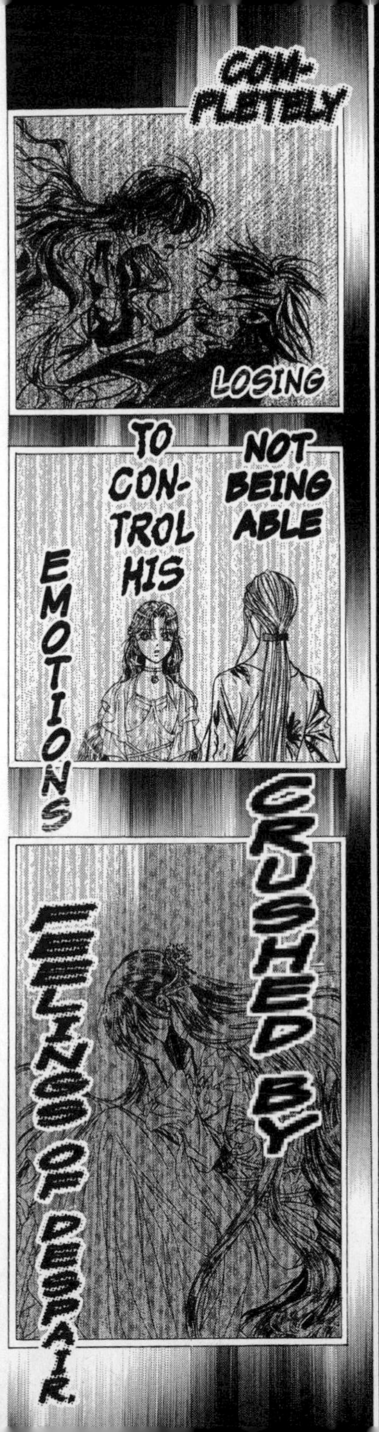
COM-PLETELY
LOSING
NOT BEING ABLE
TO CON-TROL HIS
EMOTIONS
CRUSHED BY
FEELINGS OF DESPAIR.

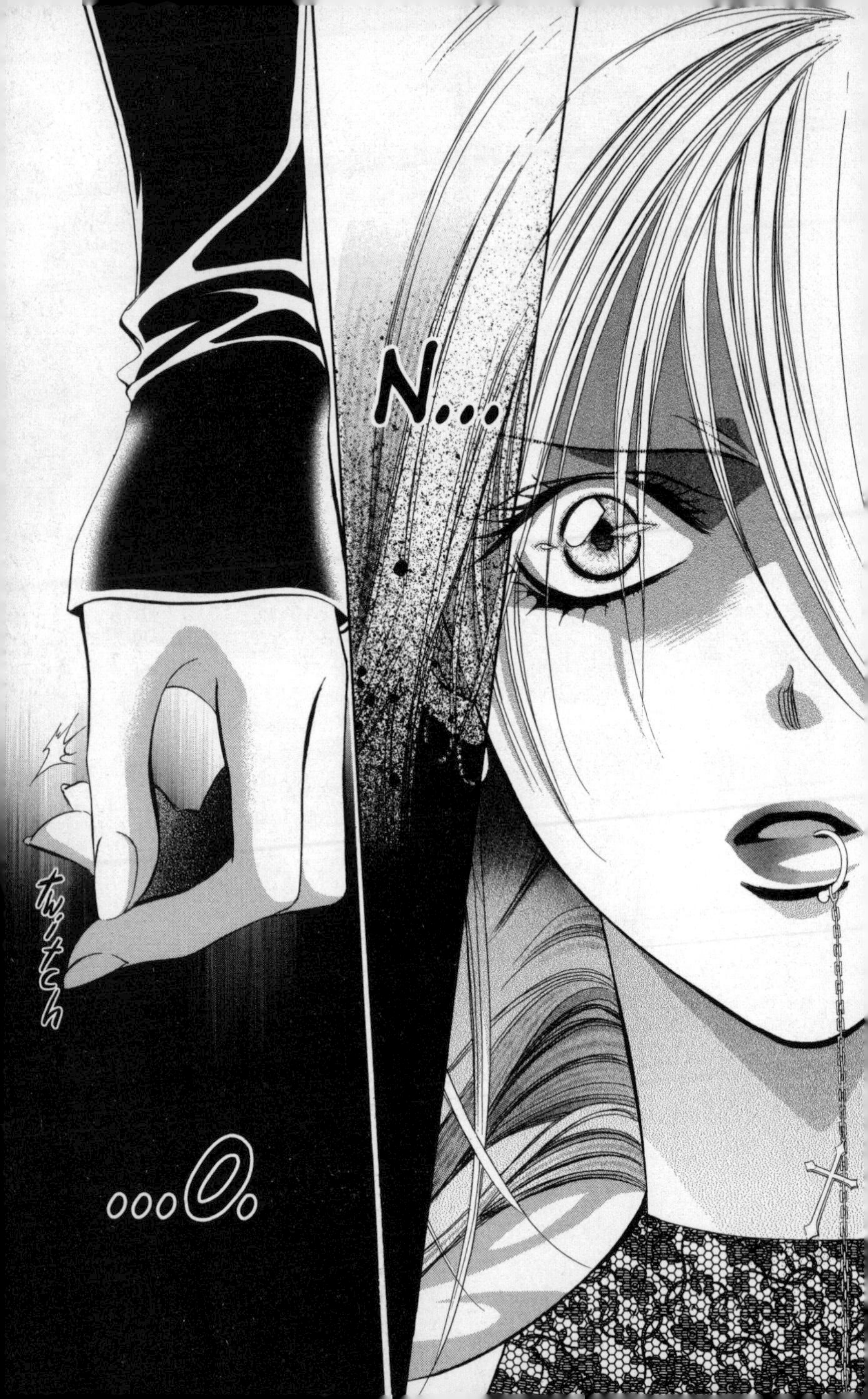
N...
twitch
...O.

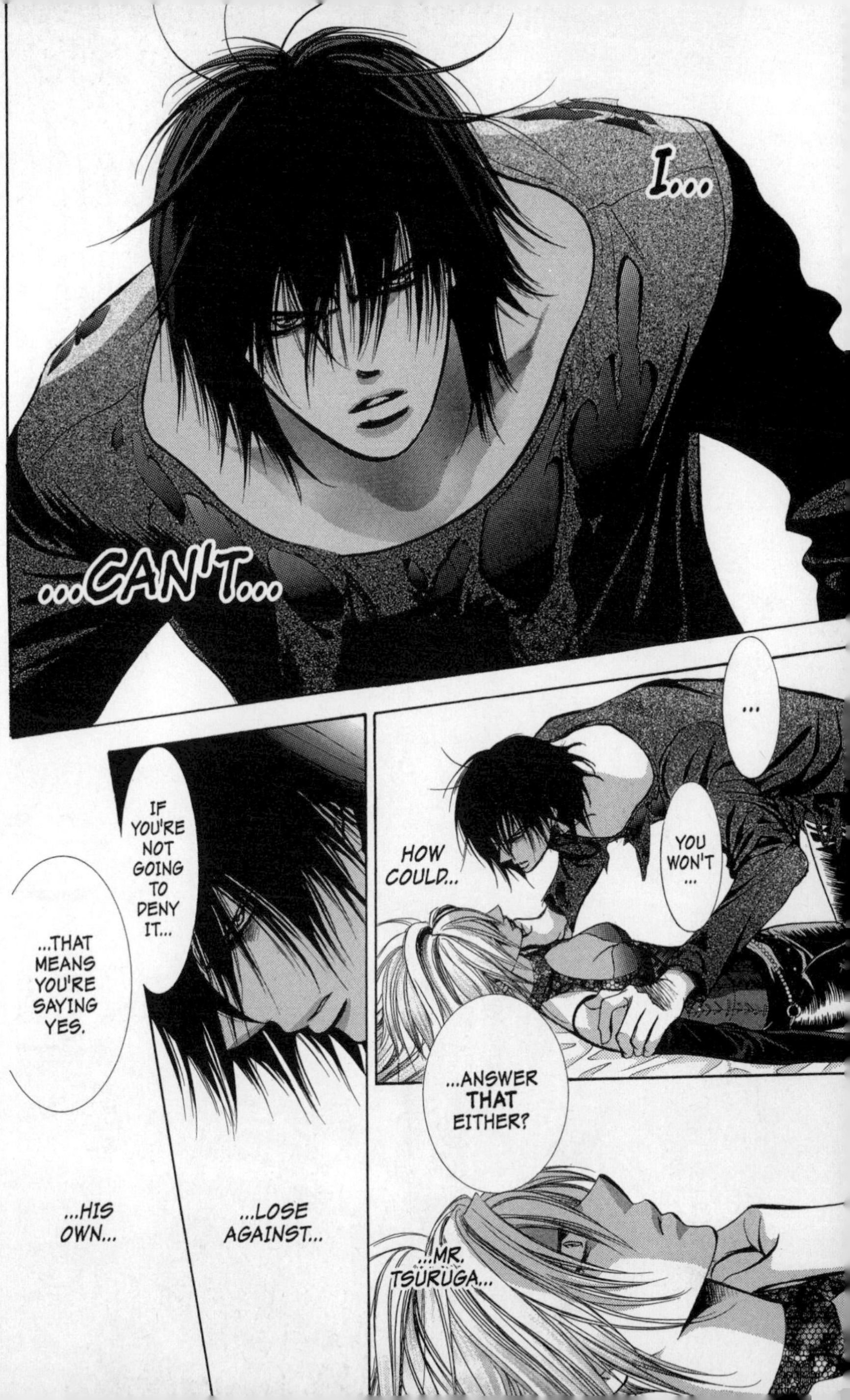
I...
...CAN'T...
...
YOU WON'T ...
HOW COULD...
...ANSWER THAT EITHER?
IF YOU'RE NOT GOING TO DENY IT...
...THAT MEANS YOU'RE SAYING YES.
...MR. TSURUGA...
...LOSE AGAINST...
...HIS OWN...

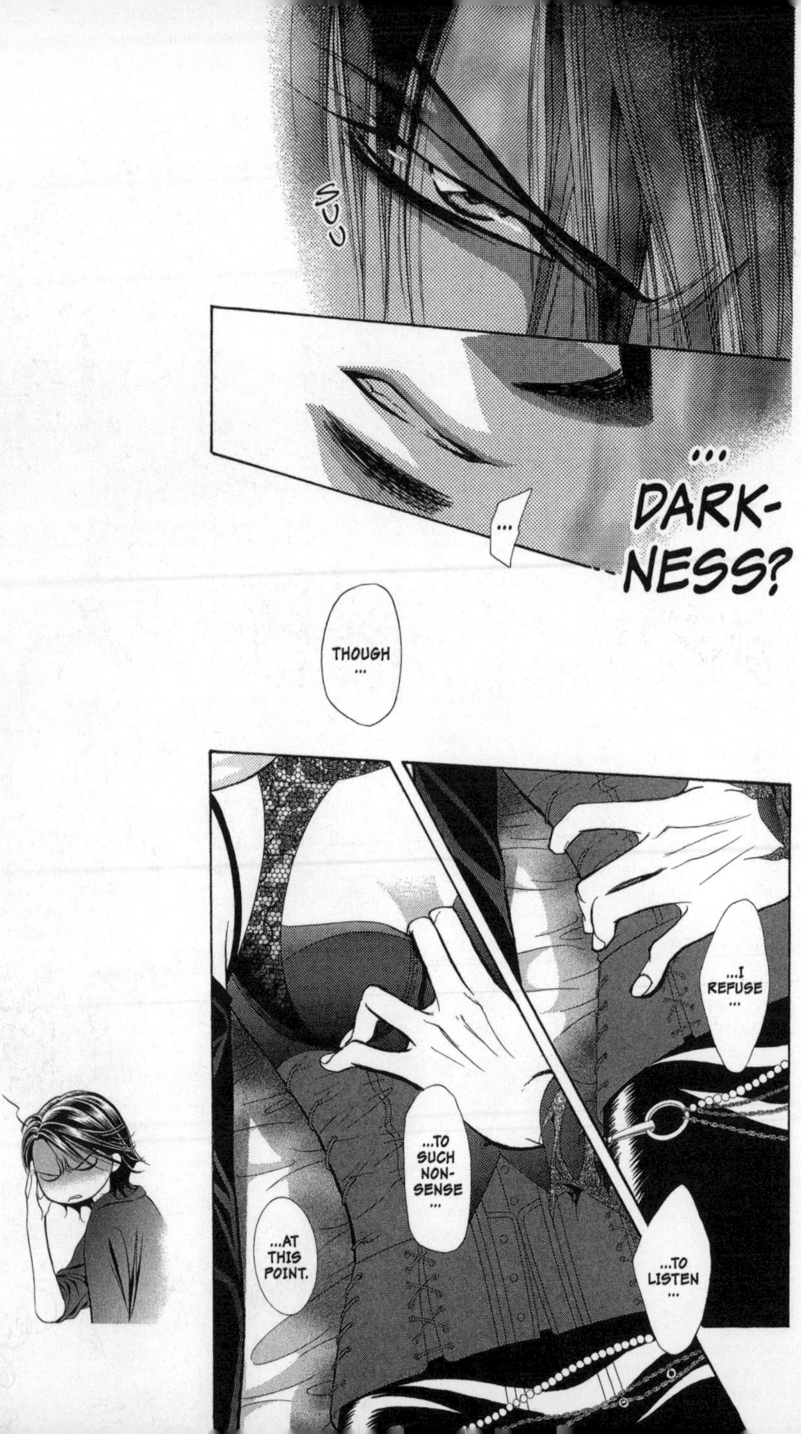
SUU
...
...DARK-NESS?
THOUGH ...
...I REFUSE ...
...TO LISTEN ...
...TO SUCH NON-SENSE ...
...AT THIS POINT.

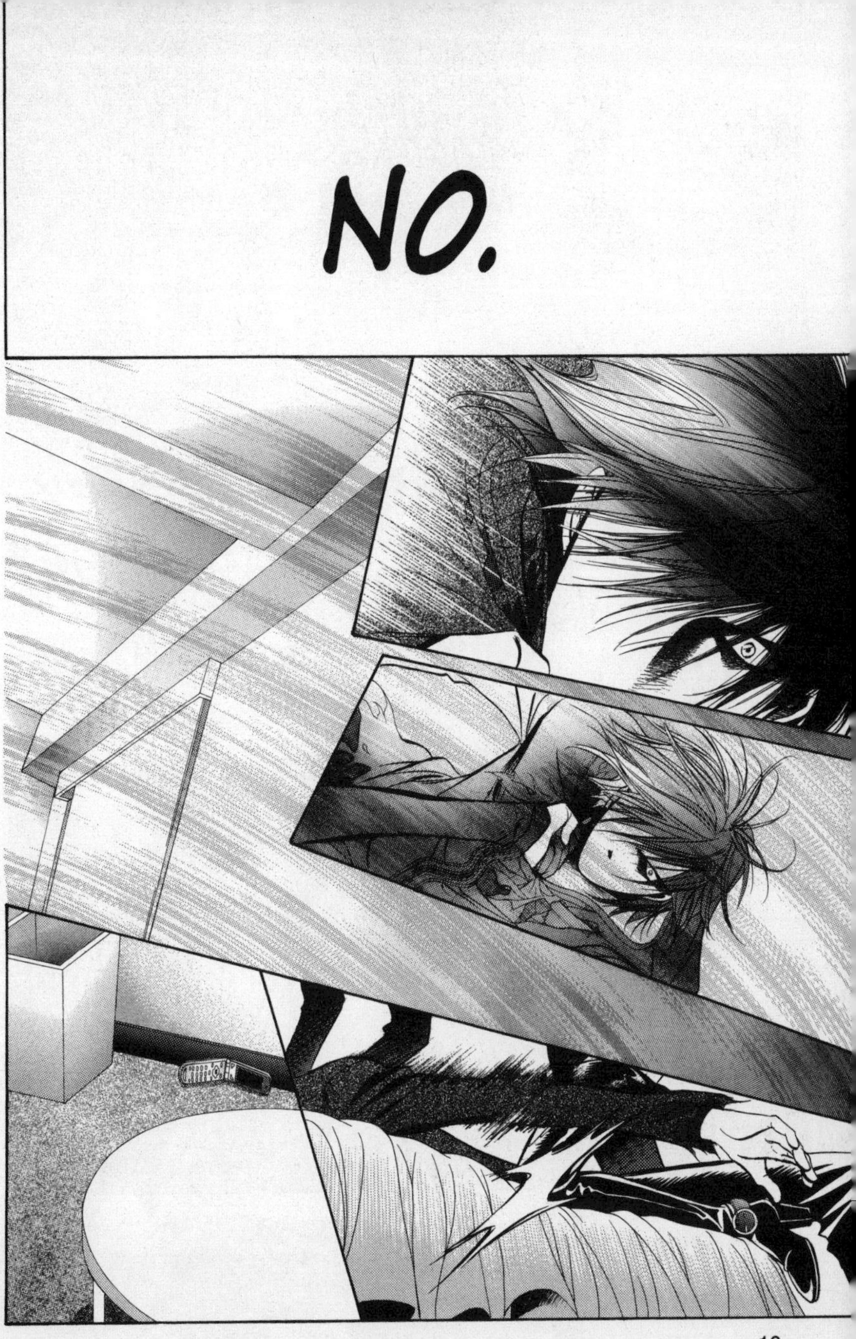
NO.

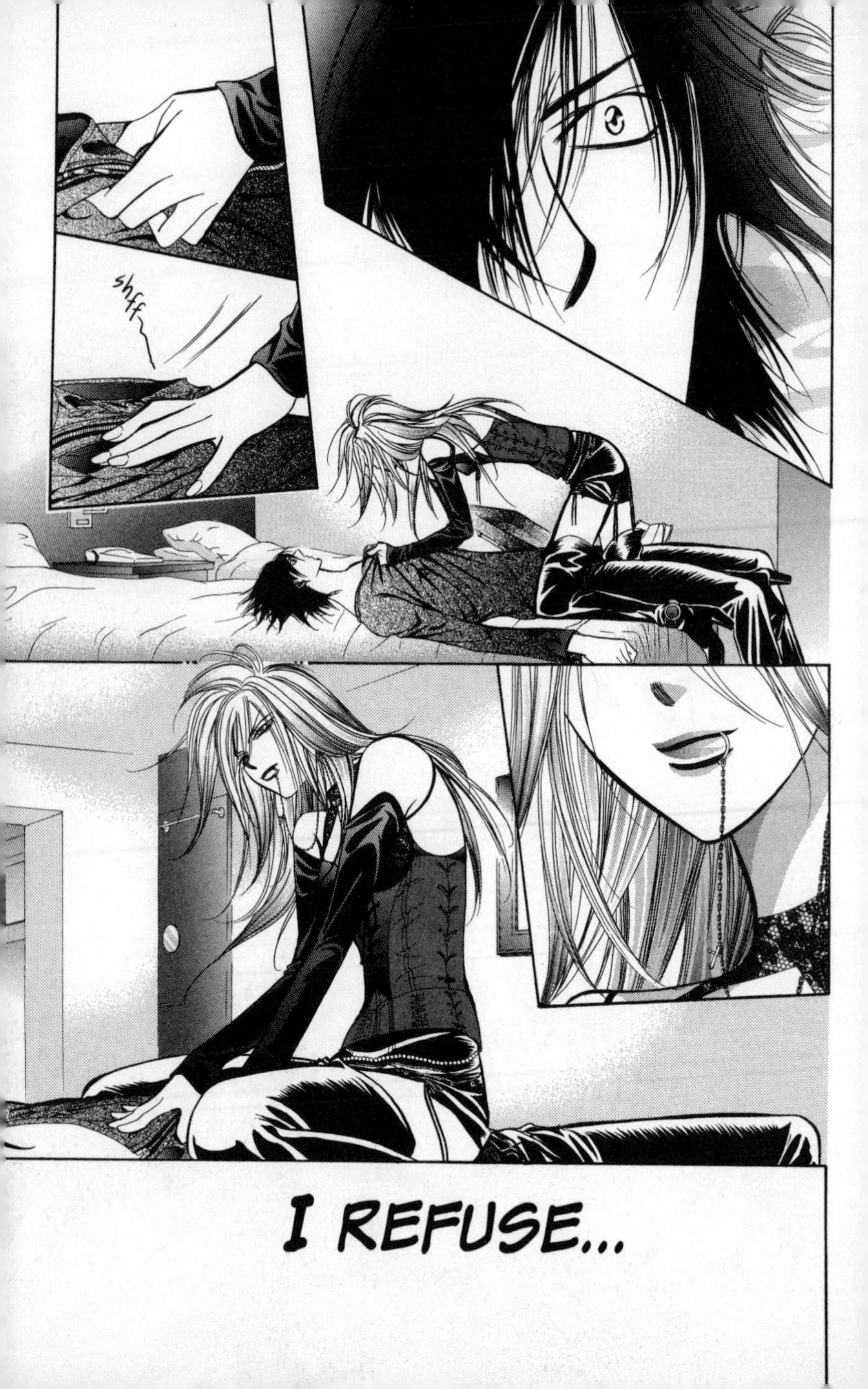
shff~
I REFUSE...

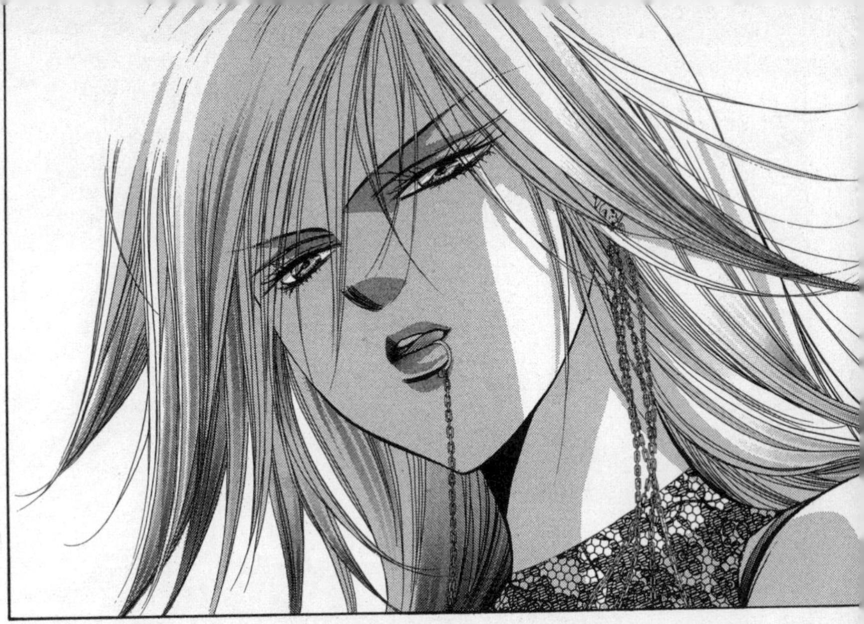

...TO ACKNOWLEDGE IT.

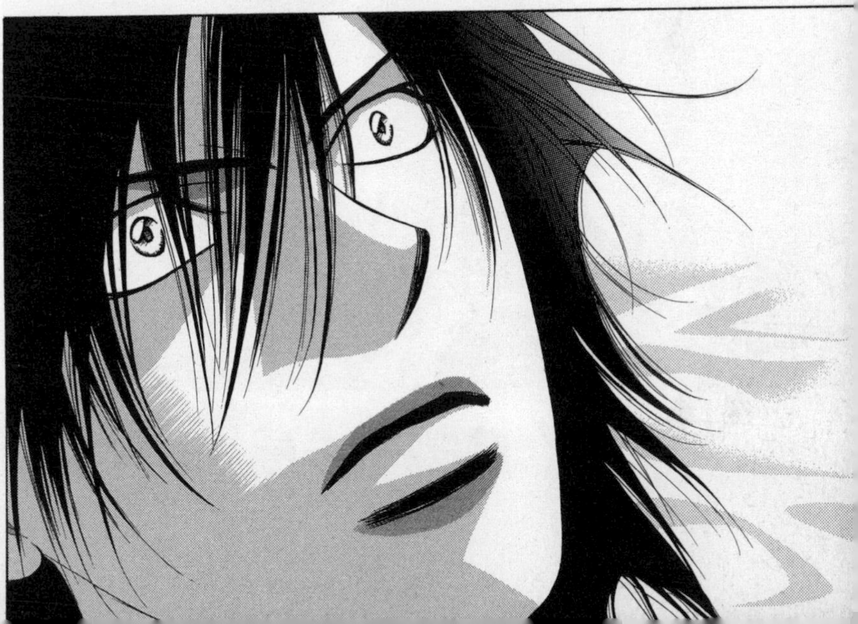

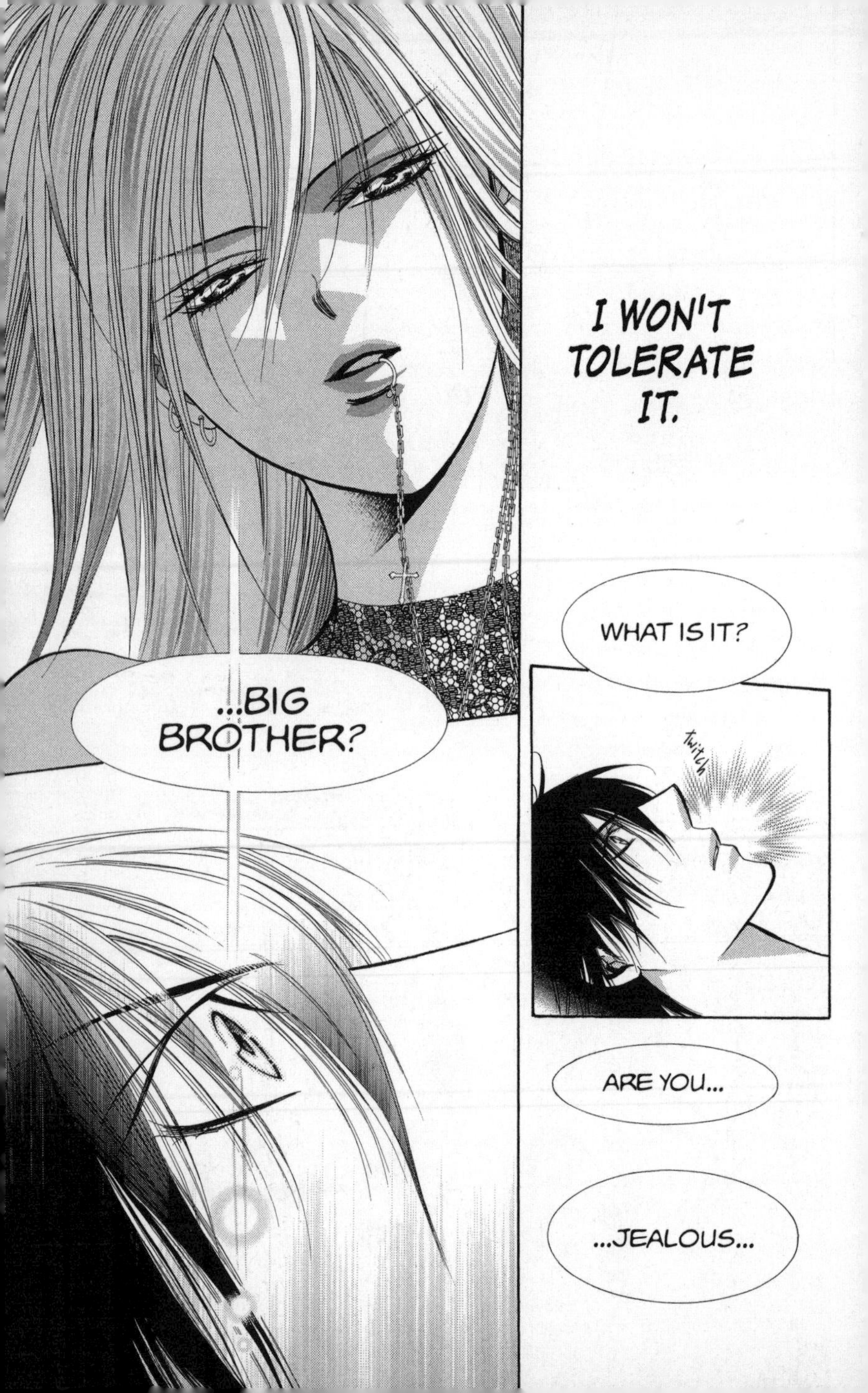
I WON'T TOLERATE IT.
WHAT IS IT?
twitch
ARE YOU...
...JEALOUS...
...BIG BROTHER?

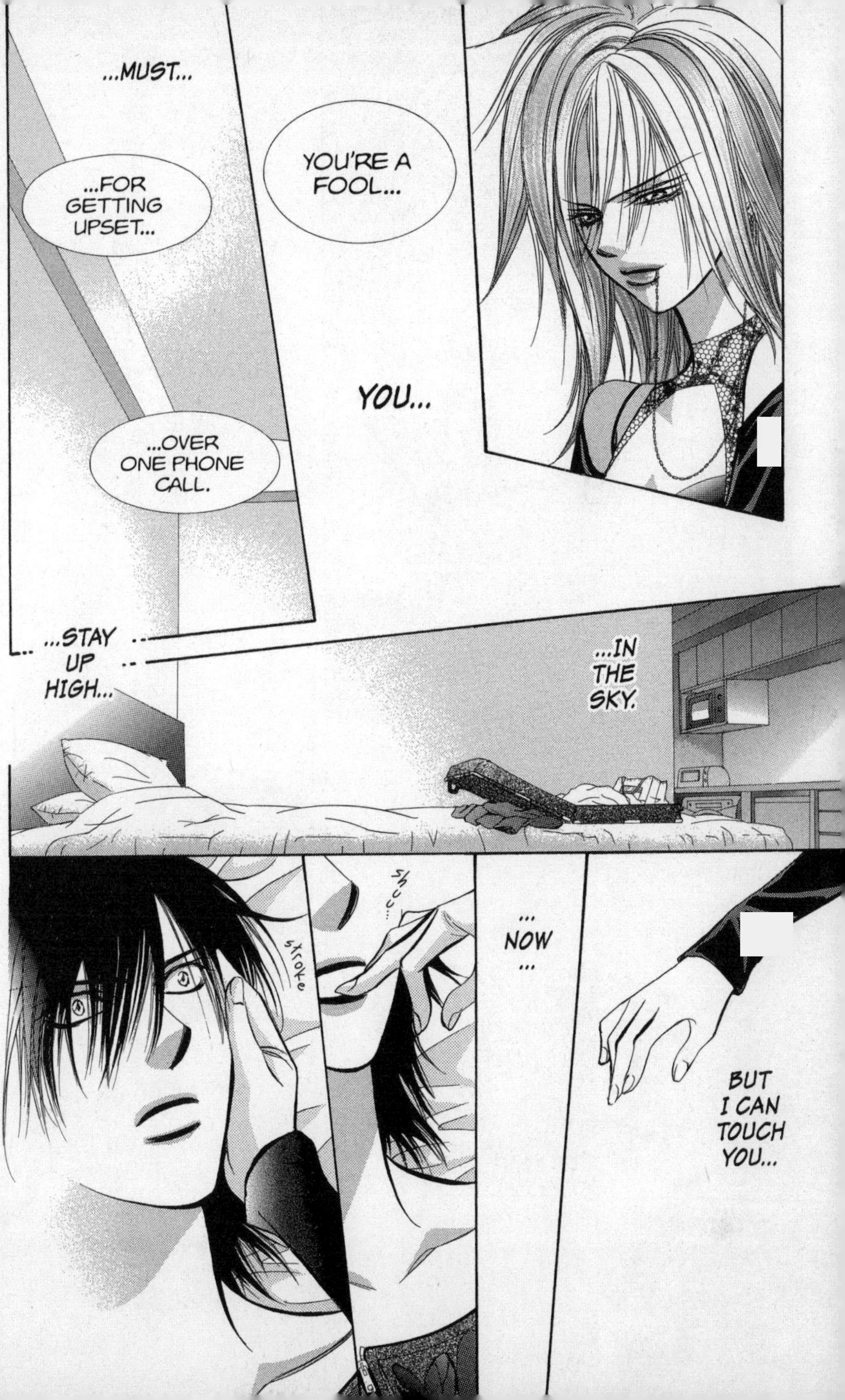
YOU'RE A FOOL...
...FOR GETTING UPSET...
...OVER ONE PHONE CALL.
YOU...
...MUST...
...STAY UP HIGH...
...IN THE SKY.
BUT I CAN TOUCH YOU...
... NOW ...
shuu...
stroke

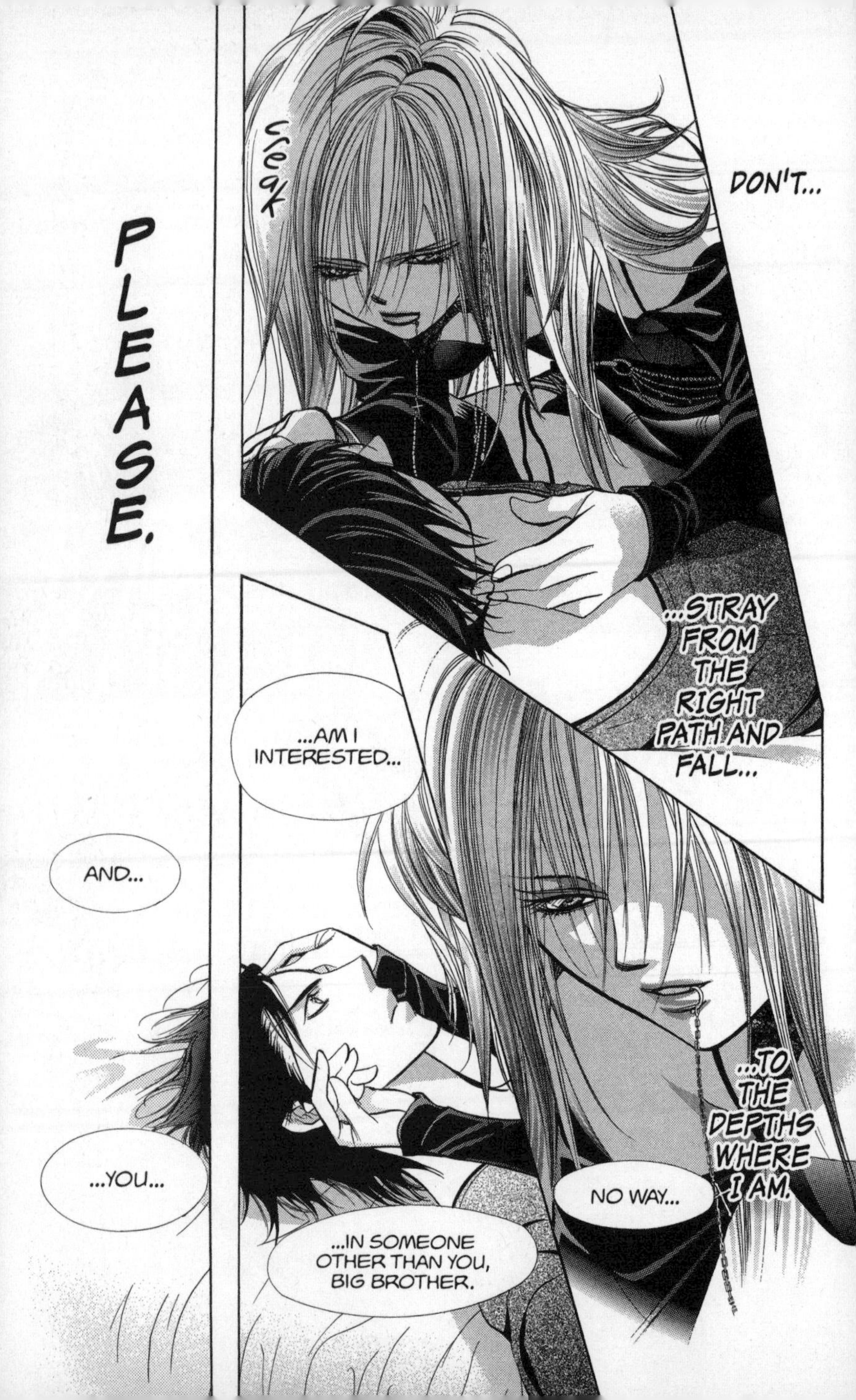
DON'T...
creak
...STRAY FROM THE RIGHT PATH AND FALL...
...AM I INTERESTED...
...TO THE DEPTHS WHERE I AM.
NO WAY...
...IN SOMEONE OTHER THAN YOU, BIG BROTHER.
PLEASE.
AND...
...YOU...

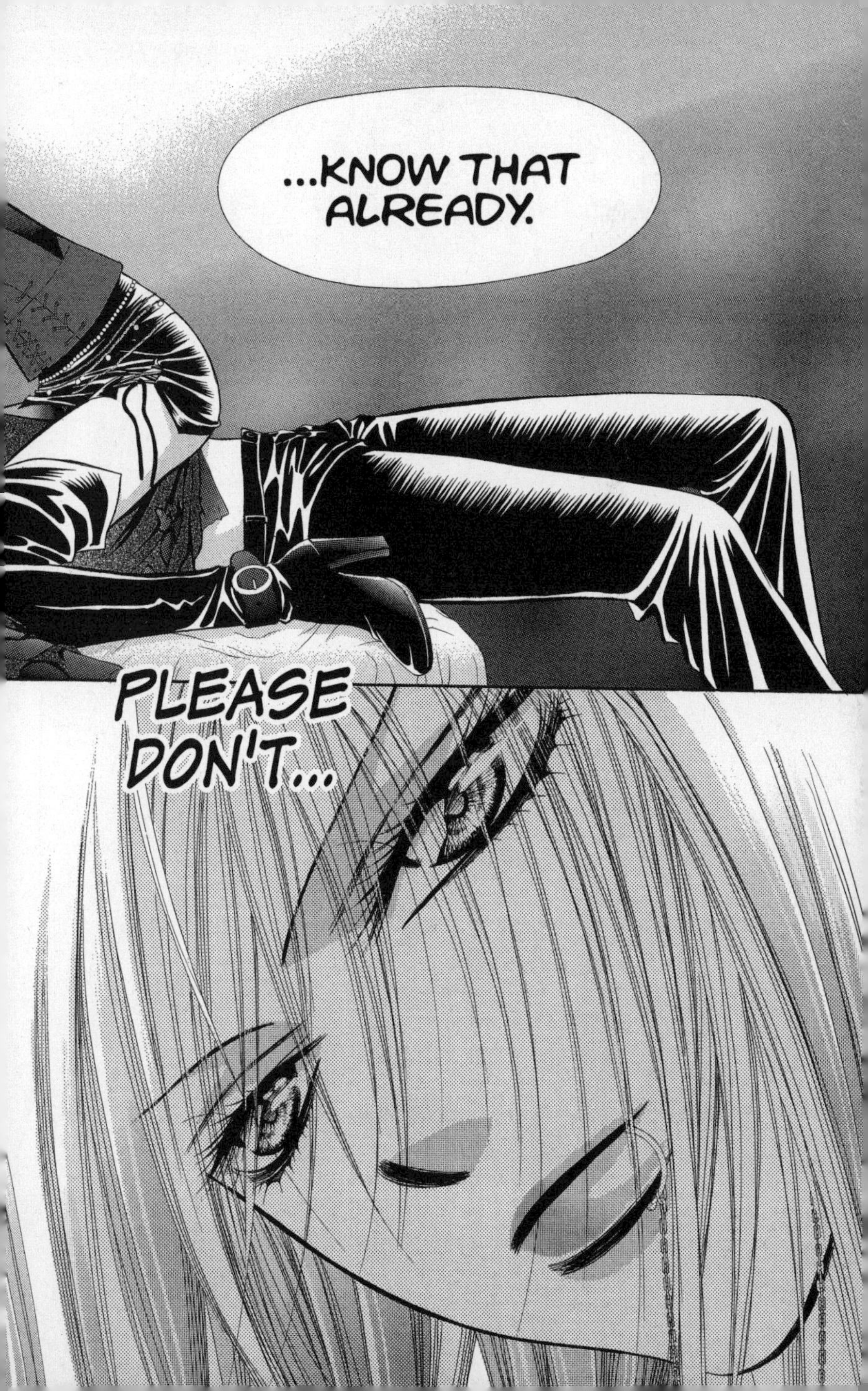
...KNOW THAT ALREADY.
PLEASE DON'T...

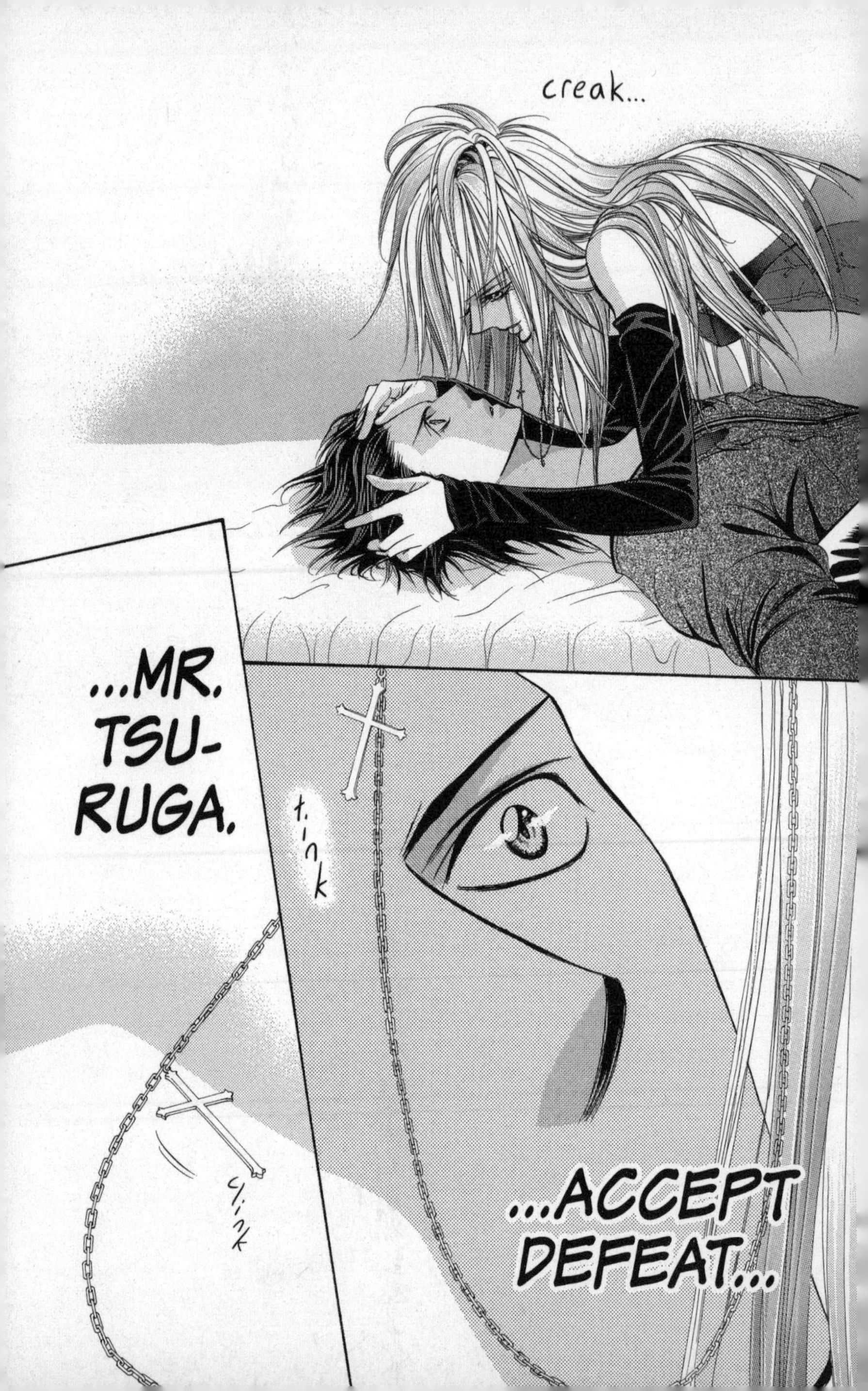
creak...
...MR. TSU-RUGA.
tink
...ACCEPT DEFEAT...
clink

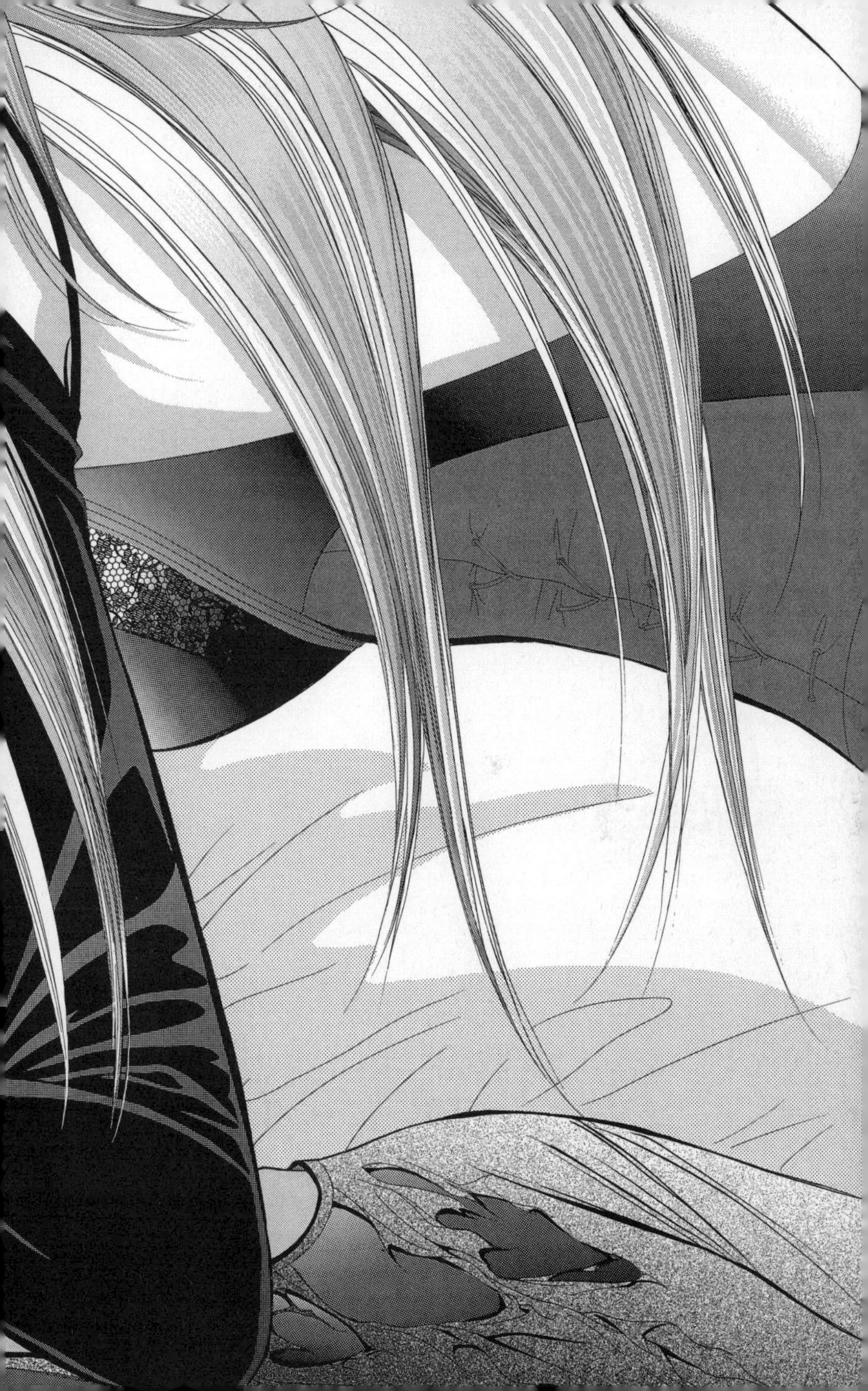

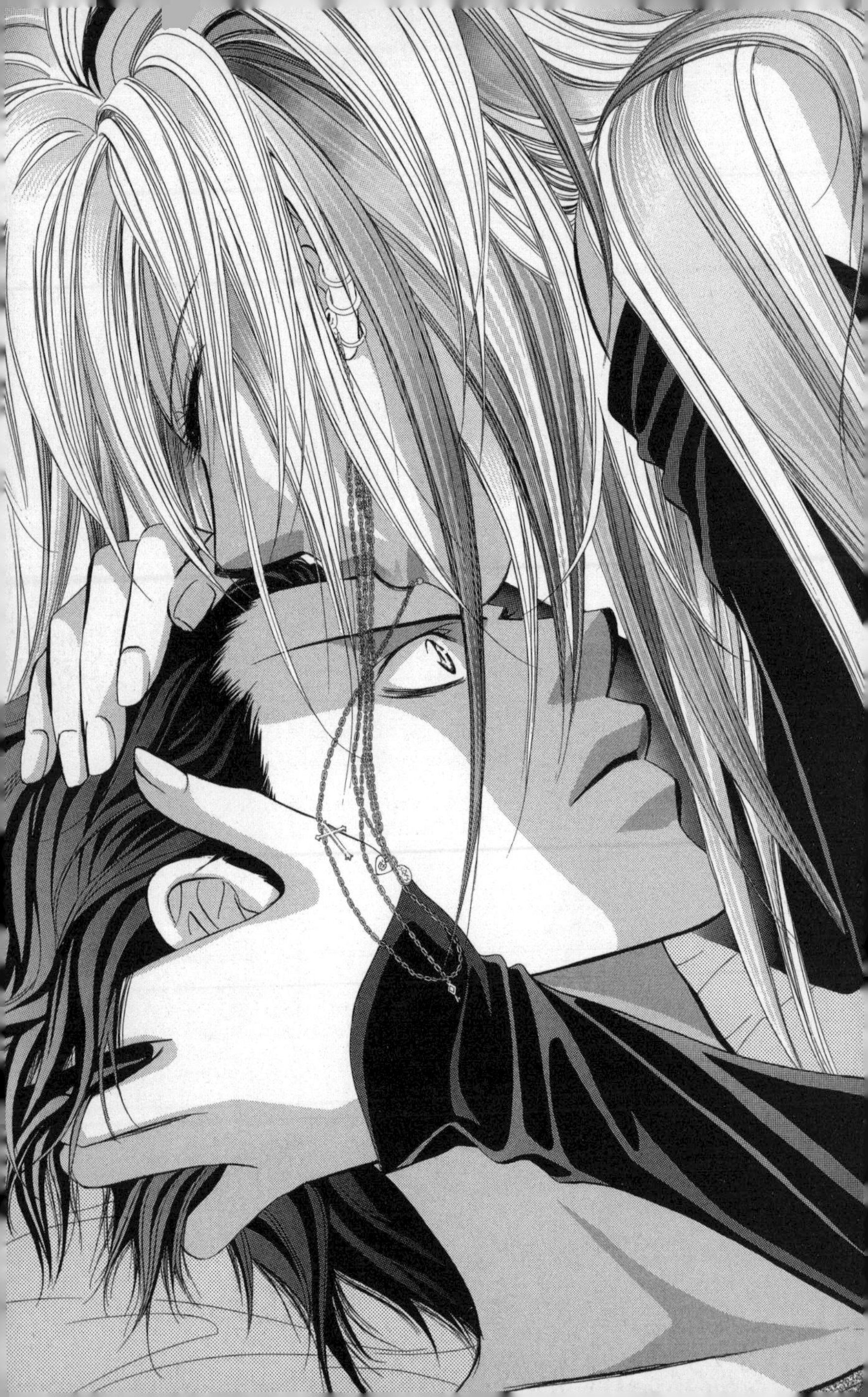

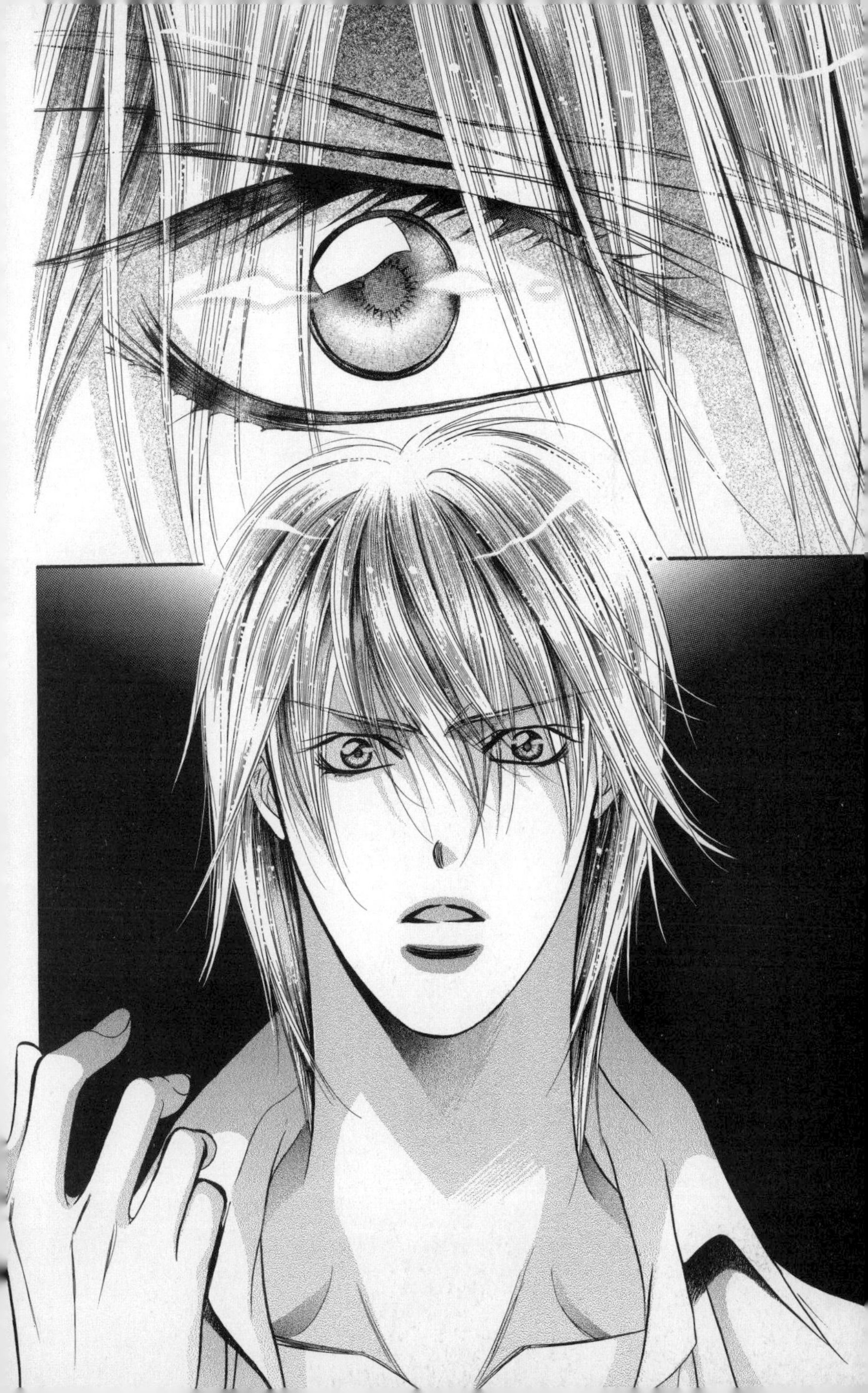

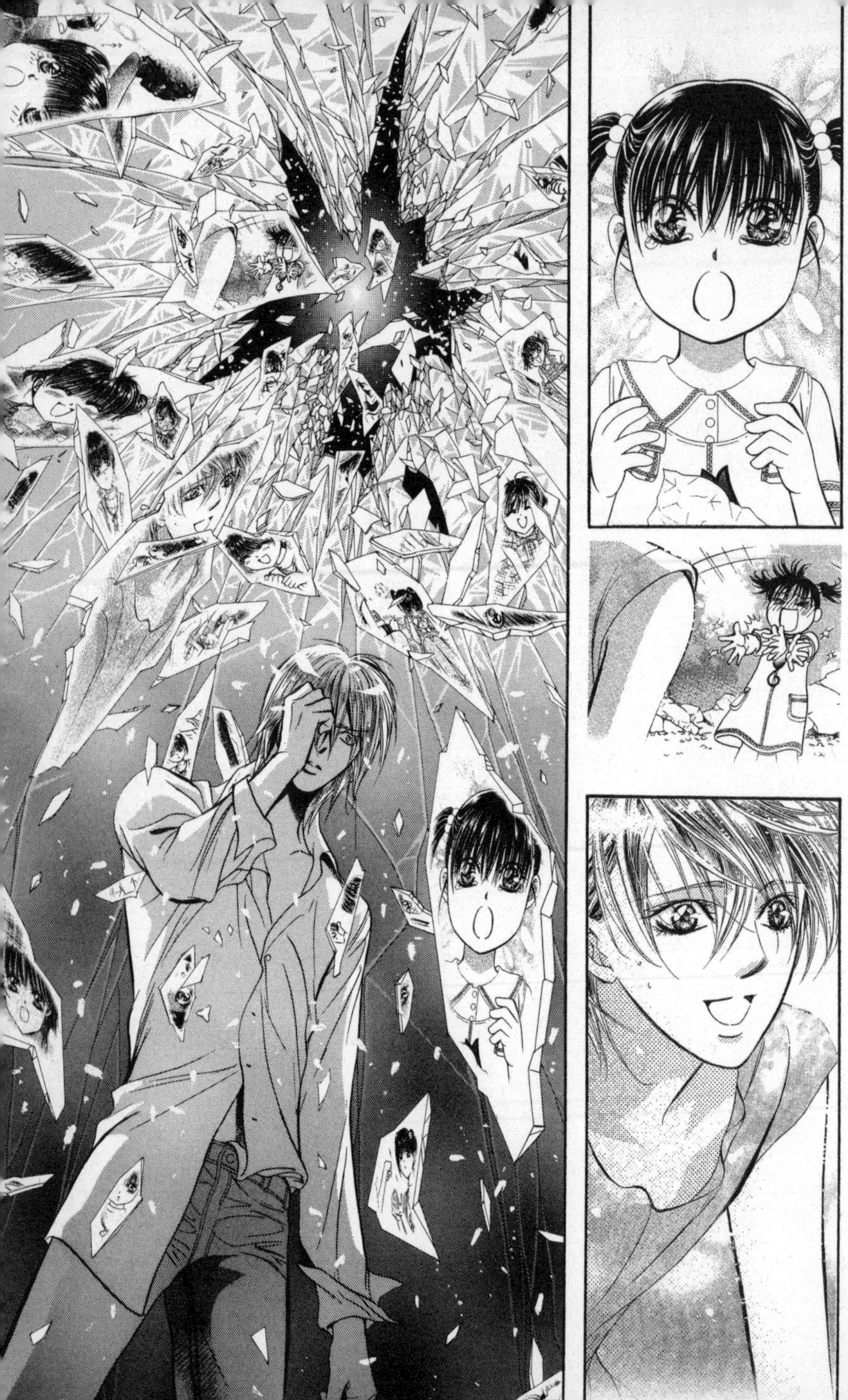

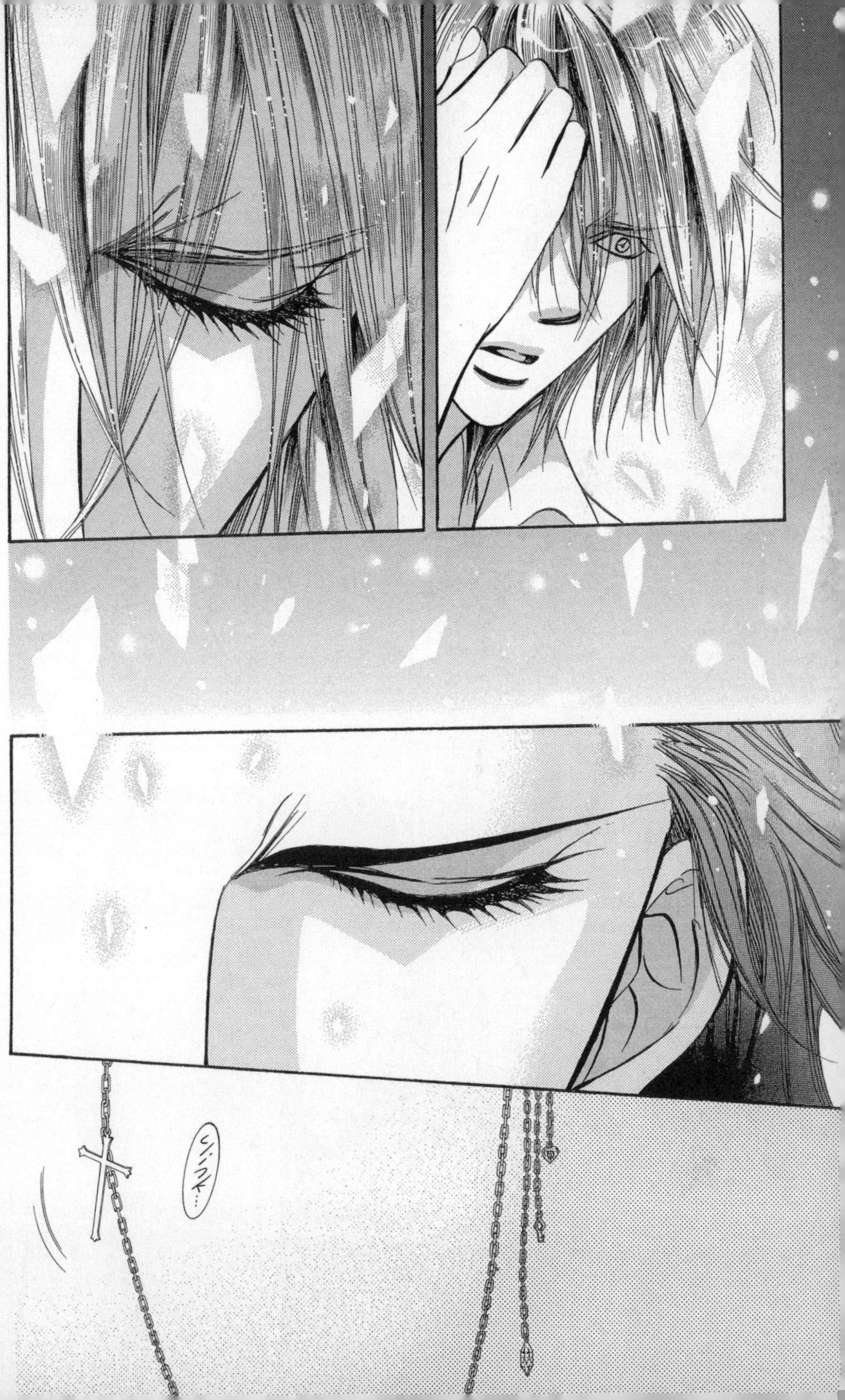
clink...

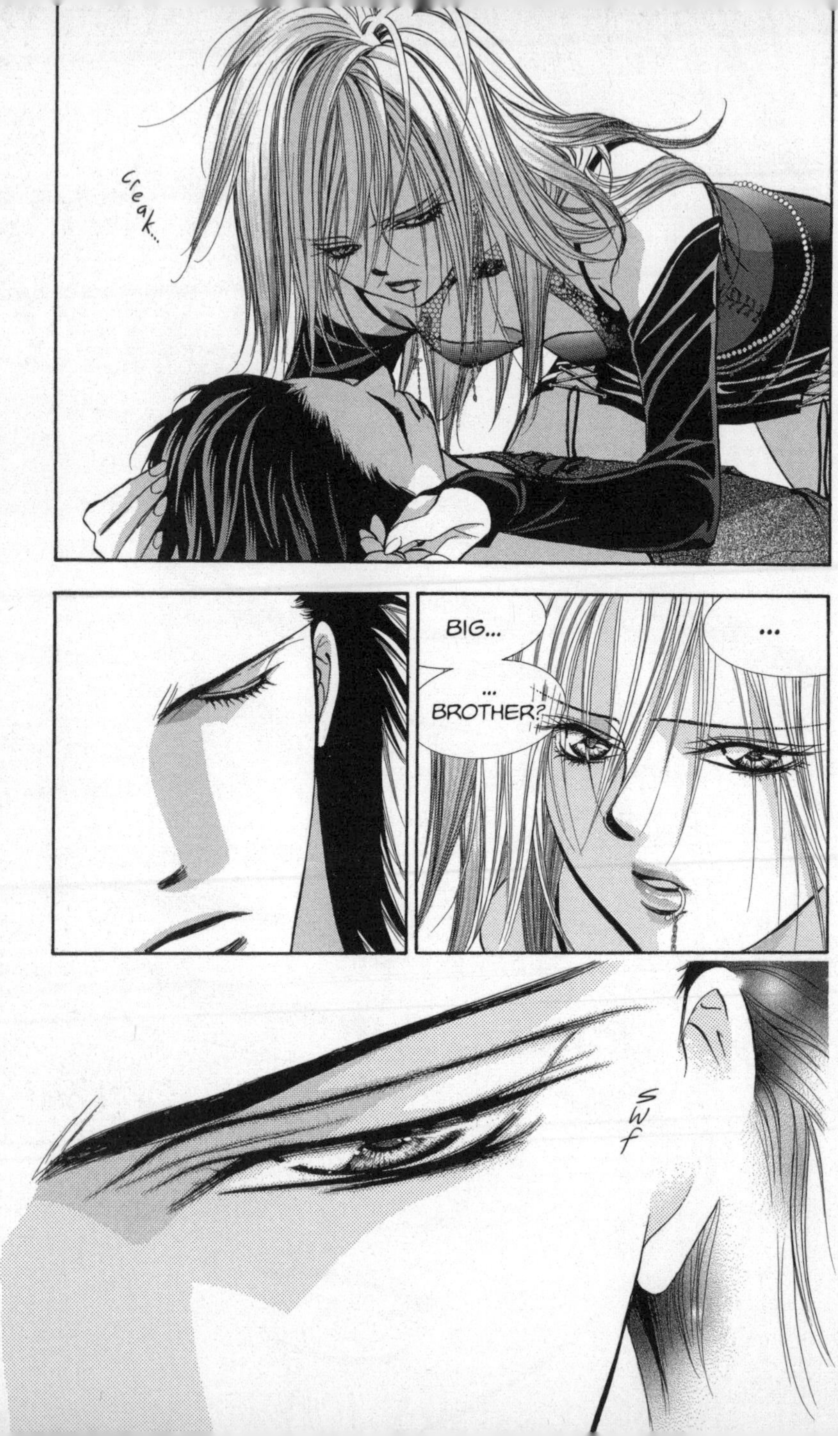
creak...
...
BIG...
... BROTHER?
SWF

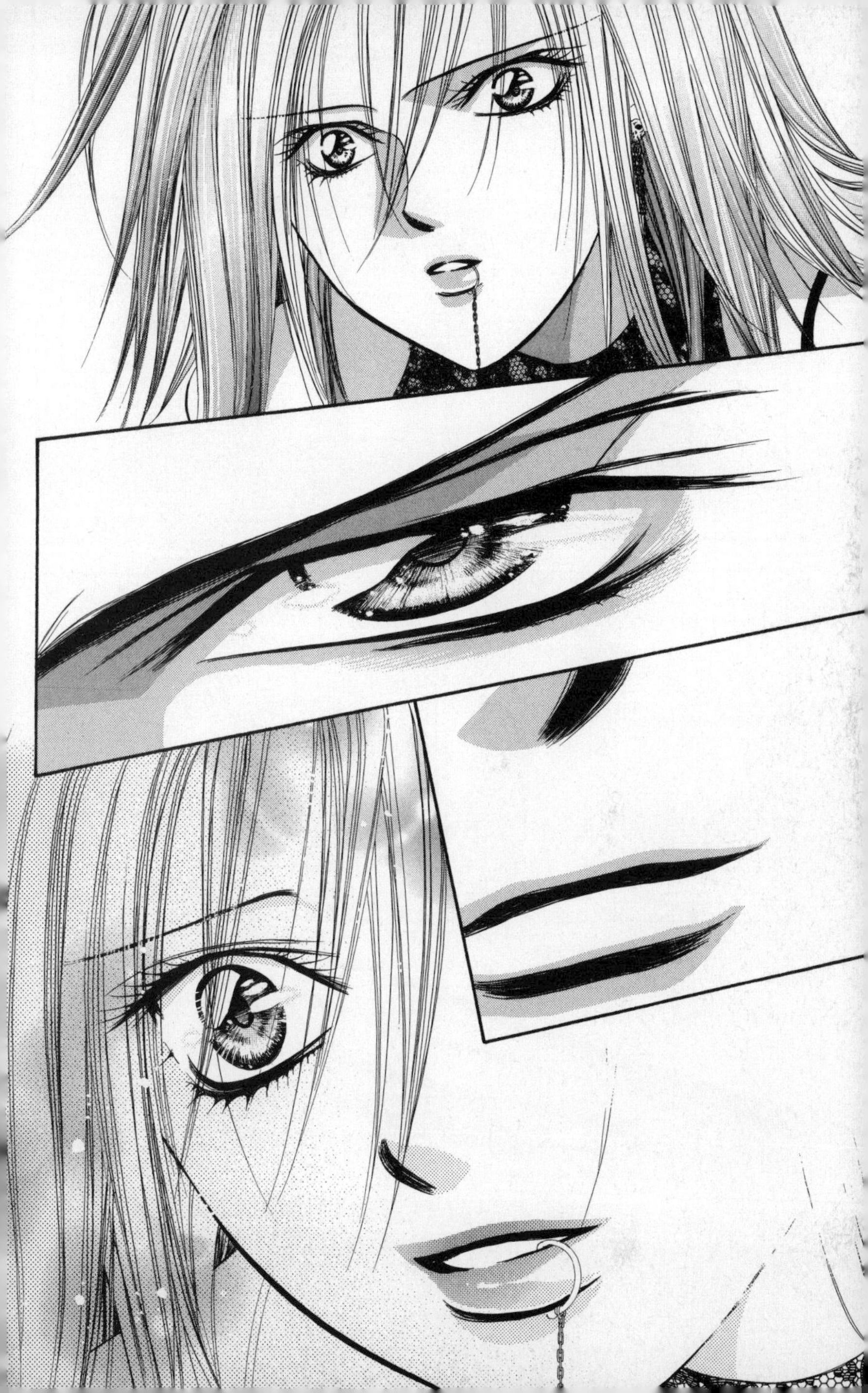

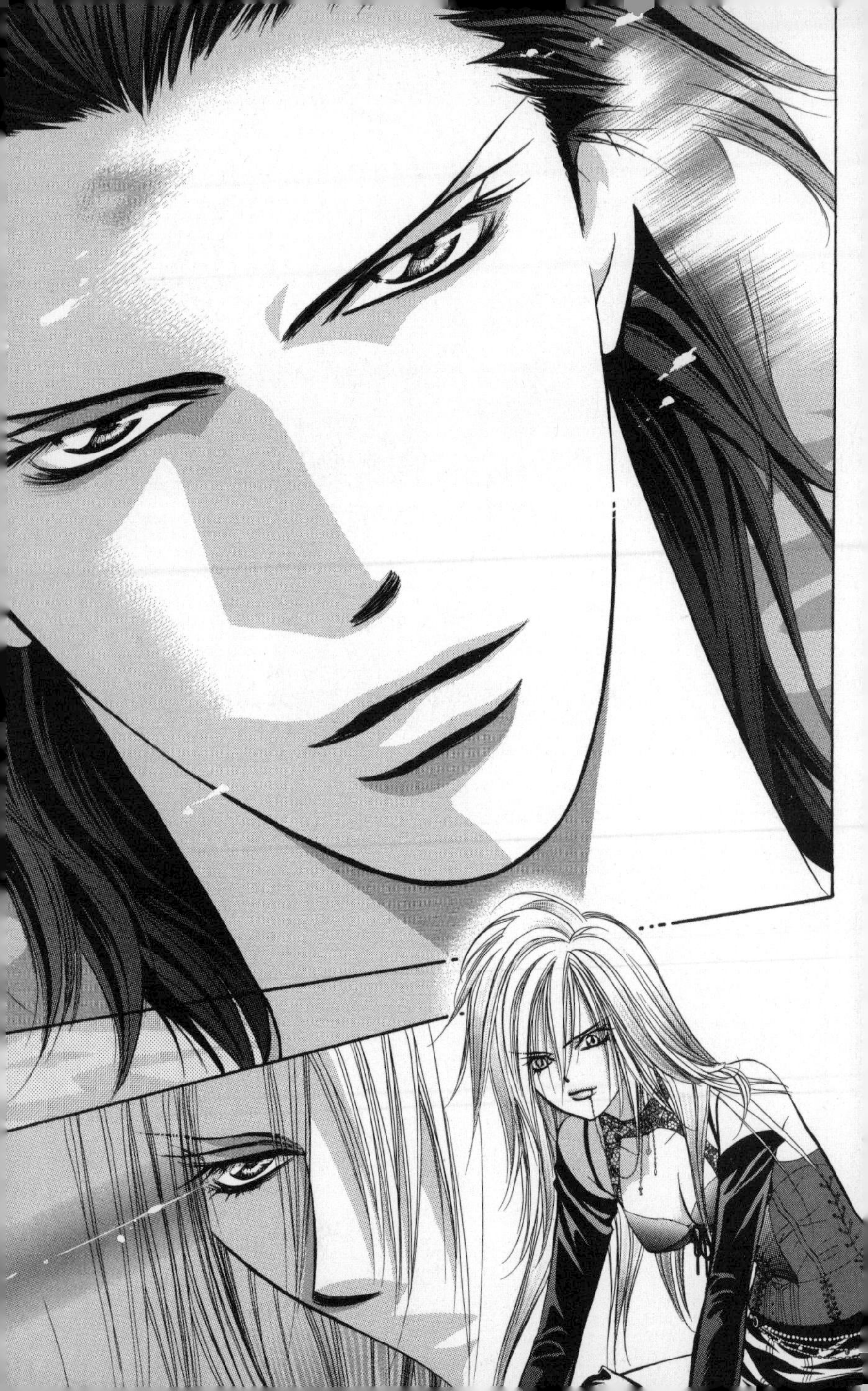

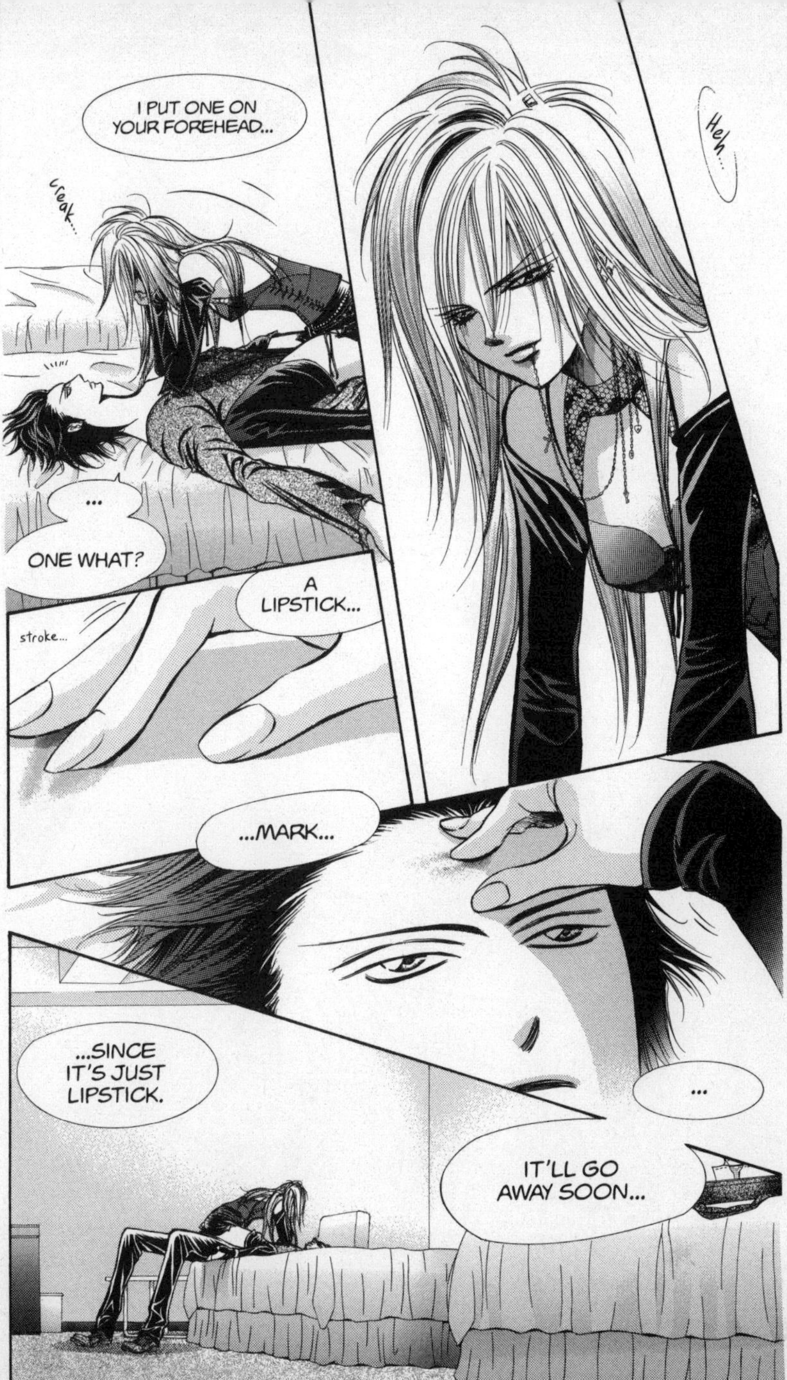
Heh...
I PUT ONE ON YOUR FOREHEAD...
creak...
...
ONE WHAT?
A LIPSTICK...
stroke...
...MARK...
...
IT'LL GO AWAY SOON...
...SINCE IT'S JUST LIPSTICK.

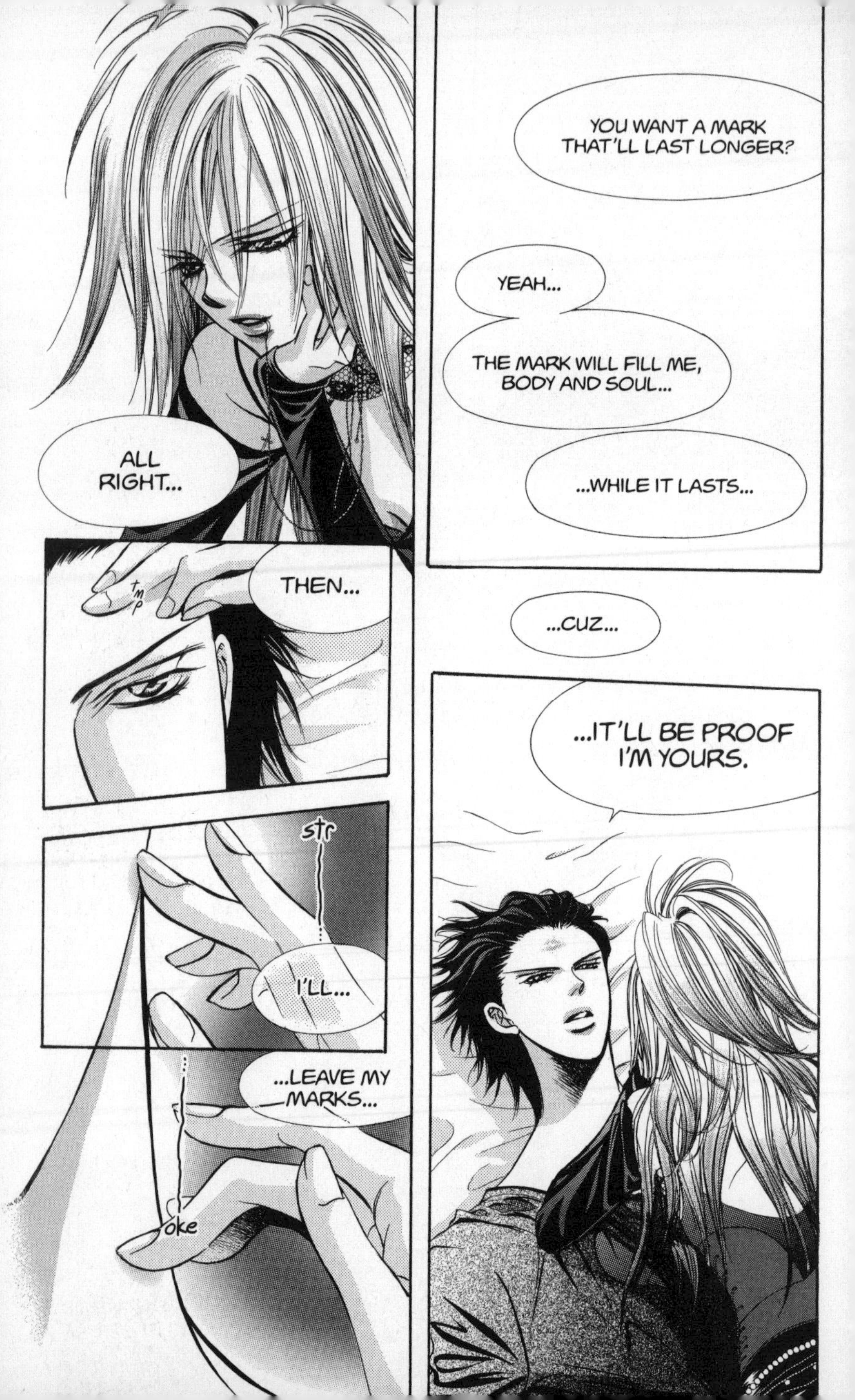
YOU WANT A MARK THAT'LL LAST LONGER?
YEAH...
THE MARK WILL FILL ME, BODY AND SOUL...
...WHILE IT LASTS...
ALL RIGHT...
THEN...
tmp
str
I'LL...
...LEAVE MY MARKS...
oke
...CUZ...
...IT'LL BE PROOF I'M YOURS.

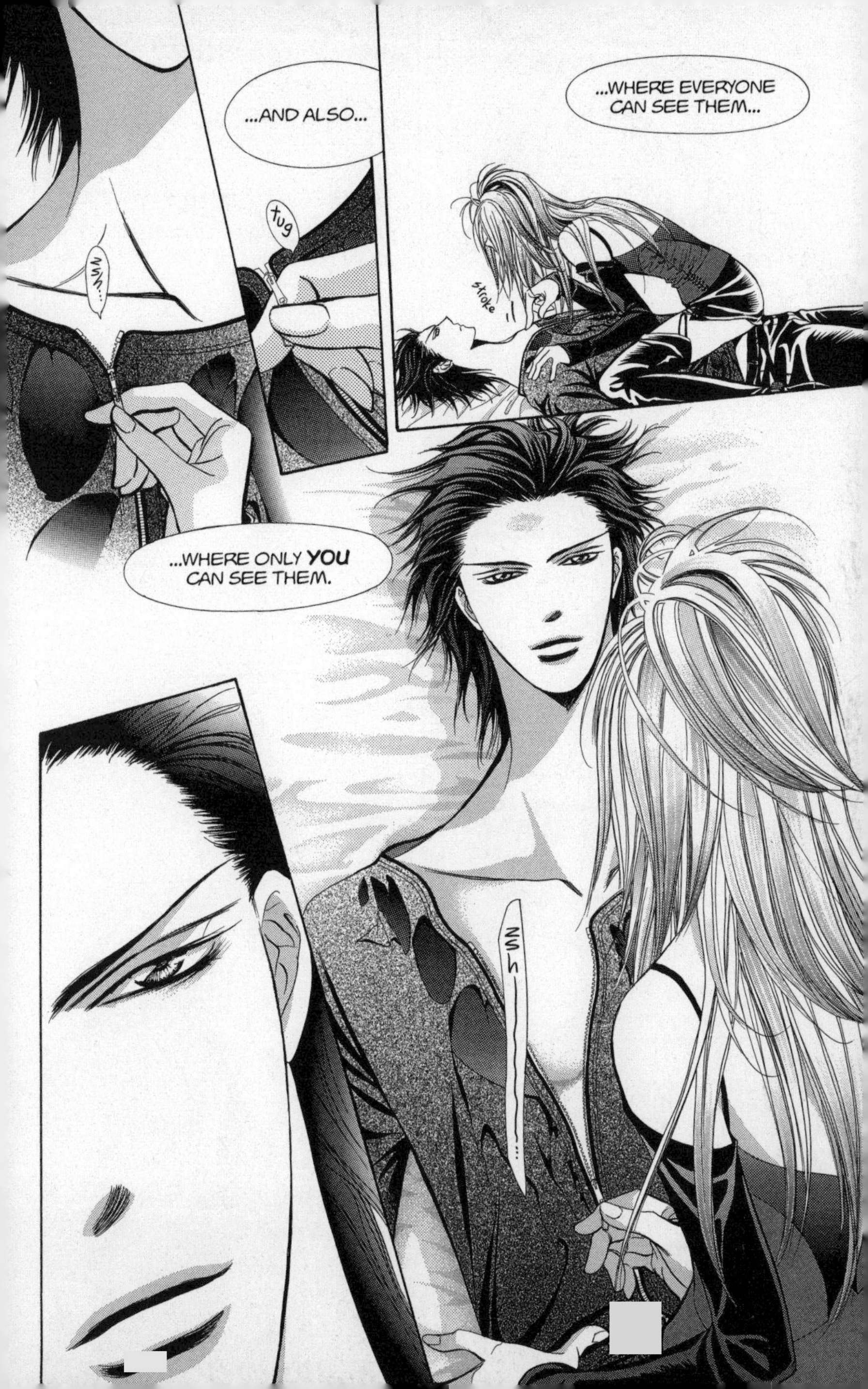
...WHERE EVERYONE CAN SEE THEM...
stroke
...AND ALSO...
tug
zsh...
...WHERE ONLY YOU CAN SEE THEM.
zsh—...

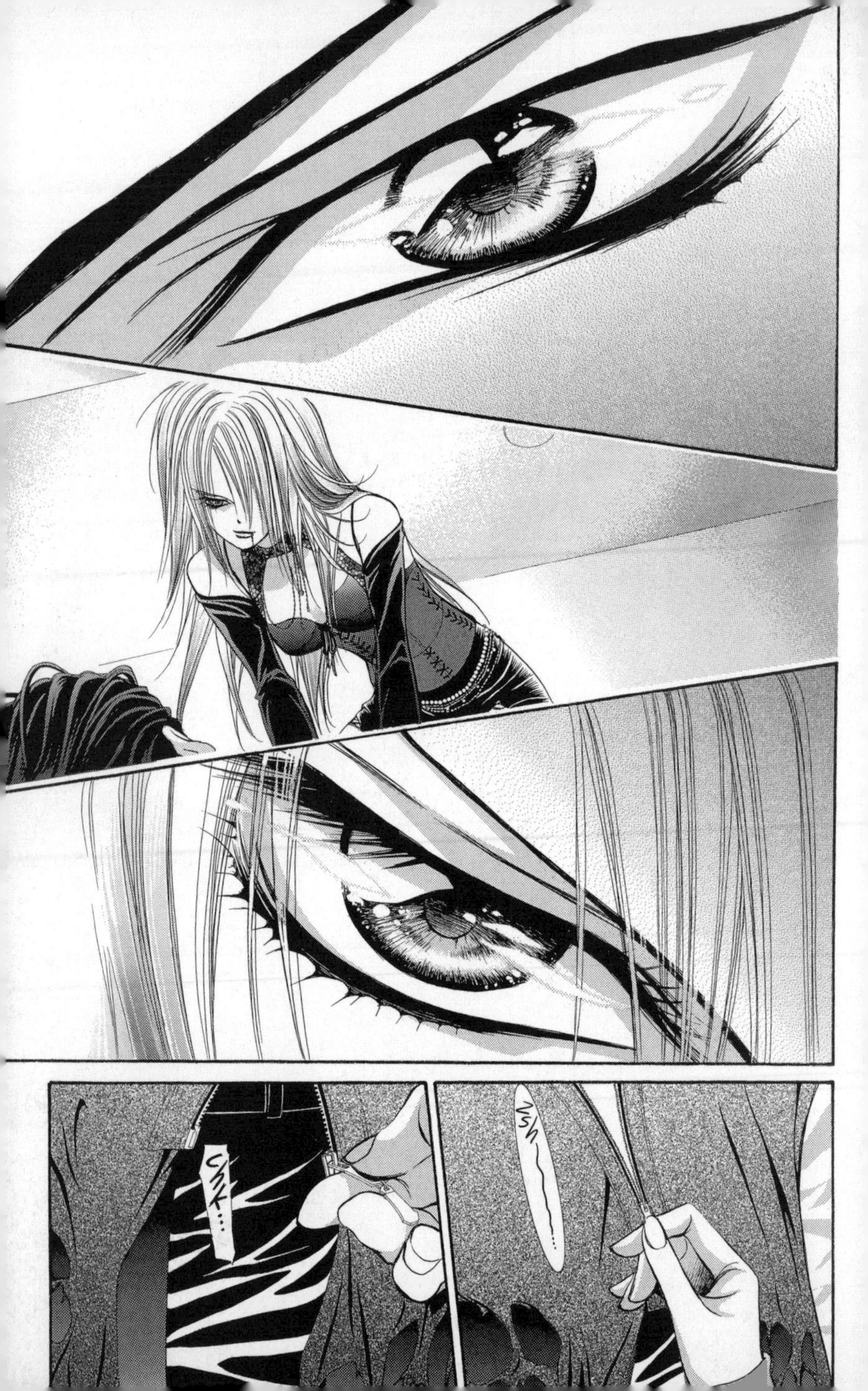
Zsh~...
Chik...

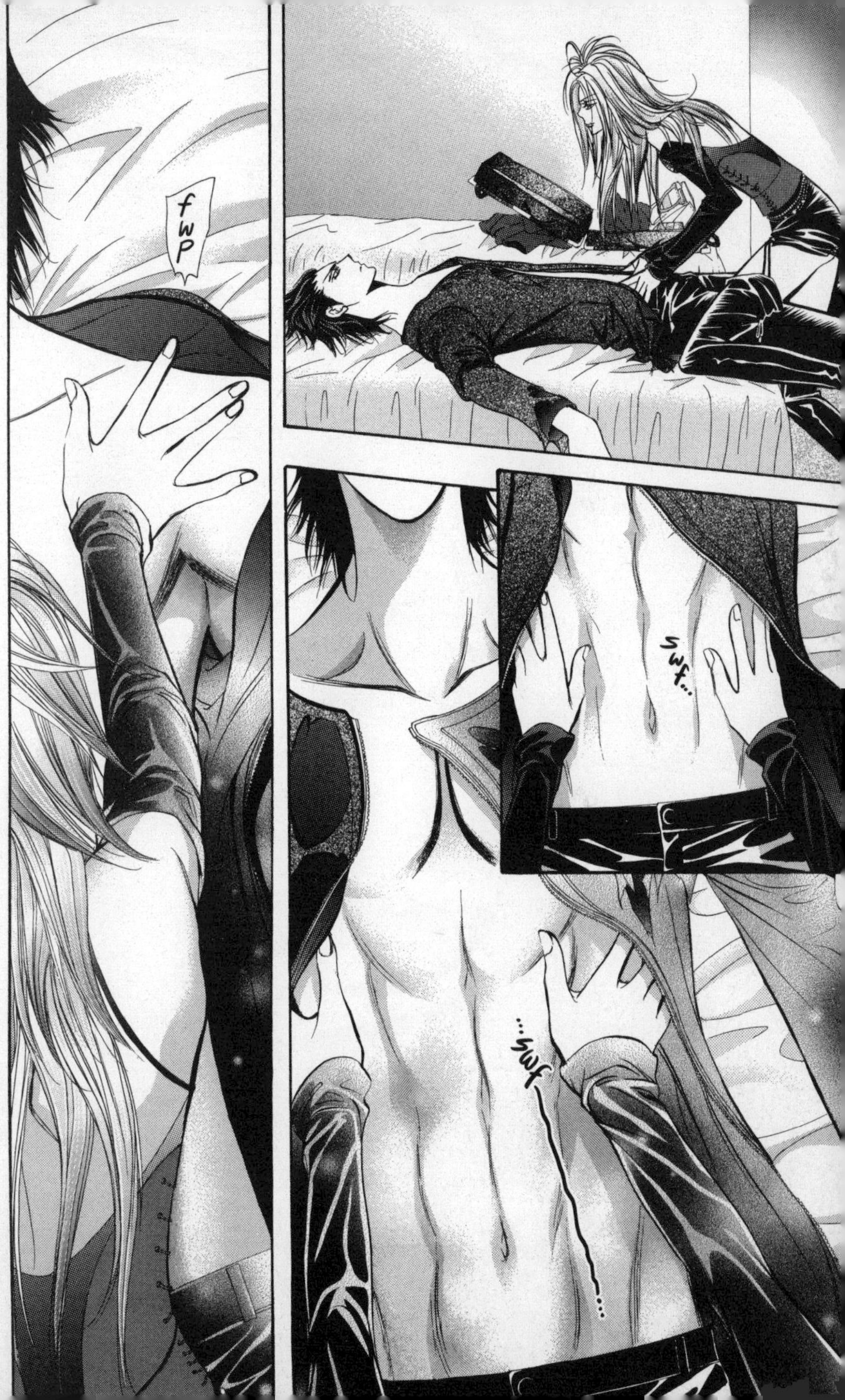
swf...
...swf...
fwp

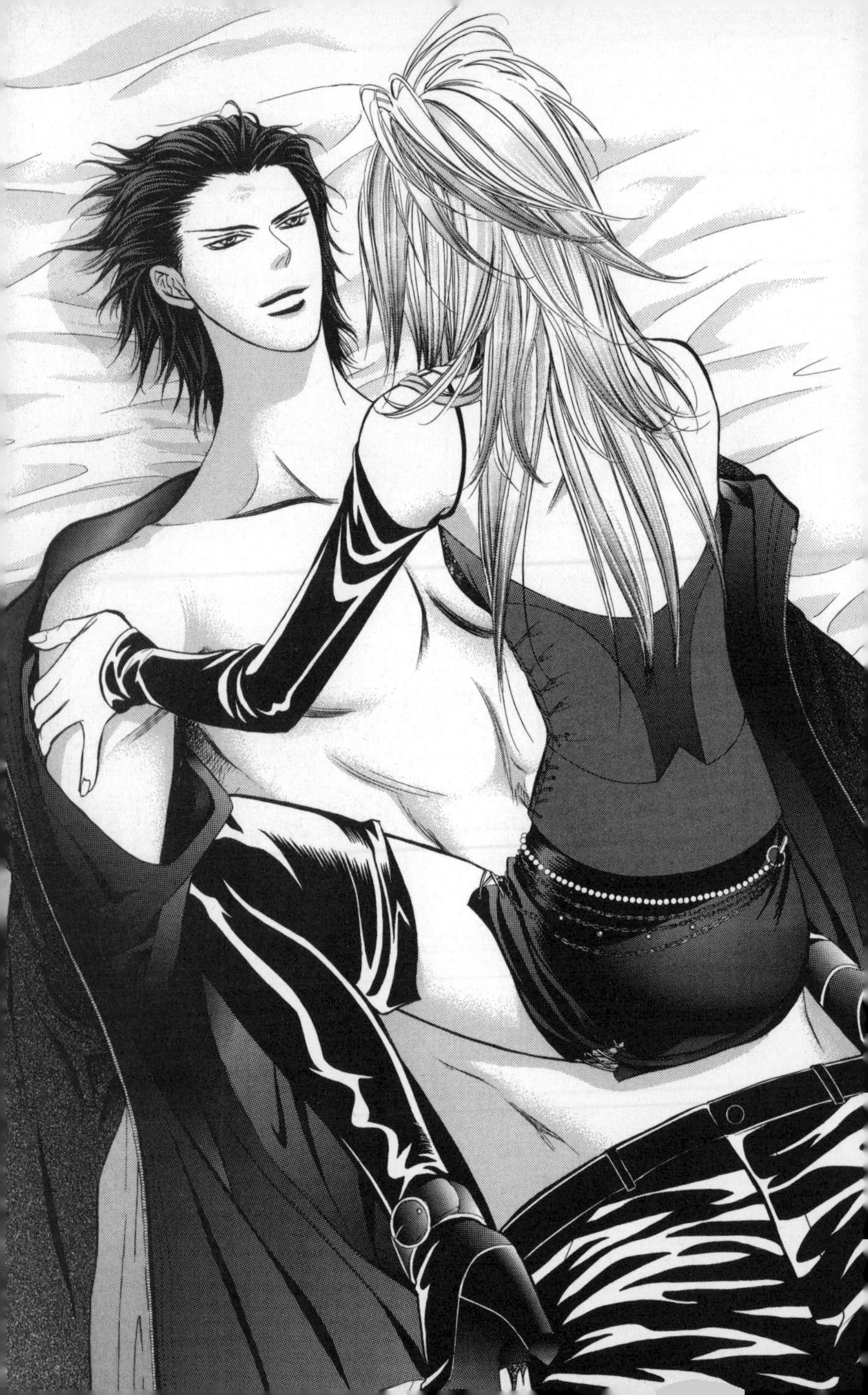

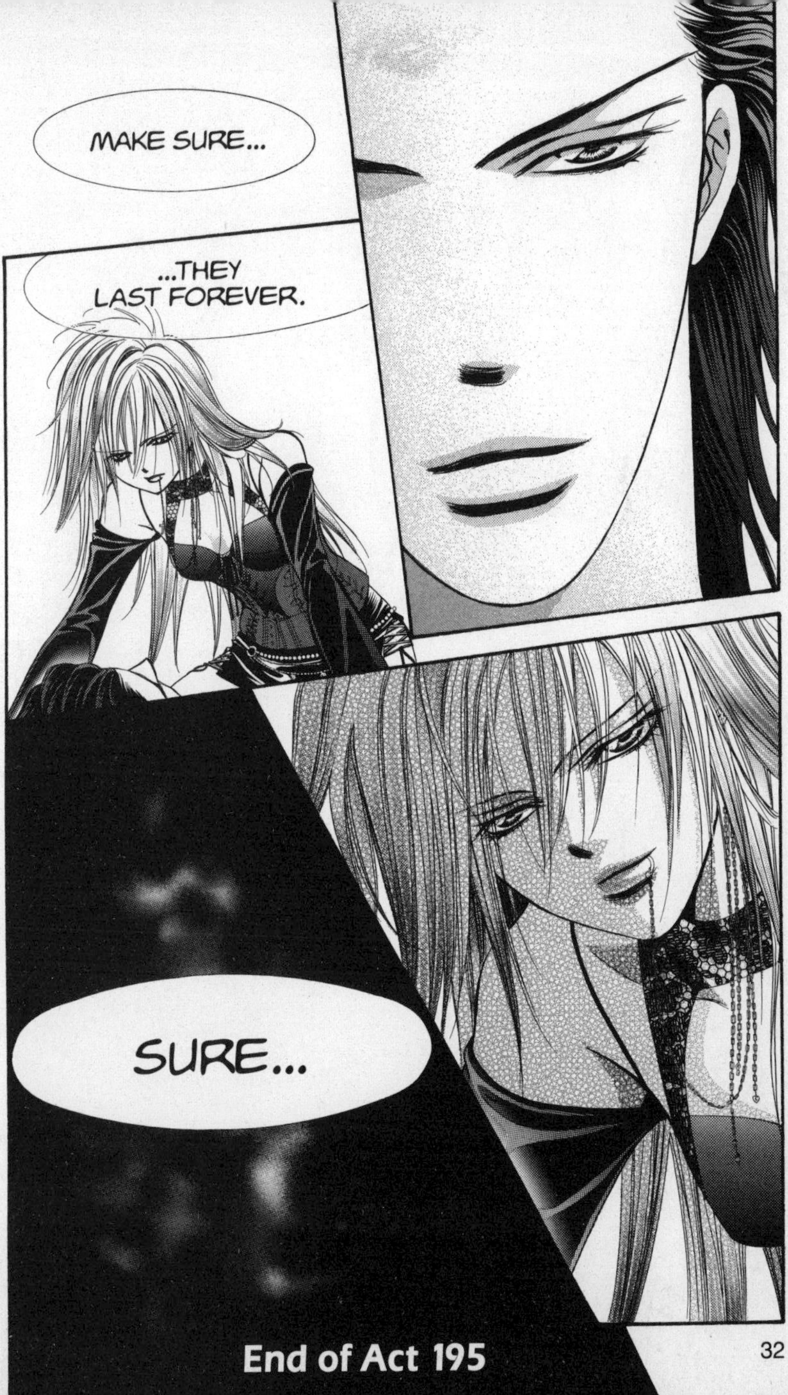
MAKE SURE...
...THEY LAST FOREVER.
SURE...

End of Act 195

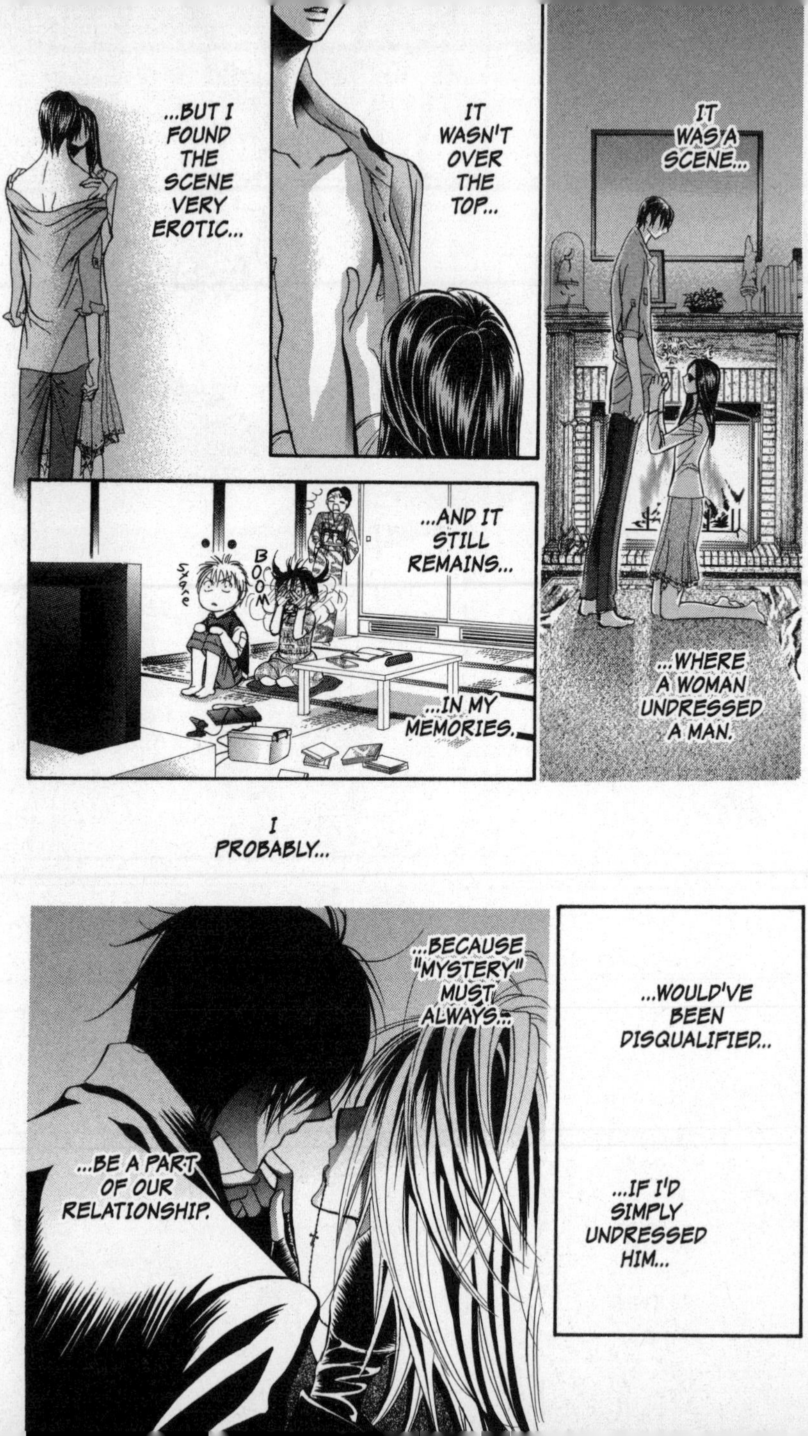
IT WAS A SCENE...
...WHERE A WOMAN UNDRESSED A MAN.
IT WASN'T OVER THE TOP...
...BUT I FOUND THE SCENE VERY EROTIC...
...AND IT STILL REMAINS...
BOOM
stare
...IN MY MEMORIES.
I PROBABLY...
...WOULD'VE BEEN DISQUALIFIED...
...IF I'D SIMPLY UNDRESSED HIM...
...BECAUSE "MYSTERY" MUST ALWAYS...
...BE A PART OF OUR RELATIONSHIP.

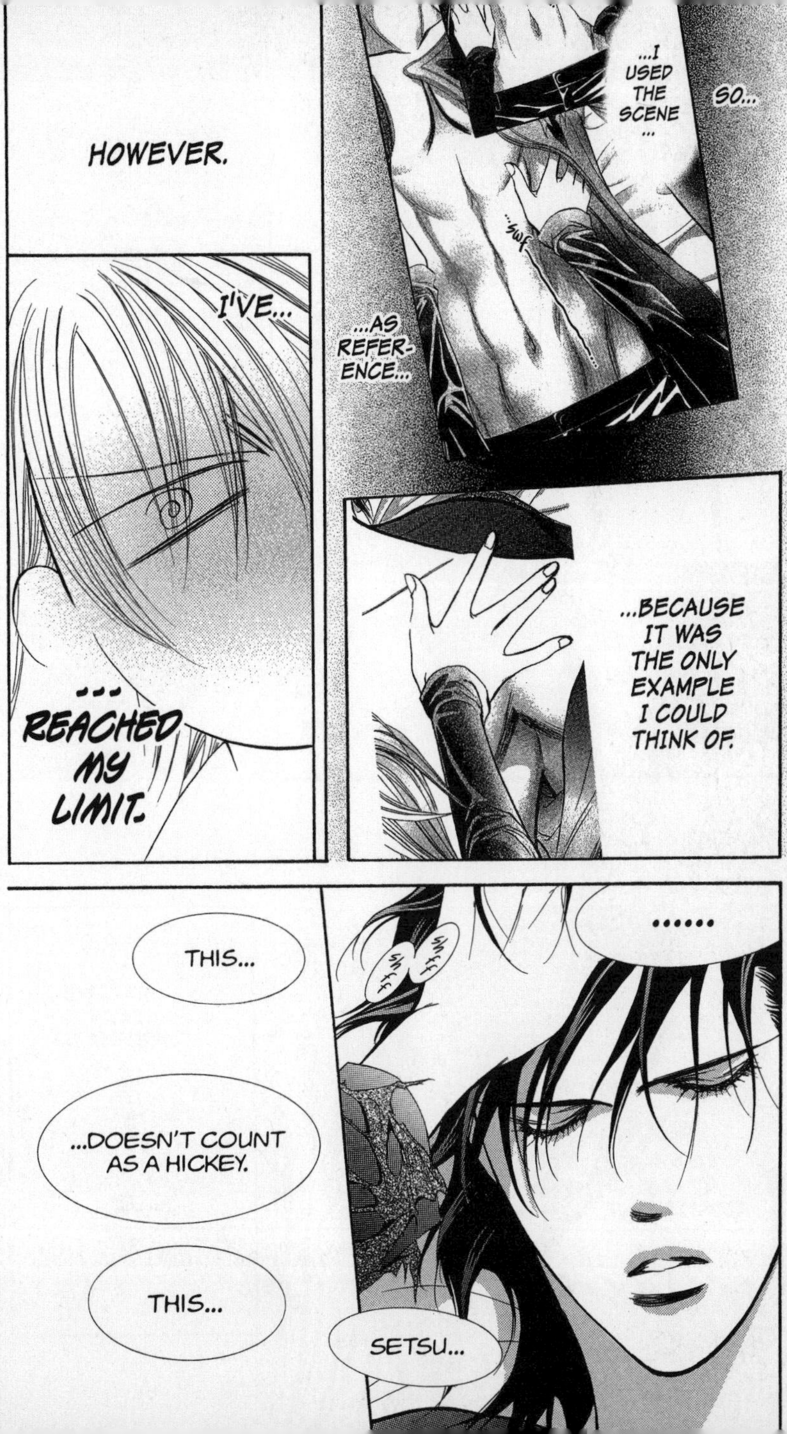
SO...
...I USED THE SCENE...
...swf
...AS REFERENCE...
...BECAUSE IT WAS THE ONLY EXAMPLE I COULD THINK OF.
HOWEVER.
I'VE...
...REACHED MY LIMIT.
......
swff
swff
THIS...
...DOESN'T COUNT AS A HICKEY.
THIS...
SETSU...

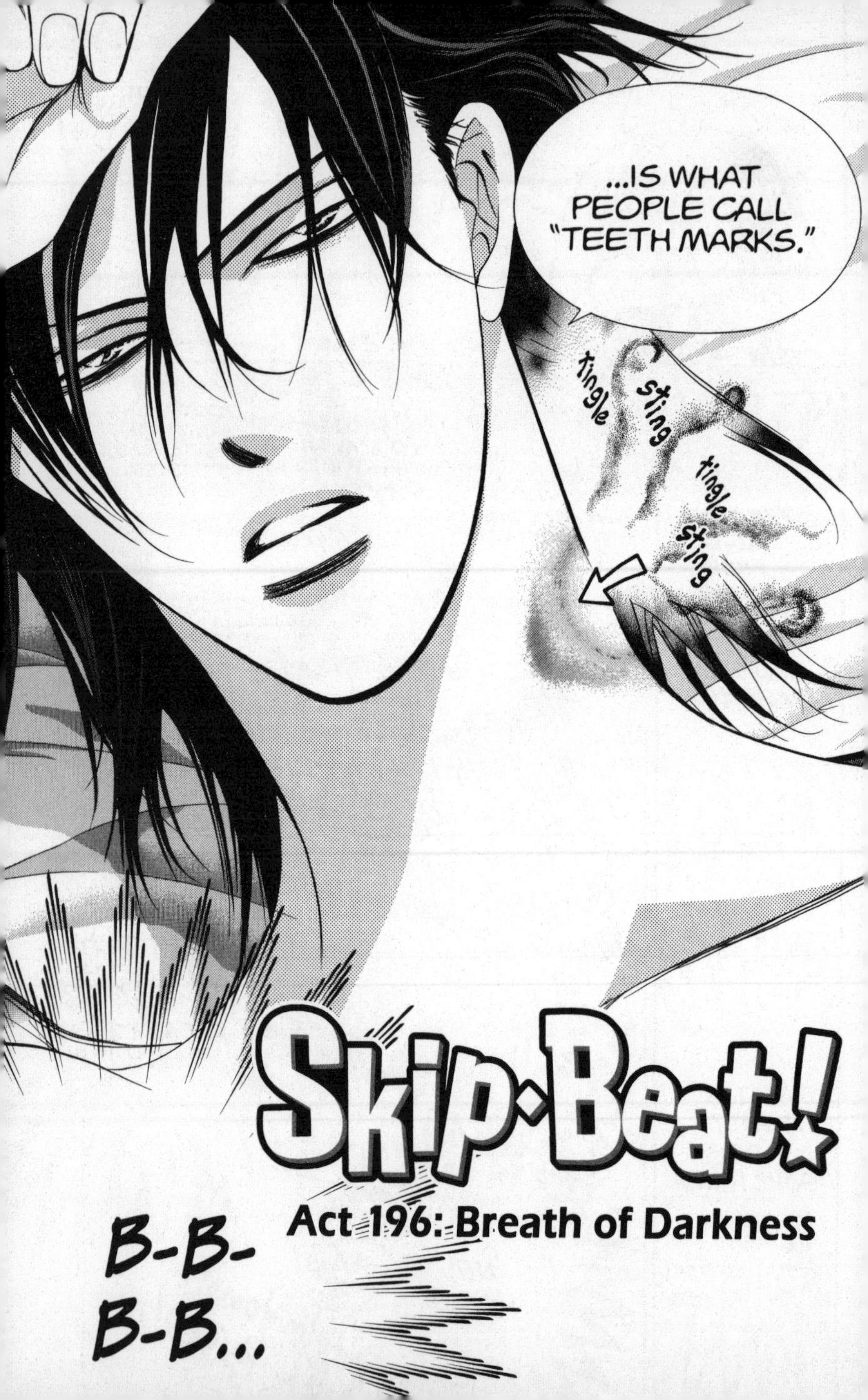
...IS WHAT PEOPLE CALL "TEETH MARKS."
tingle
sting
tingle
sting
Skip·Beat!
Act 196: Breath of Darkness
B-B-B-B...

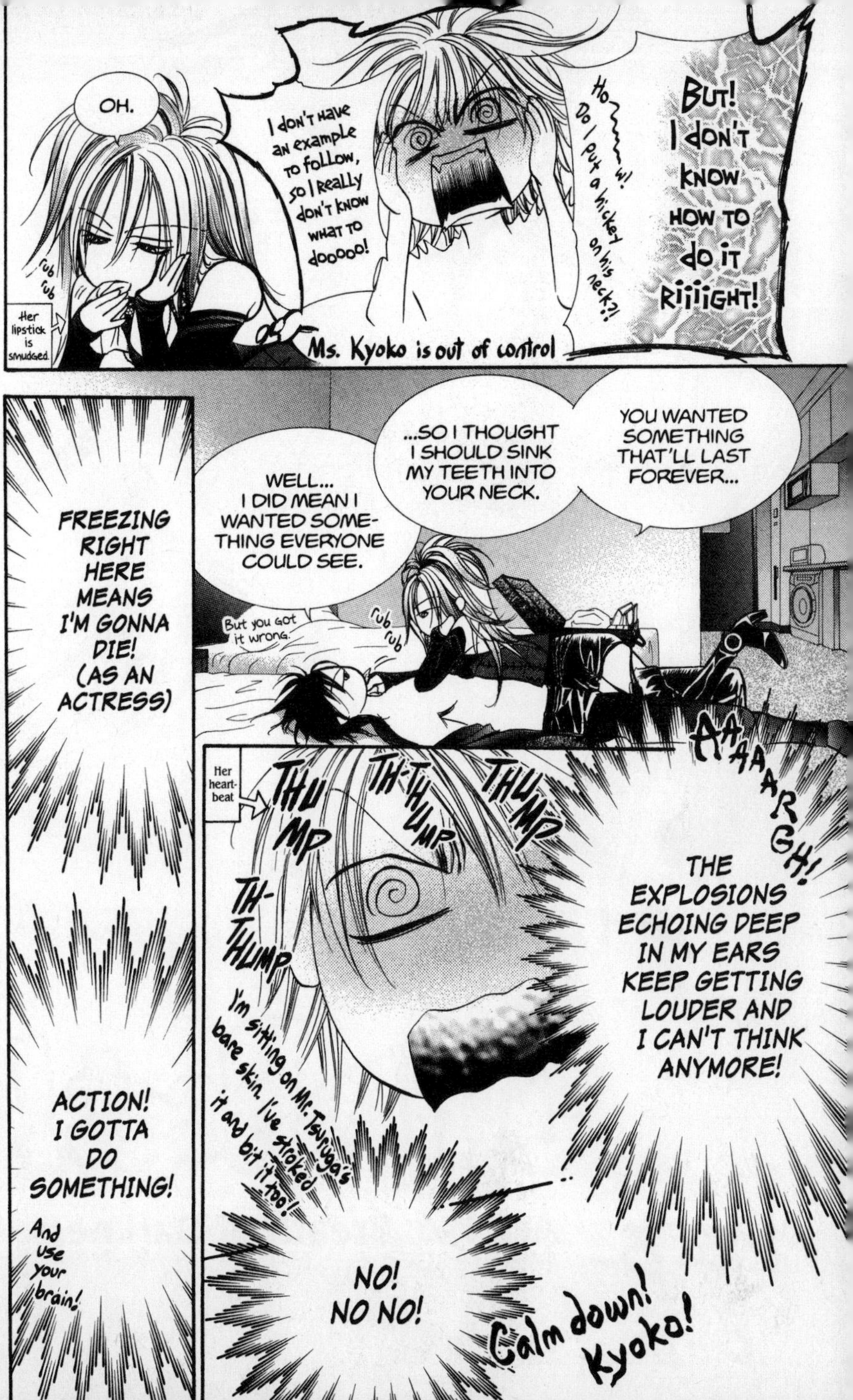
BUT! I DON'T KNOW HOW TO DO IT RIIIIGHT!
Hoooow! Do I put a hickey on his neck?!
I don't have an example to follow, so I really don't know what to doooooo!
Ms. Kyoko is out of control
OH.
rub rub
Her lipstick is smudged.
YOU WANTED SOMETHING THAT'LL LAST FOREVER...
...SO I THOUGHT I SHOULD SINK MY TEETH INTO YOUR NECK.
WELL... I DID MEAN I WANTED SOMETHING EVERYONE COULD SEE.
rub rub
But you got it wrong.
AAAAARGH!
THE EXPLOSIONS ECHOING DEEP IN MY EARS KEEP GETTING LOUDER AND I CAN'T THINK ANYMORE!
THUMP
TH-THUMP
THUMP
Her heart-beat
TH-THUMP
I'm sitting on Mr. Tsuruga's bare skin. I've stroked it and bit it too!
...
Calm down! Kyoko!
NO! NO NO!
FREEZING RIGHT HERE MEANS I'M GONNA DIE! (AS AN ACTRESS)
ACTION! I GOTTA DO SOMETHING!
And use your brain!

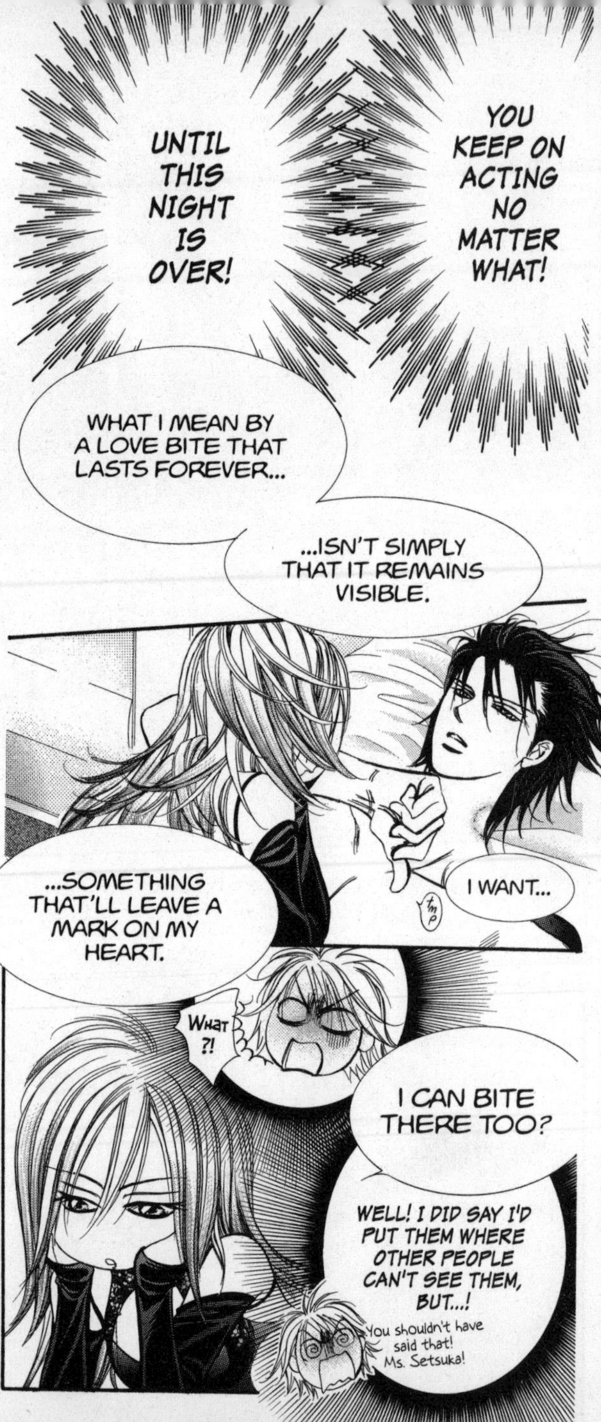
YOU KEEP ON ACTING NO MATTER WHAT!
UNTIL THIS NIGHT IS OVER!
WHAT I MEAN BY A LOVE BITE THAT LASTS FOREVER...
...ISN'T SIMPLY THAT IT REMAINS VISIBLE.
I WANT...
...SOMETHING THAT'LL LEAVE A MARK ON MY HEART.
I CAN BITE THERE TOO?
WHAT?!
WELL! I DID SAY I'D PUT THEM WHERE OTHER PEOPLE CAN'T SEE THEM, BUT...!
You shouldn't have said that! Ms. Setsuka!
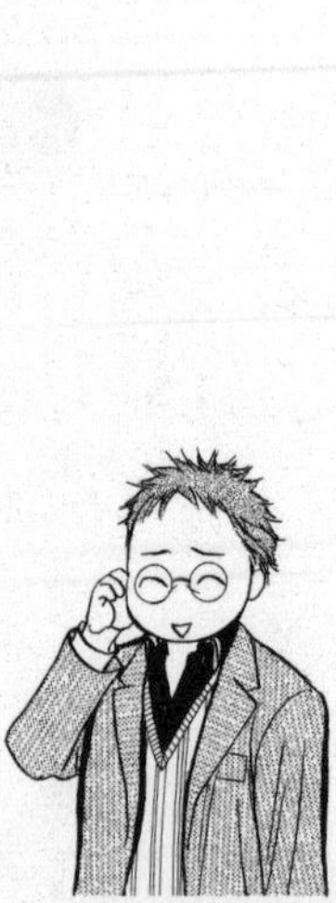

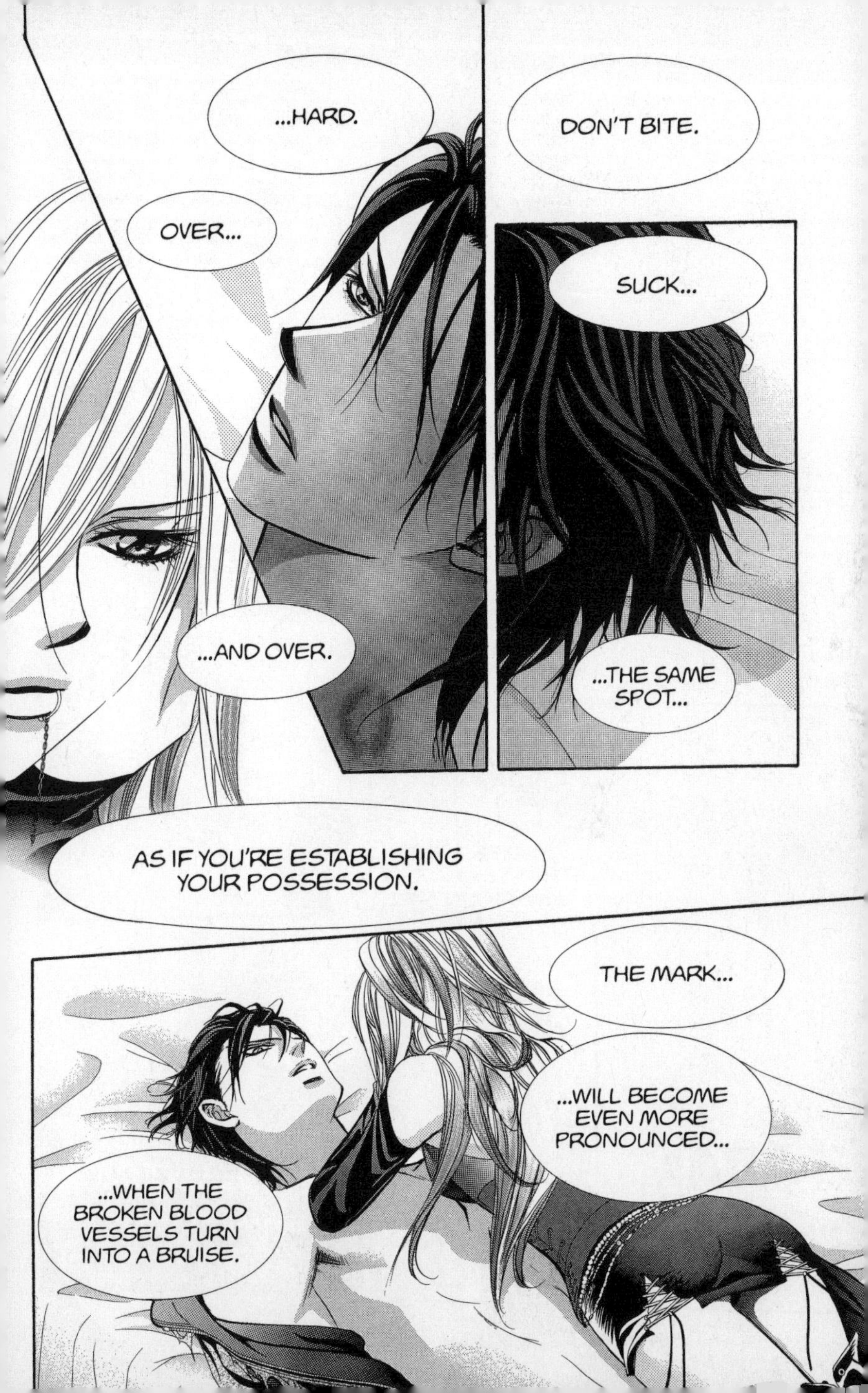
DON'T BITE.
SUCK...
...THE SAME SPOT...
...HARD.
OVER...
...AND OVER.
AS IF YOU'RE ESTABLISHING YOUR POSSESSION.
THE MARK...
...WILL BECOME EVEN MORE PRONOUNCED...
...WHEN THE BROKEN BLOOD VESSELS TURN INTO A BRUISE.

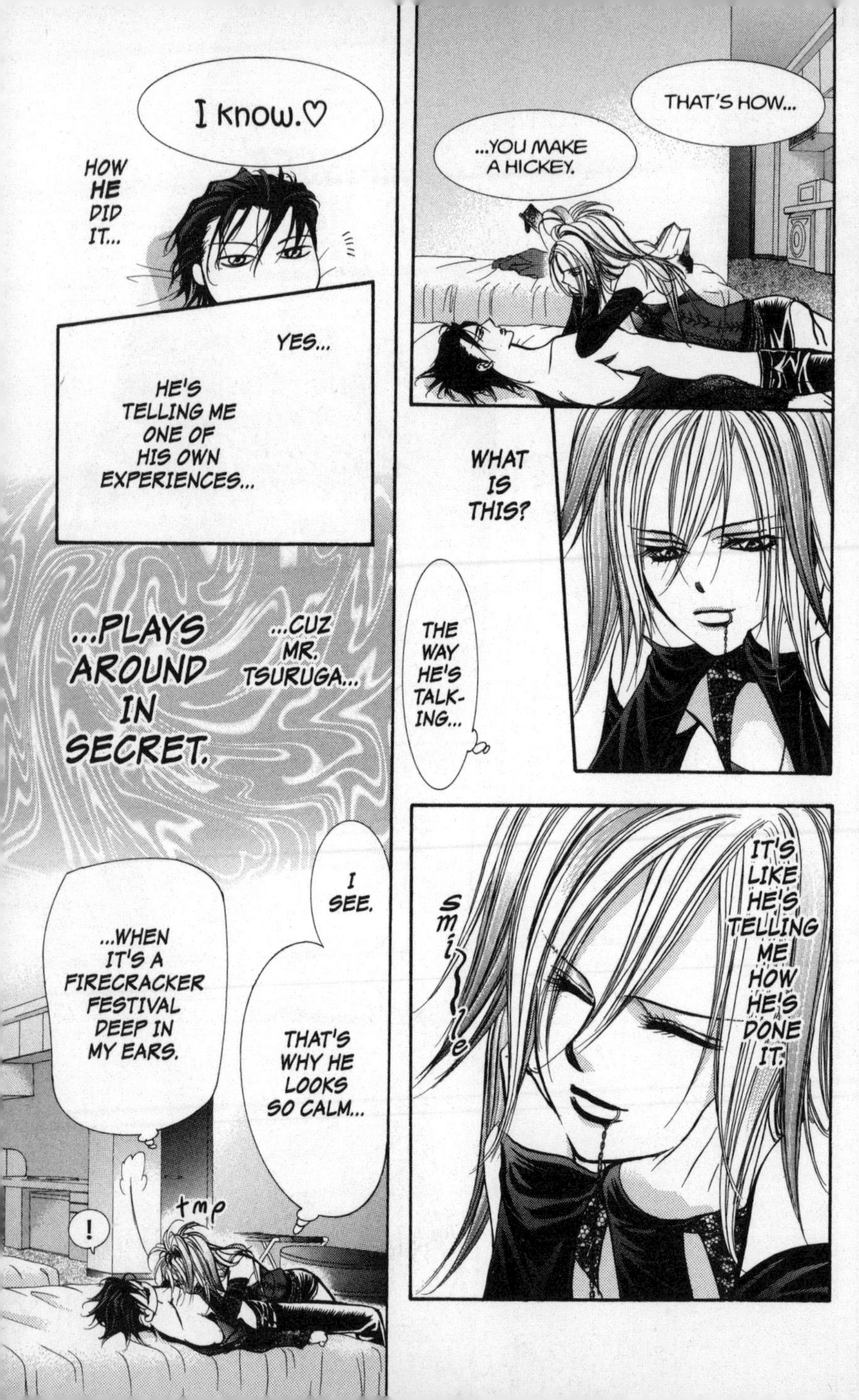
THAT'S HOW...
...YOU MAKE A HICKEY.
WHAT IS THIS?
THE WAY HE'S TALKING...
IT'S LIKE HE'S TELLING ME HOW HE'S DONE IT.
smile
I know.♡
HOW HE DID IT...
YES...
HE'S TELLING ME ONE OF HIS OWN EXPERIENCES...
...CUZ MR. TSURUGA...
...PLAYS AROUND IN SECRET.
I SEE.
THAT'S WHY HE LOOKS SO CALM...
...WHEN IT'S A FIRECRACKER FESTIVAL DEEP IN MY EARS.
tmp
!

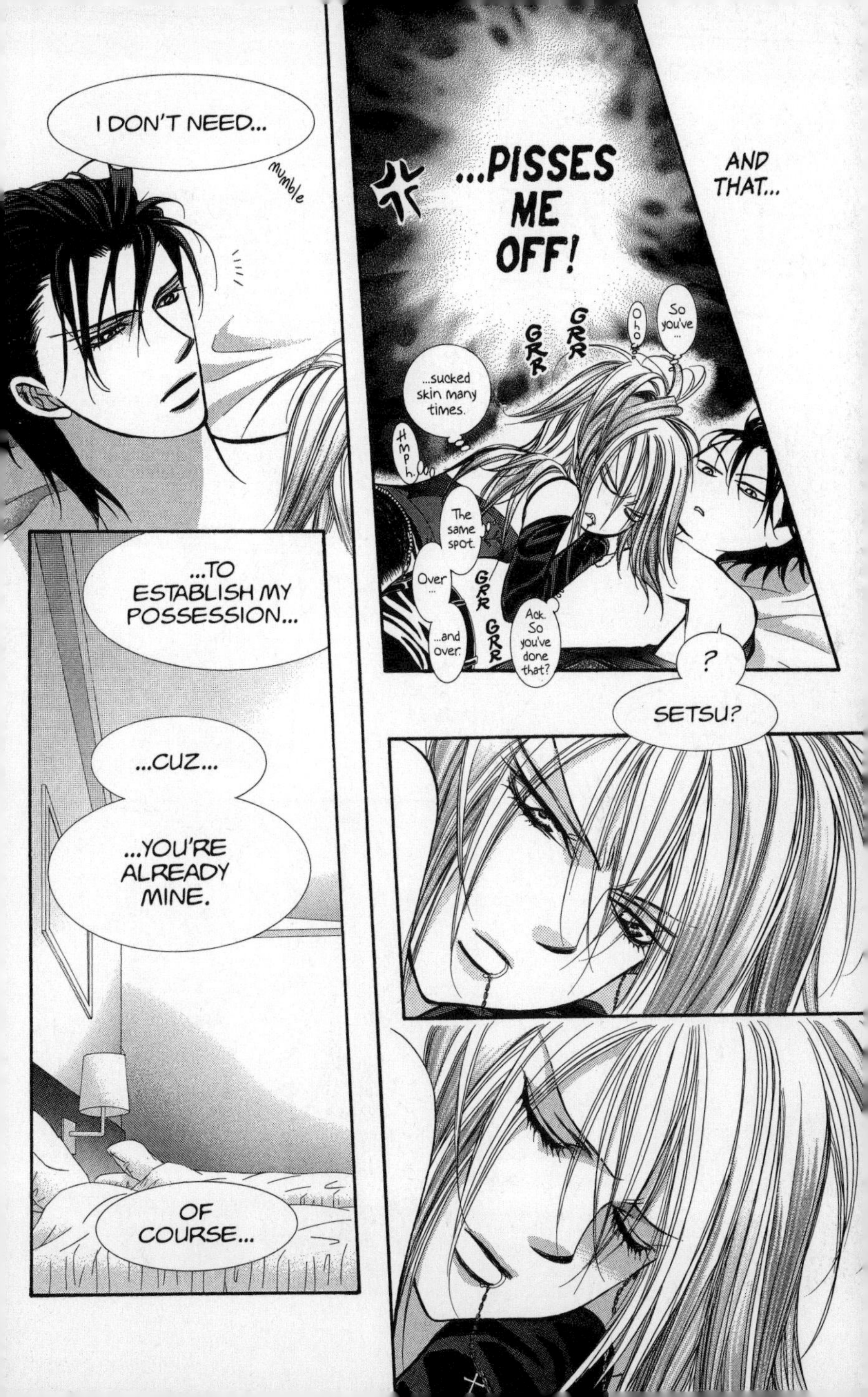
I DON'T NEED...
mumble
...TO ESTABLISH MY POSSESSION...
...CUZ...
...YOU'RE ALREADY MINE.
OF COURSE...
AND THAT...
...PISSES ME OFF!
So you've...
Oho
GRR
GRR
...sucked skin many times.
Hmph.
The same spot.
Over...
...and over.
GRR
GRR
Ack. So you've done that?
?
SETSU?

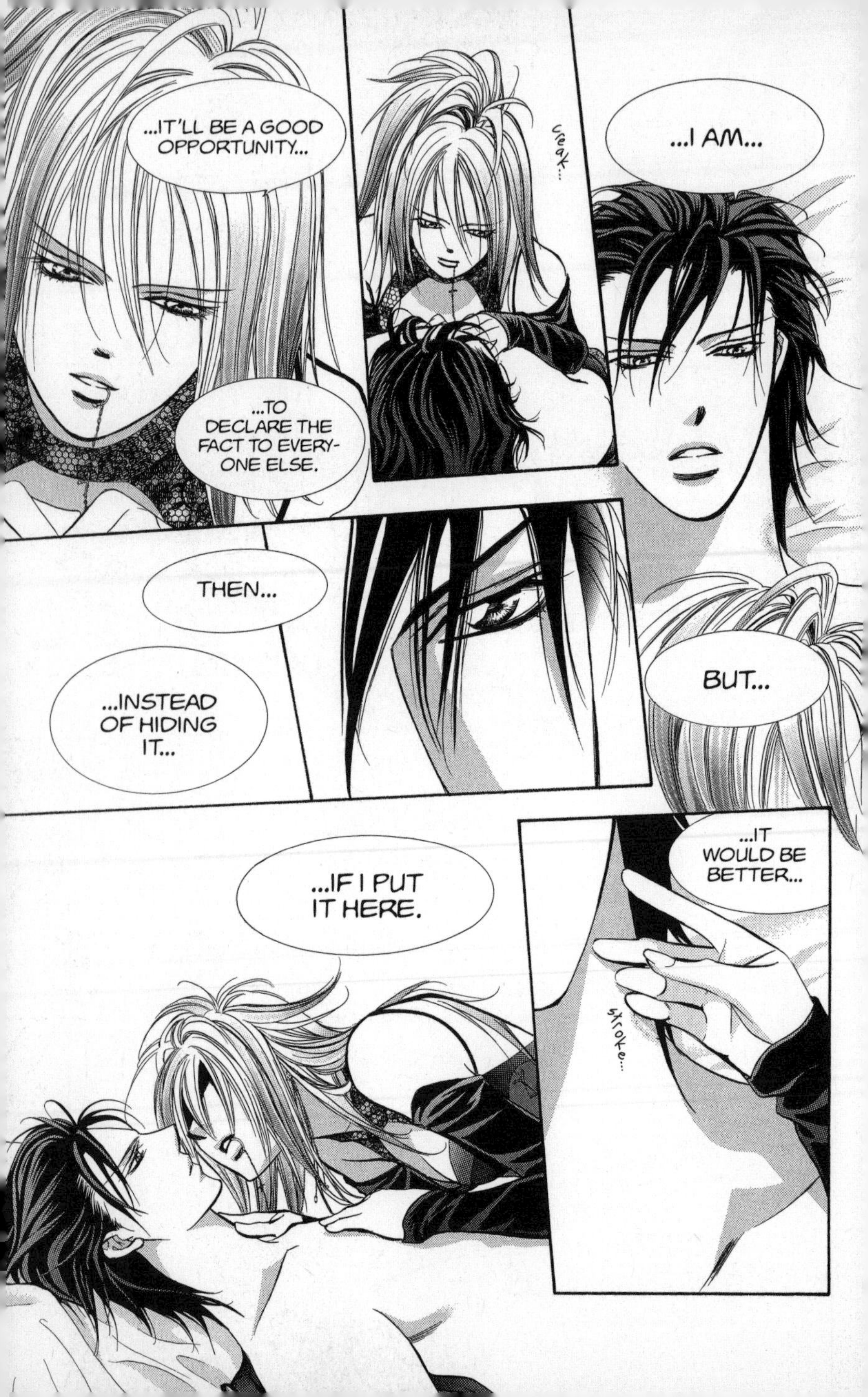
...I AM...
BUT...
creak...
...IT'LL BE A GOOD OPPORTUNITY...
...TO DECLARE THE FACT TO EVERY-ONE ELSE.
THEN...
...INSTEAD OF HIDING IT...
...IT WOULD BE BETTER...
stroke...
...IF I PUT IT HERE.

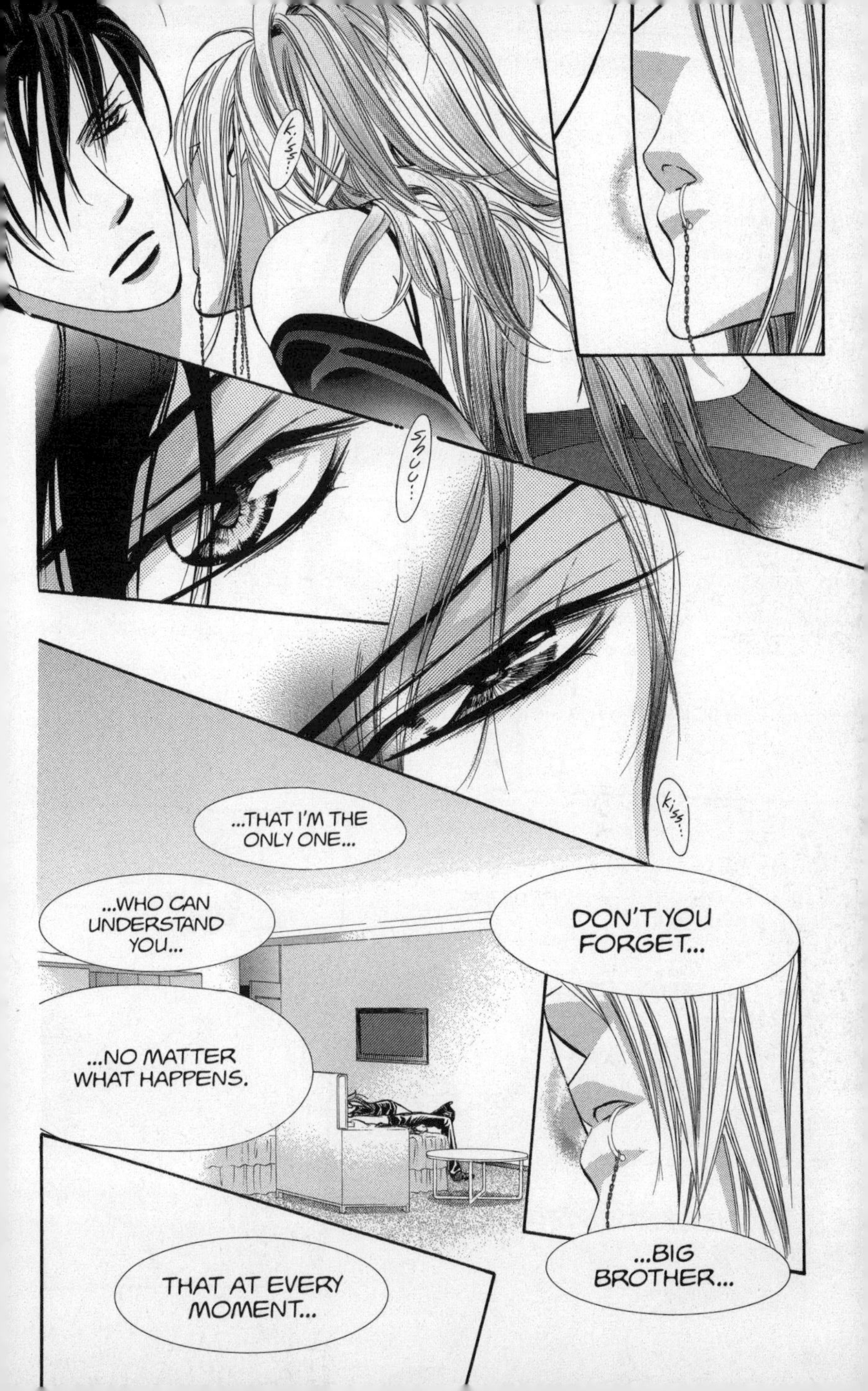
Kiss...
Shuu...
Kiss...
DON'T YOU FORGET...
...THAT I'M THE ONLY ONE...
...WHO CAN UNDERSTAND YOU...
...NO MATTER WHAT HAPPENS.
...BIG BROTHER...
THAT AT EVERY MOMENT...

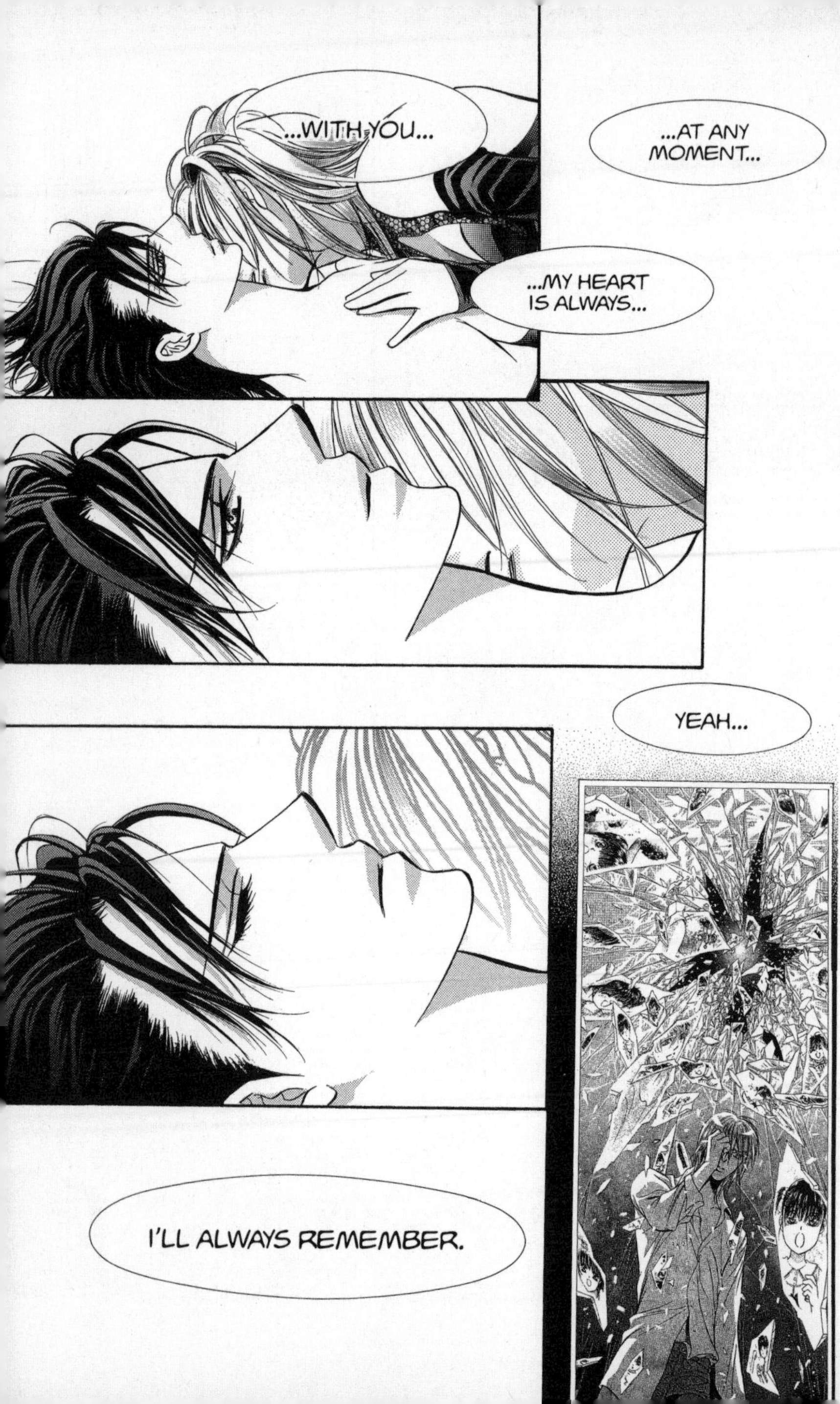
...AT ANY MOMENT...
...MY HEART IS ALWAYS...
...WITH YOU...
YEAH...
I'LL ALWAYS REMEMBER.

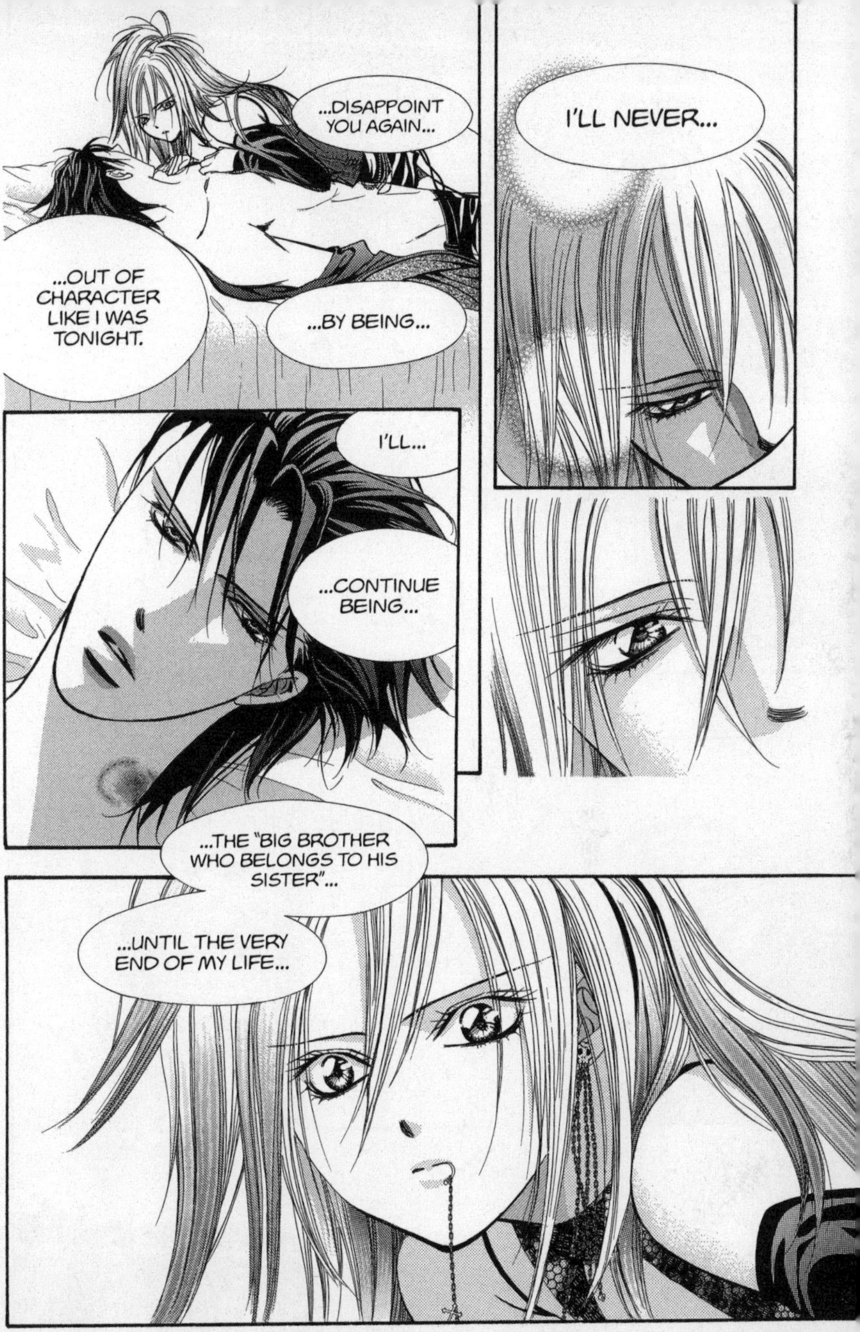
I'LL NEVER...
...DISAPPOINT YOU AGAIN...
...BY BEING...
...OUT OF CHARACTER LIKE I WAS TONIGHT.
I'LL...
...CONTINUE BEING...
...THE "BIG BROTHER WHO BELONGS TO HIS SISTER"...
...UNTIL THE VERY END OF MY LIFE...

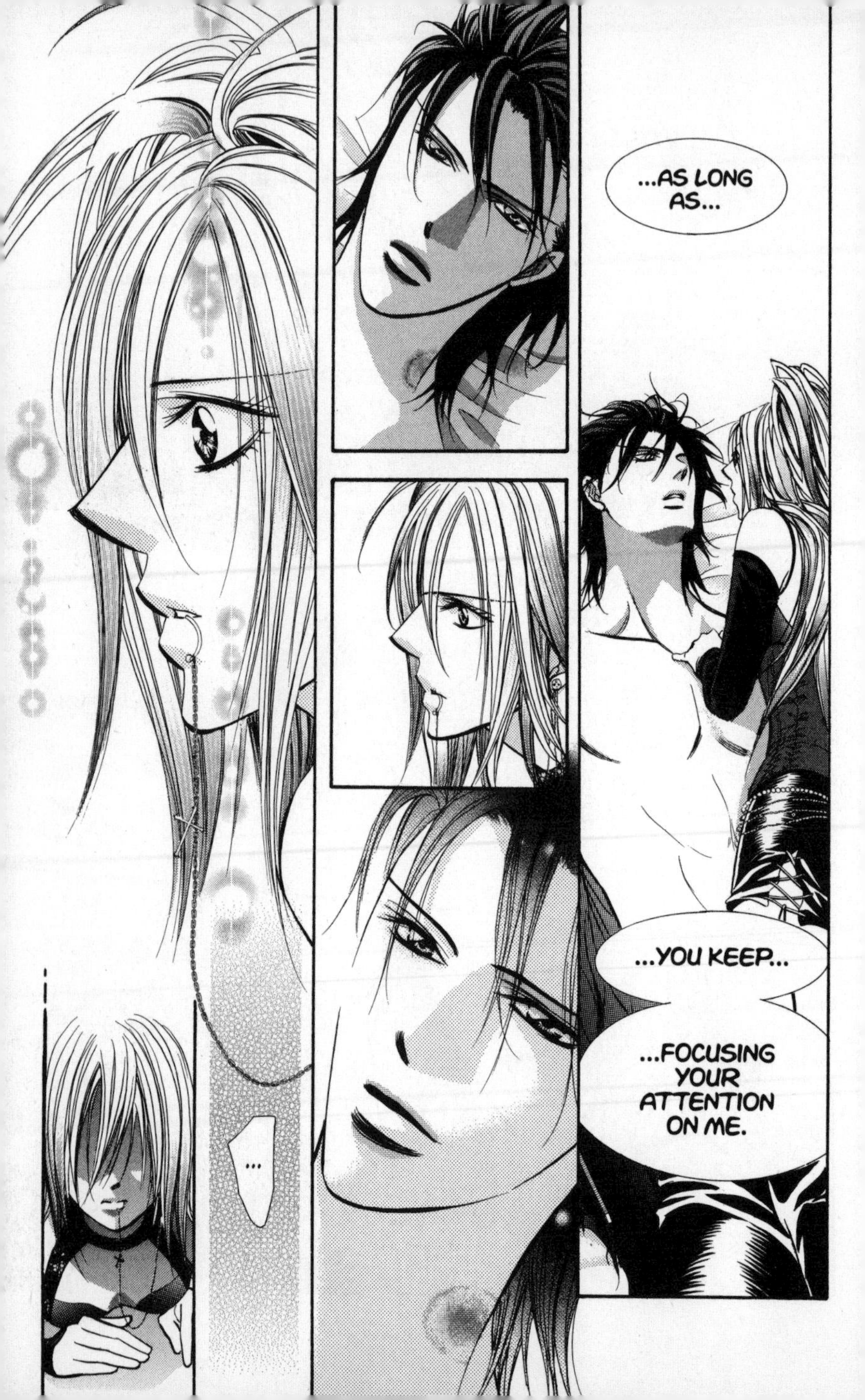
...AS LONG AS...
...YOU KEEP...
...FOCUSING YOUR ATTENTION ON ME.
...

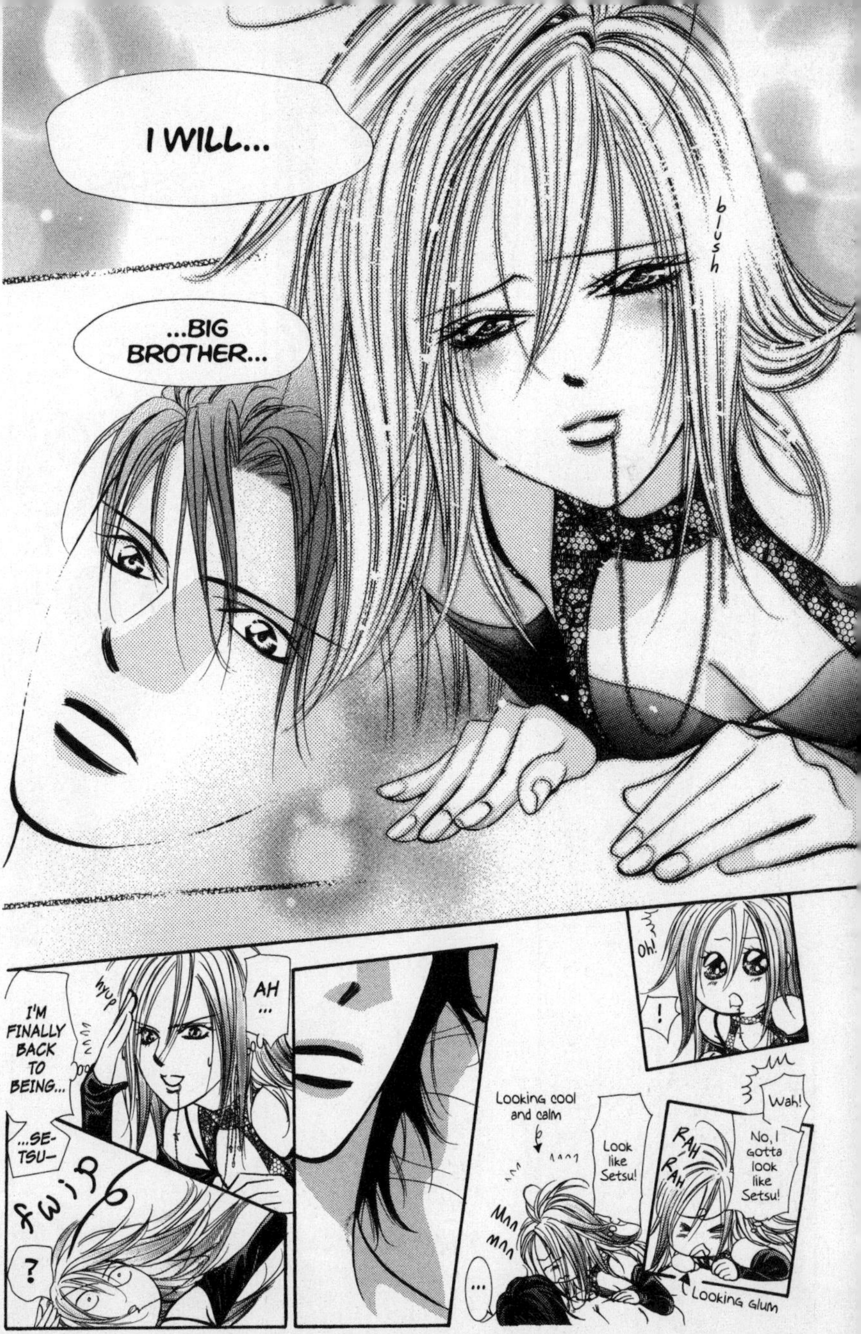

I WILL...
blush
...BIG BROTHER...
Oh!
!
Wah!
No, I gotta look like Setsu!
RAH RAH
Looking Glum
Looking cool and calm
Look like Setsu!
...
AH ...
hyup
I'M FINALLY BACK TO BEING...
...SE-TSU-
fwip
?

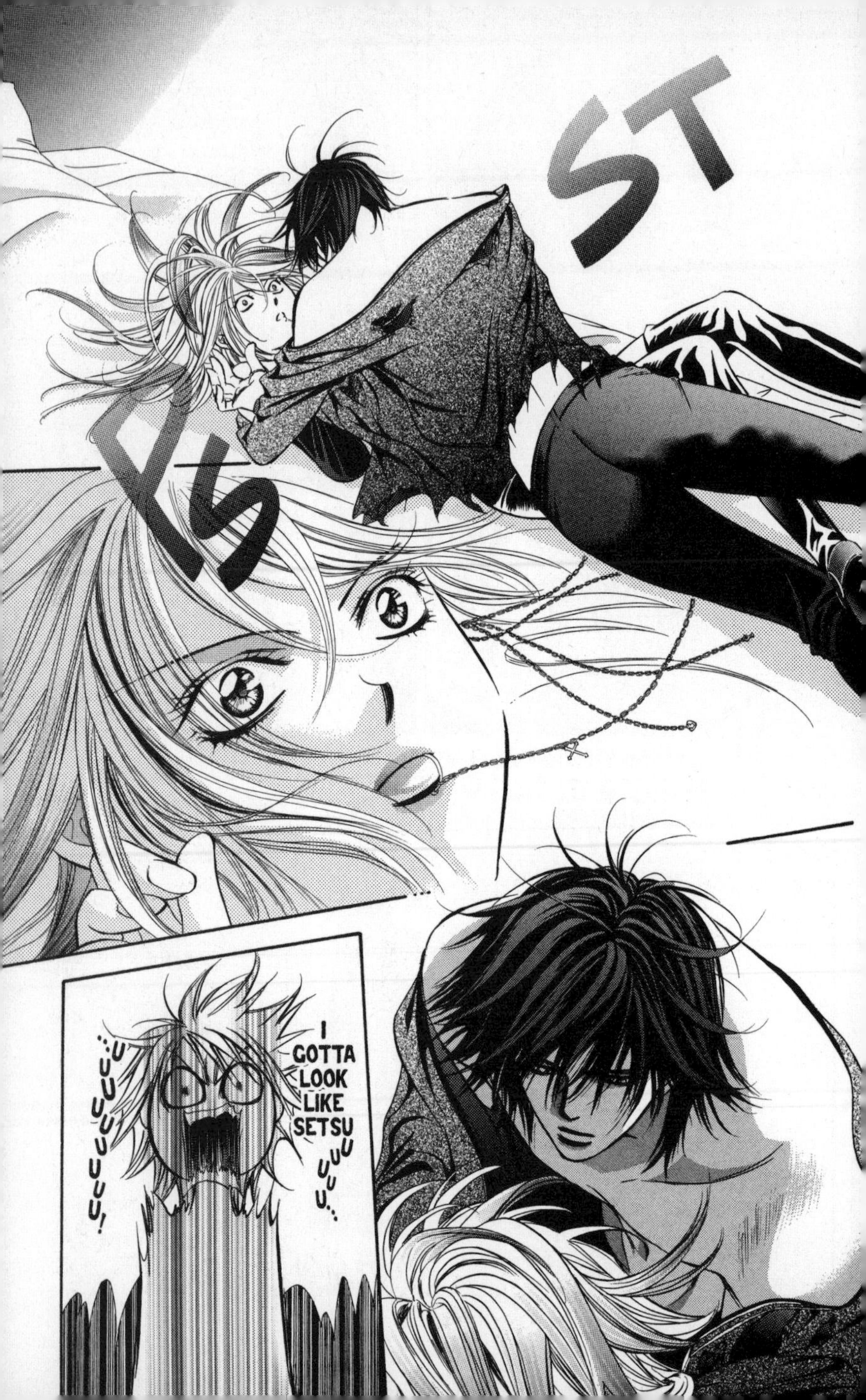
I GOTTA LOOK LIKE SETSUUUUUU...
...UUUUUUUUUU!

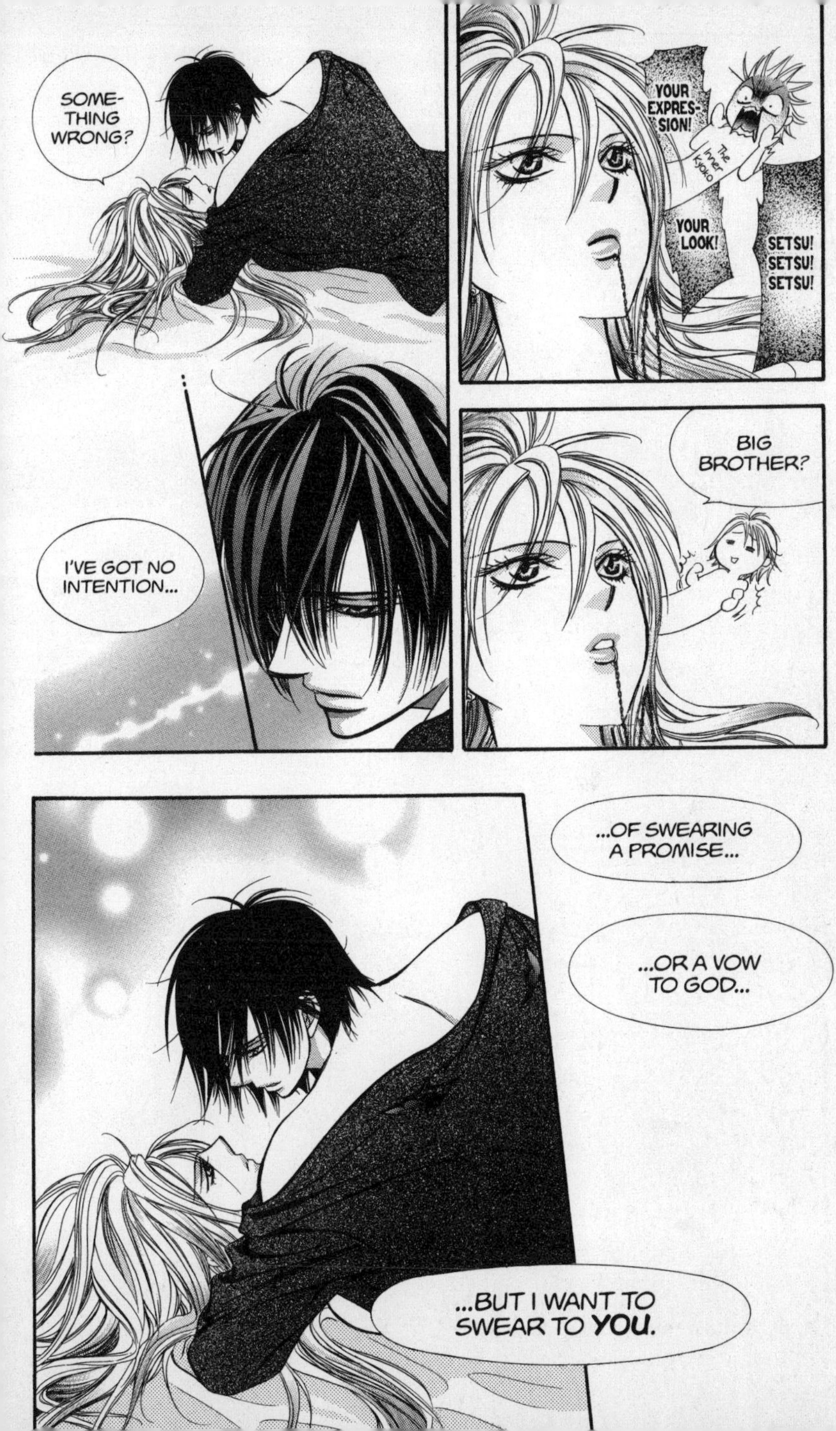
YOUR EXPRES-SION!
The Inner Kyoko
YOUR LOOK!
SETSU! SETSU! SETSU!
BIG BROTHER?
SOME-THING WRONG?
I'VE GOT NO INTENTION...
...OF SWEARING A PROMISE...
...OR A VOW TO GOD...
...BUT I WANT TO SWEAR TO **YOU**.

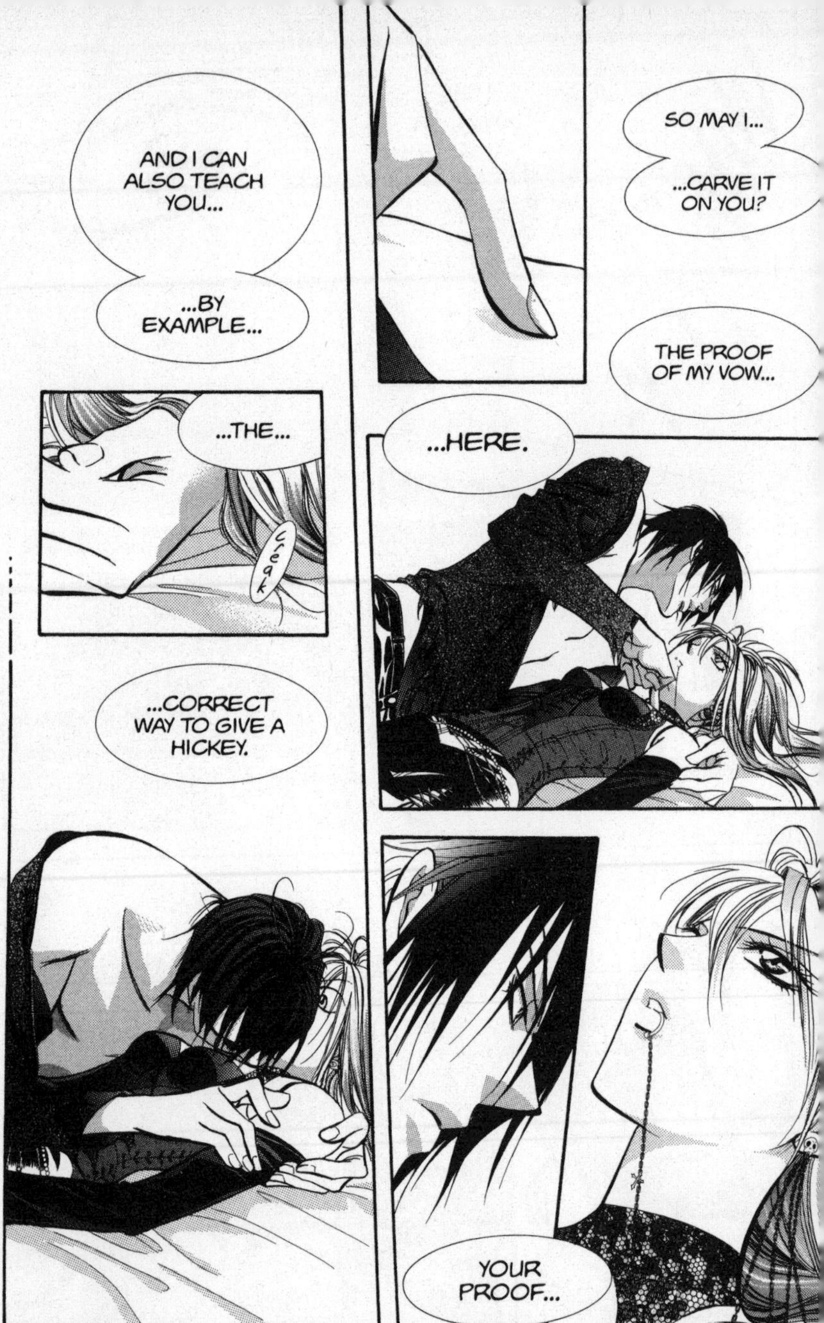
SO MAY I...
...CARVE IT ON YOU?
THE PROOF OF MY VOW...
...HERE.
YOUR PROOF...
AND I CAN ALSO TEACH YOU...
...BY EXAMPLE...
...THE...
Creak
...CORRECT WAY TO GIVE A HICKEY.

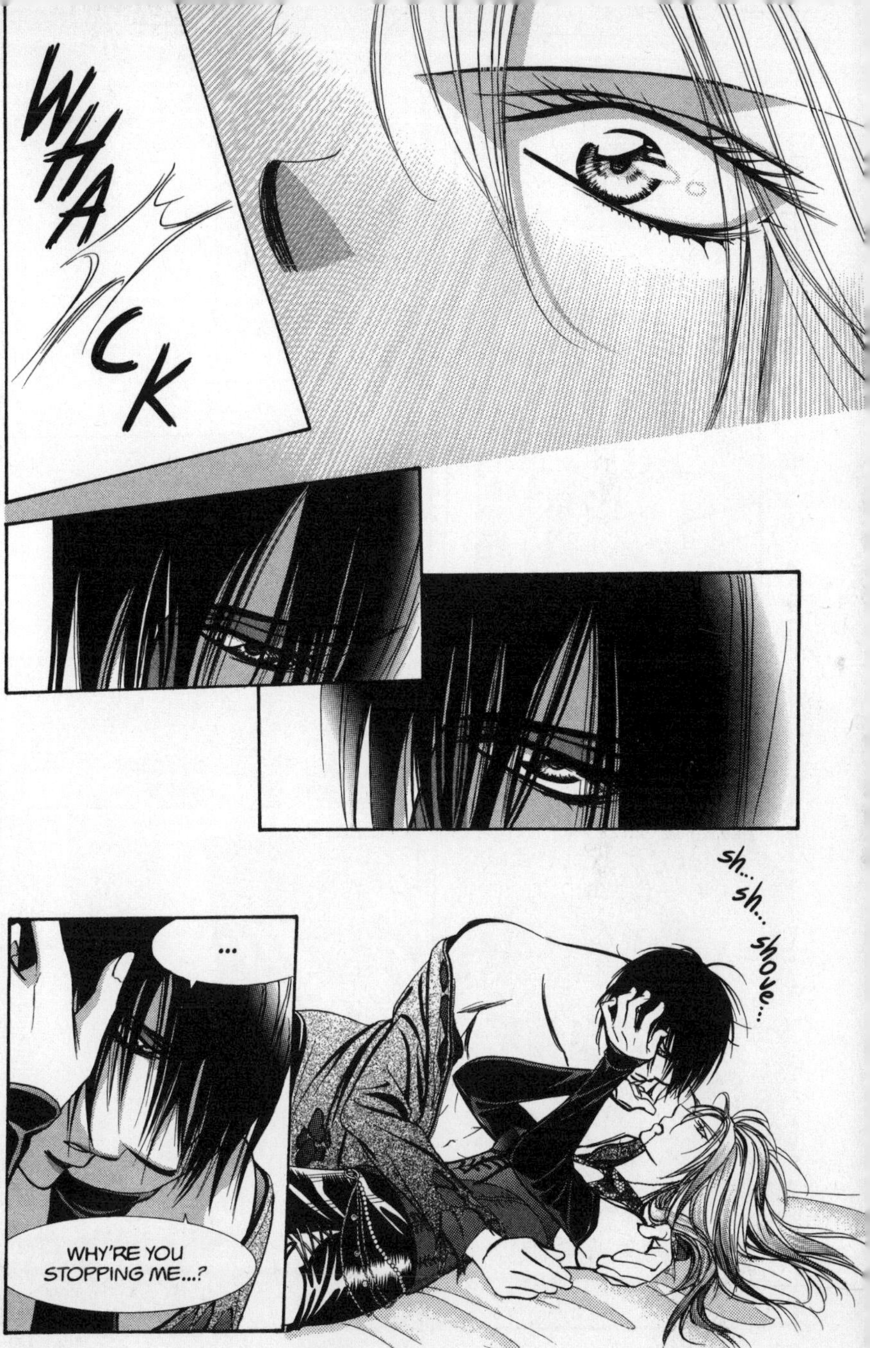
WHACK
sh... sh... shove...
...
WHY'RE YOU STOPPING ME...?

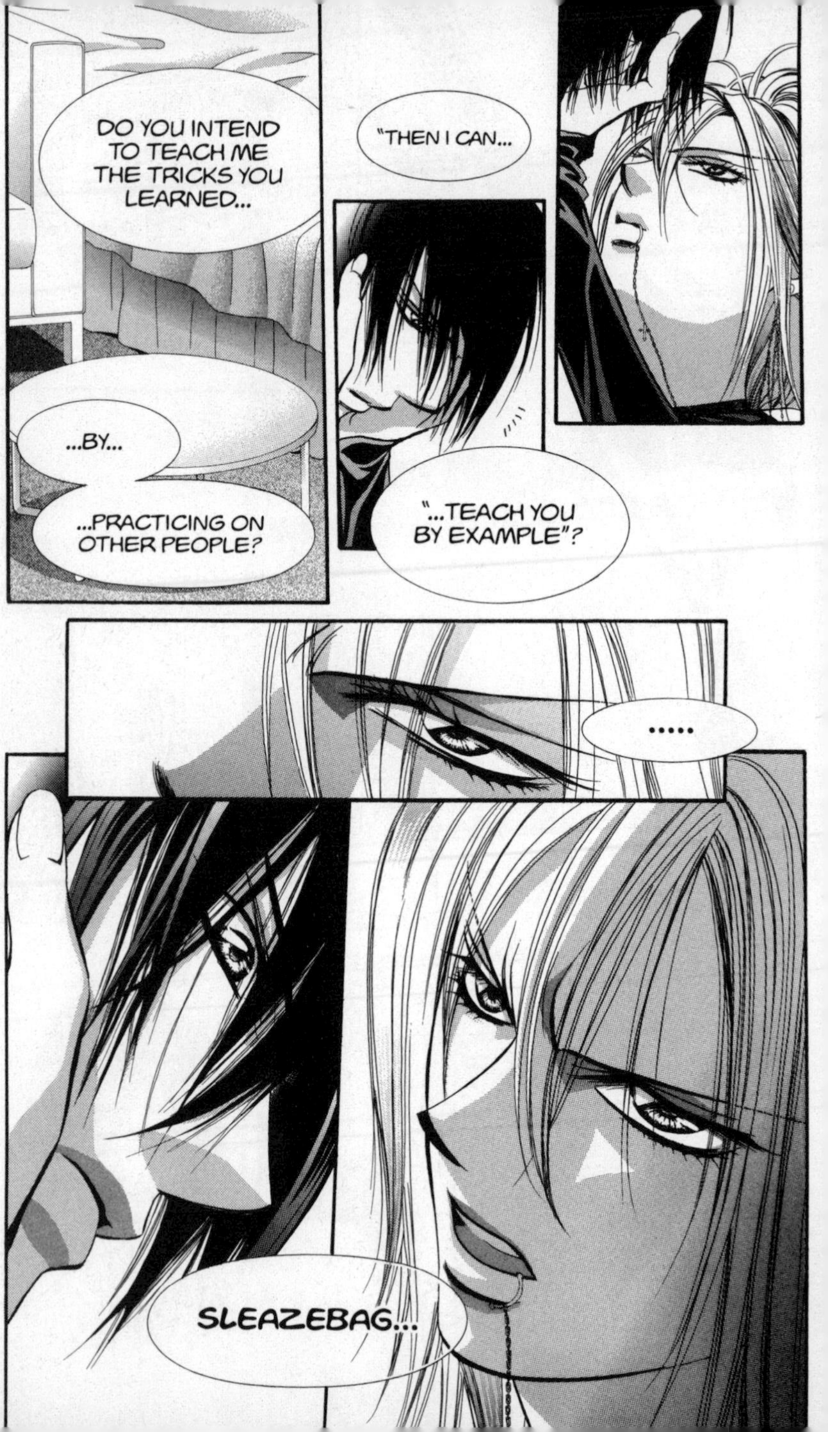
"THEN I CAN...
"...TEACH YOU BY EXAMPLE"?
DO YOU INTEND TO TEACH ME THE TRICKS YOU LEARNED...
...BY...
...PRACTICING ON OTHER PEOPLE?
......
SLEAZEBAG...

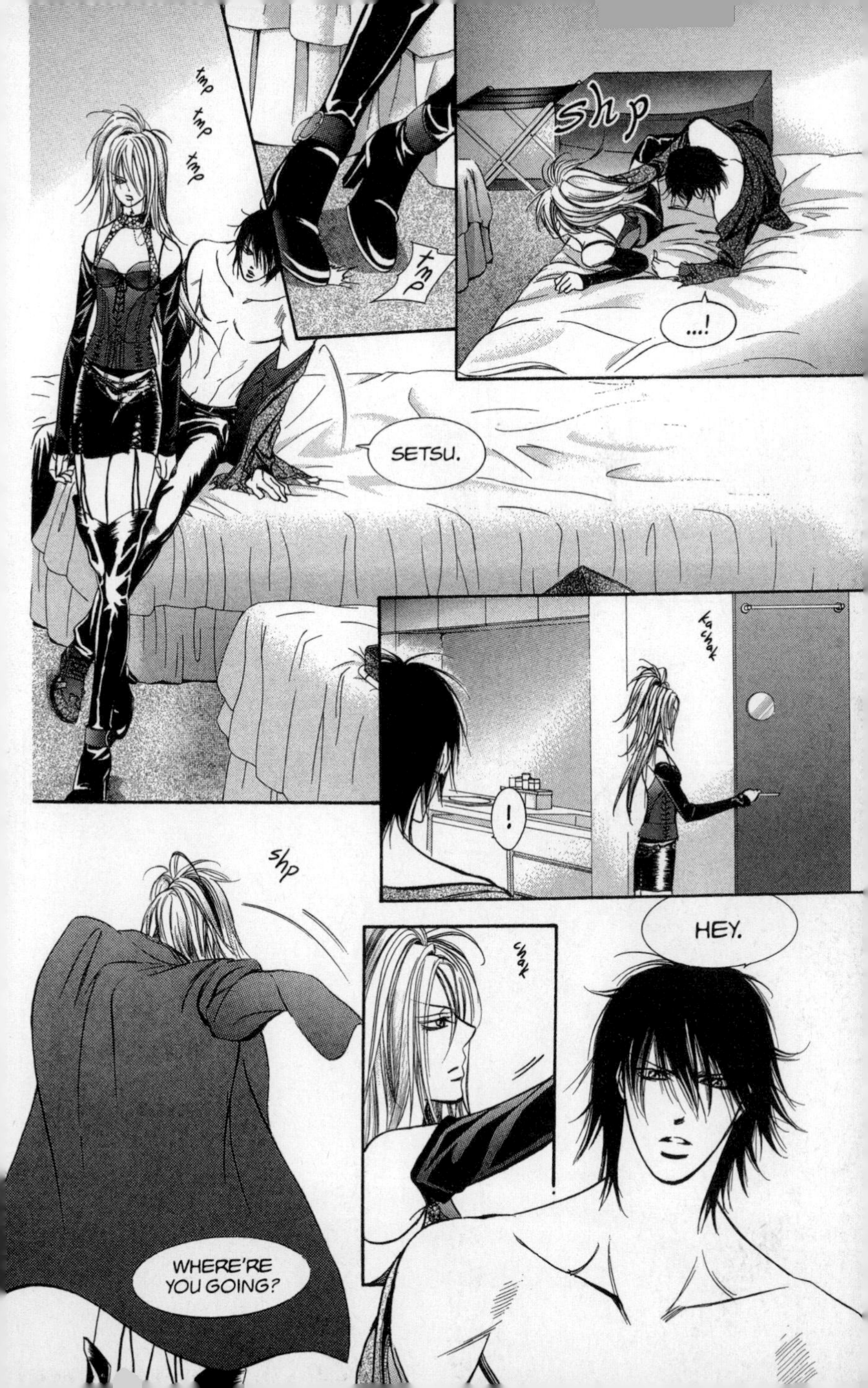
shp
...!
tmp
tmp
tmp
tmp
SETSU.
ka chak
!
HEY.
chak
shp
WHERE'RE YOU GOING?

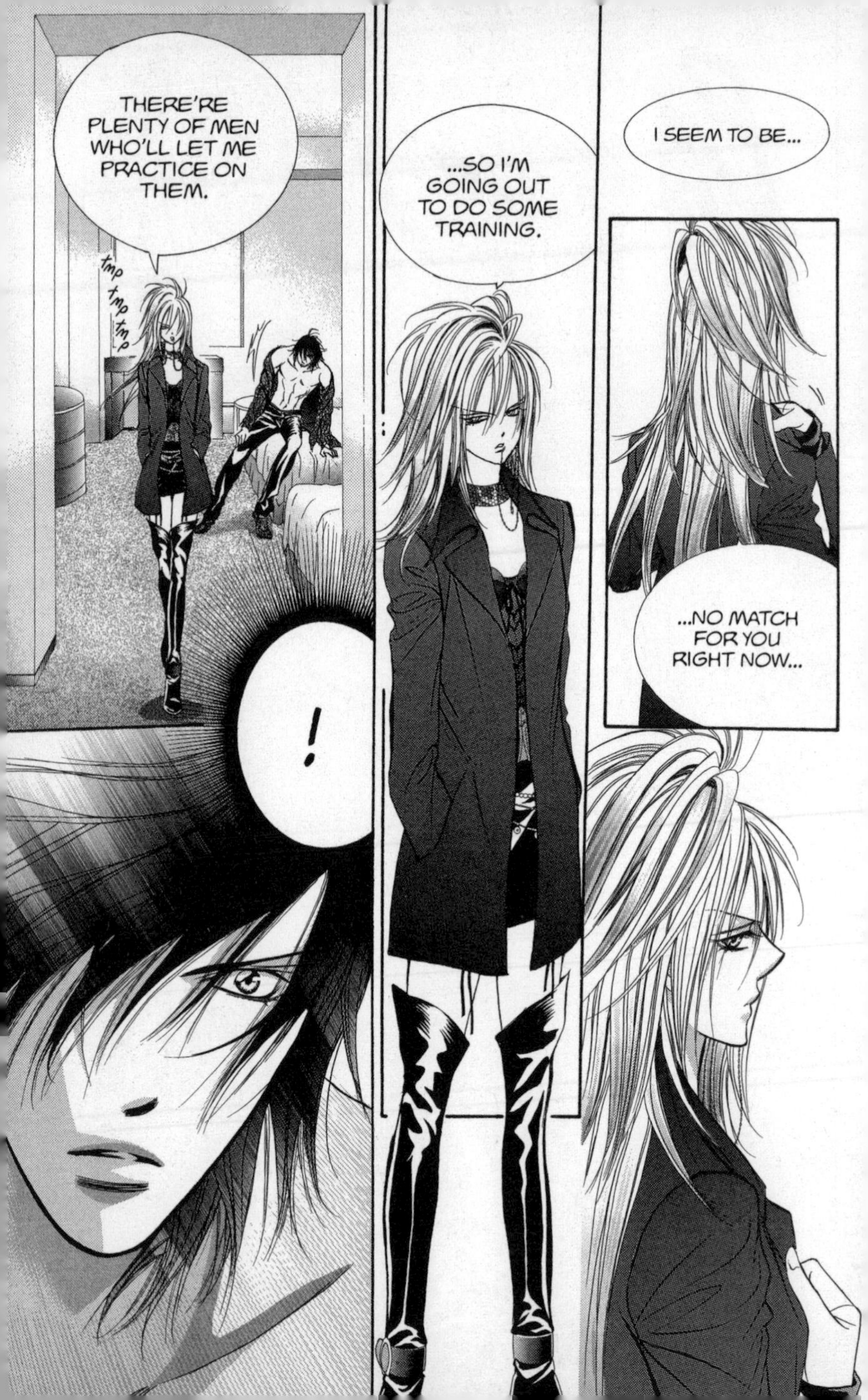
I SEEM TO BE...
...NO MATCH FOR YOU RIGHT NOW...
...SO I'M GOING OUT TO DO SOME TRAINING.
THERE'RE PLENTY OF MEN WHO'LL LET ME PRACTICE ON THEM.
tmp tmp tmp
!

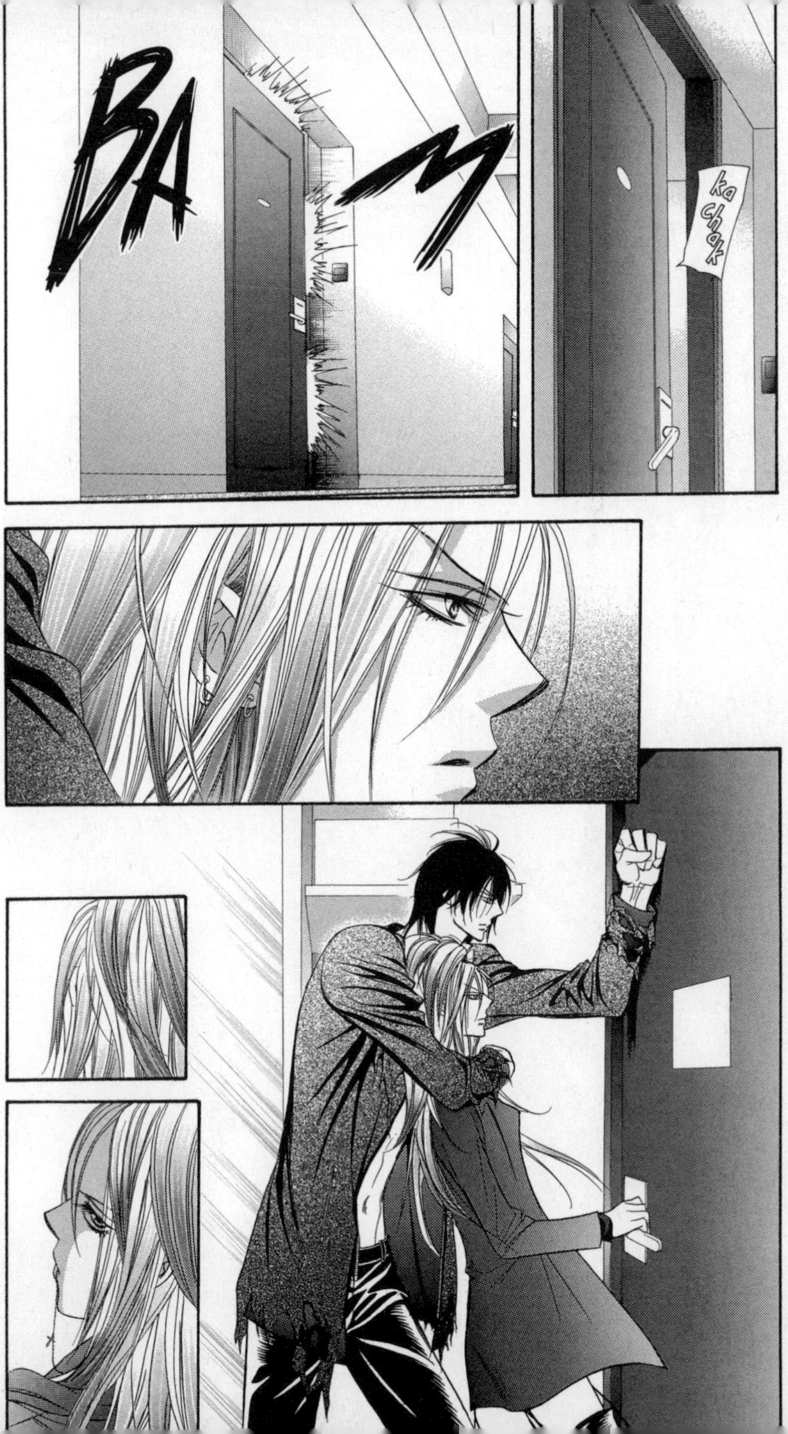
ka chak
BAM

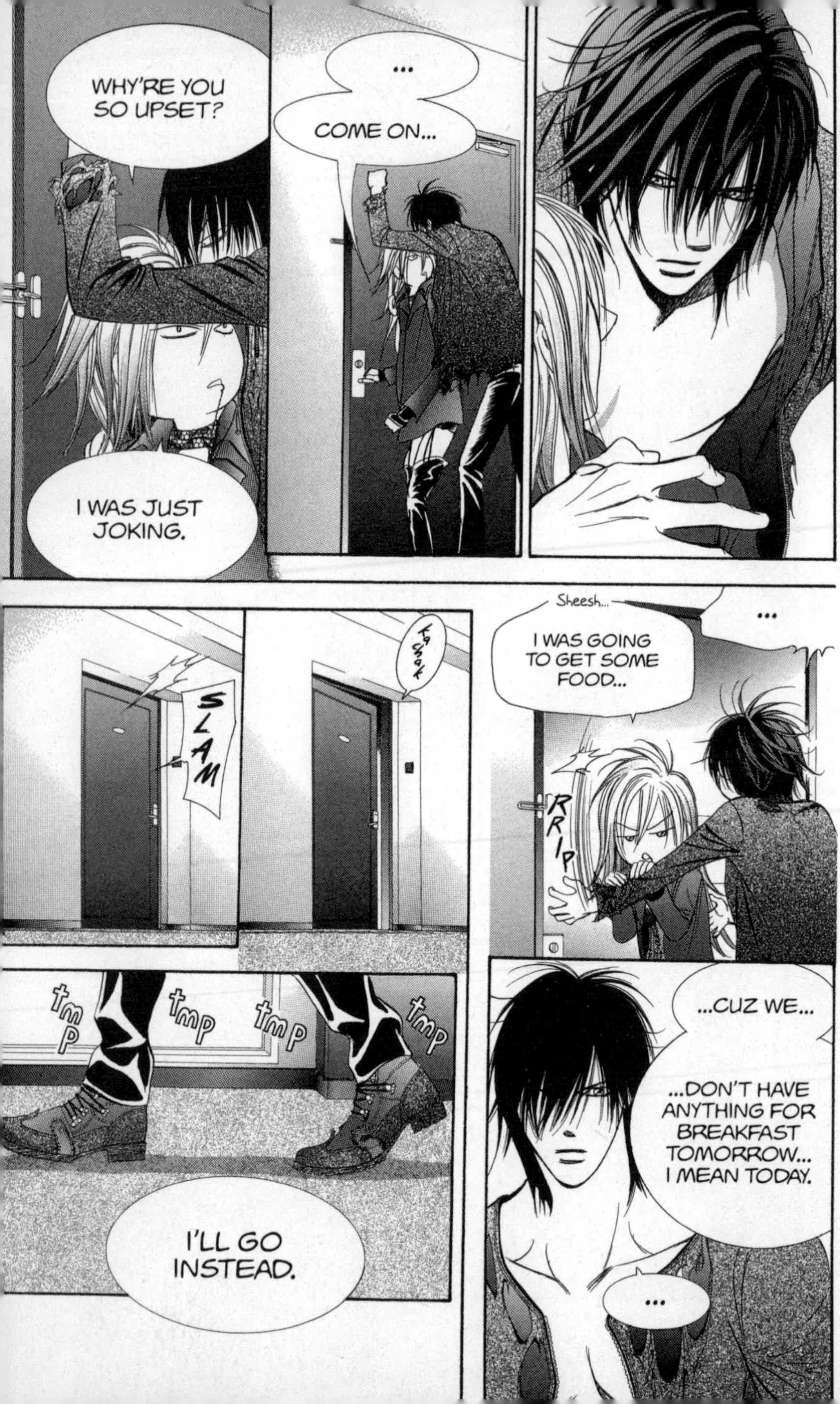
...
COME ON...
WHY'RE YOU SO UPSET?
I WAS JUST JOKING.
...
Sheesh...
I WAS GOING TO GET SOME FOOD...
RRIP
ka chak
SLAM
...CUZ WE...
...DON'T HAVE ANYTHING FOR BREAKFAST TOMORROW... I MEAN TODAY.
...
tmp tmp tmp tmp
I'LL GO INSTEAD.

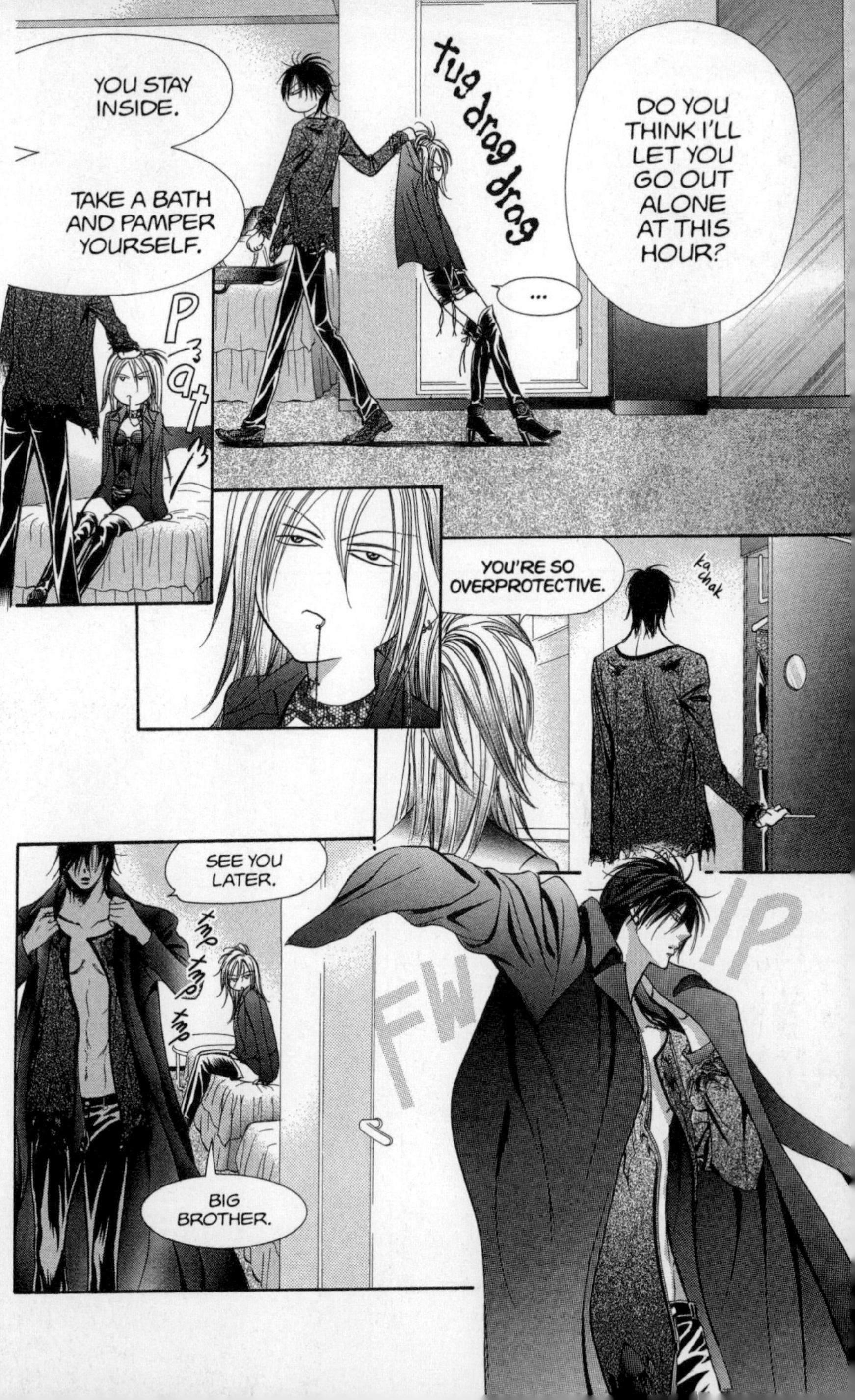
DO YOU THINK I'LL LET YOU GO OUT ALONE AT THIS HOUR?
tug drag drag
...
YOU STAY INSIDE.
TAKE A BATH AND PAMPER YOURSELF.
Pat
ka chak
YOU'RE SO OVERPROTECTIVE.
FWIP
SEE YOU LATER.
tmp tmp tmp
BIG BROTHER.

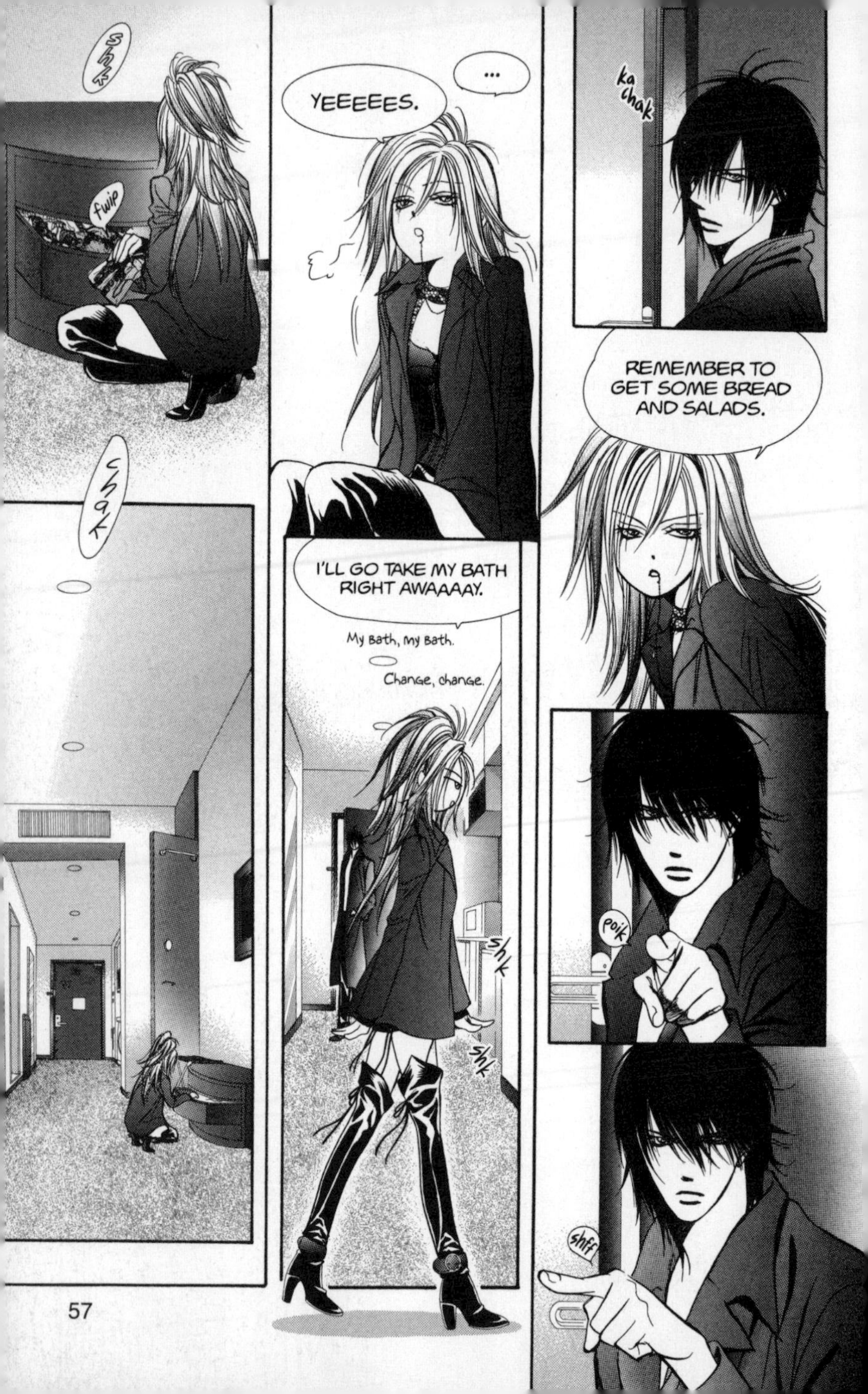
ka chak
REMEMBER TO GET SOME BREAD AND SALADS.
poik
shff
...
YEEEEEES.
I'LL GO TAKE MY BATH RIGHT AWAAAAY.
My Bath, My Bath.
Change, change.
shk
shk
shk
fwip
chak

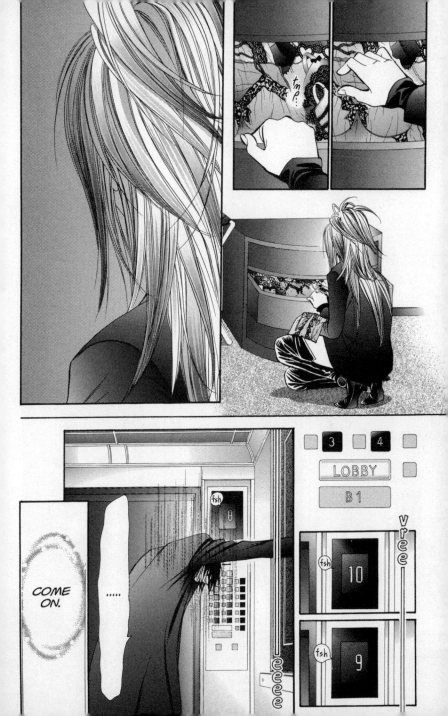

tnp...

COME
ON.

.....

3   4

LOBBY

B1

fsh

fsh   10

fsh   9

vree

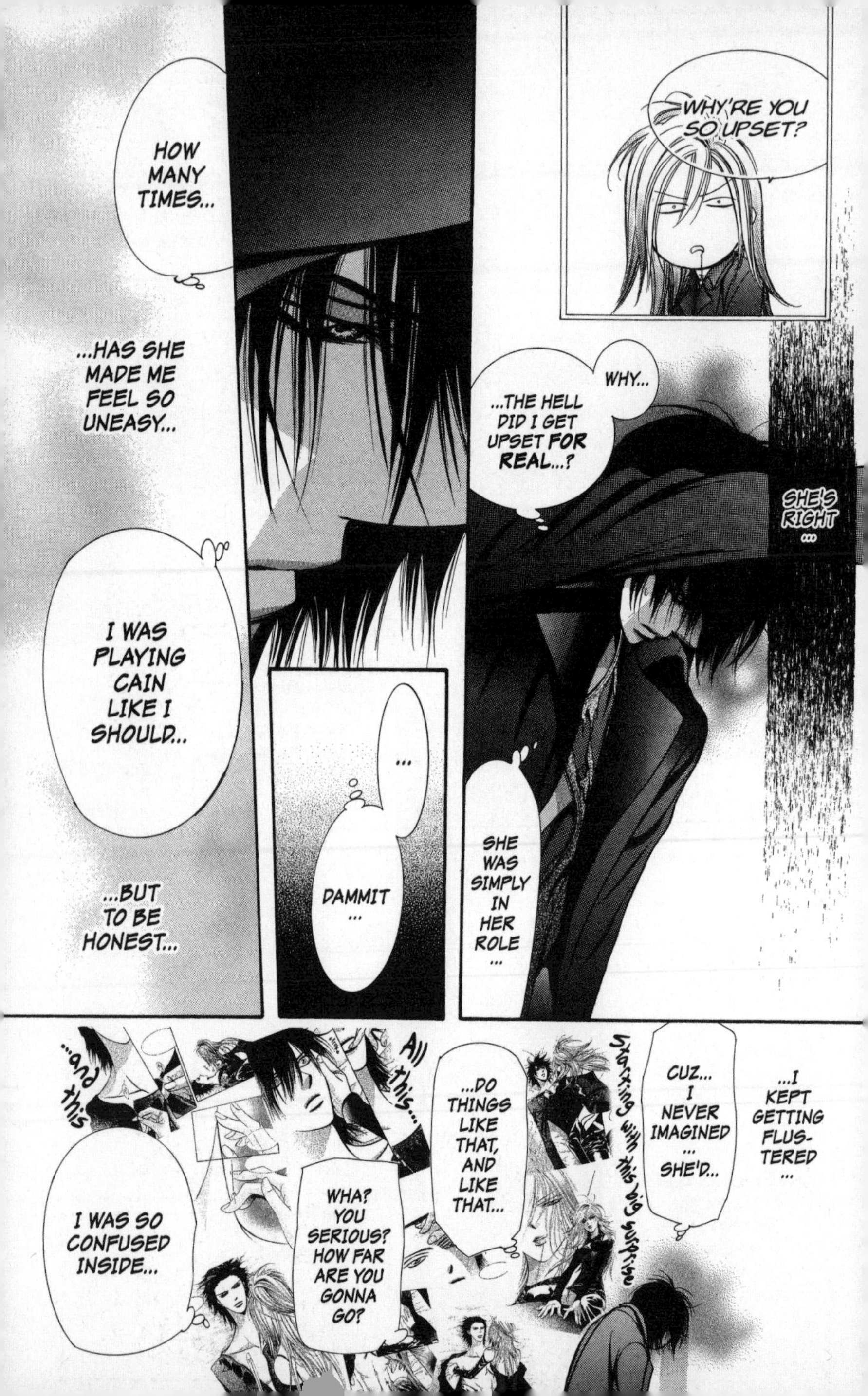
WHY'RE YOU SO UPSET?
SHE'S RIGHT ...
WHY...
...THE HELL DID I GET UPSET FOR REAL...?
SHE WAS SIMPLY IN HER ROLE ...
...
DAMMIT ...
HOW MANY TIMES...
...HAS SHE MADE ME FEEL SO UNEASY...
I WAS PLAYING CAIN LIKE I SHOULD...
...BUT TO BE HONEST...
...I KEPT GETTING FLUS-TERED ...
CUZ... I NEVER IMAGINED ... SHE'D...
Starting with this big surprise
...DO THINGS LIKE THAT, AND LIKE THAT...
WHA? YOU SERIOUS? HOW FAR ARE YOU GONNA GO?
All this...
...and this
I WAS SO CONFUSED INSIDE...

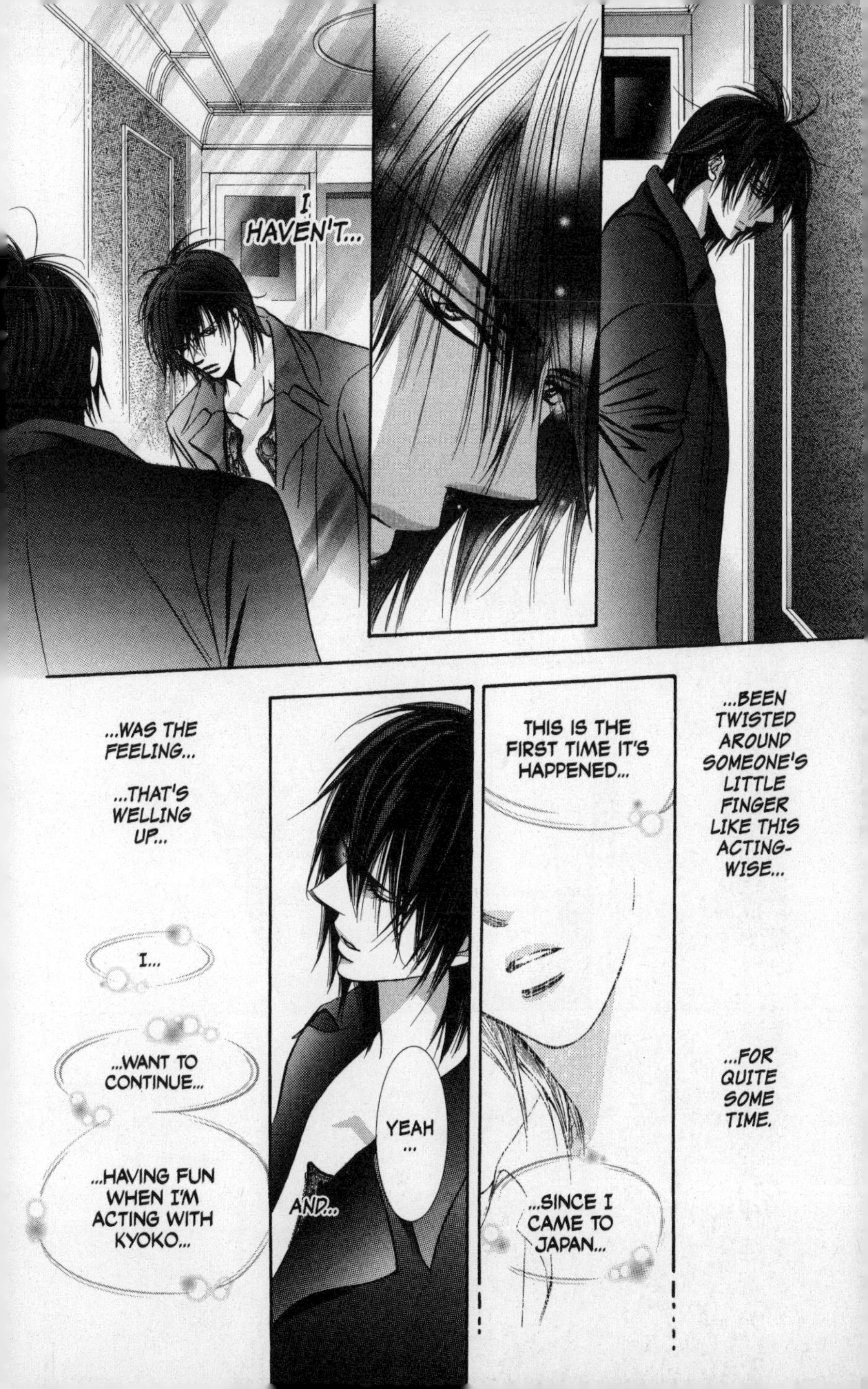
I HAVEN'T...
...BEEN TWISTED AROUND SOMEONE'S LITTLE FINGER LIKE THIS ACTING-WISE...
...FOR QUITE SOME TIME.
THIS IS THE FIRST TIME IT'S HAPPENED...
...SINCE I CAME TO JAPAN...
YEAH ...
AND...
...WAS THE FEELING...
...THAT'S WELLING UP...
I...
...WANT TO CONTINUE...
...HAVING FUN WHEN I'M ACTING WITH KYOKO...

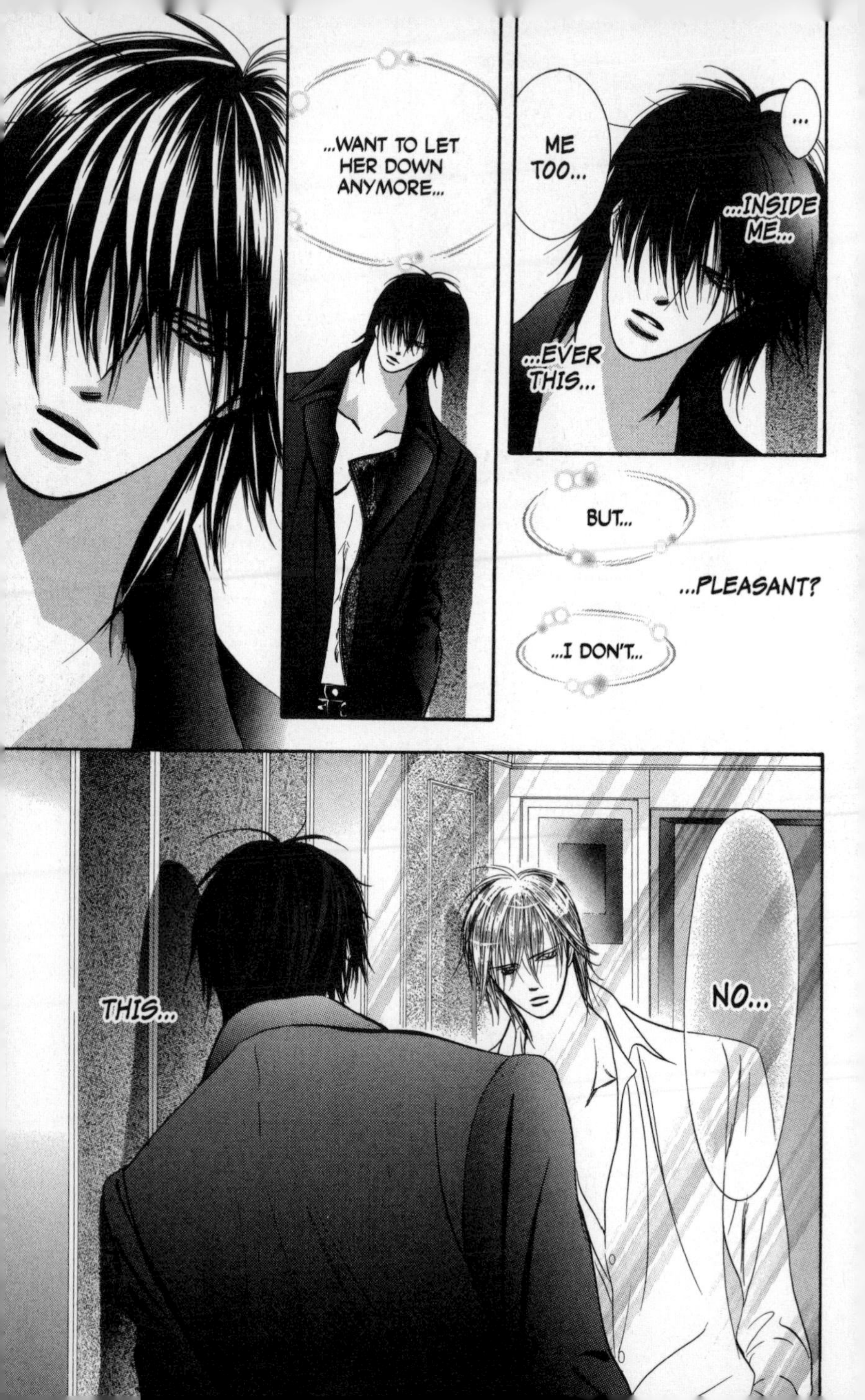
...
ME TOO...
...INSIDE ME...
...EVER THIS...
BUT...
...PLEASANT?
...I DON'T...
...WANT TO LET HER DOWN ANYMORE...
NO...
THIS...

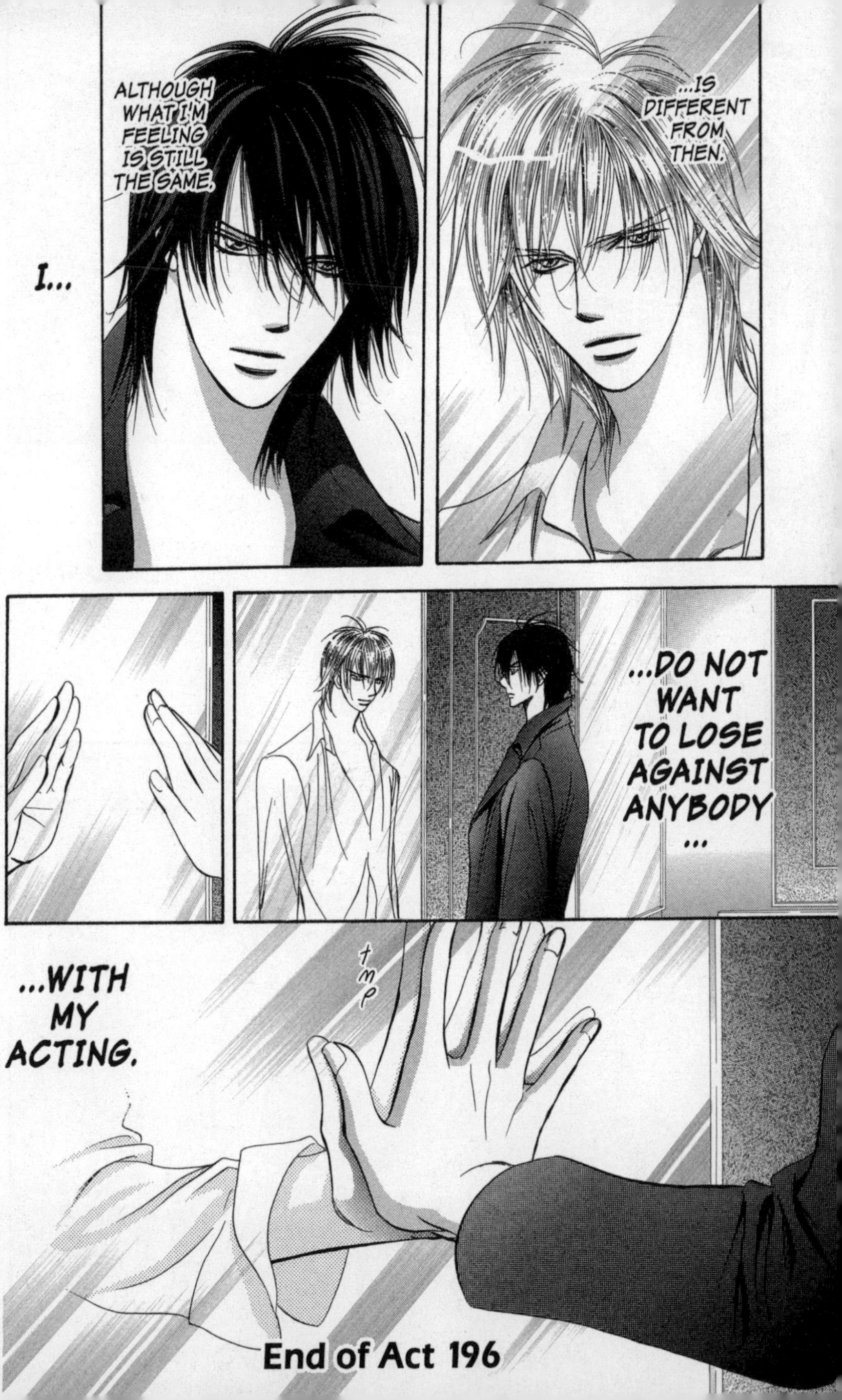
...IS DIFFERENT FROM THEN.
ALTHOUGH WHAT I'M FEELING IS STILL THE SAME.
I...
...DO NOT WANT TO LOSE AGAINST ANYBODY ...
TMP
...WITH MY ACTING.
End of Act 196

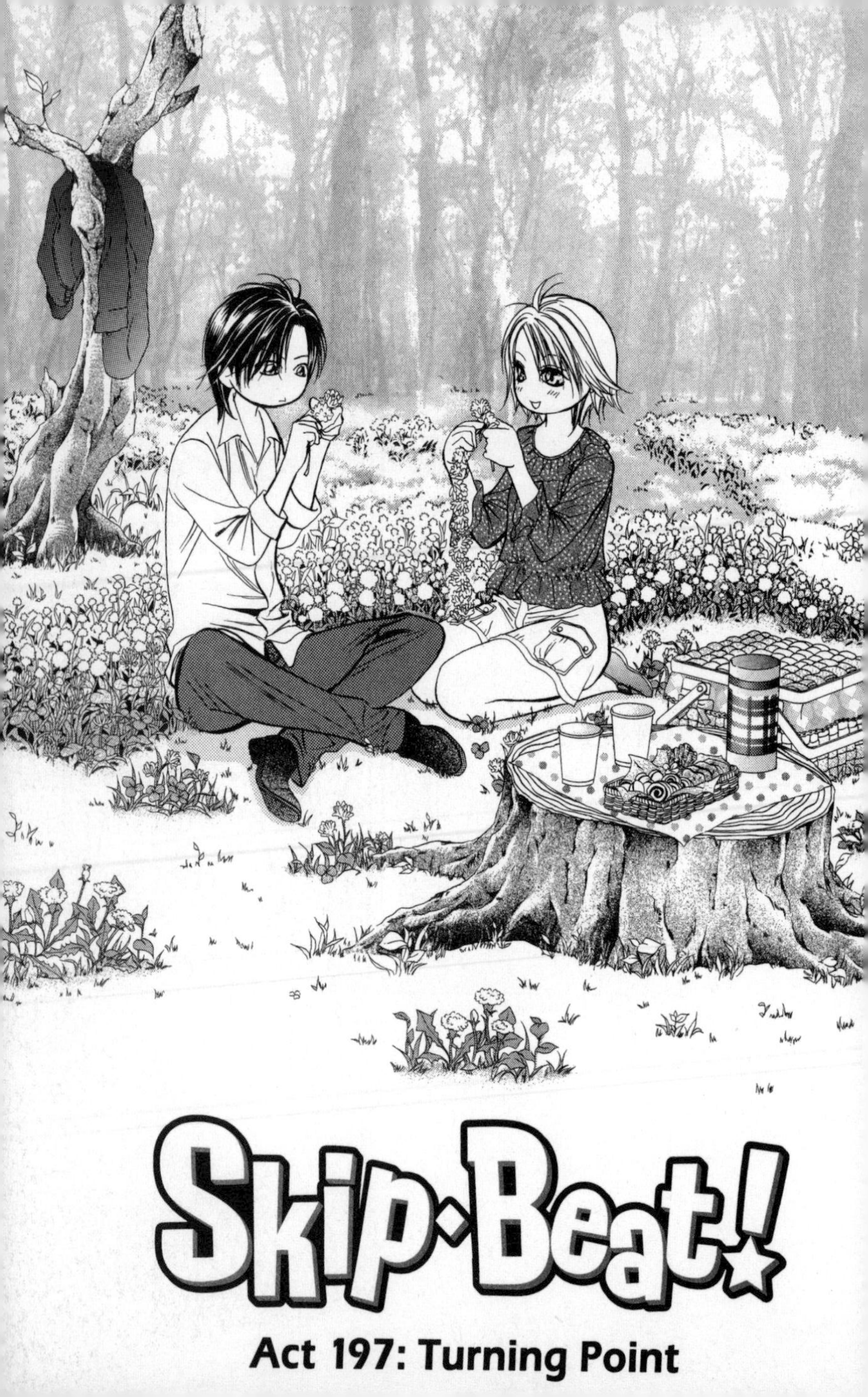

Skip·Beat!

Act 197: Turning Point

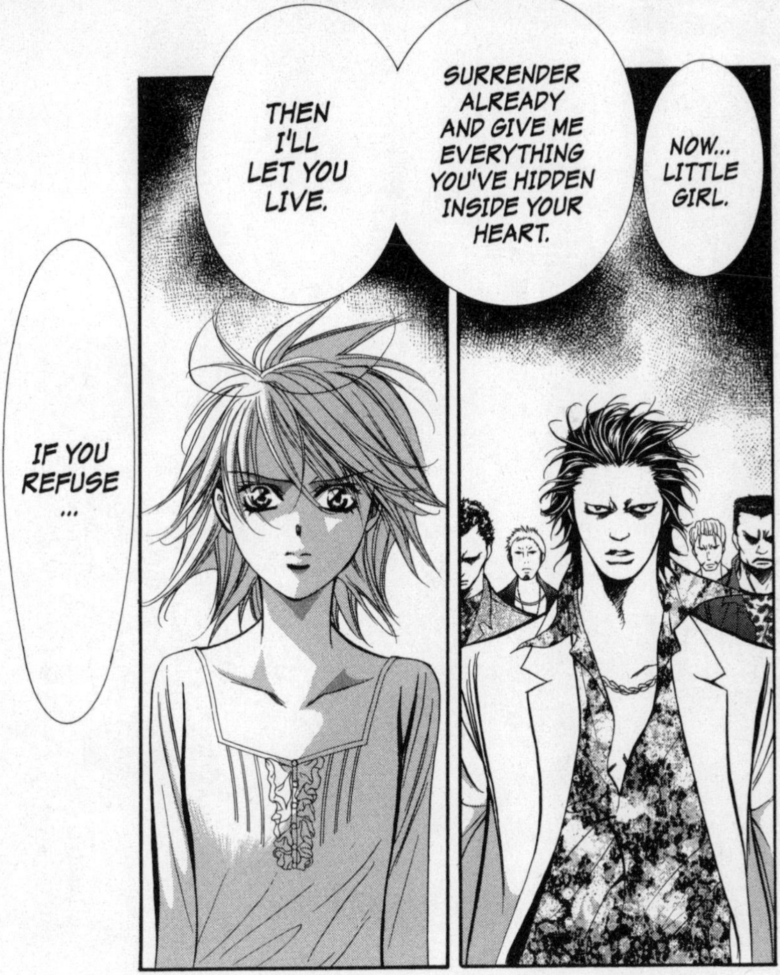
NOW... LITTLE GIRL.
SURRENDER ALREADY AND GIVE ME EVERYTHING YOU'VE HIDDEN INSIDE YOUR HEART.
THEN I'LL LET YOU LIVE.
IF YOU REFUSE ...
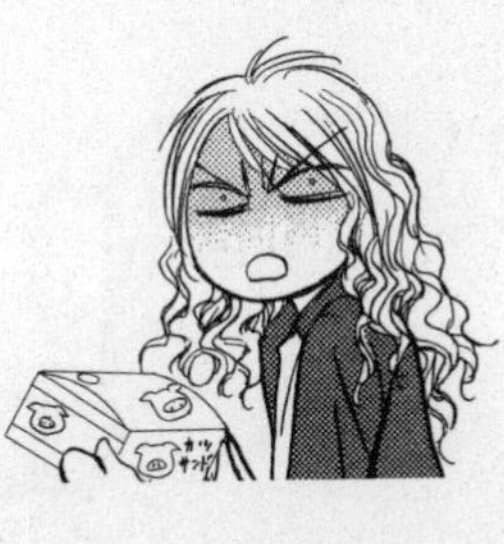

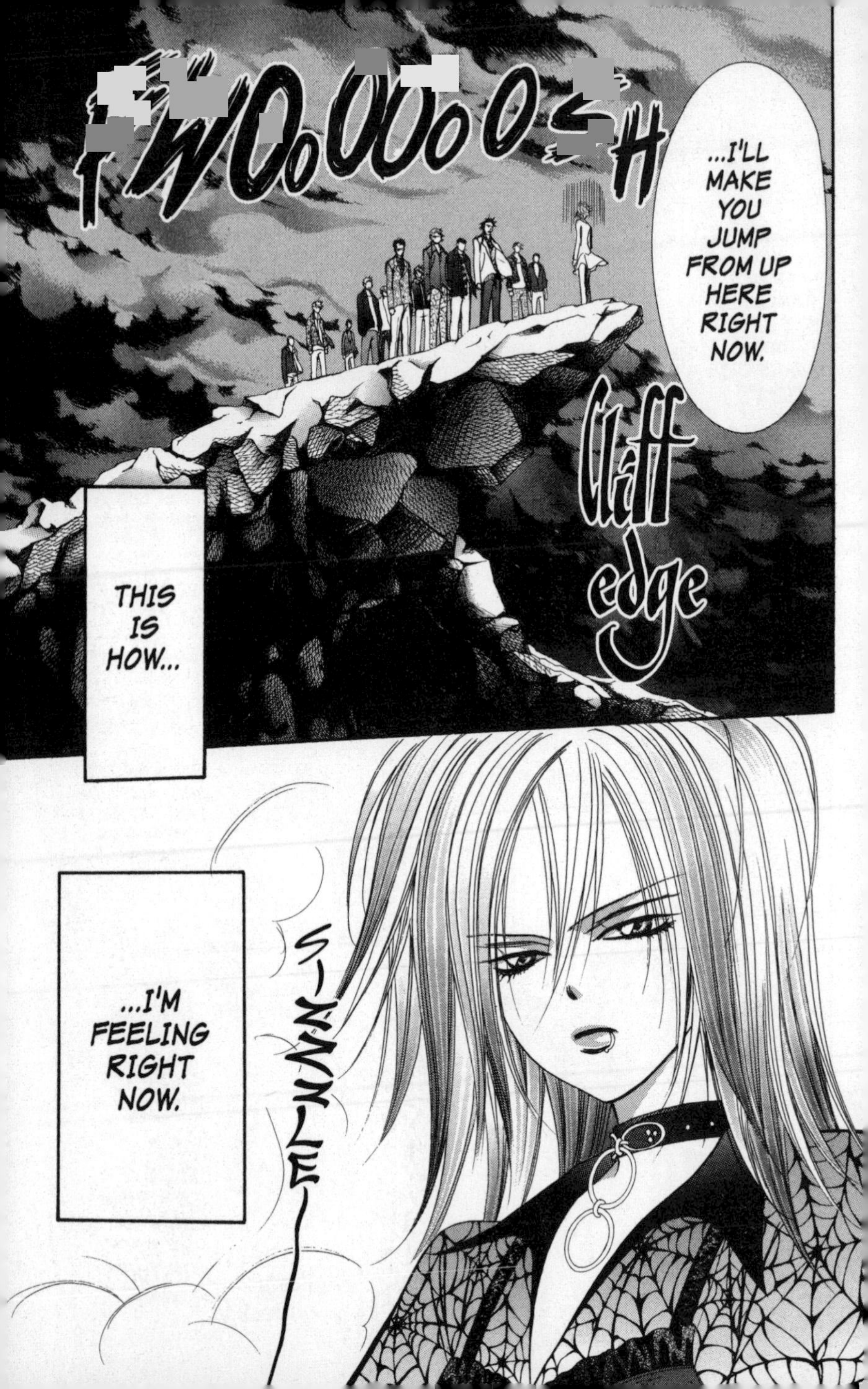
FWOOOOOOSH
...I'LL MAKE YOU JUMP FROM UP HERE RIGHT NOW.
Cliff edge
THIS IS HOW...
...I'M FEELING RIGHT NOW.
S-ZZZLE—

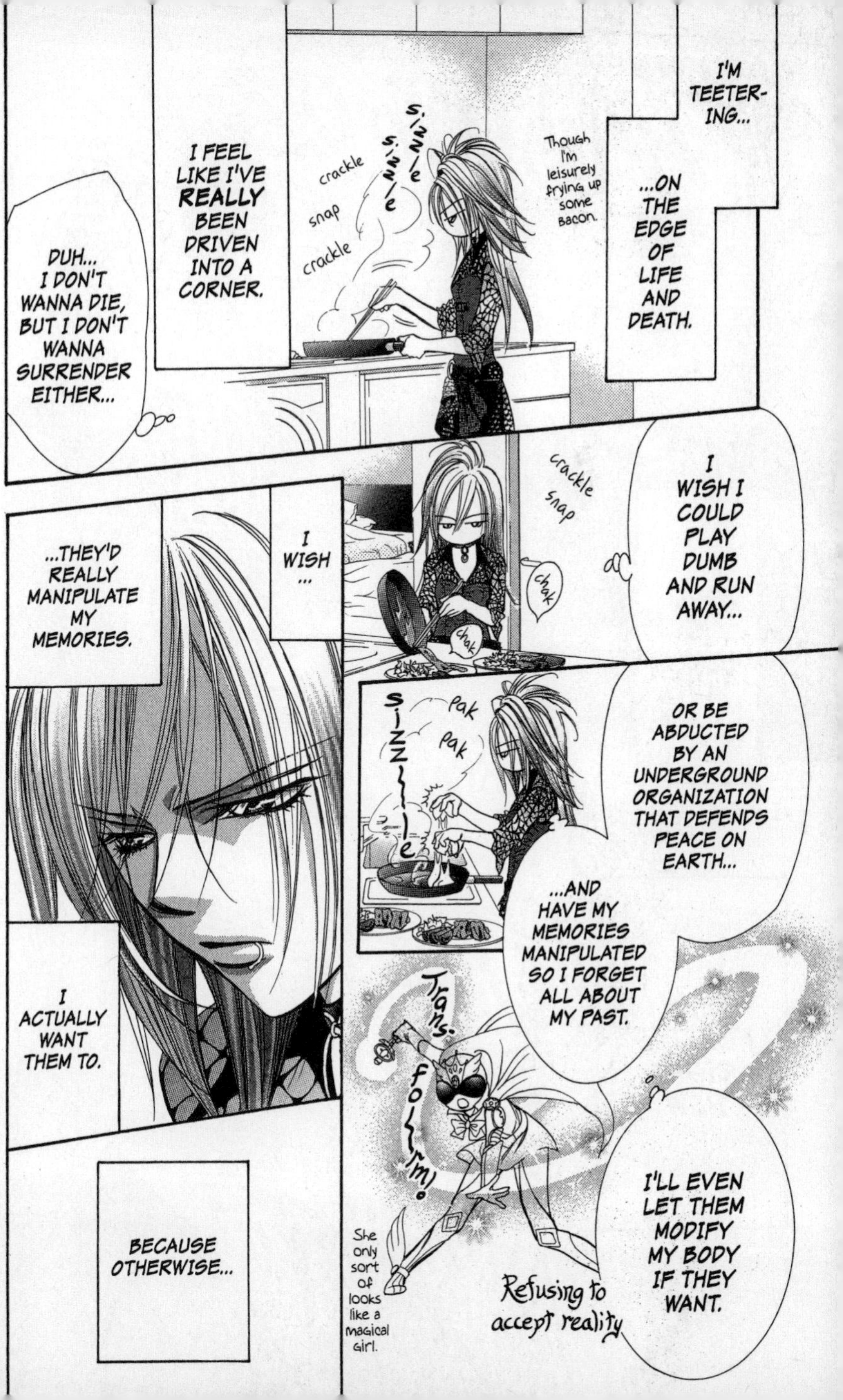
I'M TEETERING...
...ON THE EDGE OF LIFE AND DEATH.
Though I'm leisurely frying up some bacon.
sizzle
sizzle
crackle
snap
crackle
I FEEL LIKE I'VE **REALLY** BEEN DRIVEN INTO A CORNER.
DUH... I DON'T WANNA DIE, BUT I DON'T WANNA SURRENDER EITHER...
I WISH I COULD PLAY DUMB AND RUN AWAY...
crackle
snap
chak
chak
OR BE ABDUCTED BY AN UNDERGROUND ORGANIZATION THAT DEFENDS PEACE ON EARTH...
pak
pak
SIZZ~~~le
...AND HAVE MY MEMORIES MANIPULATED SO I FORGET ALL ABOUT MY PAST.
I'LL EVEN LET THEM MODIFY MY BODY IF THEY WANT.
Trans. fo~~rm!
Refusing to accept reality
She only sort of looks like a magical girl.
I WISH...
...THEY'D REALLY MANIPULATE MY MEMORIES.
I ACTUALLY WANT THEM TO.
BECAUSE OTHERWISE...

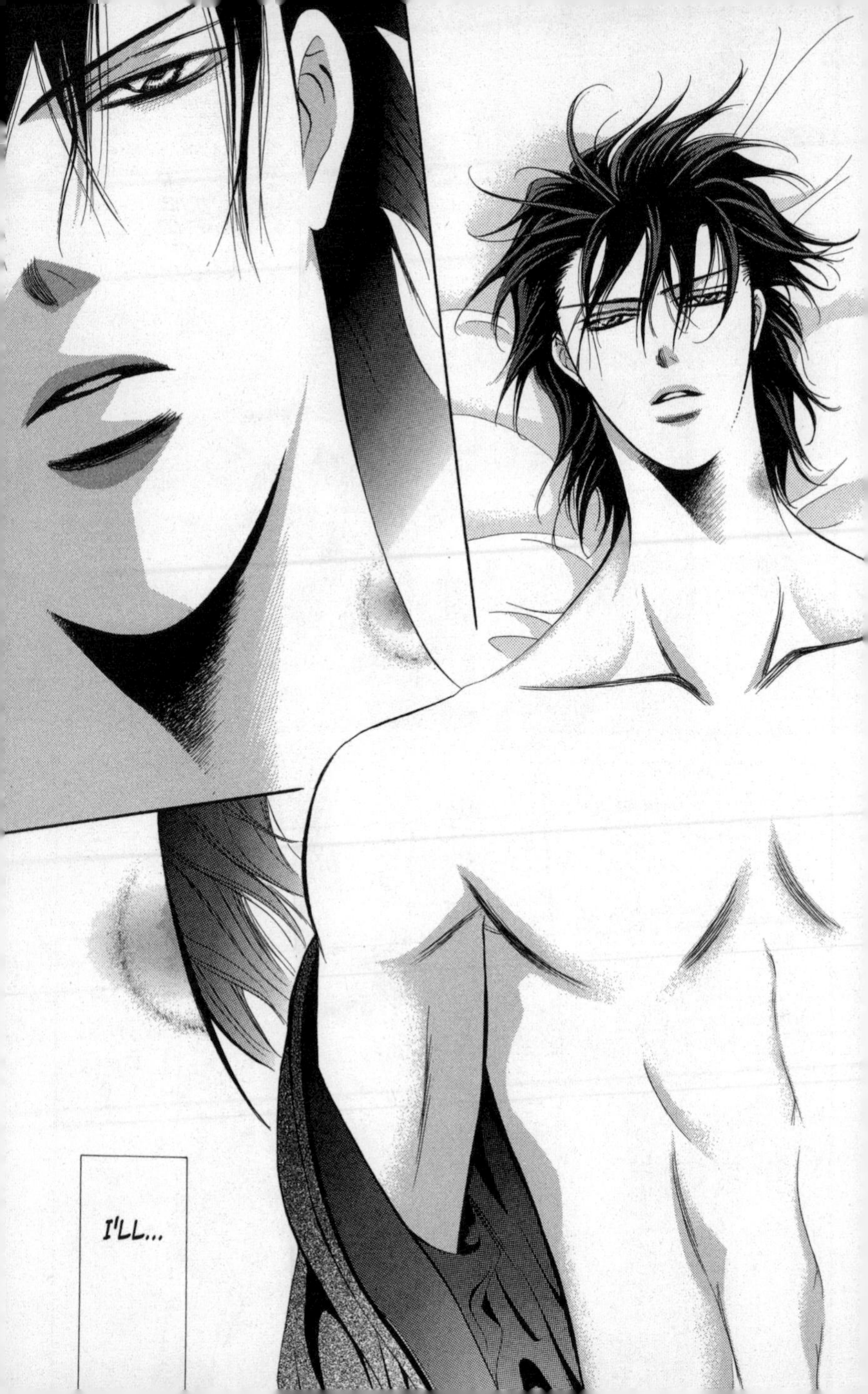
I'LL...

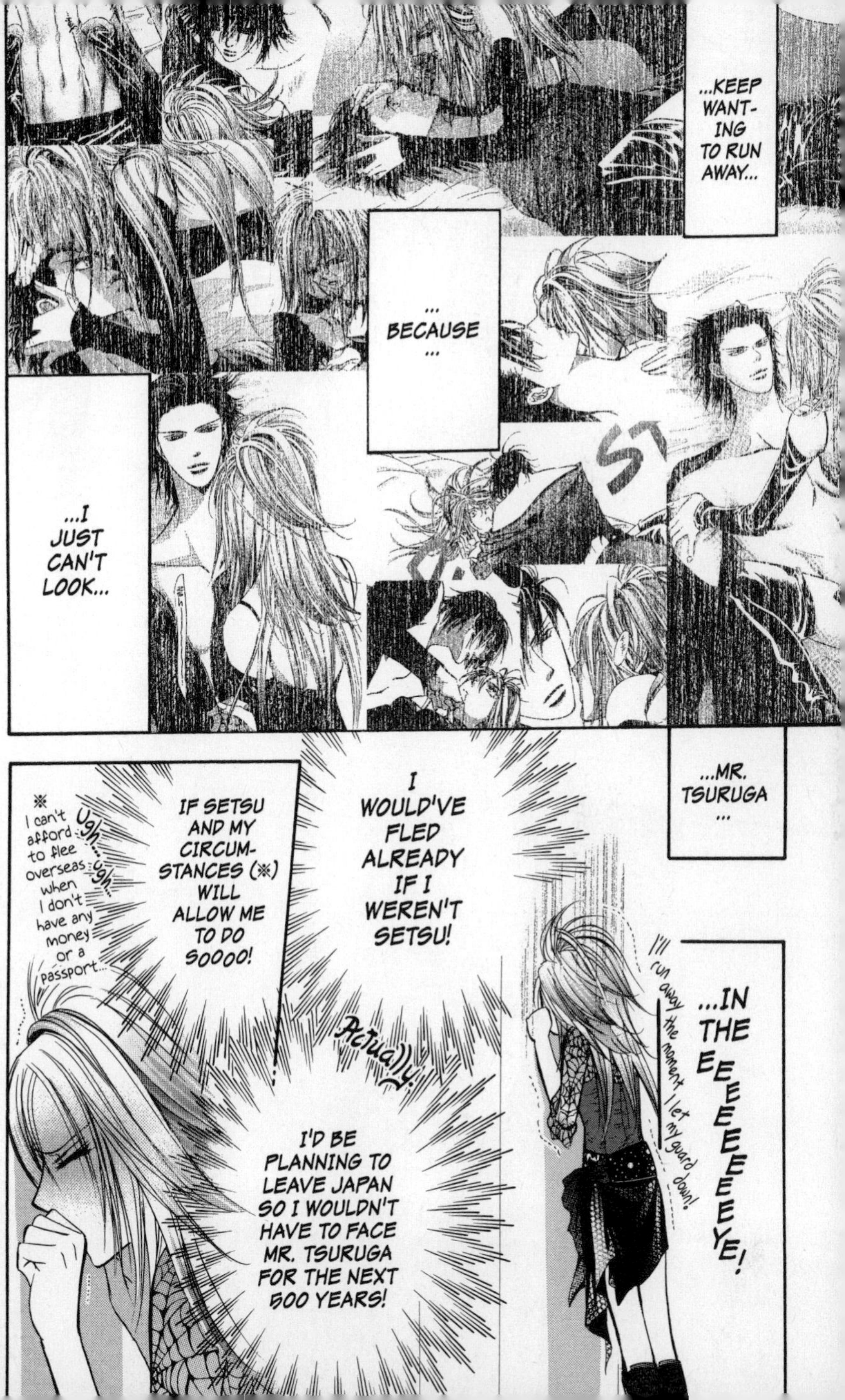
...KEEP WANT-ING TO RUN AWAY...
... BECAUSE ...
...I JUST CAN'T LOOK...
...MR. TSURUGA ...
I WOULD'VE FLED ALREADY IF I WEREN'T SETSU!
IF SETSU AND MY CIRCUM-STANCES (※) WILL ALLOW ME TO DO SOOOO!
※ I can't afford to flee overseas when I don't have any money or a passport...
Ugh...ugh...
...IN THE EEEEEEEEYE!
I'll run away the moment I let my guard down!
Actually
I'D BE PLANNING TO LEAVE JAPAN SO I WOULDN'T HAVE TO FACE MR. TSURUGA FOR THE NEXT 500 YEARS!

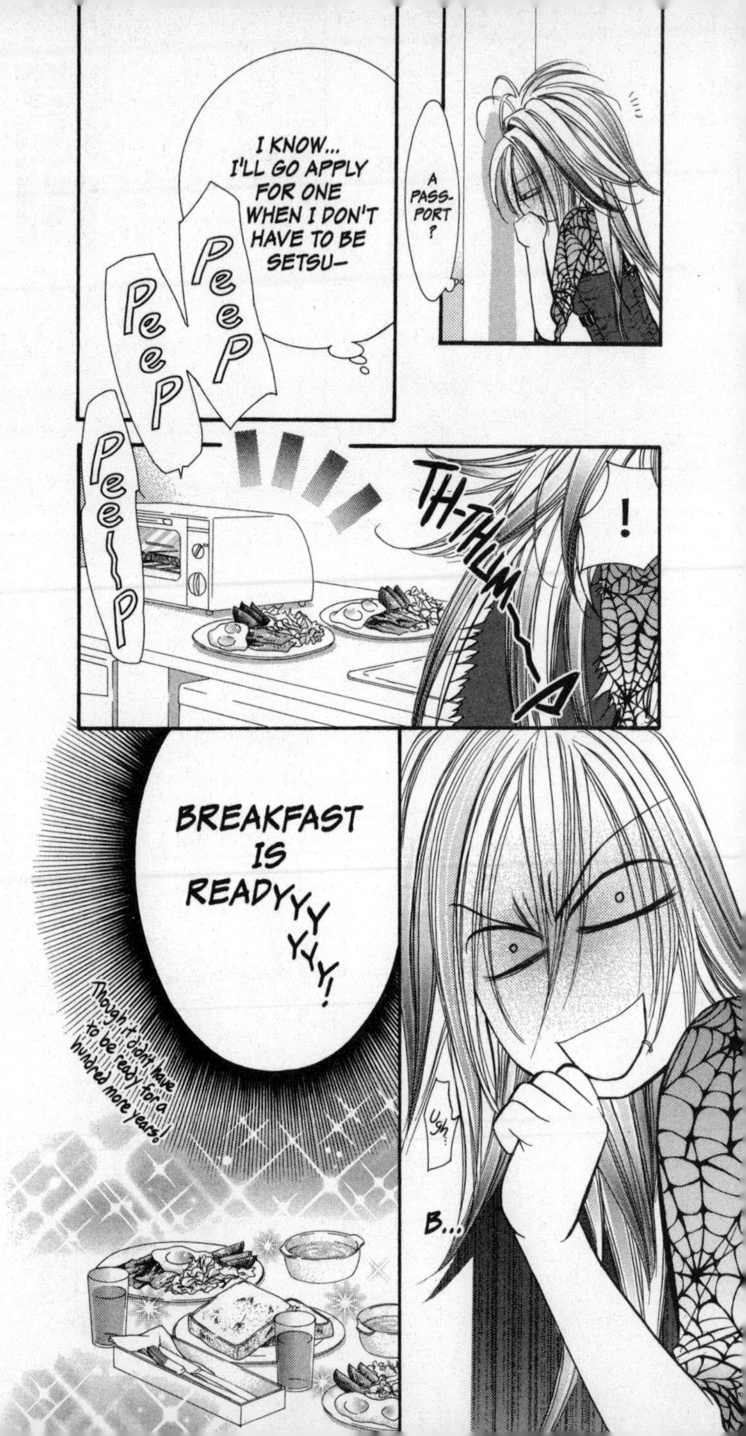
A PASS-PORT?
I KNOW... I'LL GO APPLY FOR ONE WHEN I DON'T HAVE TO BE SETSU—
Peep
Peep
!
TH-THUM~~A
Pee~~p
Ugh...
B...
BREAKFAST IS READYYYYYY!
Though it didn't have to be ready for a hundred more years!

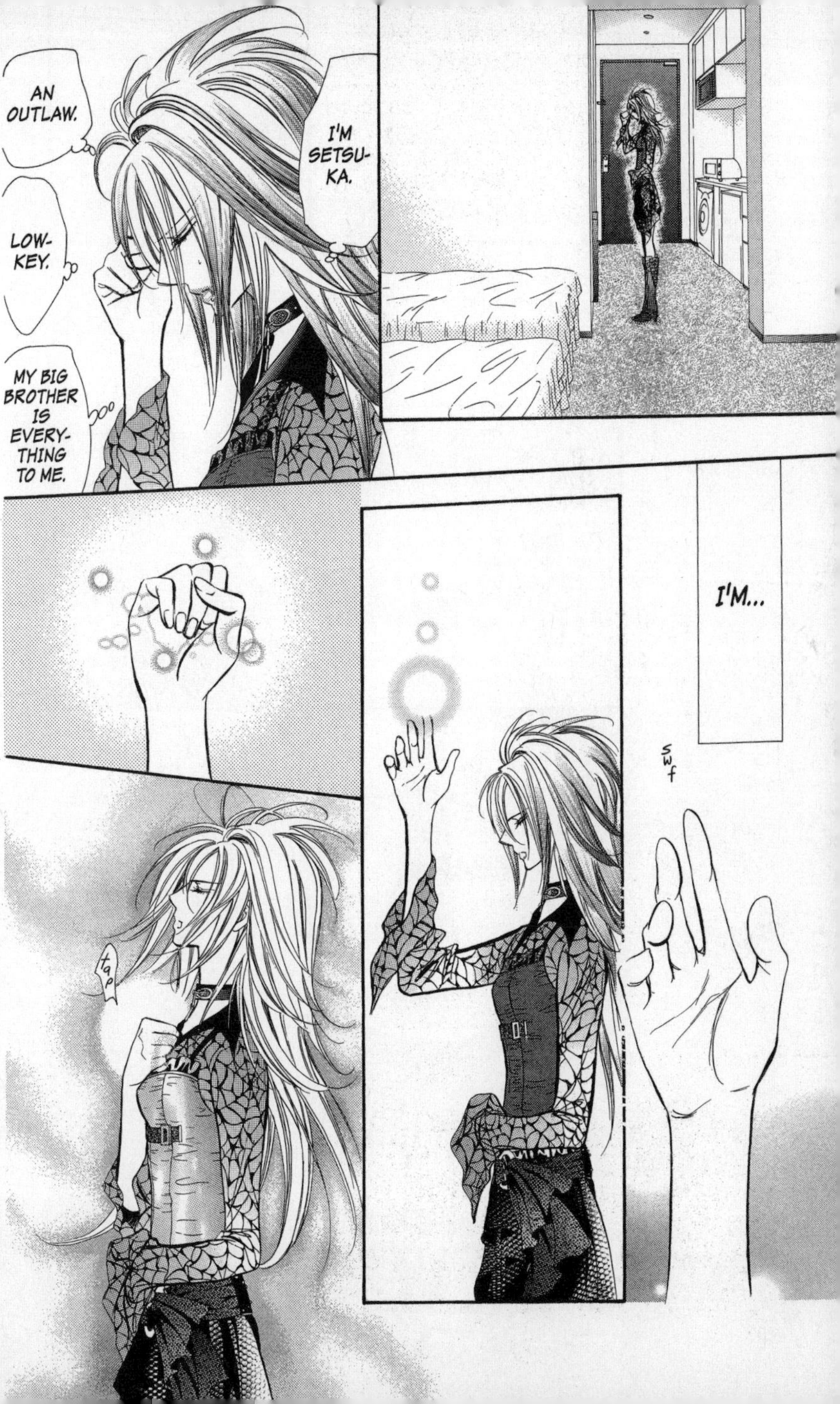
I'M SETSU-KA.
AN OUTLAW.
LOW-KEY.
MY BIG BROTHER IS EVERY-THING TO ME.
I'M...
swf
tap

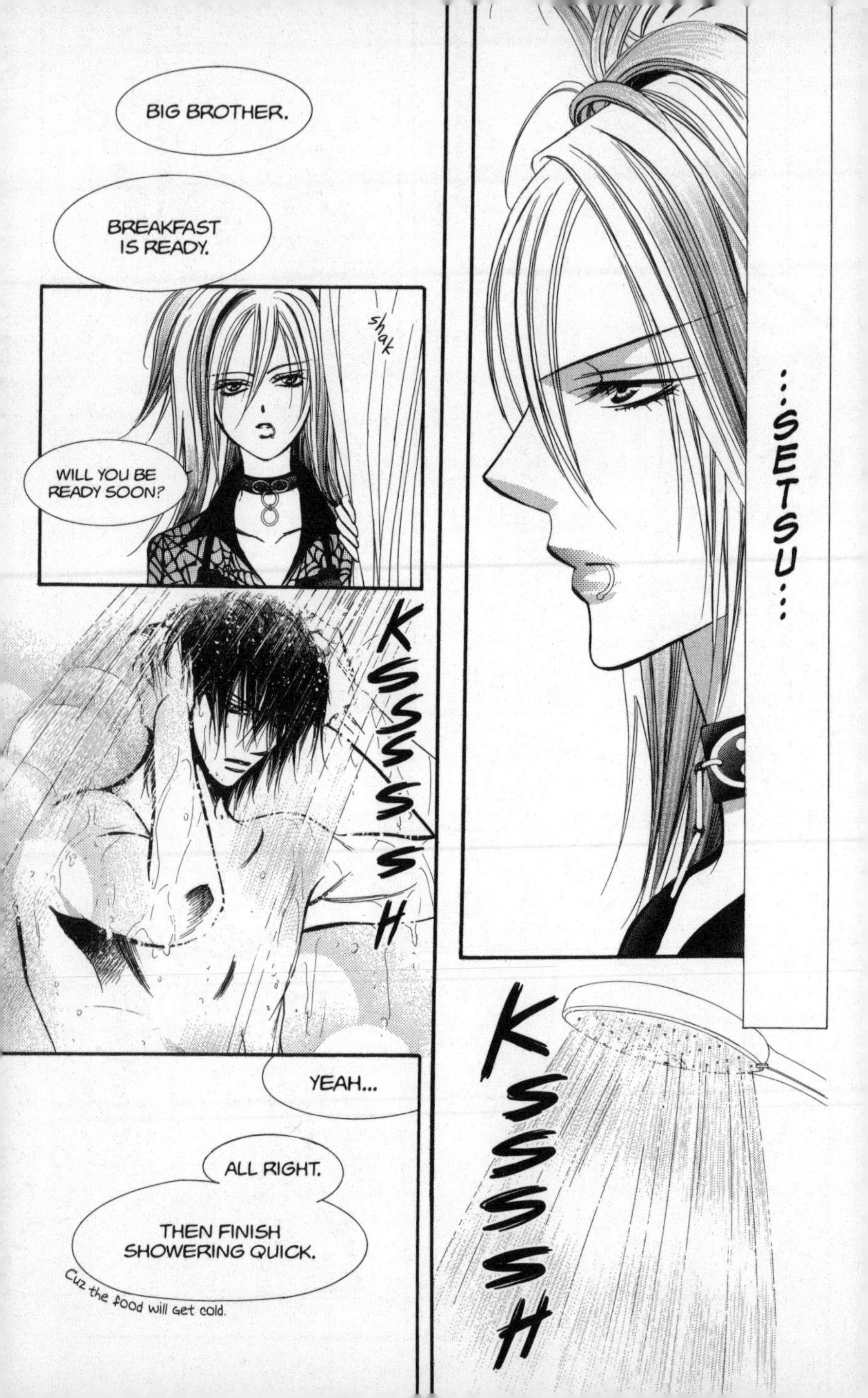
...SETSU...
BIG BROTHER.
BREAKFAST IS READY.
shak
WILL YOU BE READY SOON?
KSSSSSH
KSSSSH
YEAH...
ALL RIGHT.
THEN FINISH SHOWERING QUICK.
Cuz the food will get cold.

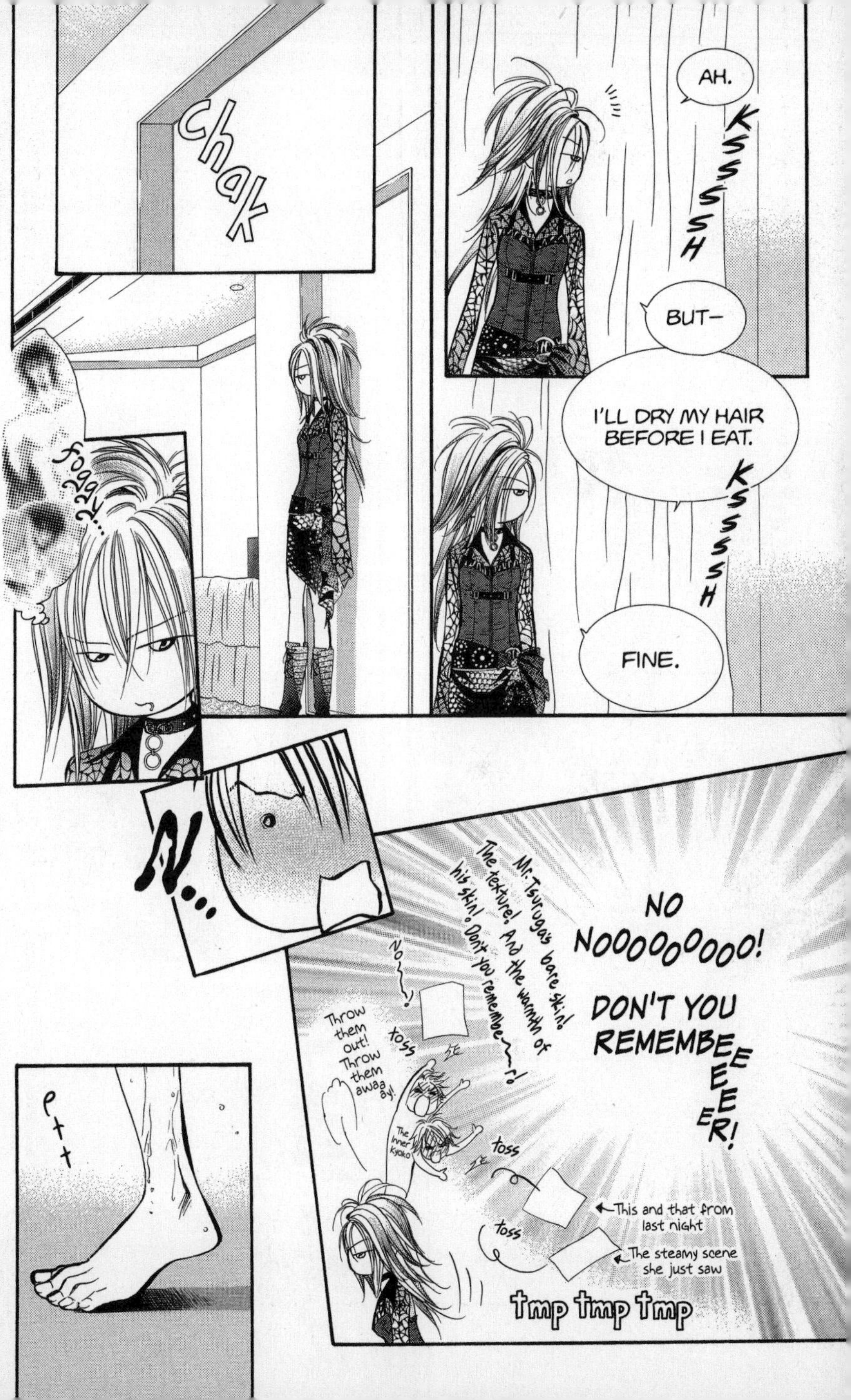
AH.
KSSSSH
BUT—
I'LL DRY MY HAIR BEFORE I EAT.
KSSSSSH
FINE.
chak
foggy...
N...
NO NOOOOOOOOO!
DON'T YOU REMEMBEEEEER!
Mr. Tsuruga's bare skin! The texture! And the warmth of his skin! Don't you remembe~~r!
No~~!
Throw them out! Throw them awaa ay!
toss
The Inner Kyoko
toss
toss
This and that from last night
The steamy scene she just saw
tmp tmp tmp
ptt

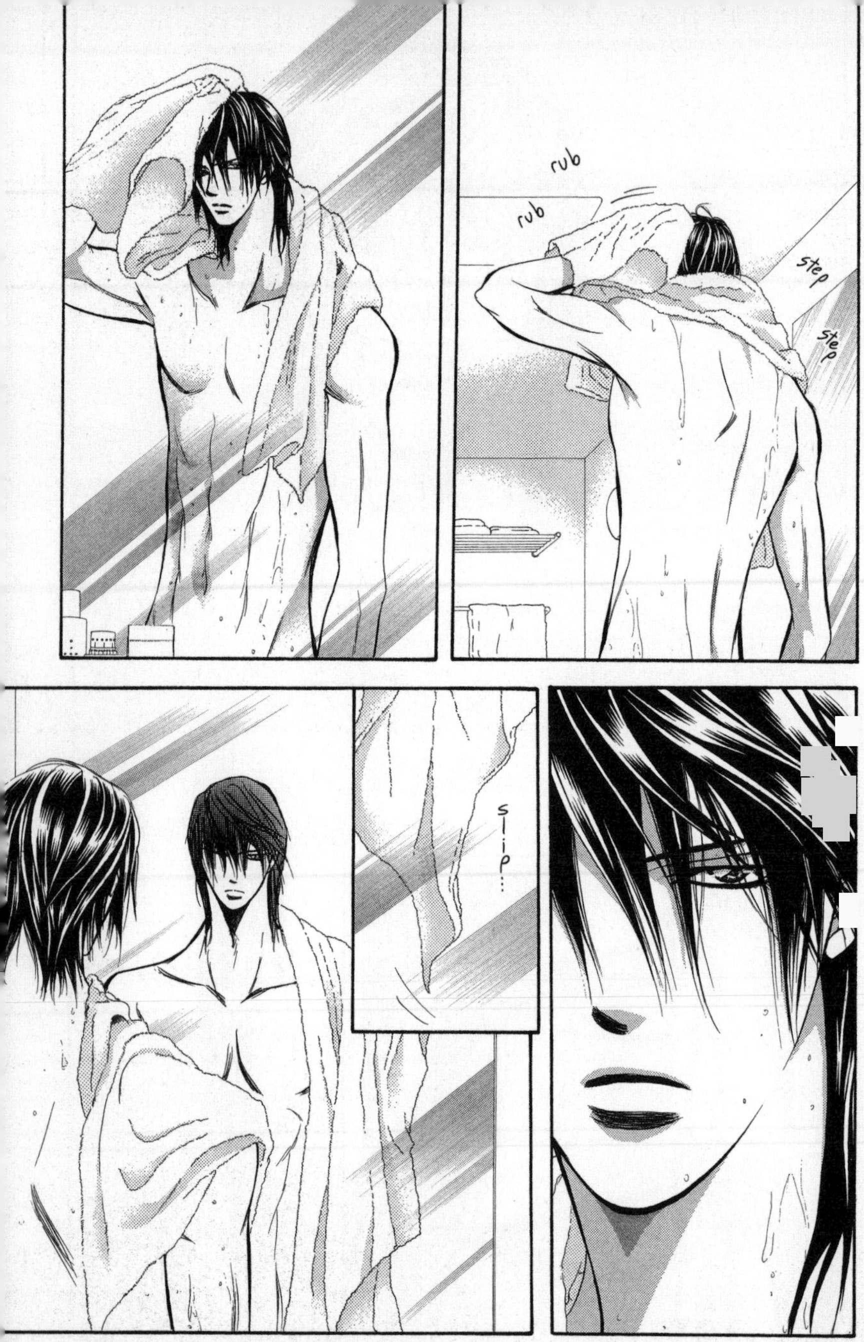
rub
rub
step
step
sl...ip...

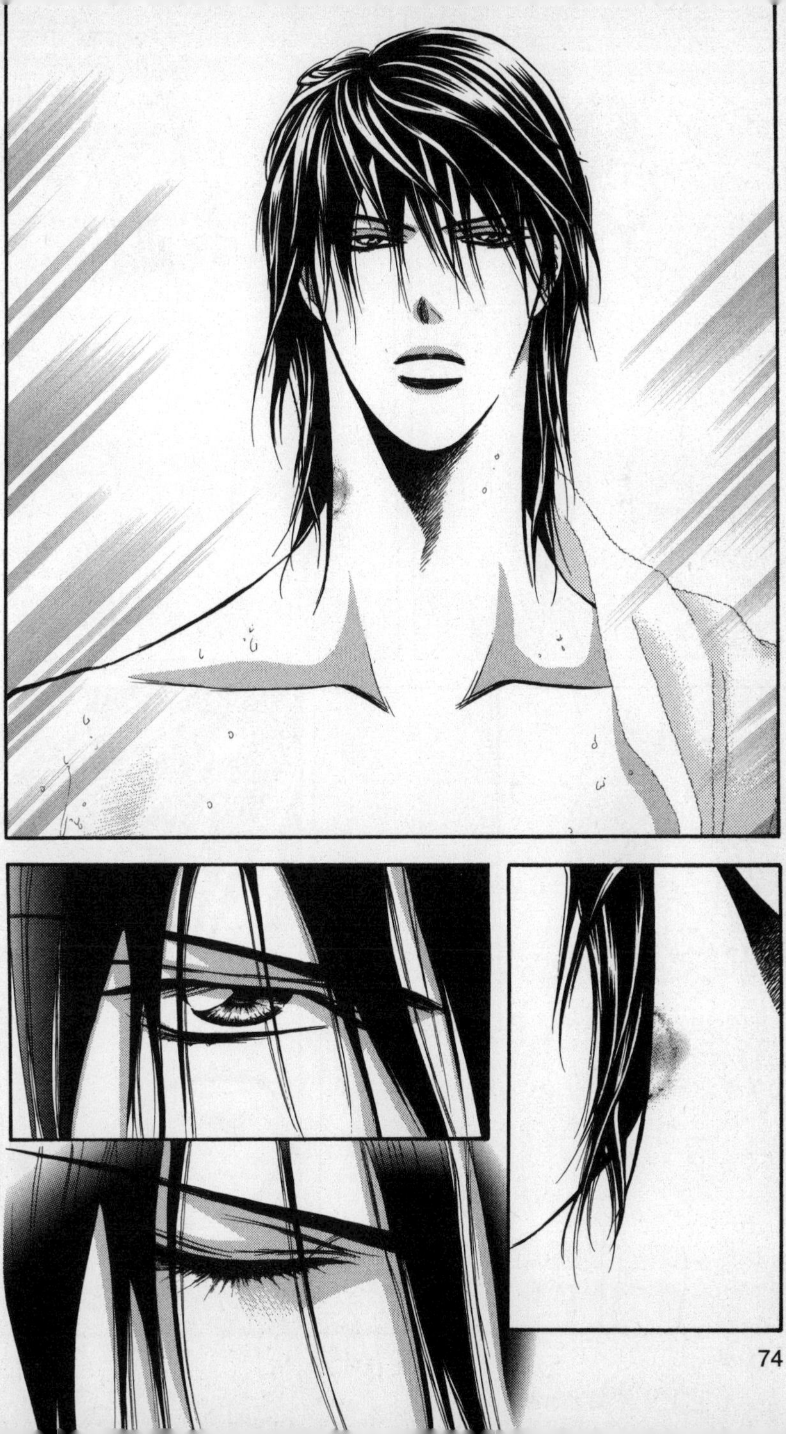

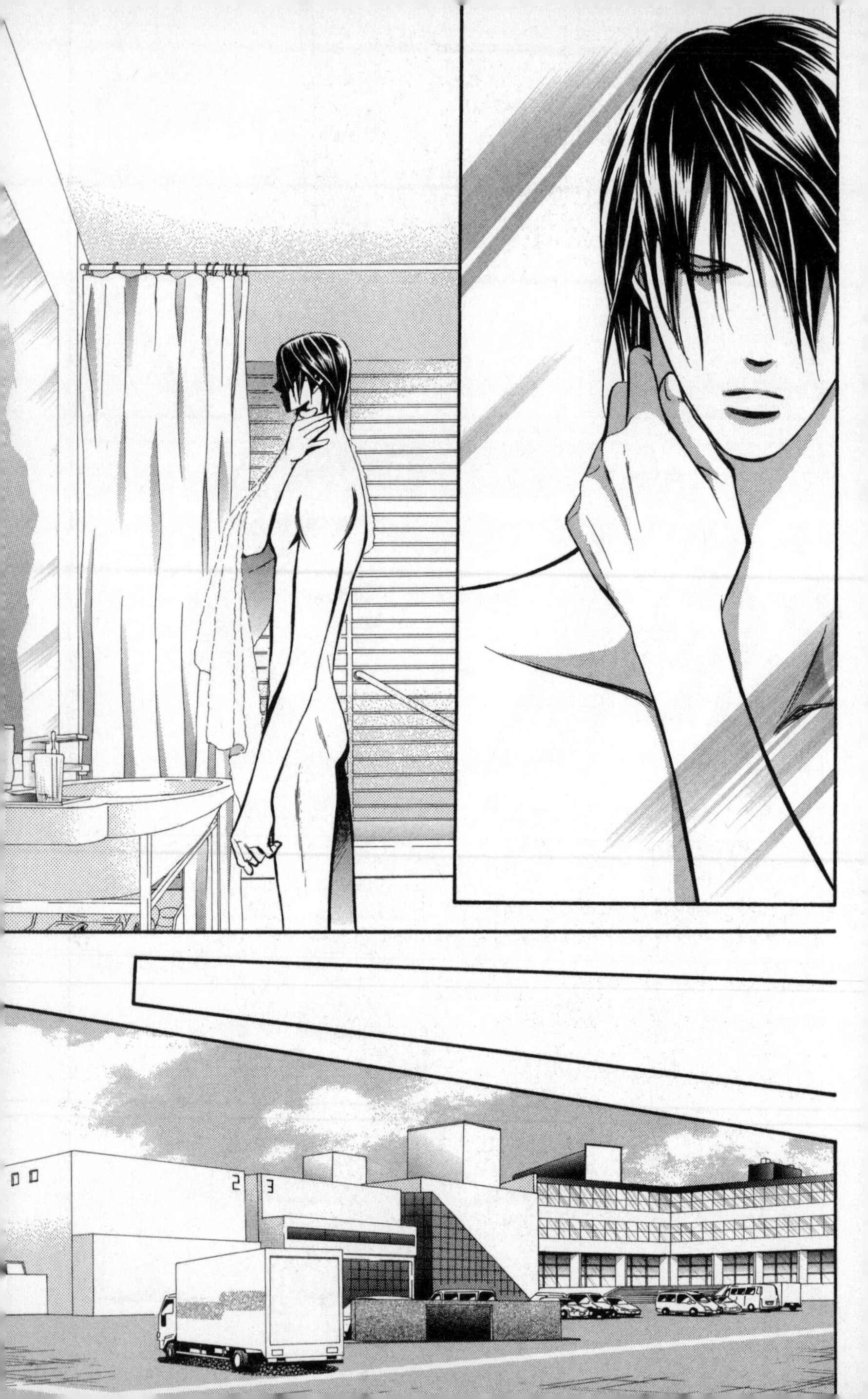

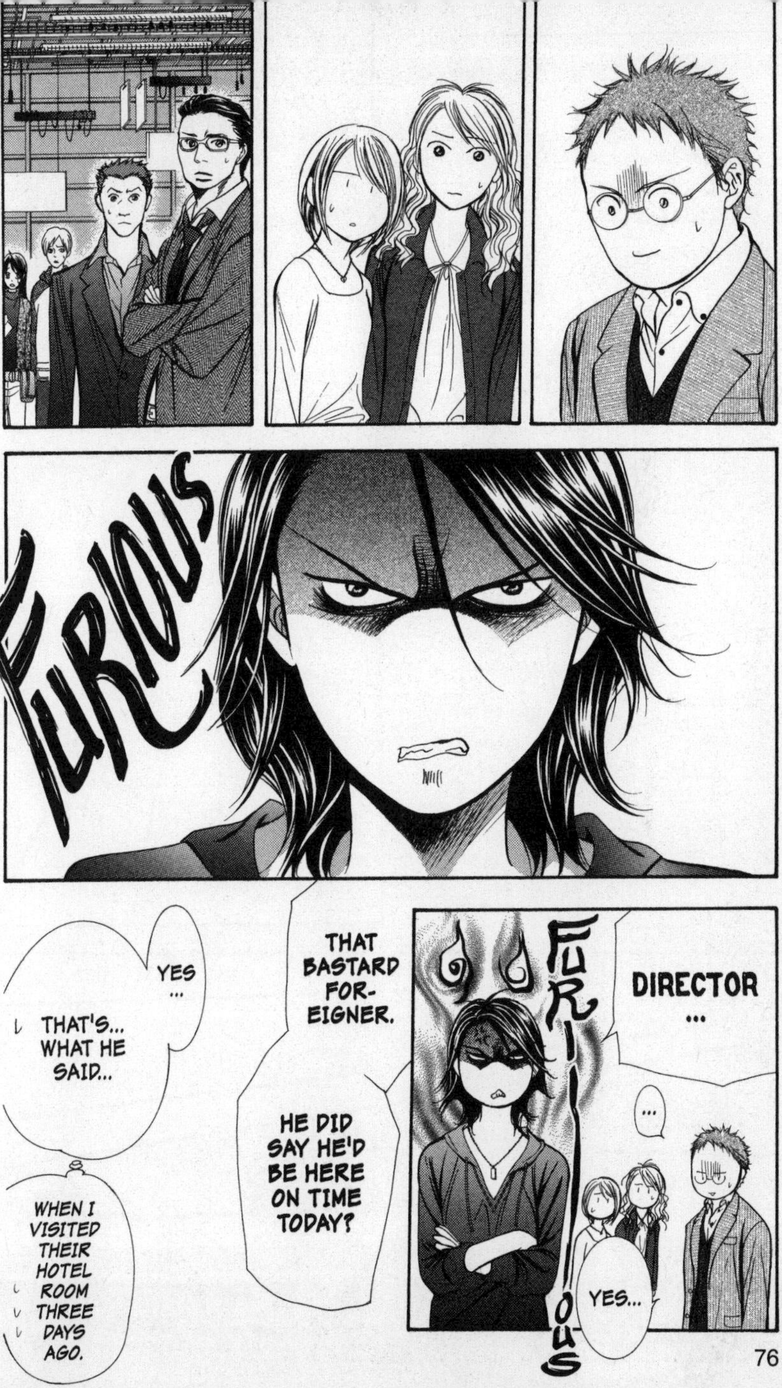
FURIOUS
DIRECTOR...
...
FURI-OUS
YES...
THAT BASTARD FOR-EIGNER.
HE DID SAY HE'D BE HERE ON TIME TODAY?
YES... THAT'S... WHAT HE SAID...
WHEN I VISITED THEIR HOTEL ROOM THREE DAYS AGO.

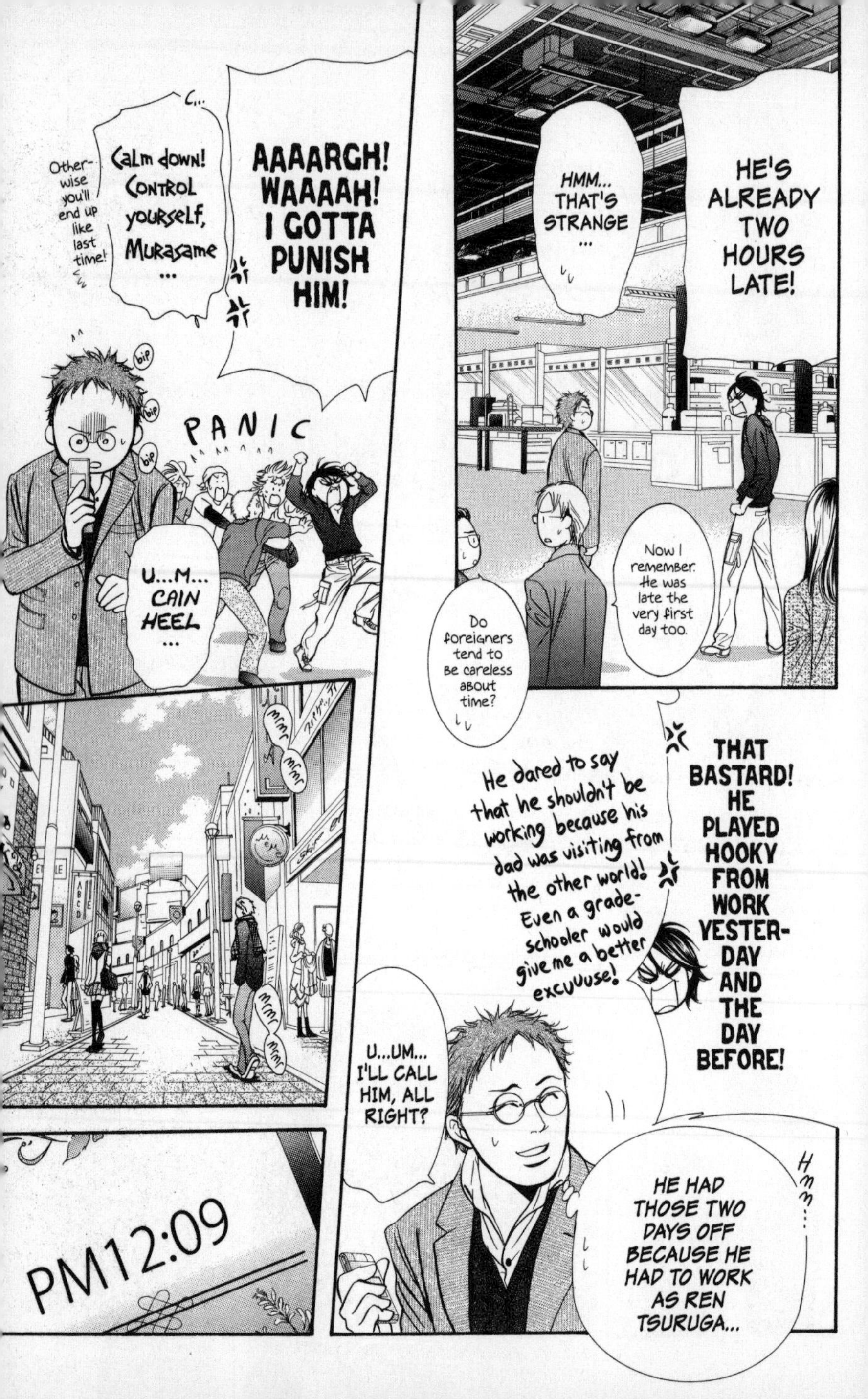
HE'S ALREADY TWO HOURS LATE!
HMM... THAT'S STRANGE...
Now I remember. He was late the very first day too.
Do foreigners tend to be careless about time?
THAT BASTARD! HE PLAYED HOOKY FROM WORK YESTERDAY AND THE DAY BEFORE!
He dared to say that he shouldn't be working because his dad was visiting from the other world! Even a grade-schooler would give me a better excuuuse!
U...UM... I'LL CALL HIM, ALL RIGHT?
HE HAD THOSE TWO DAYS OFF BECAUSE HE HAD TO WORK AS REN TSURUGA...
Hmm...
AAAARGH! WAAAAH! I GOTTA PUNISH HIM!
C...
Calm down! Control yourself, Murasame...
Other-wise you'll end up like last time!
bip
bip
bip
PANIC
U...M... CAIN HEEL...
mumu
mumu
mumu
mumu
PM12:09

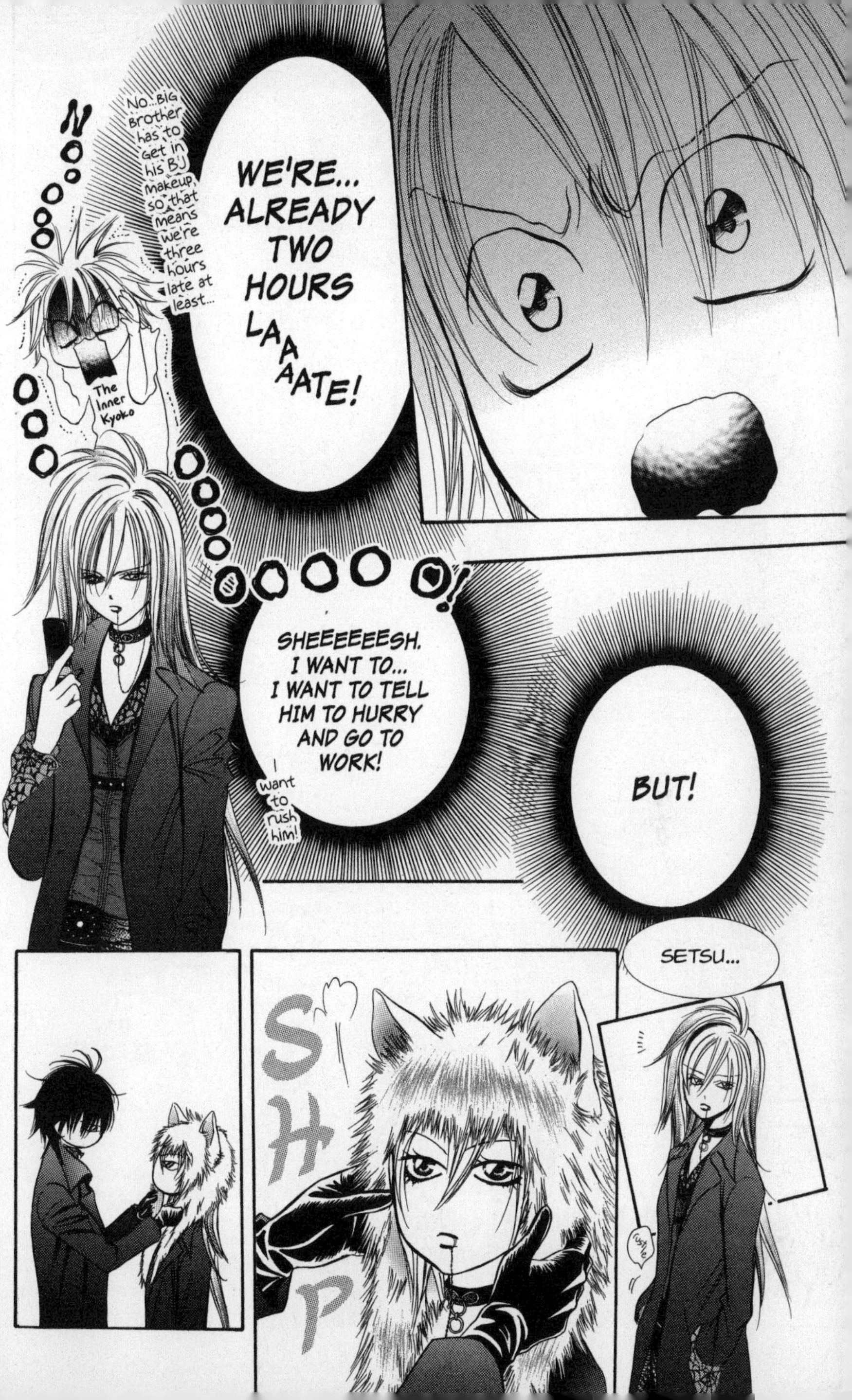
WE'RE... ALREADY TWO HOURS LAAAATE!
No...BIG Brother has to get in his BJ makeup, so that means we're three hours late at least...
The Inner Kyoko
NOOOOOOOOOOOOOOOOO!
SHEEEEEESH. I WANT TO... I WANT TO TELL HIM TO HURRY AND GO TO WORK!
I want to rush him!
BUT!
SETSU...
rustle
SHP

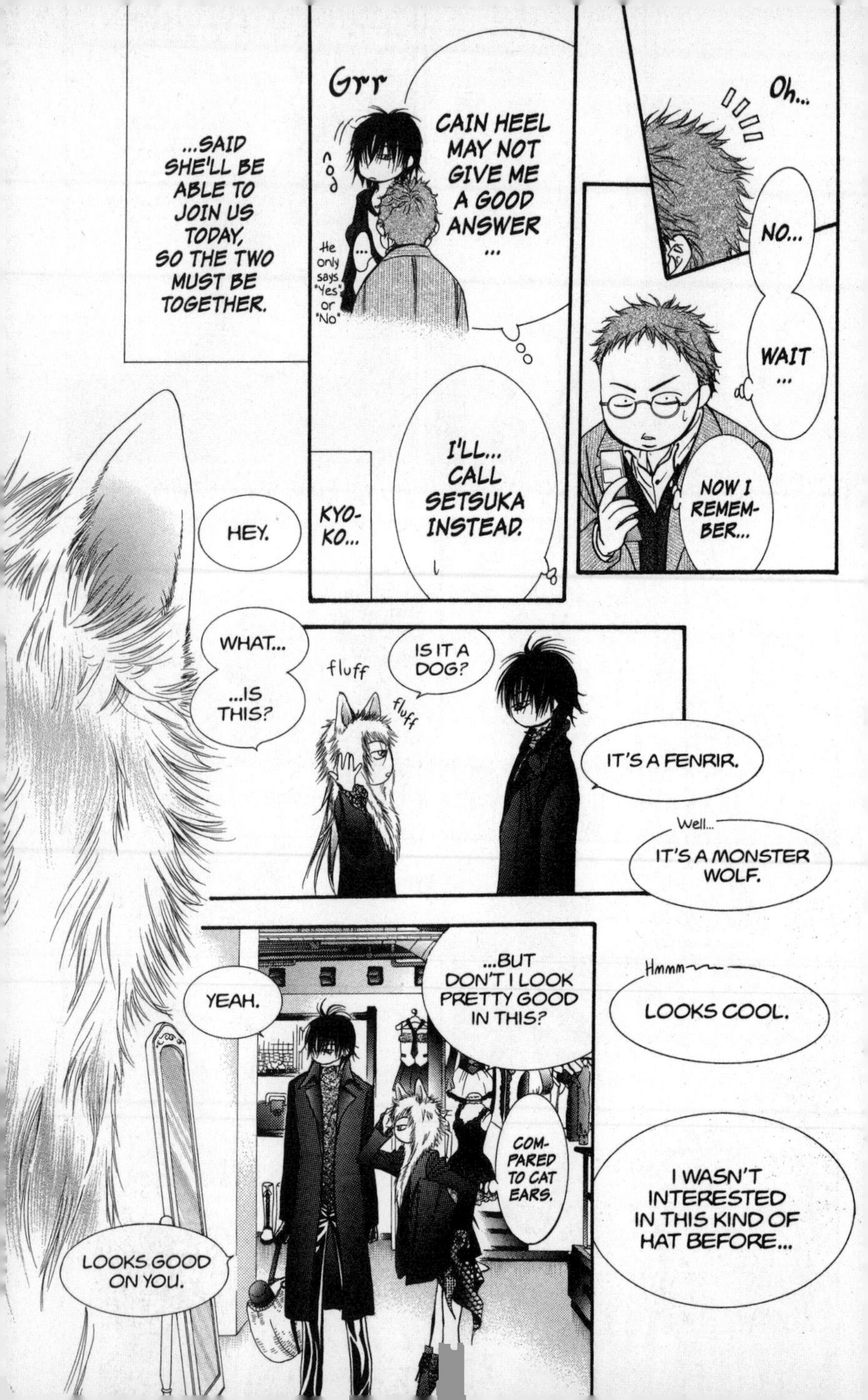
Oh...
NO...
WAIT...
NOW I REMEMBER...
Grr
He only says "Yes" or "No"
...
CAIN HEEL MAY NOT GIVE ME A GOOD ANSWER...
I'LL... CALL SETSUKA INSTEAD.
...SAID SHE'LL BE ABLE TO JOIN US TODAY, SO THE TWO MUST BE TOGETHER.
KYO-KO...
HEY.
WHAT...
...IS THIS?
fluff fluff
IS IT A DOG?
IT'S A FENRIR.
Well...
IT'S A MONSTER WOLF.
Hmmm
LOOKS COOL.
I WASN'T INTERESTED IN THIS KIND OF HAT BEFORE...
COMPARED TO CAT EARS.
...BUT DON'T I LOOK PRETTY GOOD IN THIS?
YEAH.
LOOKS GOOD ON YOU.

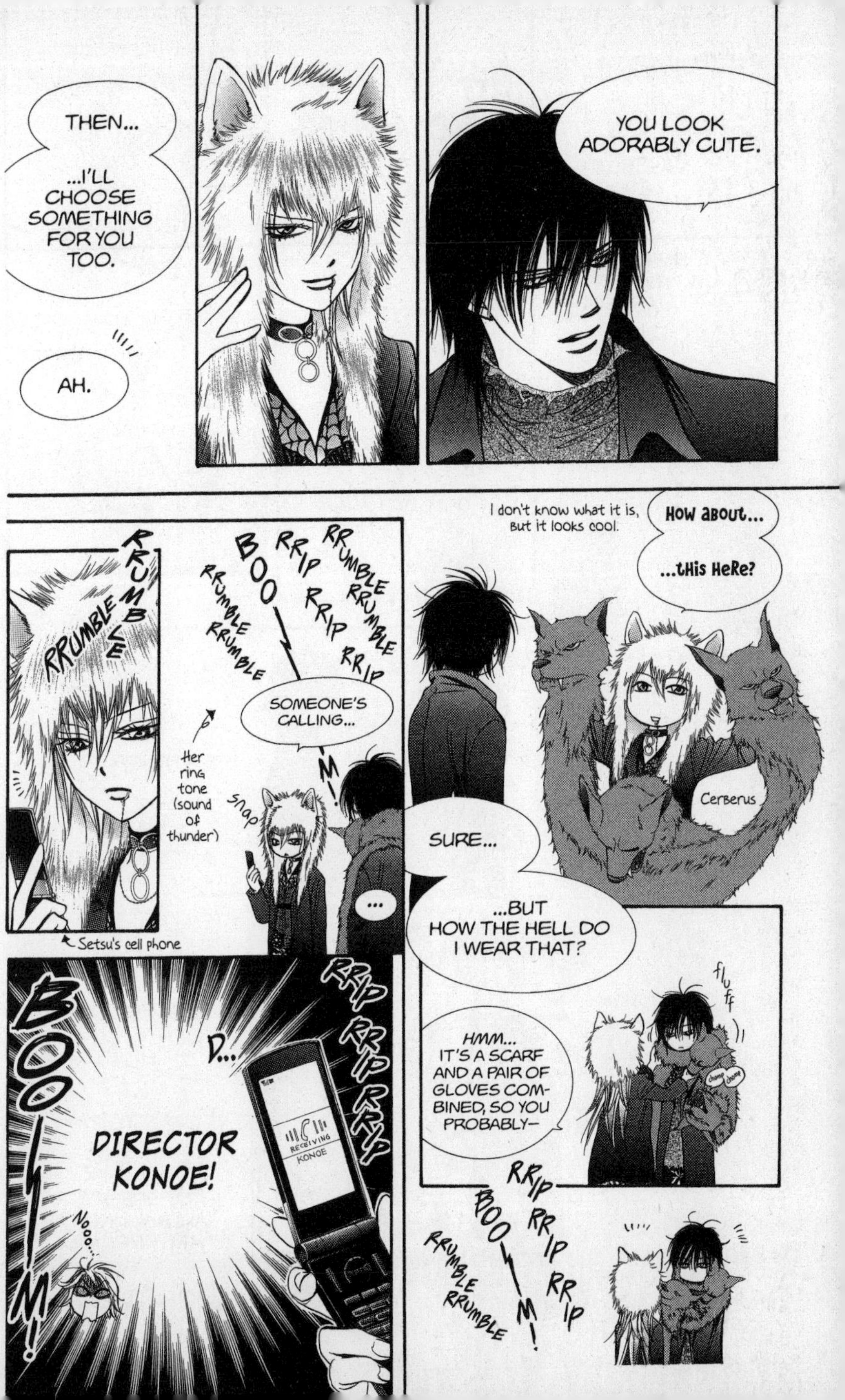
YOU LOOK ADORABLY CUTE.
THEN...
...I'LL CHOOSE SOMETHING FOR YOU TOO.
AH.
I don't know what it is, but it looks cool.
HOW ABOUT...
...THIS HERE?
Cerberus
SURE...
...BUT HOW THE HELL DO I WEAR THAT?
fluff
HMM... IT'S A SCARF AND A PAIR OF GLOVES COMBINED, SO YOU PROBABLY—
RRIP RRIP RRIP
BOOM!
RRUMBLE RRUMBLE
RRUMBLE RRUMBLE
BOOM RRIP RRIP RRIP
RRUMBLE RRUMBLE RRUMBLE
SOMEONE'S CALLING...
Her ring tone (sound of thunder)
snap
...
RRUMBLE RRUMBLE
Setsu's cell phone
RRIP RRIP RRIP
D...
RECEIVING KONOE
DIRECTOR KONOE!
Nooo...
BOOM!

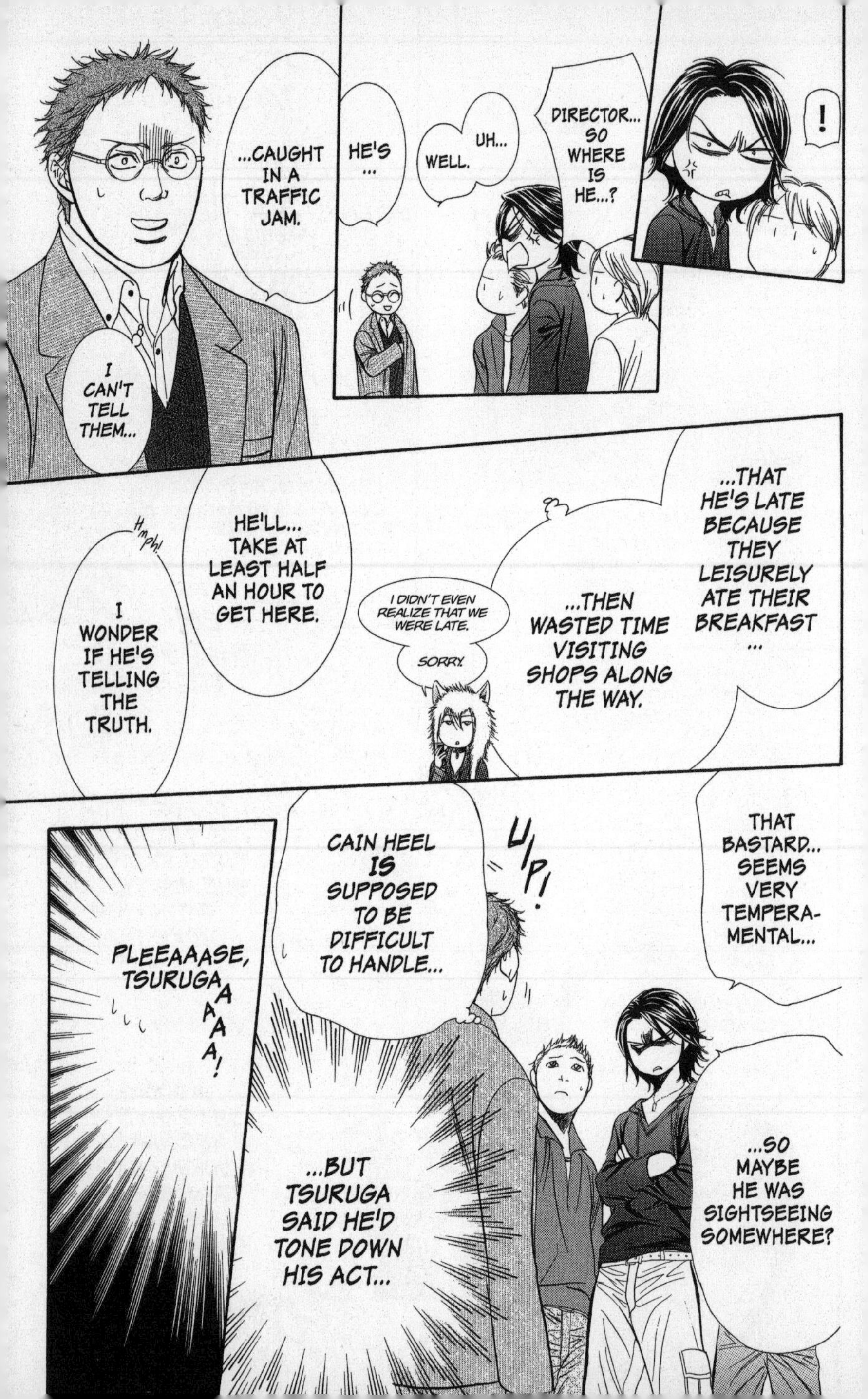
!
DIRECTOR... SO WHERE IS HE...?
UH... WELL.
HE'S ...
...CAUGHT IN A TRAFFIC JAM.
I CAN'T TELL THEM...
...THAT HE'S LATE BECAUSE THEY LEISURELY ATE THEIR BREAKFAST ...
...THEN WASTED TIME VISITING SHOPS ALONG THE WAY.
I DIDN'T EVEN REALIZE THAT WE WERE LATE.
SORRY.
HE'LL... TAKE AT LEAST HALF AN HOUR TO GET HERE.
Hmph!
I WONDER IF HE'S TELLING THE TRUTH.
THAT BASTARD... SEEMS VERY TEMPERA-MENTAL...
...SO MAYBE HE WAS SIGHTSEEING SOMEWHERE?
UP!
CAIN HEEL IS SUPPOSED TO BE DIFFICULT TO HANDLE...
...BUT TSURUGA SAID HE'D TONE DOWN HIS ACT...
PLEEAAASE, TSURUGAAAAA!

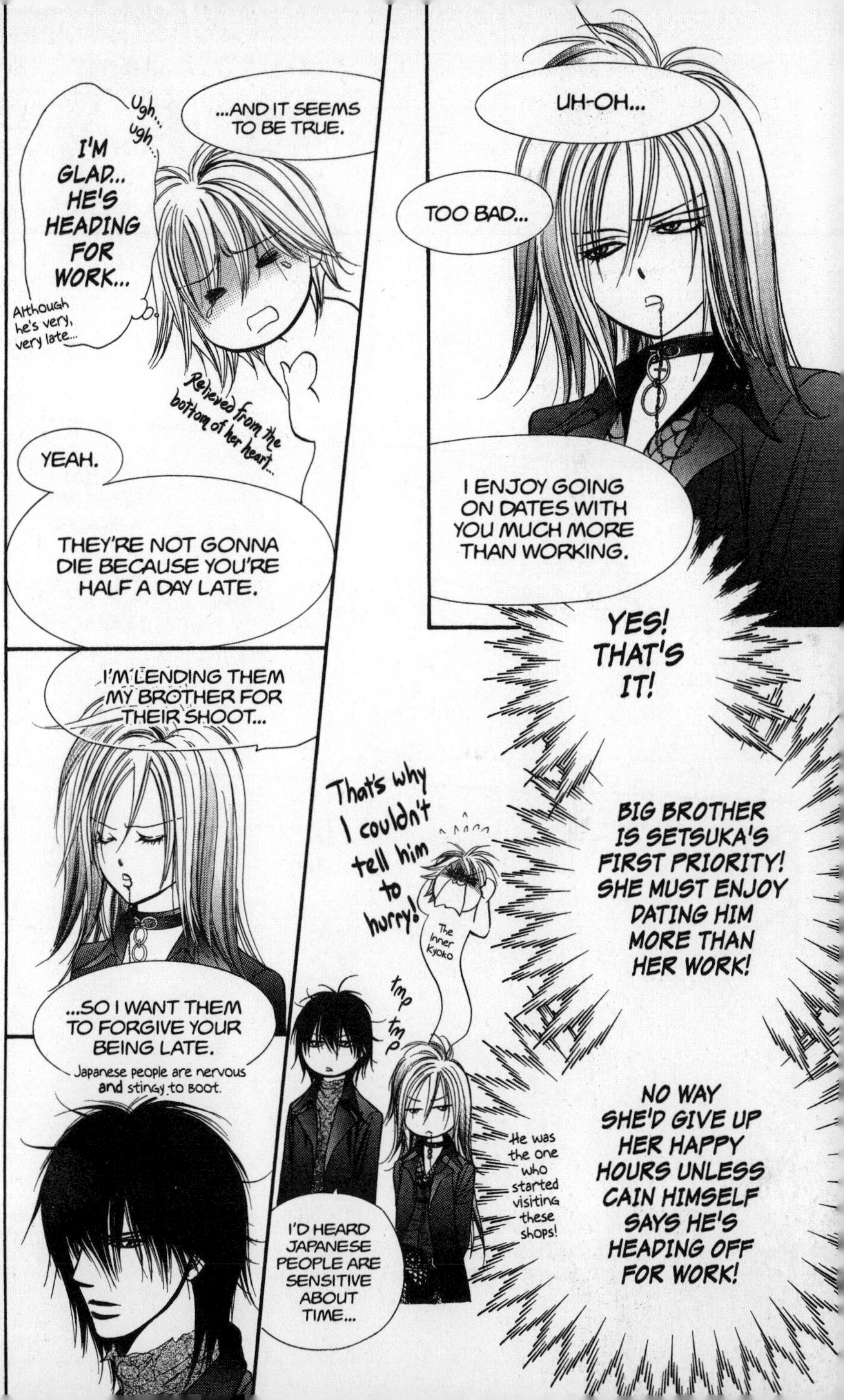
UH-OH...
TOO BAD...
I ENJOY GOING ON DATES WITH YOU MUCH MORE THAN WORKING.
...AND IT SEEMS TO BE TRUE.
Ugh... ugh...
I'M GLAD... HE'S HEADING FOR WORK...
Although he's very, very late...
Relieved from the bottom of her heart...
YEAH.
THEY'RE NOT GONNA DIE BECAUSE YOU'RE HALF A DAY LATE.
YES! THAT'S IT!
BIG BROTHER IS SETSUKA'S FIRST PRIORITY! SHE MUST ENJOY DATING HIM MORE THAN HER WORK!
NO WAY SHE'D GIVE UP HER HAPPY HOURS UNLESS CAIN HIMSELF SAYS HE'S HEADING OFF FOR WORK!
That's why I couldn't tell him to hurry!
The Inner Kyoko
tmp tmp
He was the one who started visiting these shops!
I'D HEARD JAPANESE PEOPLE ARE SENSITIVE ABOUT TIME...
I'M LENDING THEM MY BROTHER FOR THEIR SHOOT...
...SO I WANT THEM TO FORGIVE YOUR BEING LATE.
Japanese people are nervous and stingy to boot.

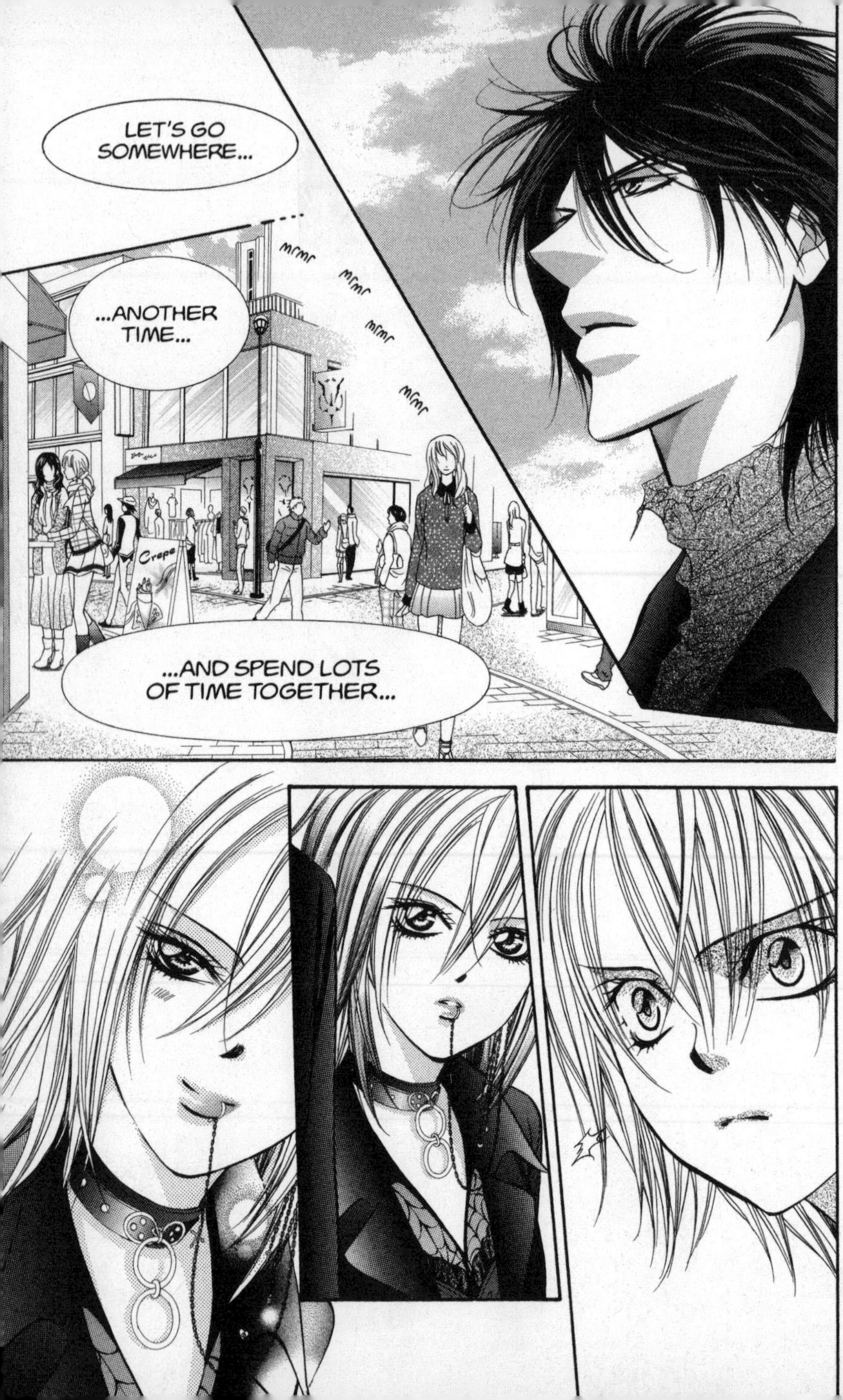
LET'S GO SOMEWHERE...
...ANOTHER TIME...
...AND SPEND LOTS OF TIME TOGETHER...
mrmr
mrmr
mrmr
mrmr
Crepe

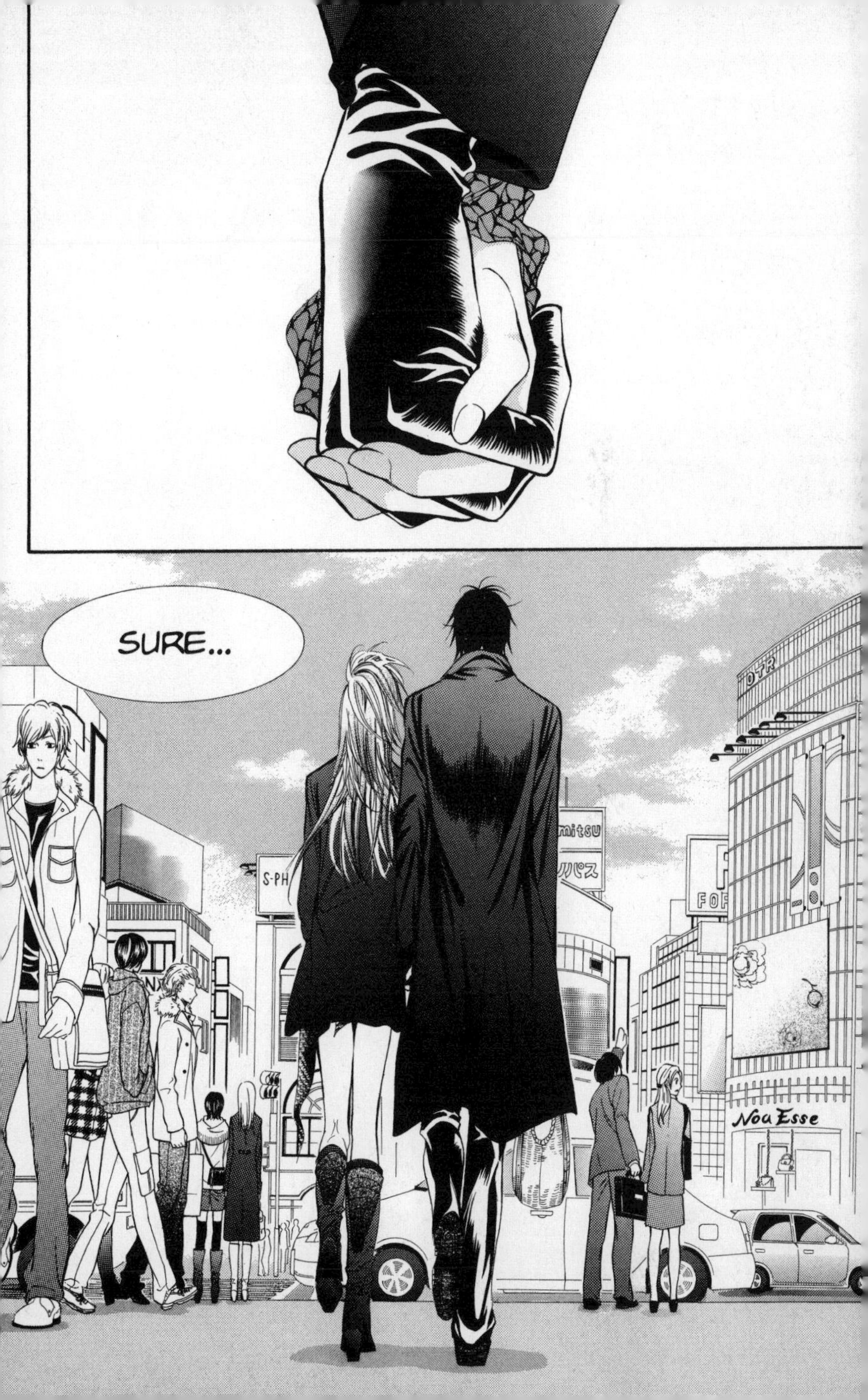
SURE...

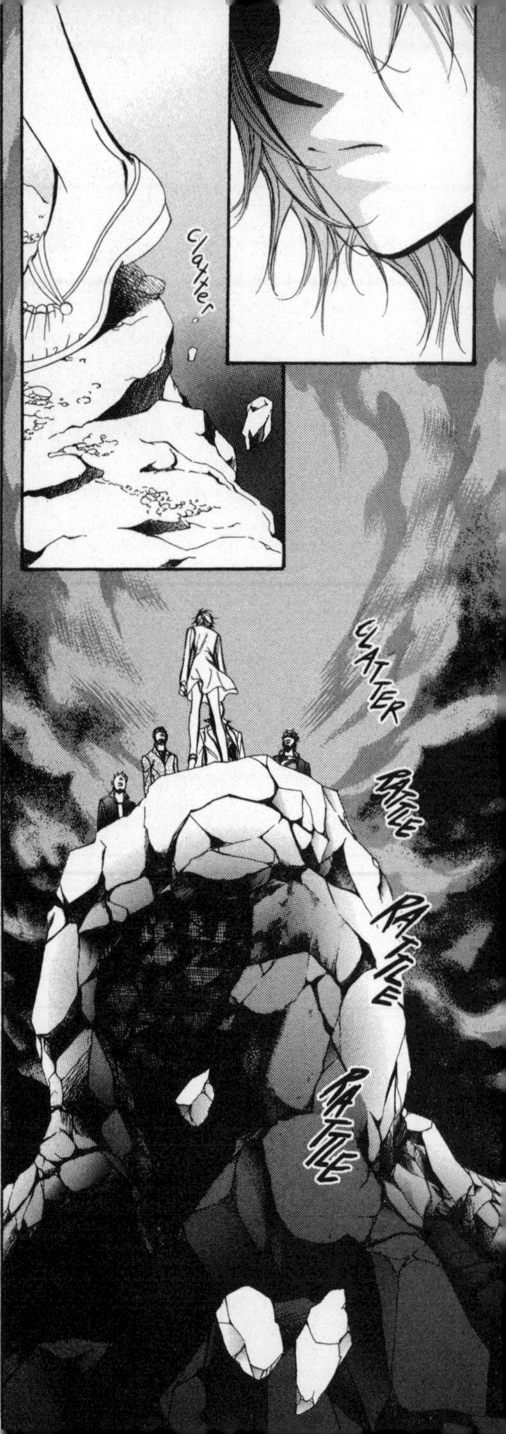
clatter
CLATTER
RATTLE
RATTLE
RATTLE

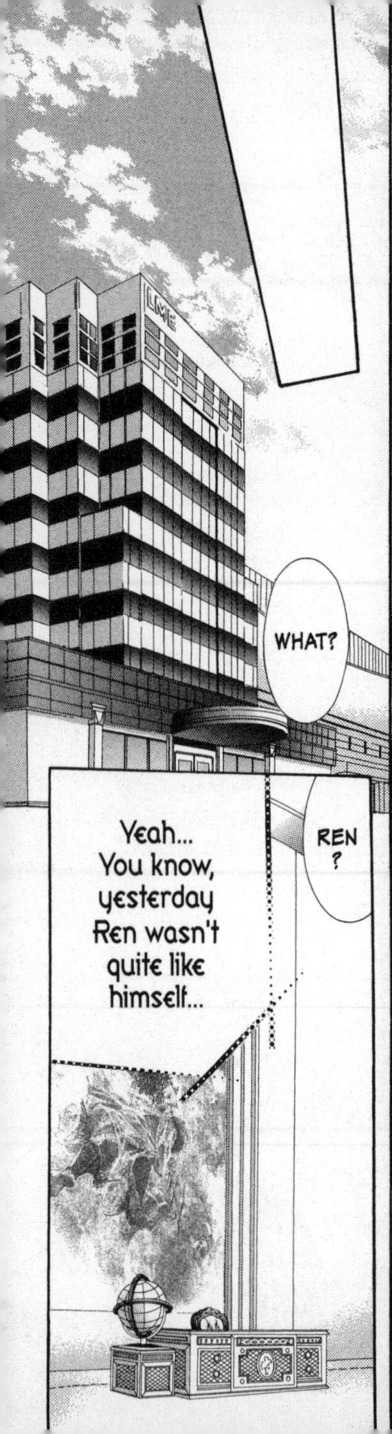
WHAT?
REN?
Yeah... You know, yesterday Ren wasn't quite like himself...

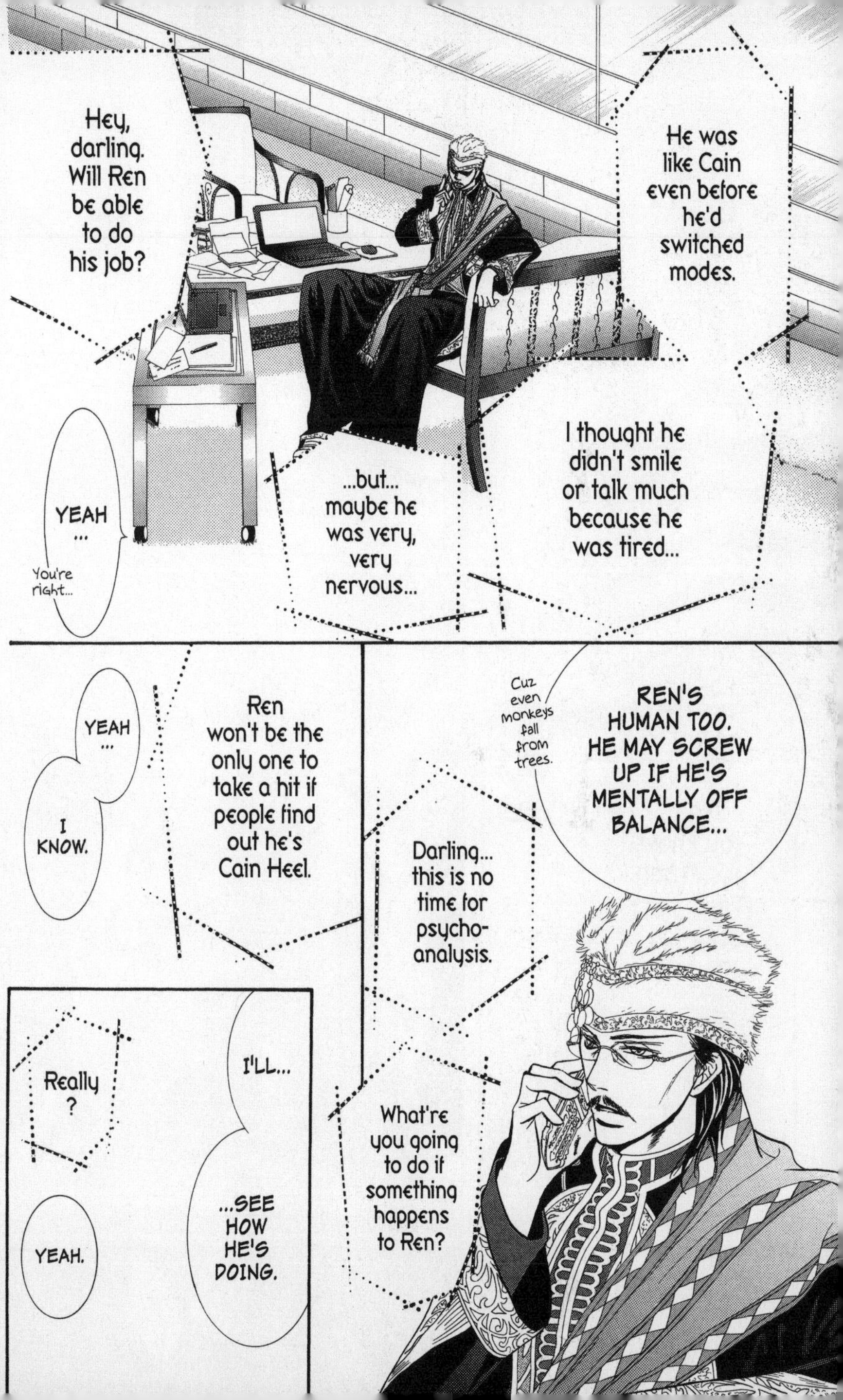
He was like Cain even before he'd switched modes.
I thought he didn't smile or talk much because he was tired...
...but... maybe he was very, very nervous...
Hey, darling. Will Ren be able to do his job?
YEAH...
You're right...
REN'S HUMAN TOO. HE MAY SCREW UP IF HE'S MENTALLY OFF BALANCE...
Cuz even monkeys fall from trees.
Darling... this is no time for psycho-analysis.
What're you going to do if something happens to Ren?
Ren won't be the only one to take a hit if people find out he's Cain Heel.
YEAH...
I KNOW.
I'LL...
...SEE HOW HE'S DOING.
Really?
YEAH.

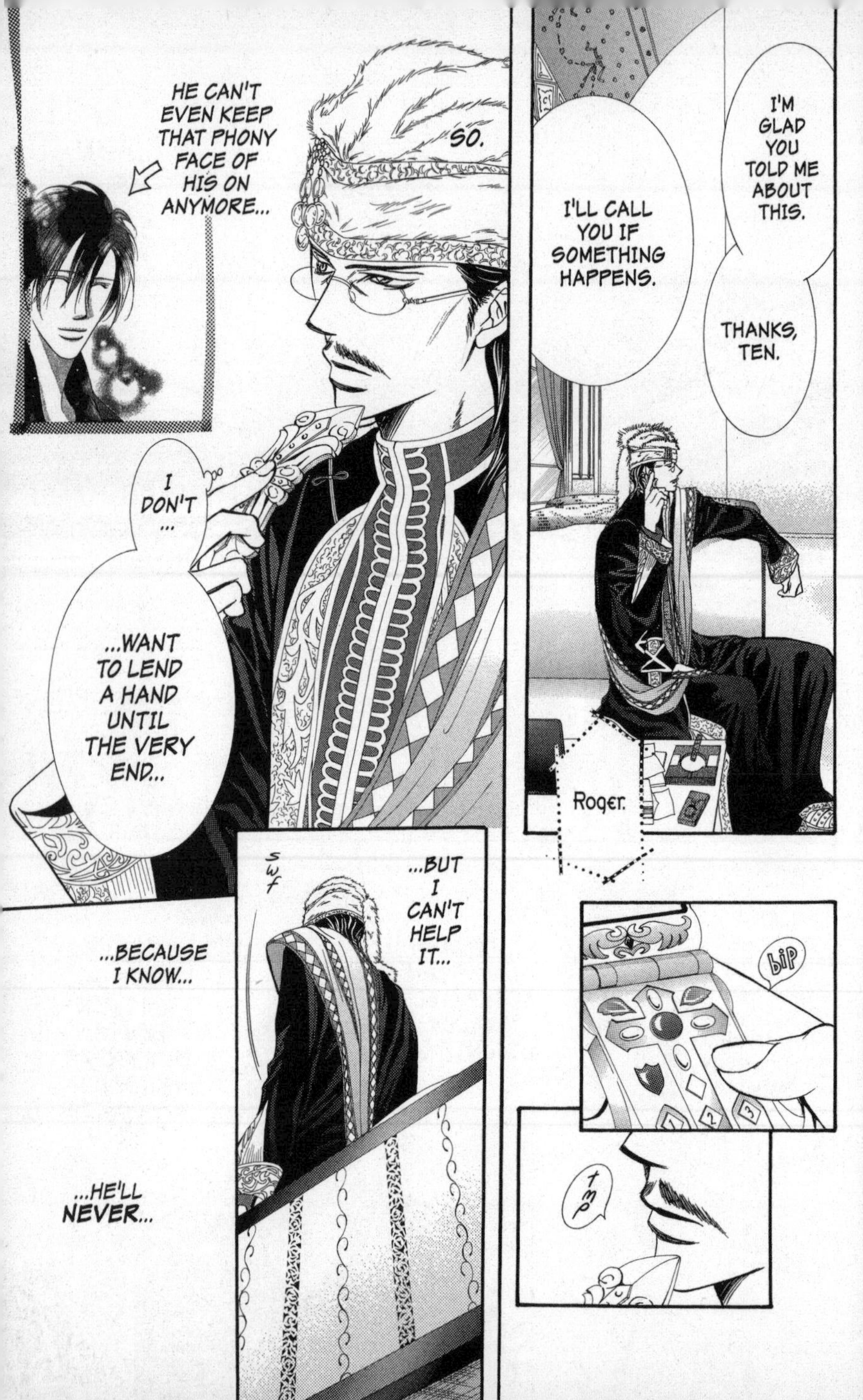

I'M GLAD YOU TOLD ME ABOUT THIS.
THANKS, TEN.
I'LL CALL YOU IF SOMETHING HAPPENS.
Roger.
bip
tmp
SO.
HE CAN'T EVEN KEEP THAT PHONY FACE OF HIS ON ANYMORE...
I DON'T...
...WANT TO LEND A HAND UNTIL THE VERY END...
swf
...BUT I CAN'T HELP IT...
...BECAUSE I KNOW...
...HE'LL NEVER...

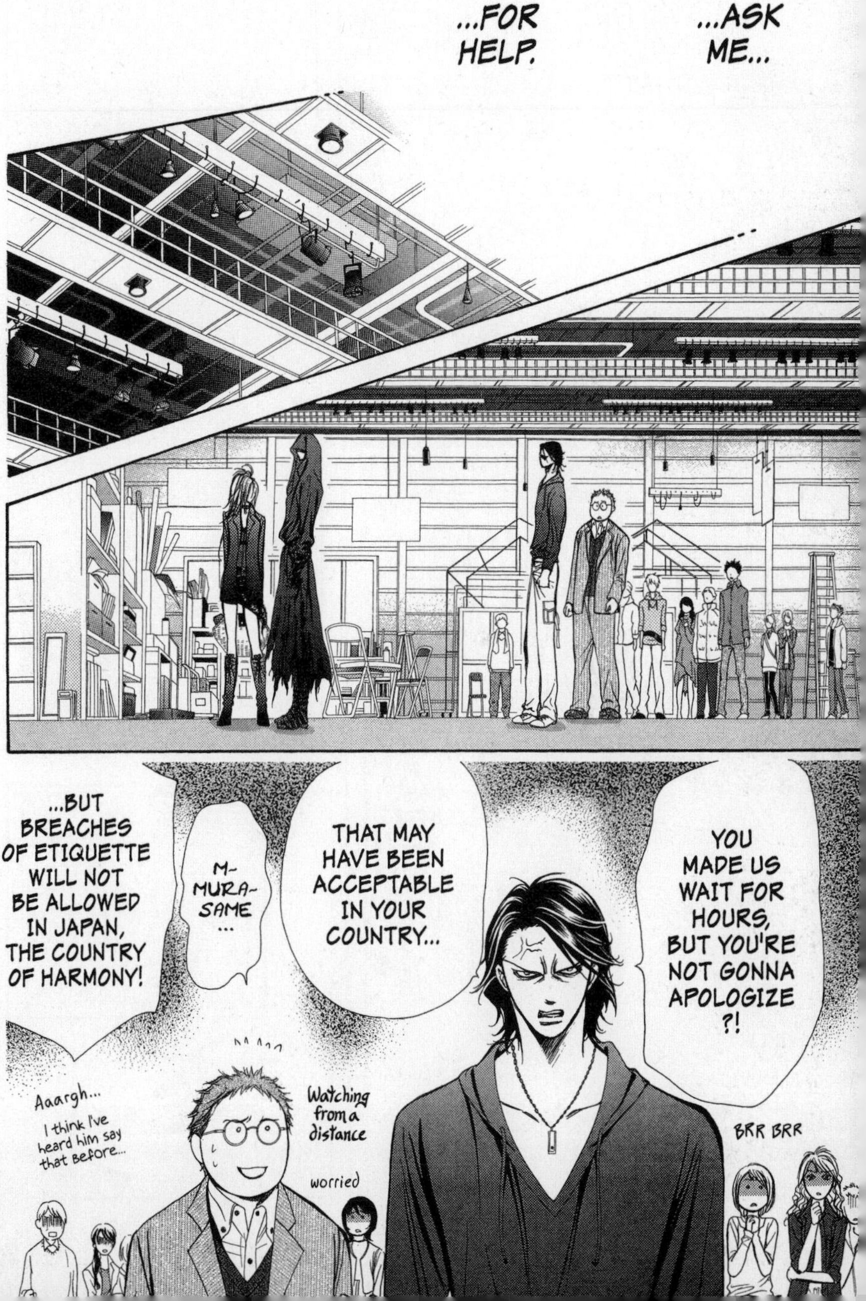
...ASK ME...
...FOR HELP.
YOU MADE US WAIT FOR HOURS, BUT YOU'RE NOT GONNA APOLOGIZE?!
THAT MAY HAVE BEEN ACCEPTABLE IN YOUR COUNTRY...
M-MURASAME...
...BUT BREACHES OF ETIQUETTE WILL NOT BE ALLOWED IN JAPAN, THE COUNTRY OF HARMONY!
BRR BRR
worried
Watching from a distance
Aaargh...
I think I've heard him say that before...

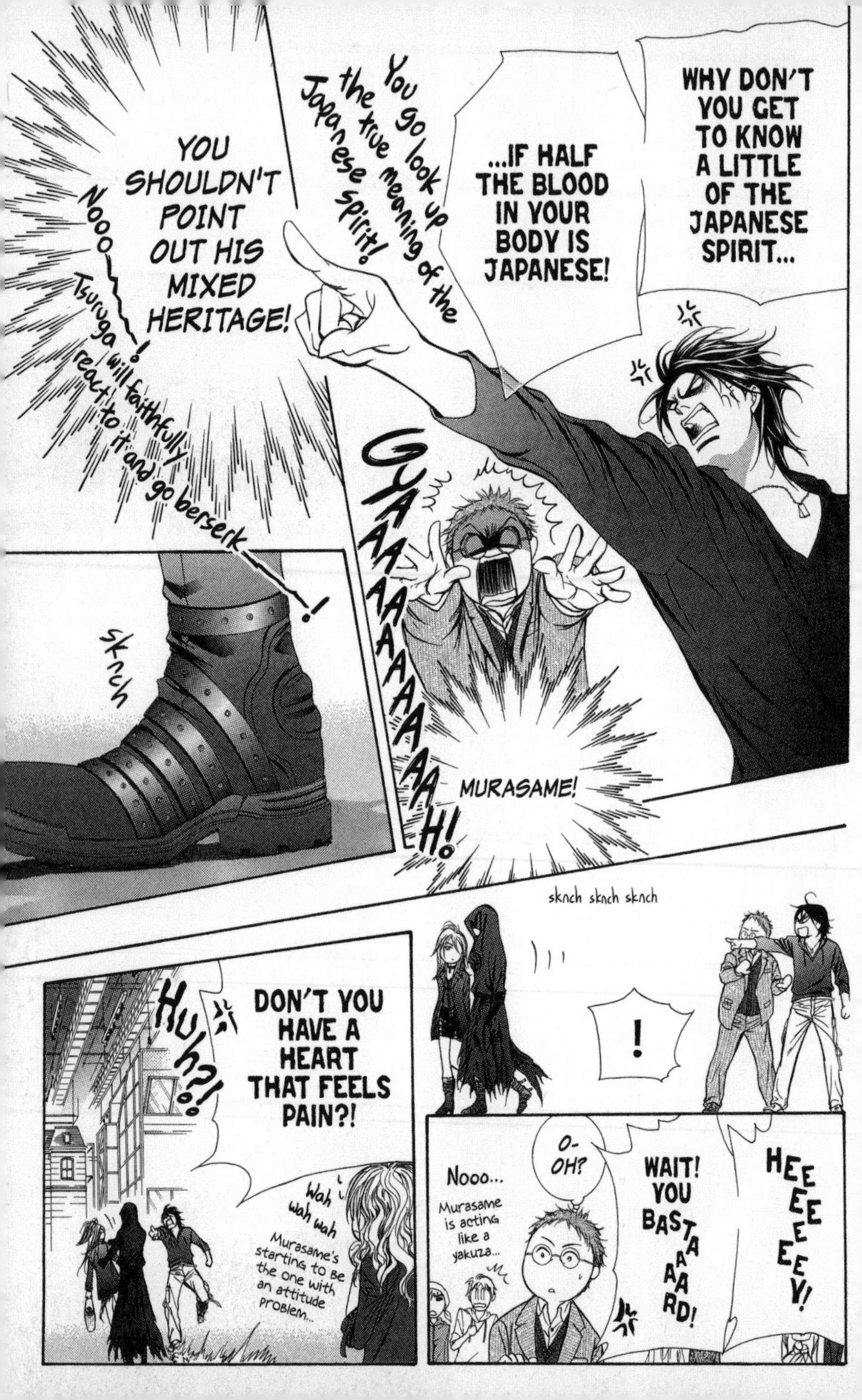
WHY DON'T YOU GET TO KNOW A LITTLE OF THE JAPANESE SPIRIT...
...IF HALF THE BLOOD IN YOUR BODY IS JAPANESE!
You go look up the true meaning of the Japanese spirit!
MURASAME!
GYAAAAAAAAAAAAAH!
YOU SHOULDN'T POINT OUT HIS MIXED HERITAGE!
Nooo—! Tsuruga will faithfully react to it and go berserk—!
sknch
sknch sknch sknch
!
HEEEEEEEY!
WAIT! YOU BASTAAAARD!
O-OH?
Nooo... Murasame is acting like a yakuza...
Huh?!
DON'T YOU HAVE A HEART THAT FEELS PAIN?!
Wah wah wah
Murasame's starting to be the one with an attitude problem...

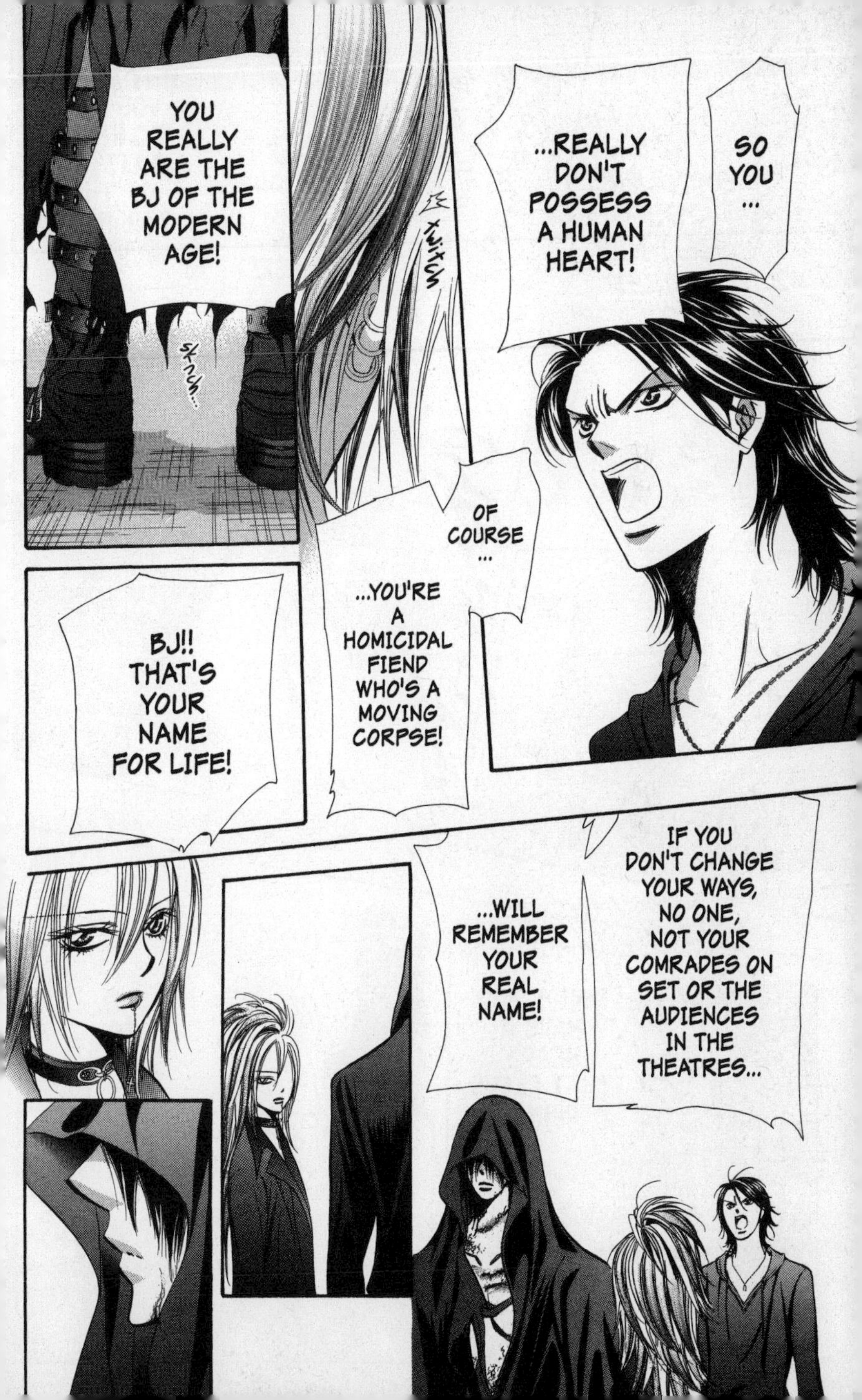
SO YOU ...
...REALLY DON'T POSSESS A HUMAN HEART!
TWITCH
YOU REALLY ARE THE BJ OF THE MODERN AGE!
OF COURSE ...
...YOU'RE A HOMICIDAL FIEND WHO'S A MOVING CORPSE!
BJ!! THAT'S YOUR NAME FOR LIFE!
IF YOU DON'T CHANGE YOUR WAYS, NO ONE, NOT YOUR COMRADES ON SET OR THE AUDIENCES IN THE THEATRES...
...WILL REMEMBER YOUR REAL NAME!

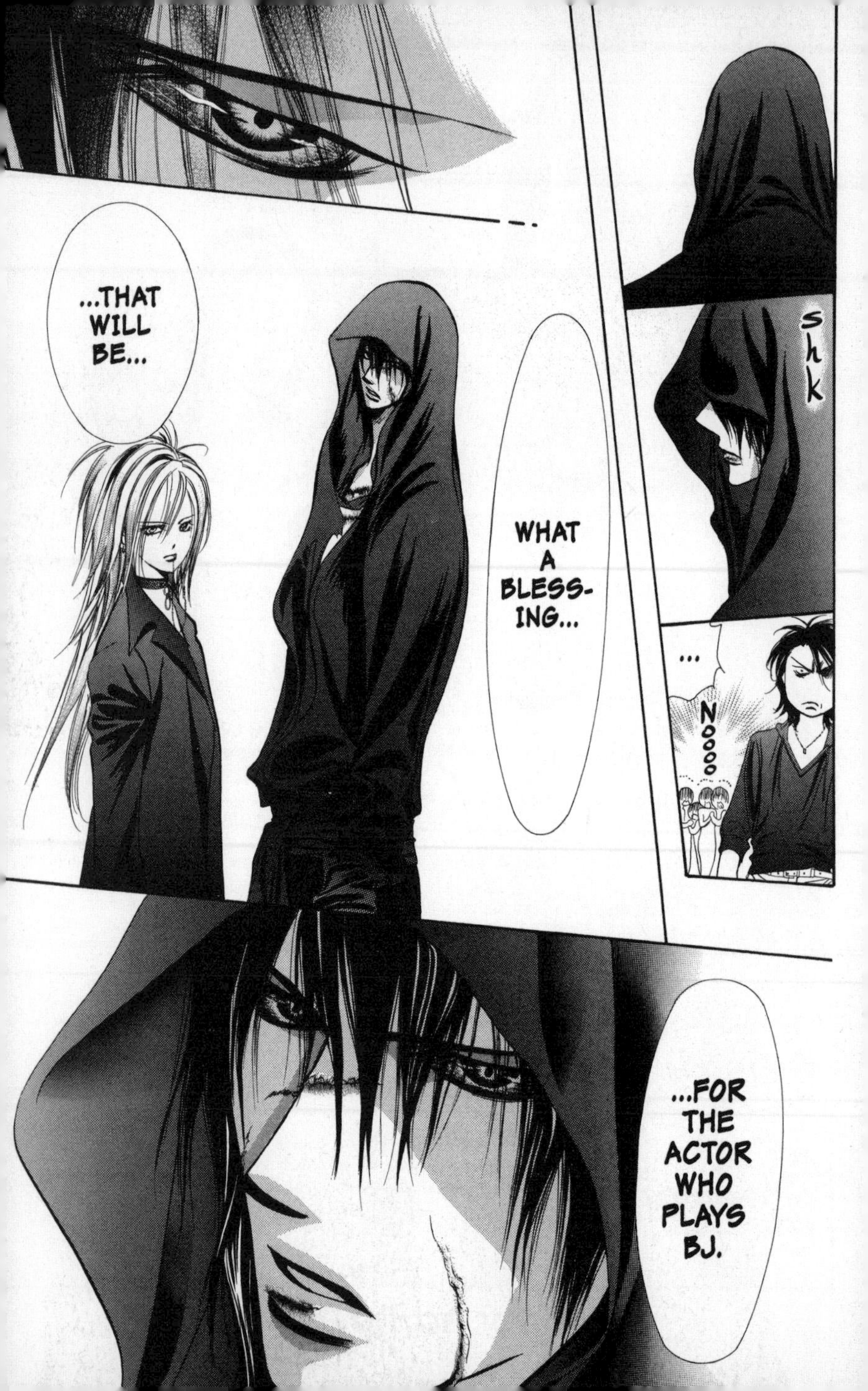
Shk
...
Noooo
...THAT WILL BE...
WHAT A BLESS-ING...
...FOR THE ACTOR WHO PLAYS BJ.

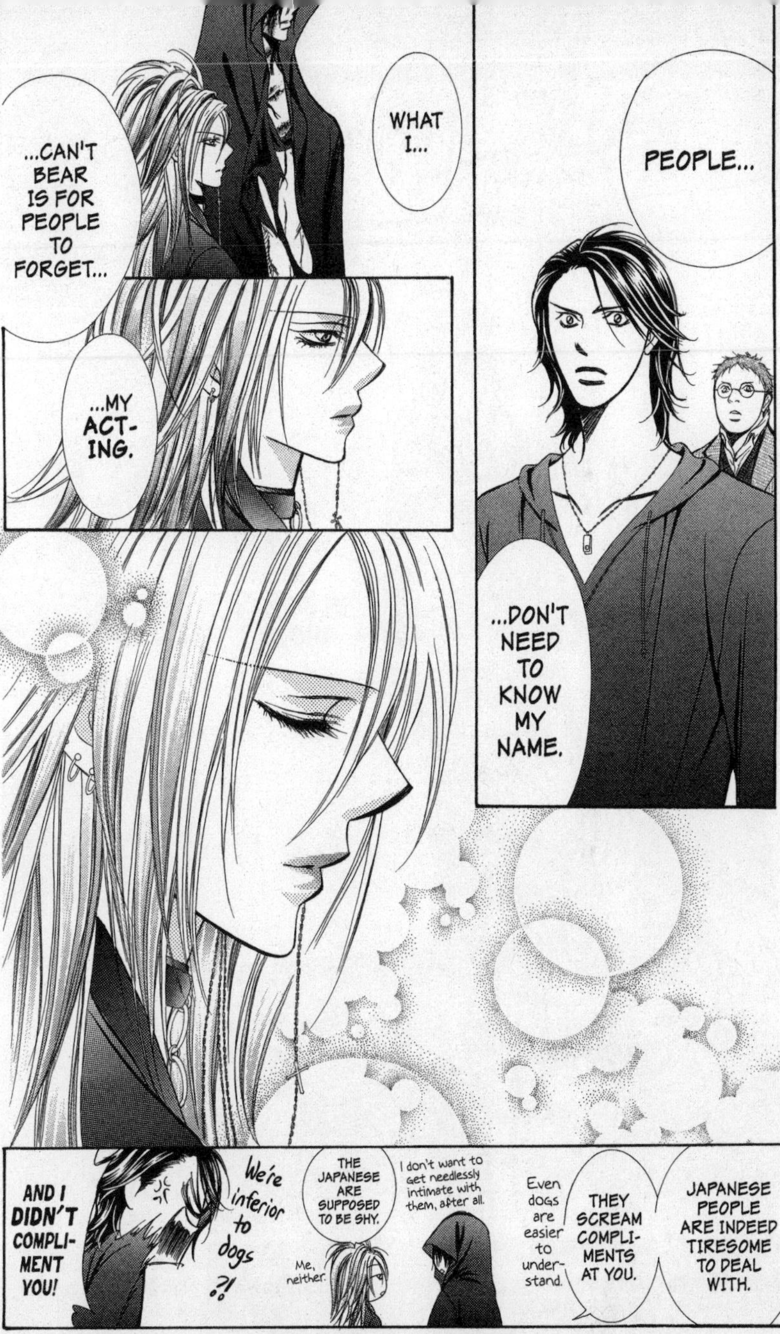
PEOPLE...
...DON'T NEED TO KNOW MY NAME.
WHAT I...
...CAN'T BEAR IS FOR PEOPLE TO FORGET...
...MY ACTING.
JAPANESE PEOPLE ARE INDEED TIRESOME TO DEAL WITH.
THEY SCREAM COMPLIMENTS AT YOU.
Even dogs are easier to understand.
I don't want to get needlessly intimate with them, after all.
THE JAPANESE ARE SUPPOSED TO BE SHY.
Me, neither.
We're inferior to dogs?!
AND I DIDN'T COMPLIMENT YOU!

End of Act 197

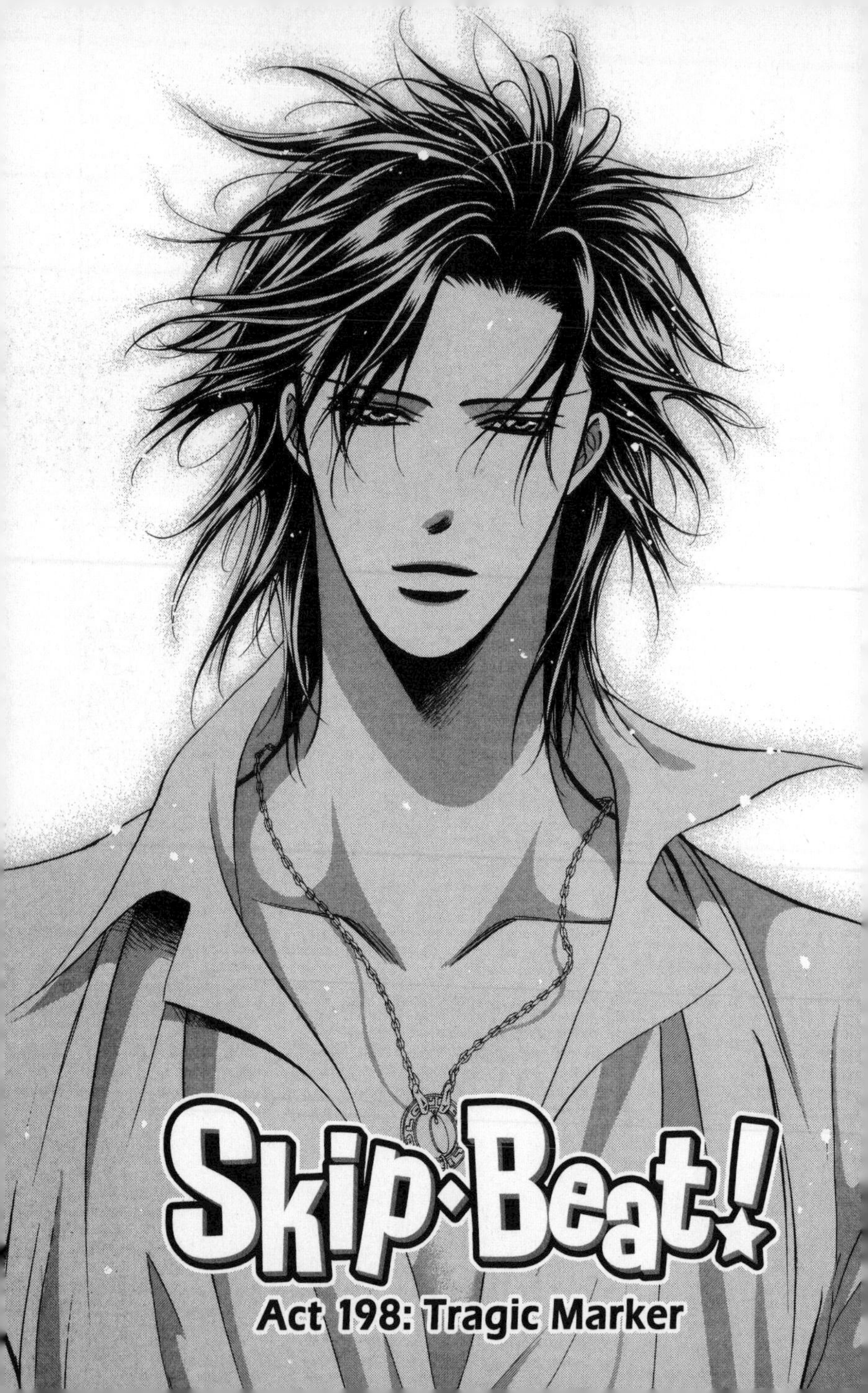
Skip·Beat!
Act 198: Tragic Marker

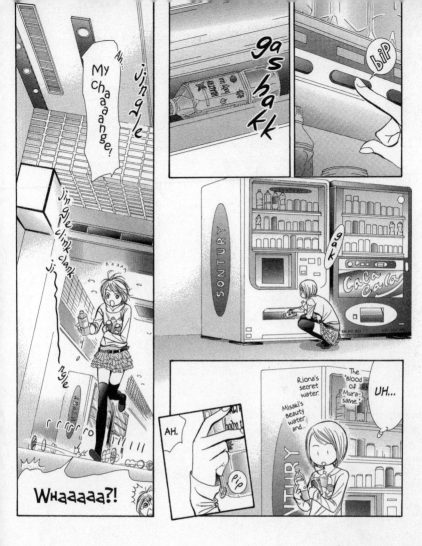

biP
gashakk
gak
UH...
The "Blood of Mura-same."
Riona's secret water.
Misaki's Beauty water and...
AH.
pip
jingle
Ah... My chaaaange!
jingle clink clank
ji
ngle
rrrrrrro
Whaaaaa?!

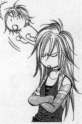

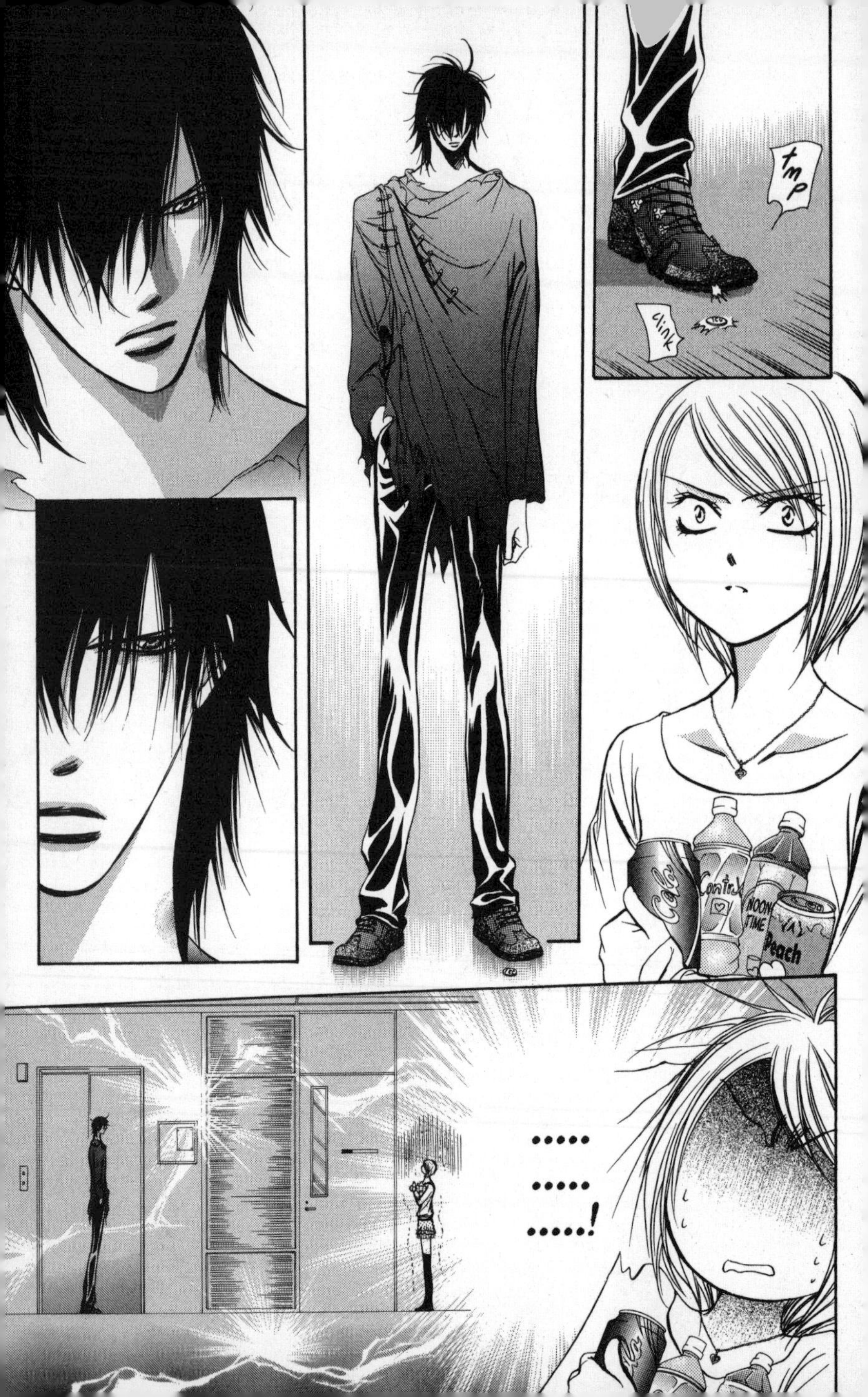
tmp
clink
NOON TIME
Peach
.....
.....
.....!

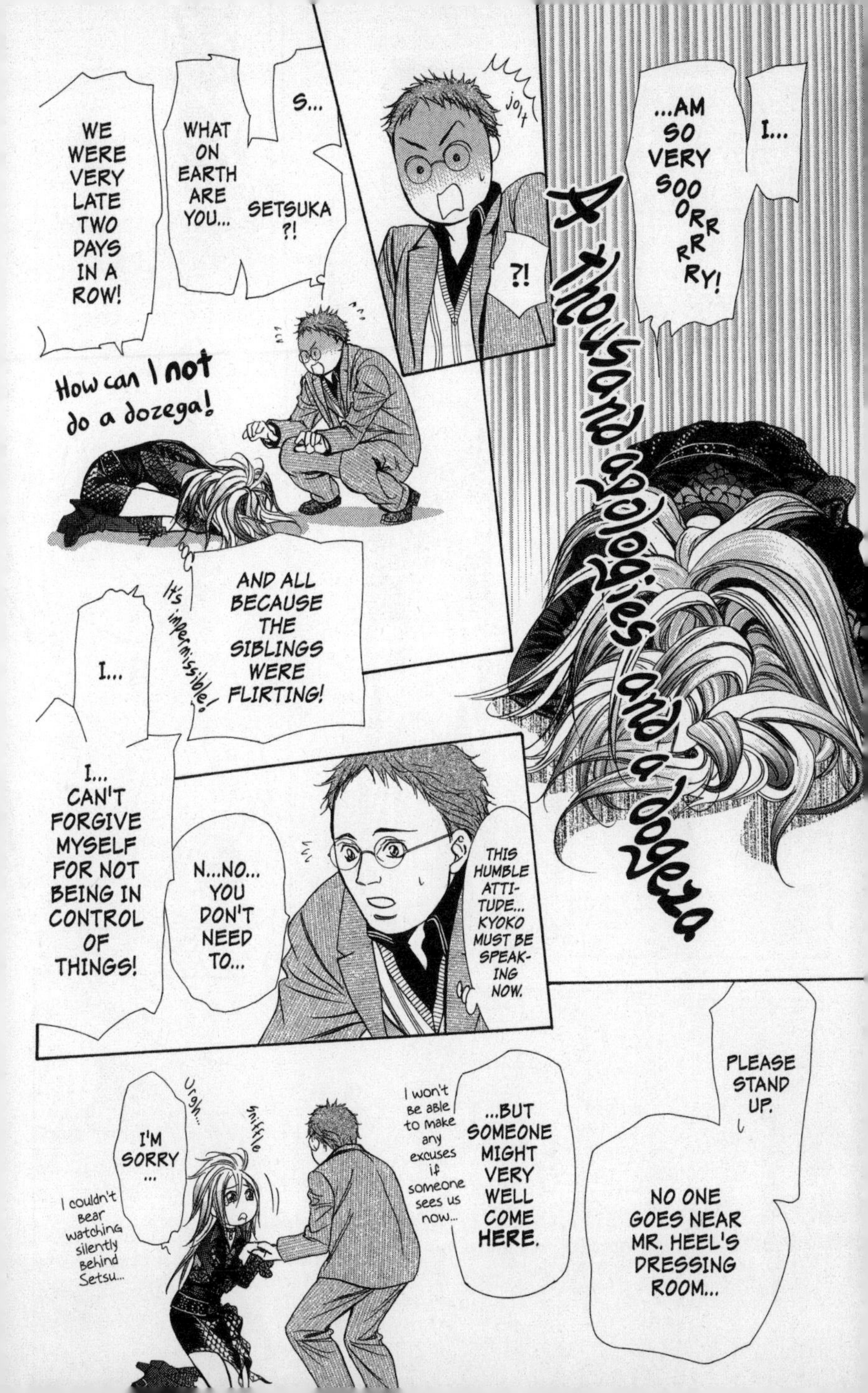
I...
...AM SO VERY SOOORRRRRY!
A thousand apologies and a dogeza
jolt
?!
S...
SETSUKA ?!
WHAT ON EARTH ARE YOU...
WE WERE VERY LATE TWO DAYS IN A ROW!
How can I not do a dozega!
AND ALL BECAUSE THE SIBLINGS WERE FLIRTING!
It's impermissible!
I...
THIS HUMBLE ATTITUDE... KYOKO MUST BE SPEAKING NOW.
N...NO... YOU DON'T NEED TO...
I... CAN'T FORGIVE MYSELF FOR NOT BEING IN CONTROL OF THINGS!
PLEASE STAND UP.
NO ONE GOES NEAR MR. HEEL'S DRESSING ROOM...
...BUT SOMEONE MIGHT VERY WELL COME HERE.
I won't be able to make any excuses if someone sees us now...
sniffle
Urgh...
I'M SORRY...
I couldn't bear watching silently behind Setsu...

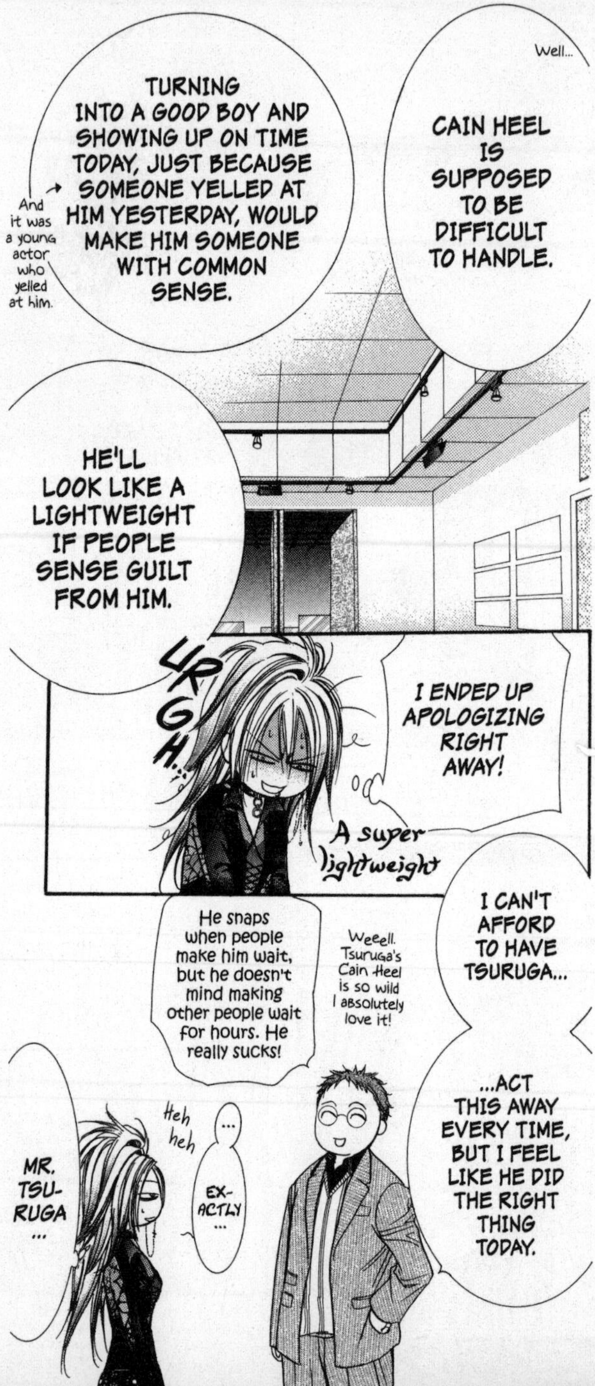
Well...
CAIN HEEL IS SUPPOSED TO BE DIFFICULT TO HANDLE.
TURNING INTO A GOOD BOY AND SHOWING UP ON TIME TODAY, JUST BECAUSE SOMEONE YELLED AT HIM YESTERDAY, WOULD MAKE HIM SOMEONE WITH COMMON SENSE.
And it was a young actor who yelled at him.
HE'LL LOOK LIKE A LIGHTWEIGHT IF PEOPLE SENSE GUILT FROM HIM.
I ENDED UP APOLOGIZING RIGHT AWAY!
URGH...
A super lightweight
I CAN'T AFFORD TO HAVE TSURUGA...
...ACT THIS AWAY EVERY TIME, BUT I FEEL LIKE HE DID THE RIGHT THING TODAY.
Weeell. Tsuruga's Cain Heel is so wild I absolutely love it!
He snaps when people make him wait, but he doesn't mind making other people wait for hours. He really sucks!
...
Heh heh
EX-ACTLY...
MR. TSU-RUGA...

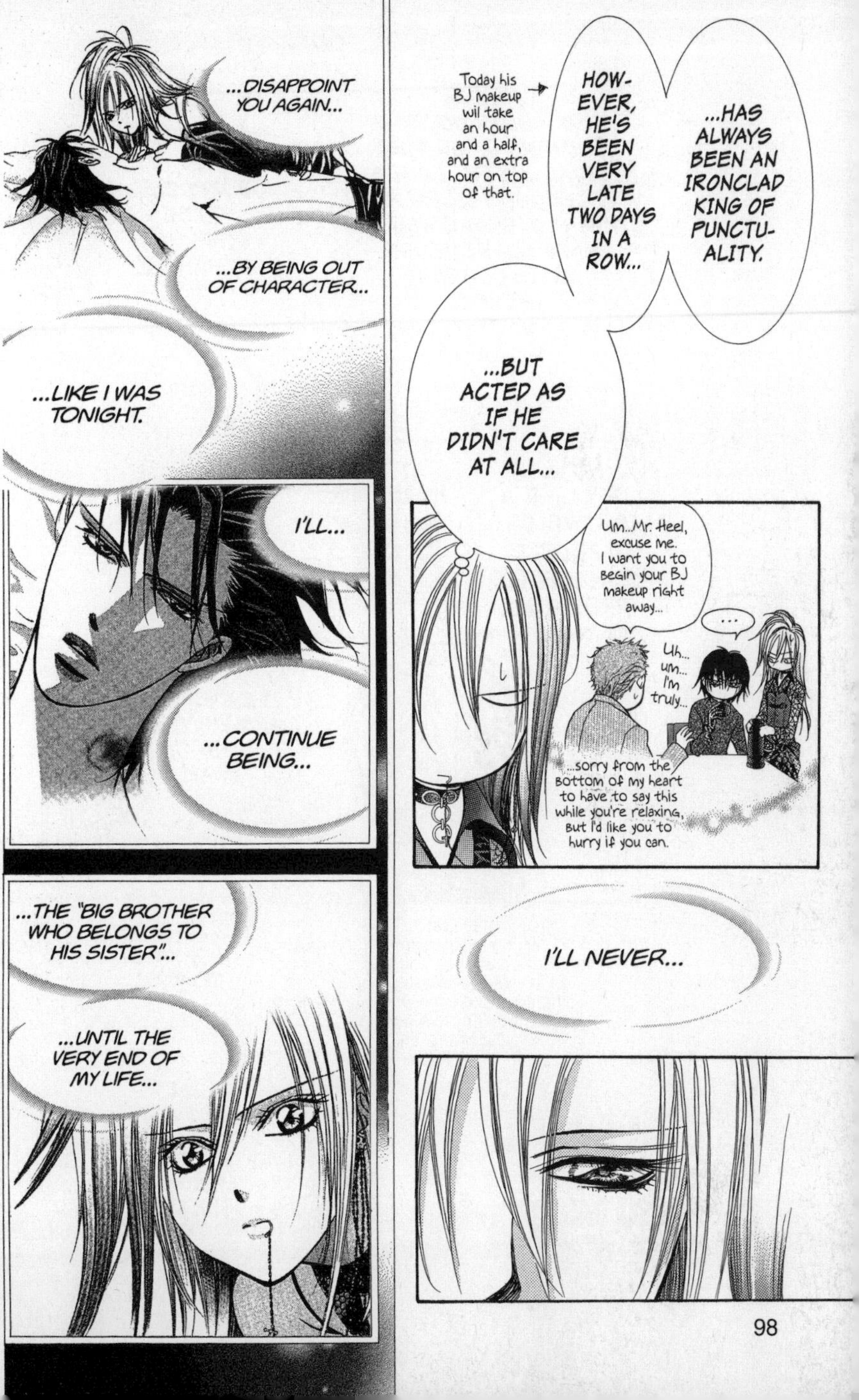
...HAS ALWAYS BEEN AN IRONCLAD KING OF PUNCTUALITY.
HOW-EVER, HE'S BEEN VERY LATE TWO DAYS IN A ROW...
Today his BJ makeup wil take an hour and a half, and an extra hour on top of that.
...BUT ACTED AS IF HE DIDN'T CARE AT ALL...
Um...Mr. Heel, excuse me. I want you to begin your BJ makeup right away...
...
Uh... um... I'm truly...
...sorry from the bottom of my heart to have to say this while you're relaxing, but I'd like you to hurry if you can.
I'LL NEVER...
...DISAPPOINT YOU AGAIN...
...BY BEING OUT OF CHARACTER...
...LIKE I WAS TONIGHT.
I'LL...
...CONTINUE BEING...
...THE "BIG BROTHER WHO BELONGS TO HIS SISTER"...
...UNTIL THE VERY END OF MY LIFE...

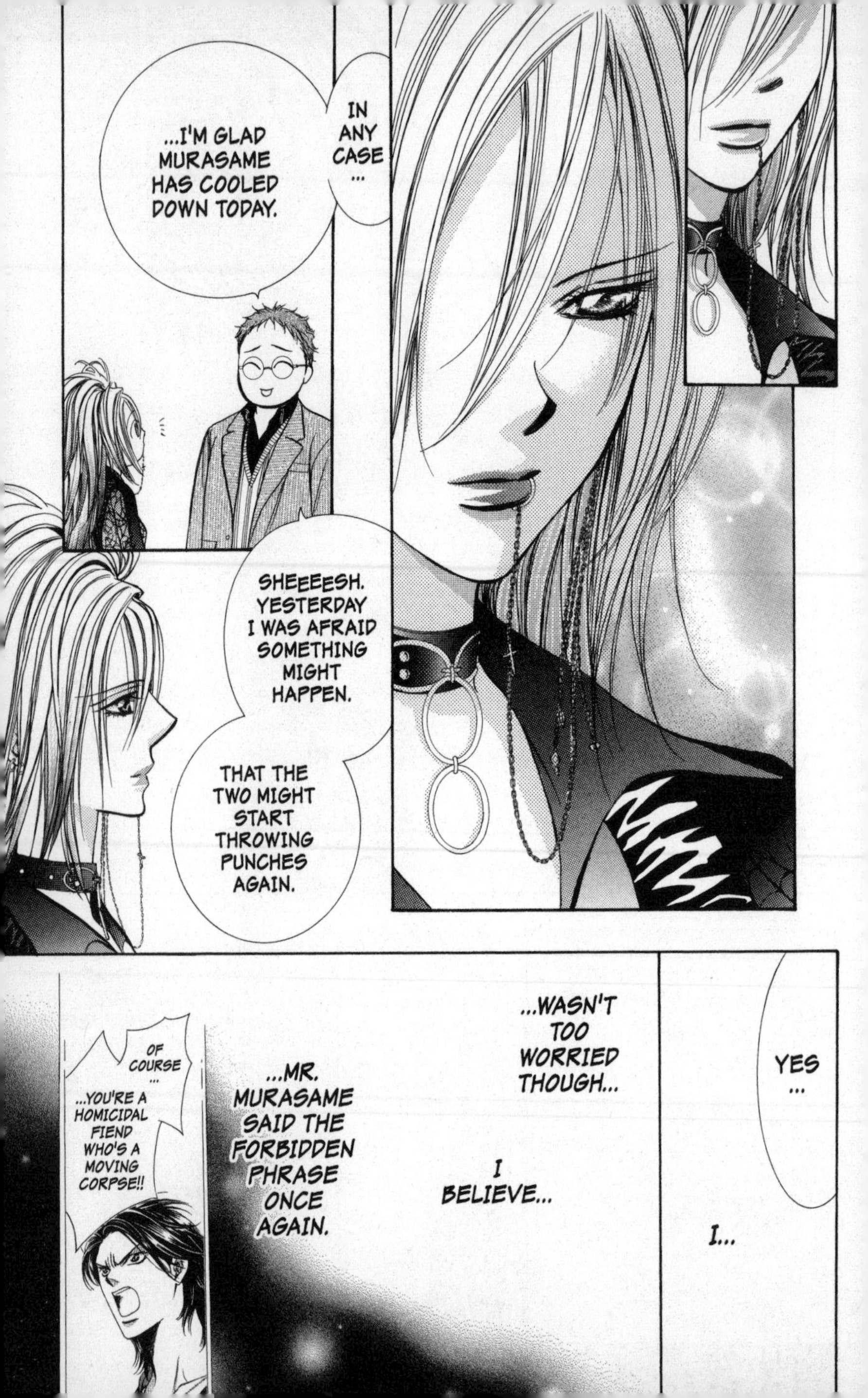
IN ANY CASE...
...I'M GLAD MURASAME HAS COOLED DOWN TODAY.
SHEEEESH. YESTERDAY I WAS AFRAID SOMETHING MIGHT HAPPEN.
THAT THE TWO MIGHT START THROWING PUNCHES AGAIN.
YES...
I...
...WASN'T TOO WORRIED THOUGH...
I BELIEVE...
...MR. MURASAME SAID THE FORBIDDEN PHRASE ONCE AGAIN.
OF COURSE...
...YOU'RE A HOMICIDAL FIEND WHO'S A MOVING CORPSE!!

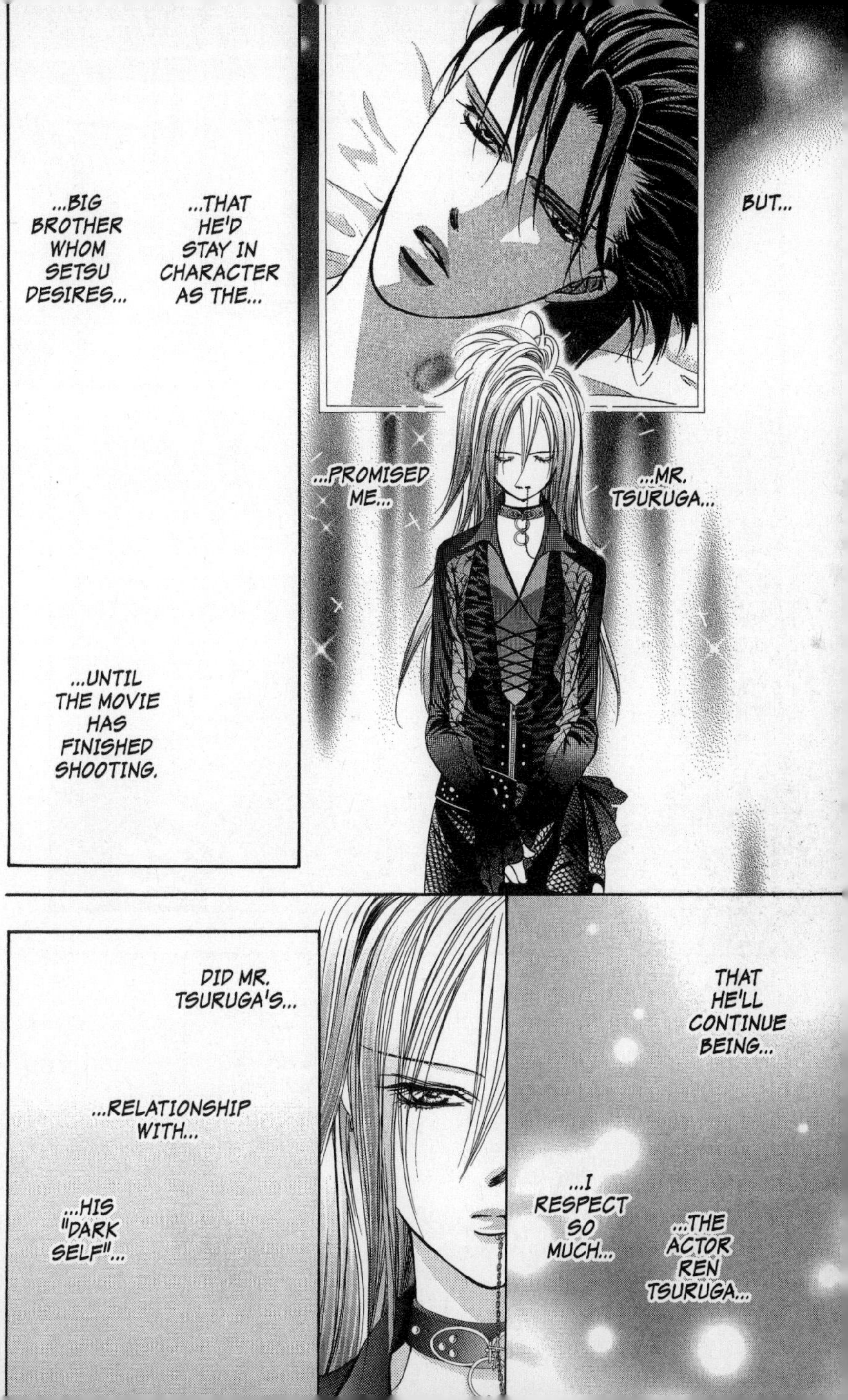
BUT...
...MR. TSURUGA...
...PROMISED ME...
...THAT HE'D STAY IN CHARACTER AS THE...
...BIG BROTHER WHOM SETSU DESIRES...
...UNTIL THE MOVIE HAS FINISHED SHOOTING.
THAT HE'LL CONTINUE BEING...
...THE ACTOR REN TSURUGA...
...I RESPECT SO MUCH...
DID MR. TSURUGA'S...
...RELATIONSHIP WITH...
...HIS "DARK SELF"...

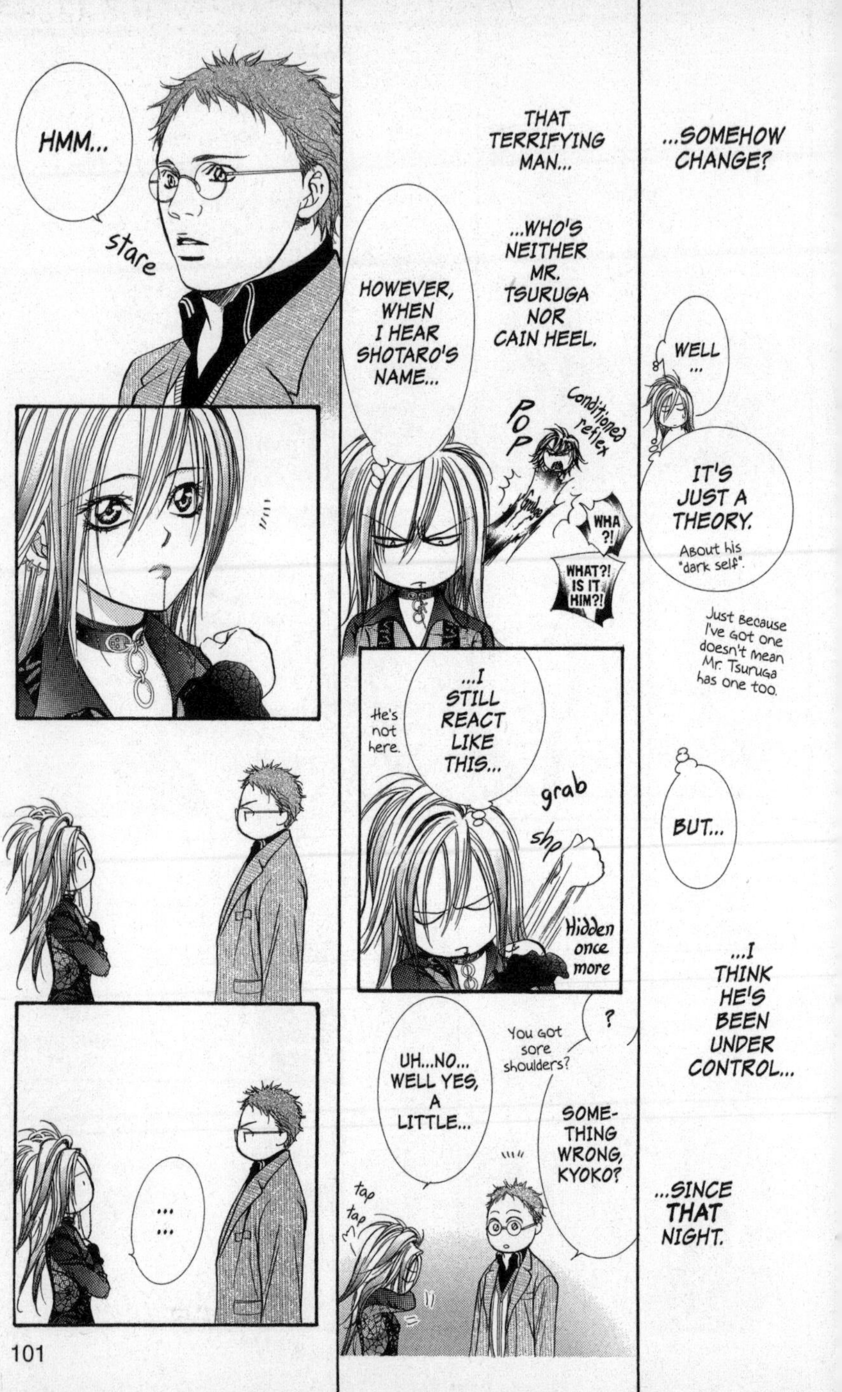
...SOMEHOW CHANGE?
WELL...
IT'S JUST A THEORY.
About his "dark self".
Just because I've got one doesn't mean Mr. Tsuruga has one too.
BUT...
...I THINK HE'S BEEN UNDER CONTROL...
...SINCE THAT NIGHT.
THAT TERRIFYING MAN...
...WHO'S NEITHER MR. TSURUGA NOR CAIN HEEL.
HOWEVER, WHEN I HEAR SHOTARO'S NAME...
Conditioned reflex
POP
WHA?!
WHAT?! IS IT HIM?!
...I STILL REACT LIKE THIS...
He's not here.
grab
shp
Hidden once more
?
You got sore shoulders?
SOMETHING WRONG, KYOKO?
UH...NO... WELL YES, A LITTLE...
tap
tap
HMM...
stare
...
...

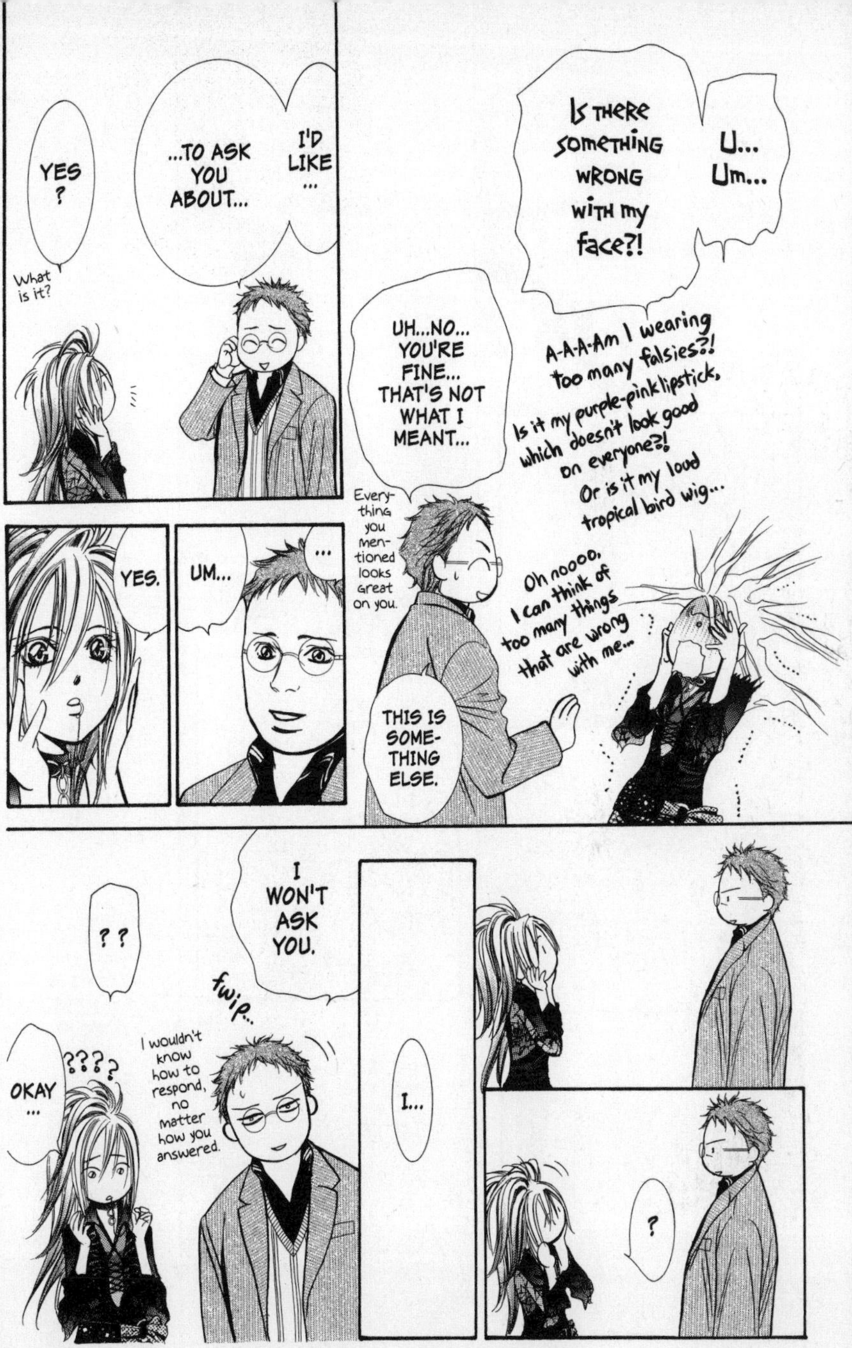
U... Um...
Is there something wrong with my face?!
A-A-A-Am I wearing too many falsies?! Is it my purple-pink lipstick, which doesn't look good on everyone?! Or is it my loud tropical bird wig...
UH...NO... YOU'RE FINE... THAT'S NOT WHAT I MEANT...
Everything you mentioned looks great on you.
Oh noooo, I can think of too many things that are wrong with me...
THIS IS SOMETHING ELSE.
I'D LIKE ...
...TO ASK YOU ABOUT...
YES ?
What is it?
...
UM...
YES.
?
I...
I WON'T ASK YOU.
fwip...
??
I wouldn't know how to respond, no matter how you answered.
????
OKAY ...

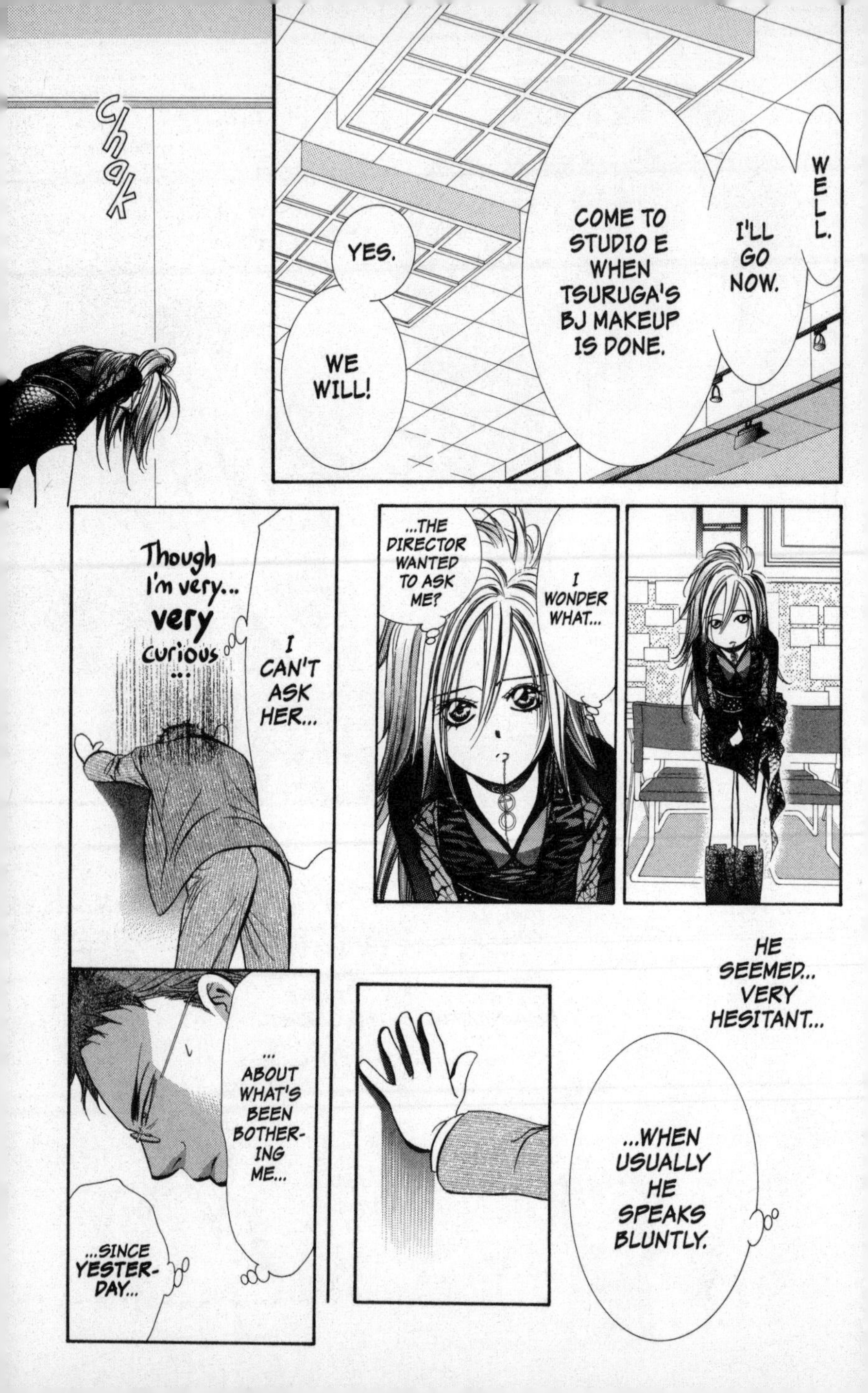
WELL.
I'LL GO NOW.
COME TO STUDIO E WHEN TSURUGA'S BJ MAKEUP IS DONE.
YES.
WE WILL!
Chak
I WONDER WHAT...
...THE DIRECTOR WANTED TO ASK ME?
I CAN'T ASK HER...
Though I'm very... very curious...
HE SEEMED... VERY HESITANT...
...WHEN USUALLY HE SPEAKS BLUNTLY.
... ABOUT WHAT'S BEEN BOTHER-ING ME...
...SINCE YESTER-DAY...

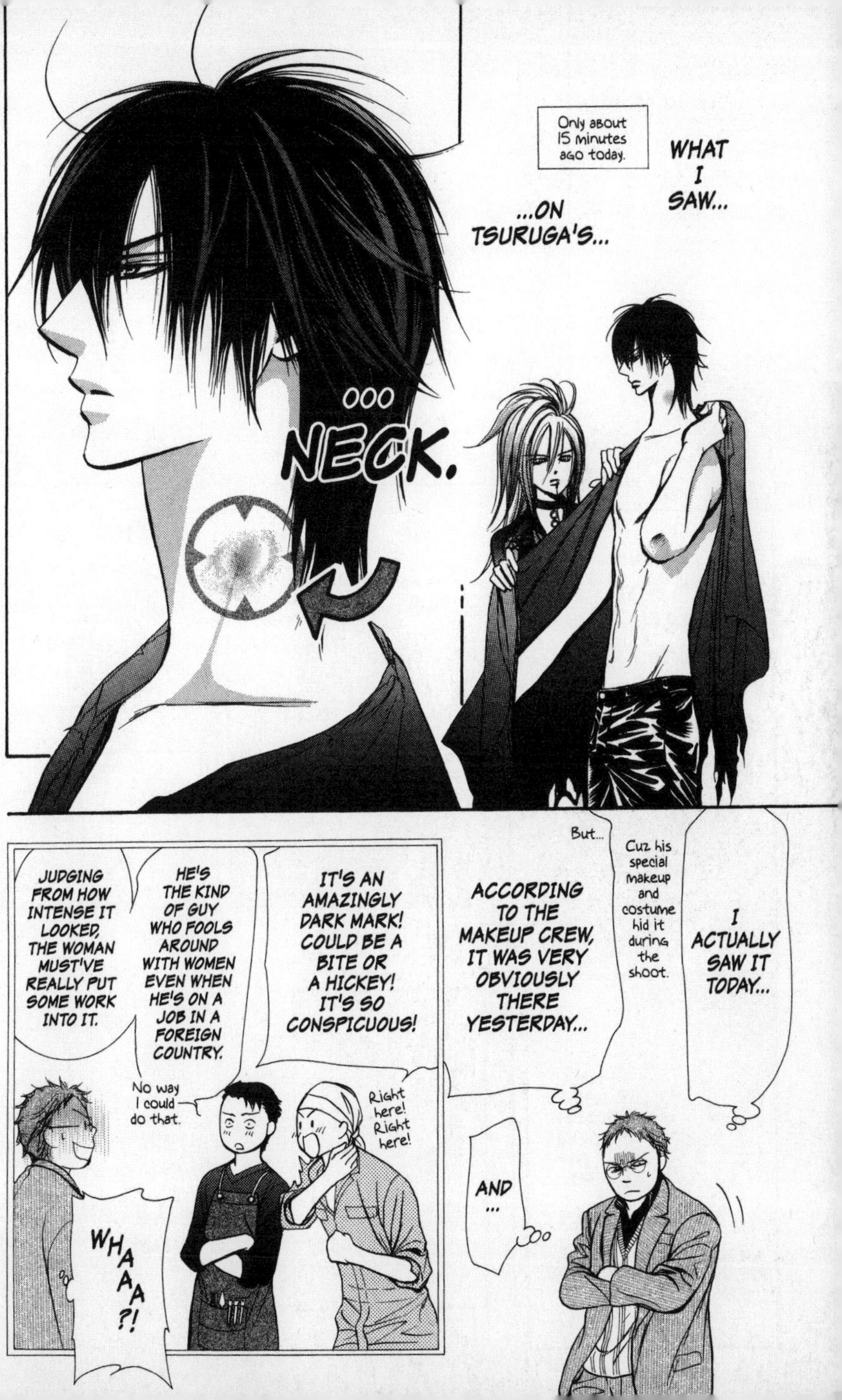
Only about 15 minutes ago today.
WHAT I SAW...
...ON TSURUGA'S...
ooo NECK.
I ACTUALLY SAW IT TODAY...
Cuz his special makeup and costume hid it during the shoot.
But...
ACCORDING TO THE MAKEUP CREW, IT WAS VERY OBVIOUSLY THERE YESTERDAY...
AND ...
IT'S AN AMAZINGLY DARK MARK! COULD BE A BITE OR A HICKEY! IT'S SO CONSPICUOUS!
Right here! Right here!
HE'S THE KIND OF GUY WHO FOOLS AROUND WITH WOMEN EVEN WHEN HE'S ON A JOB IN A FOREIGN COUNTRY.
No way I could do that.
JUDGING FROM HOW INTENSE IT LOOKED, THE WOMAN MUST'VE REALLY PUT SOME WORK INTO IT.
WHAAA?!

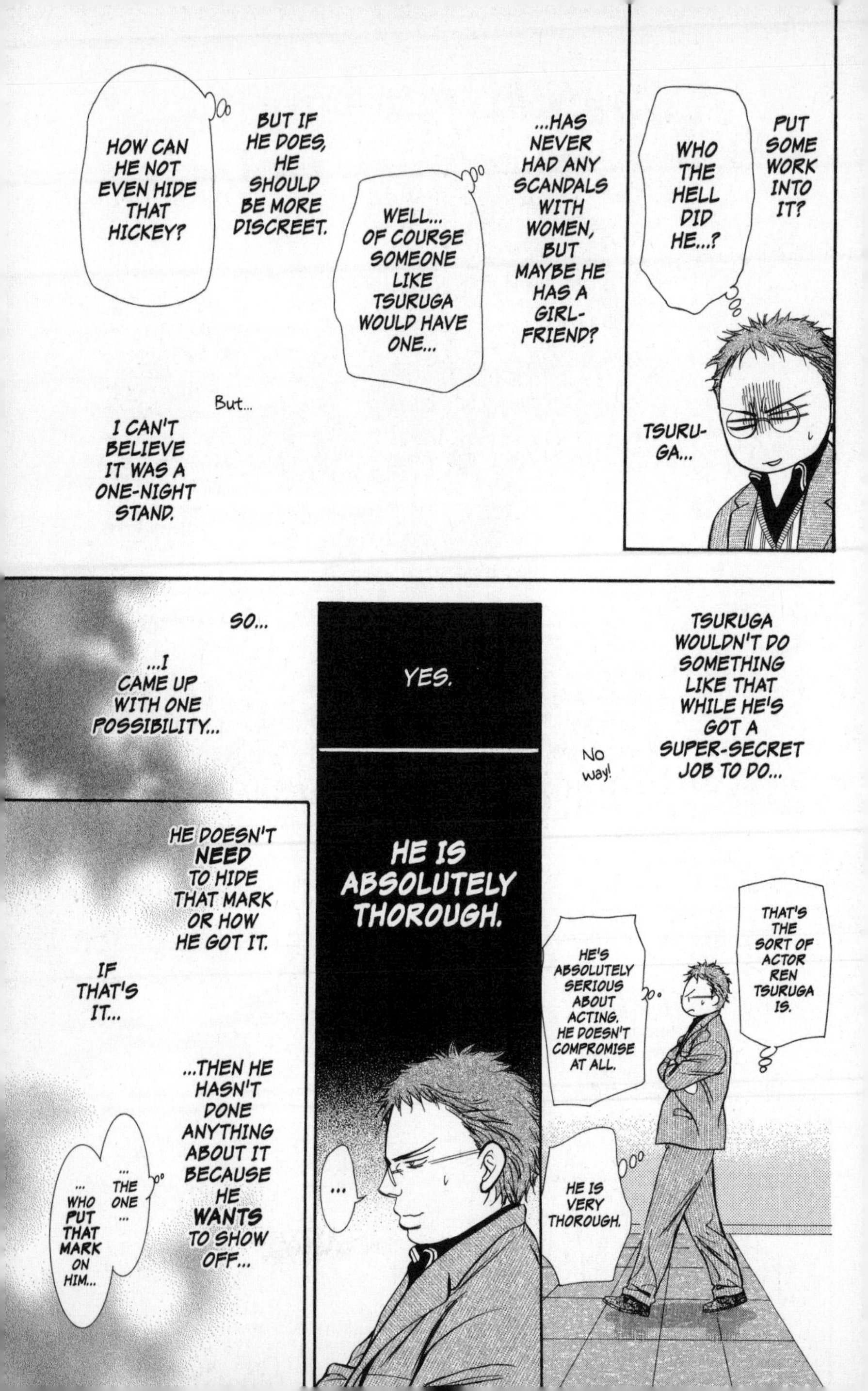
PUT SOME WORK INTO IT?
WHO THE HELL DID HE...?
TSURU-GA...
...HAS NEVER HAD ANY SCANDALS WITH WOMEN, BUT MAYBE HE HAS A GIRL-FRIEND?
WELL... OF COURSE SOMEONE LIKE TSURUGA WOULD HAVE ONE...
BUT IF HE DOES, HE SHOULD BE MORE DISCREET.
HOW CAN HE NOT EVEN HIDE THAT HICKEY?
But...
I CAN'T BELIEVE IT WAS A ONE-NIGHT STAND.
TSURUGA WOULDN'T DO SOMETHING LIKE THAT WHILE HE'S GOT A SUPER-SECRET JOB TO DO...
No way!
THAT'S THE SORT OF ACTOR REN TSURUGA IS.
HE'S ABSOLUTELY SERIOUS ABOUT ACTING. HE DOESN'T COMPROMISE AT ALL.
HE IS VERY THOROUGH.
YES.
HE IS ABSOLUTELY THOROUGH.
...
SO...
...I CAME UP WITH ONE POSSIBILITY...
HE DOESN'T NEED TO HIDE THAT MARK OR HOW HE GOT IT.
IF THAT'S IT...
...THEN HE HASN'T DONE ANYTHING ABOUT IT BECAUSE HE WANTS TO SHOW OFF...
... THE ONE ...
... WHO PUT THAT MARK ON HIM...

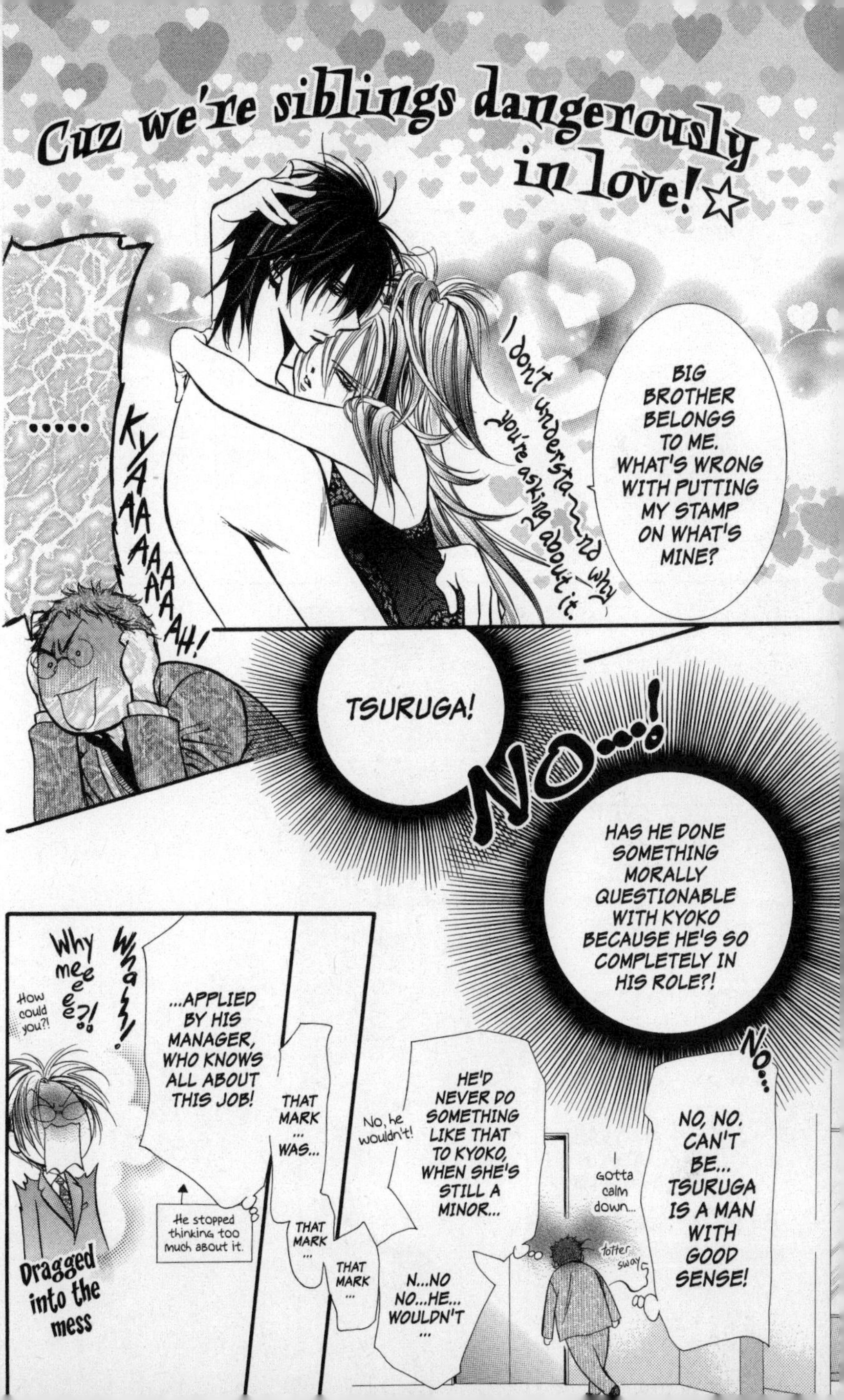
Cuz we're siblings dangerously in love!☆
BIG BROTHER BELONGS TO ME. WHAT'S WRONG WITH PUTTING MY STAMP ON WHAT'S MINE?
I don't understa~~nd why you're asking about it.
KYAAAAAAAAAAAH!
.....
TSURUGA!
NO...!
HAS HE DONE SOMETHING MORALLY QUESTIONABLE WITH KYOKO BECAUSE HE'S SO COMPLETELY IN HIS ROLE?!
No...
NO, NO. CAN'T BE... TSURUGA IS A MAN WITH GOOD SENSE!
I gotta calm down...
totter sway
HE'D NEVER DO SOMETHING LIKE THAT TO KYOKO, WHEN SHE'S STILL A MINOR...
No, he wouldn't!
N...NO NO...HE... WOULDN'T ...
THAT MARK ... WAS...
THAT MARK ...
THAT MARK ...
...APPLIED BY HIS MANAGER, WHO KNOWS ALL ABOUT THIS JOB!
He stopped thinking too much about it.
Whaaa!
Why meeee?!
How could you?!
Dragged into the mess

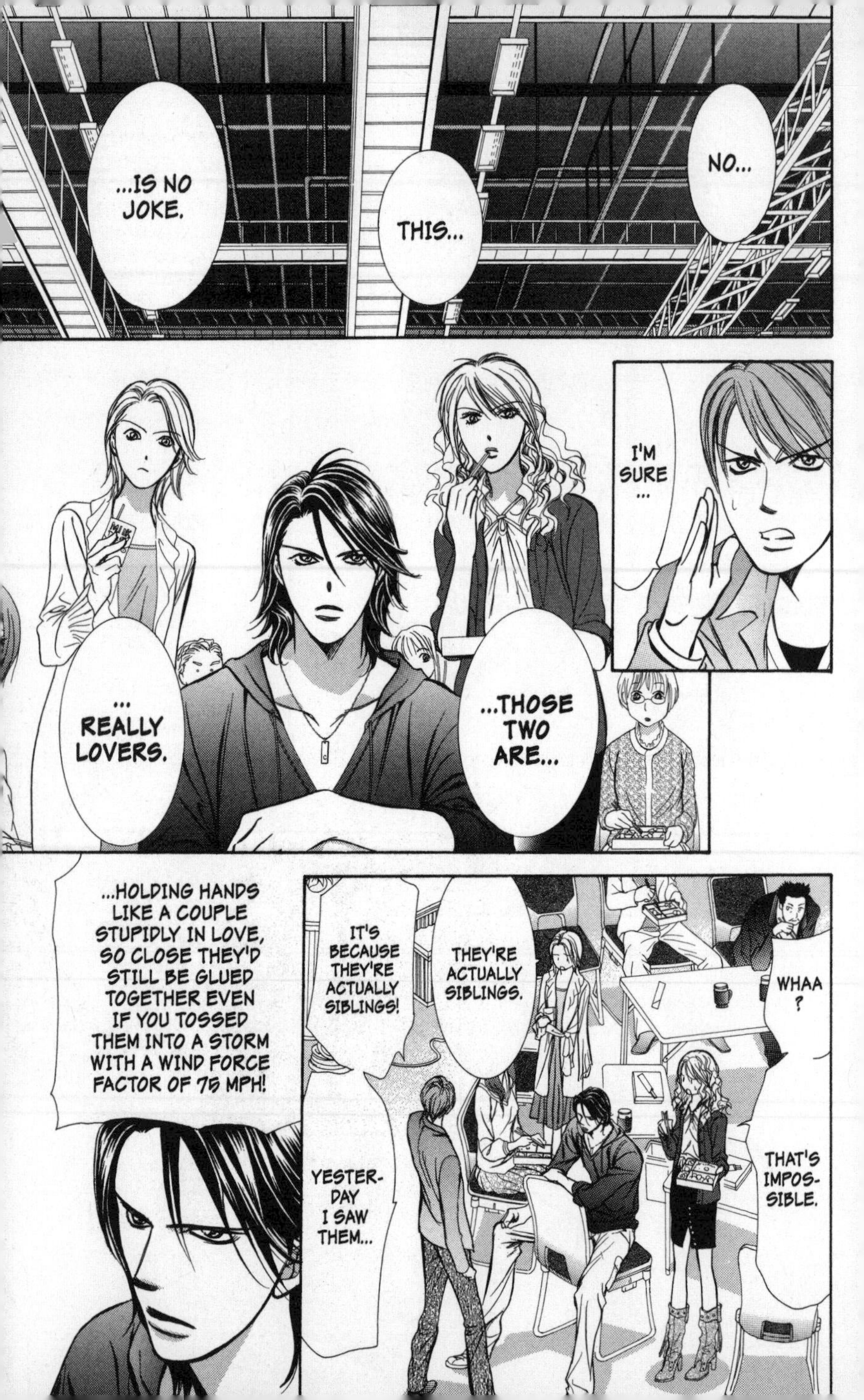

NO...
THIS...
...IS NO JOKE.
I'M SURE ...
...THOSE TWO ARE...
... REALLY LOVERS.
WHAA ?
THEY'RE ACTUALLY SIBLINGS.
IT'S BECAUSE THEY'RE ACTUALLY SIBLINGS!
THAT'S IMPOS-SIBLE.
YESTER-DAY I SAW THEM...
...HOLDING HANDS LIKE A COUPLE STUPIDLY IN LOVE, SO CLOSE THEY'D STILL BE GLUED TOGETHER EVEN IF YOU TOSSED THEM INTO A STORM WITH A WIND FORCE FACTOR OF 75 MPH!

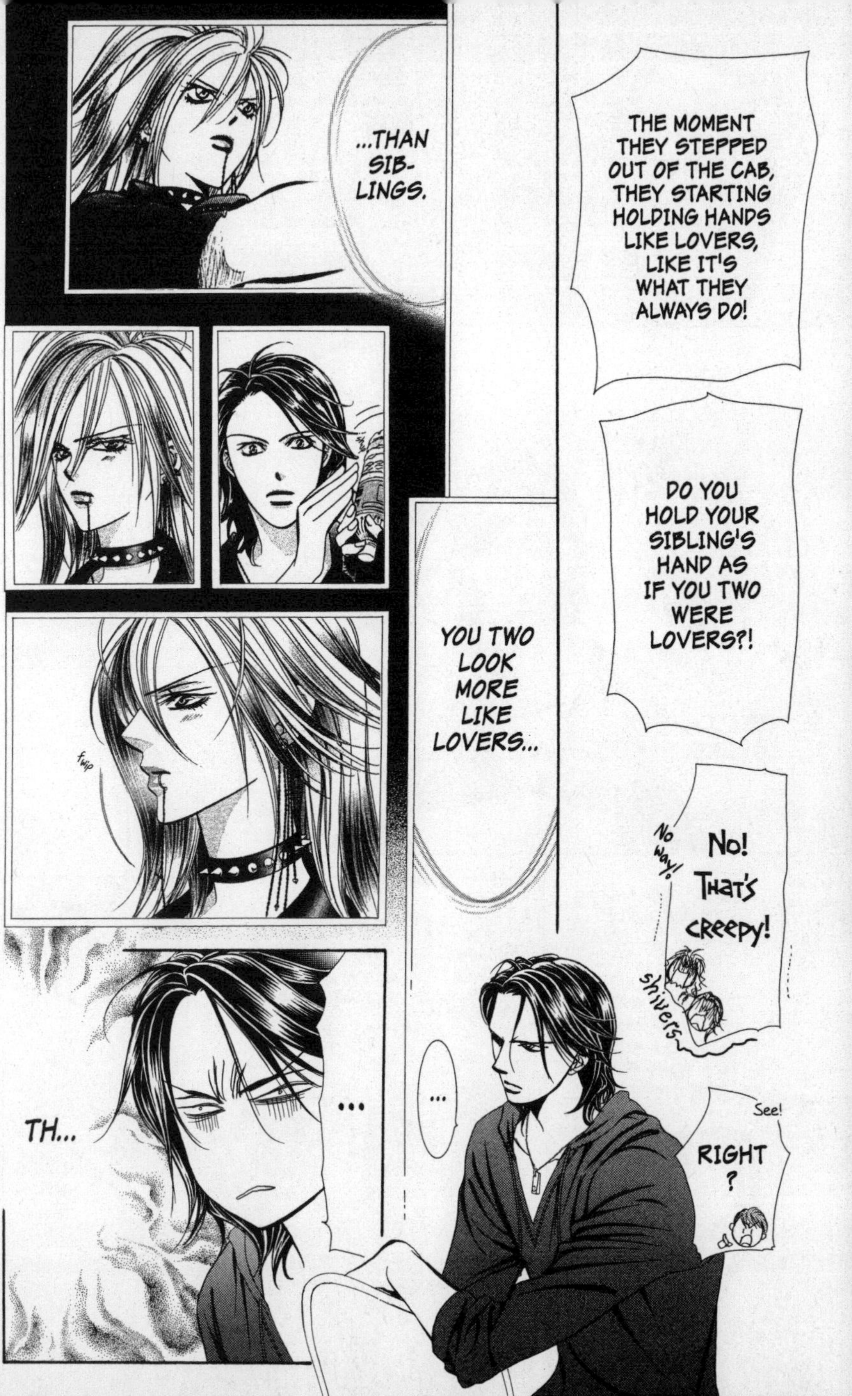
THE MOMENT THEY STEPPED OUT OF THE CAB, THEY STARTING HOLDING HANDS LIKE LOVERS, LIKE IT'S WHAT THEY ALWAYS DO!
...THAN SIB-LINGS.
DO YOU HOLD YOUR SIBLING'S HAND AS IF YOU TWO WERE LOVERS?!
YOU TWO LOOK MORE LIKE LOVERS...
fwip
No way!
No! That's creepy!
shivers
See!
RIGHT?
...
...
TH...

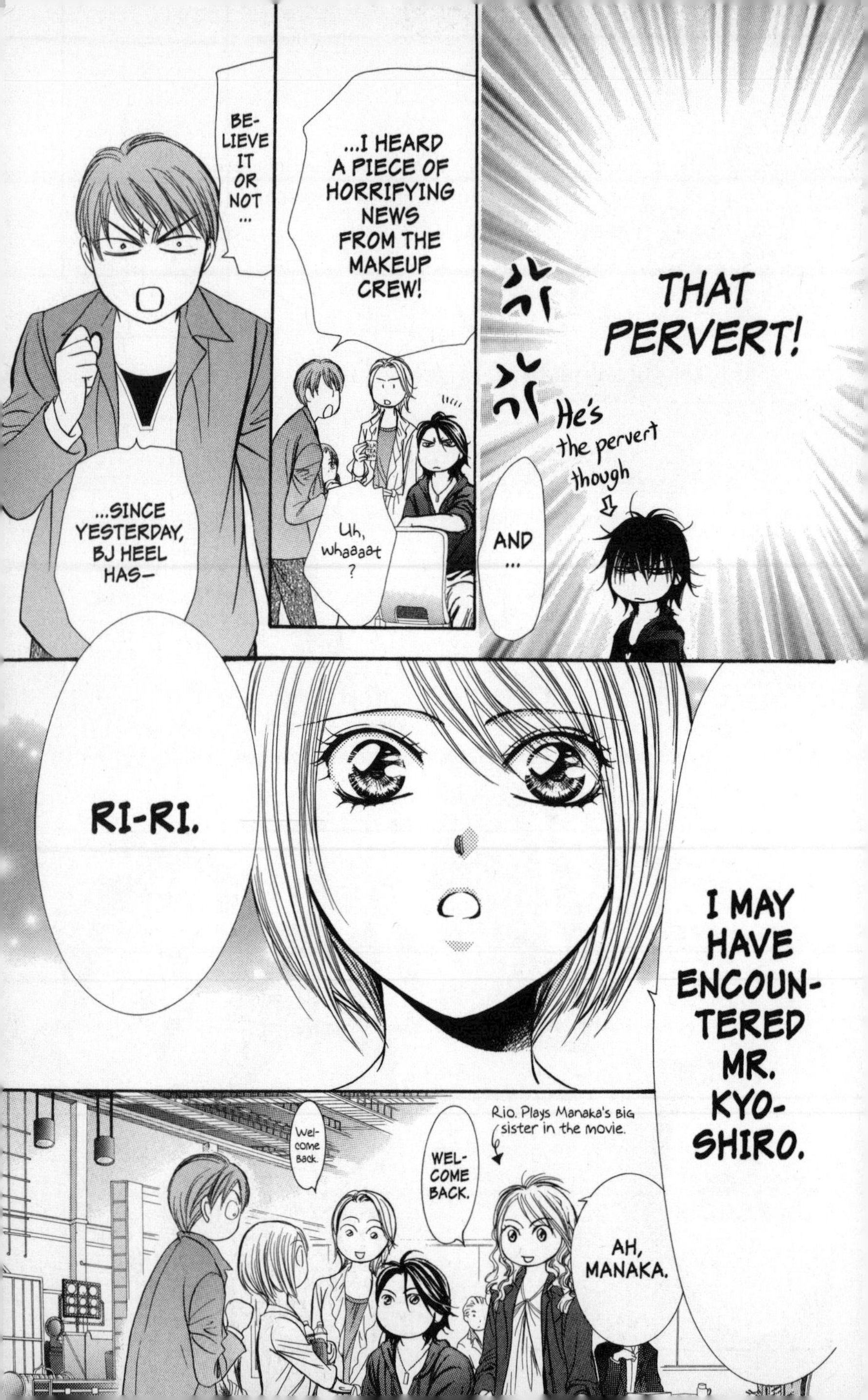
THAT PERVERT!
He's the pervert though
AND ...
...I HEARD A PIECE OF HORRIFYING NEWS FROM THE MAKEUP CREW!
Uh, whaaaat?
BE-LIEVE IT OR NOT ...
...SINCE YESTERDAY, BJ HEEL HAS—
I MAY HAVE ENCOUN-TERED MR. KYO-SHIRO.
RI-RI.
AH, MANAKA.
Rio. Plays Manaka's BIG sister in the movie.
WEL-COME BACK.
Wel-come back.

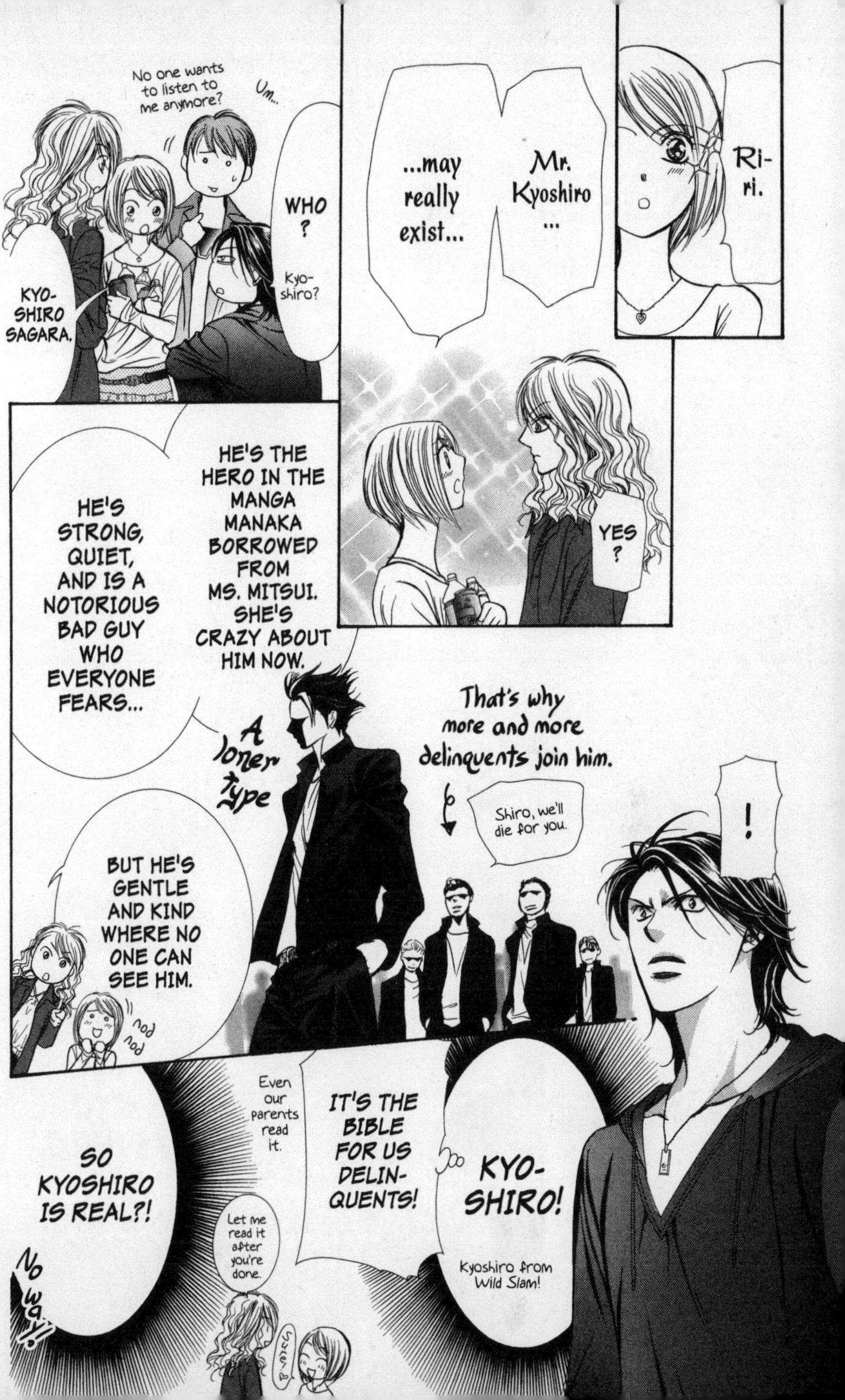
Ri-ri.
Mr. Kyoshiro ...
...may really exist...
YES?
Um...
WHO?
Kyo-shiro?
No one wants to listen to me anymore?
KYO-SHIRO SAGARA.
HE'S THE HERO IN THE MANGA MANAKA BORROWED FROM MS. MITSUI. SHE'S CRAZY ABOUT HIM NOW.
HE'S STRONG, QUIET, AND IS A NOTORIOUS BAD GUY WHO EVERYONE FEARS...
A loner type
That's why more and more delinquents join him.
Shiro, we'll die for you.
!
BUT HE'S GENTLE AND KIND WHERE NO ONE CAN SEE HIM.
nod nod
KYO-SHIRO!
Kyoshiro from Wild Slam!
IT'S THE BIBLE FOR US DELIN-QUENTS!
Even our parents read it.
Let me read it after you're done.
SO KYOSHIRO IS REAL?!
No way!!

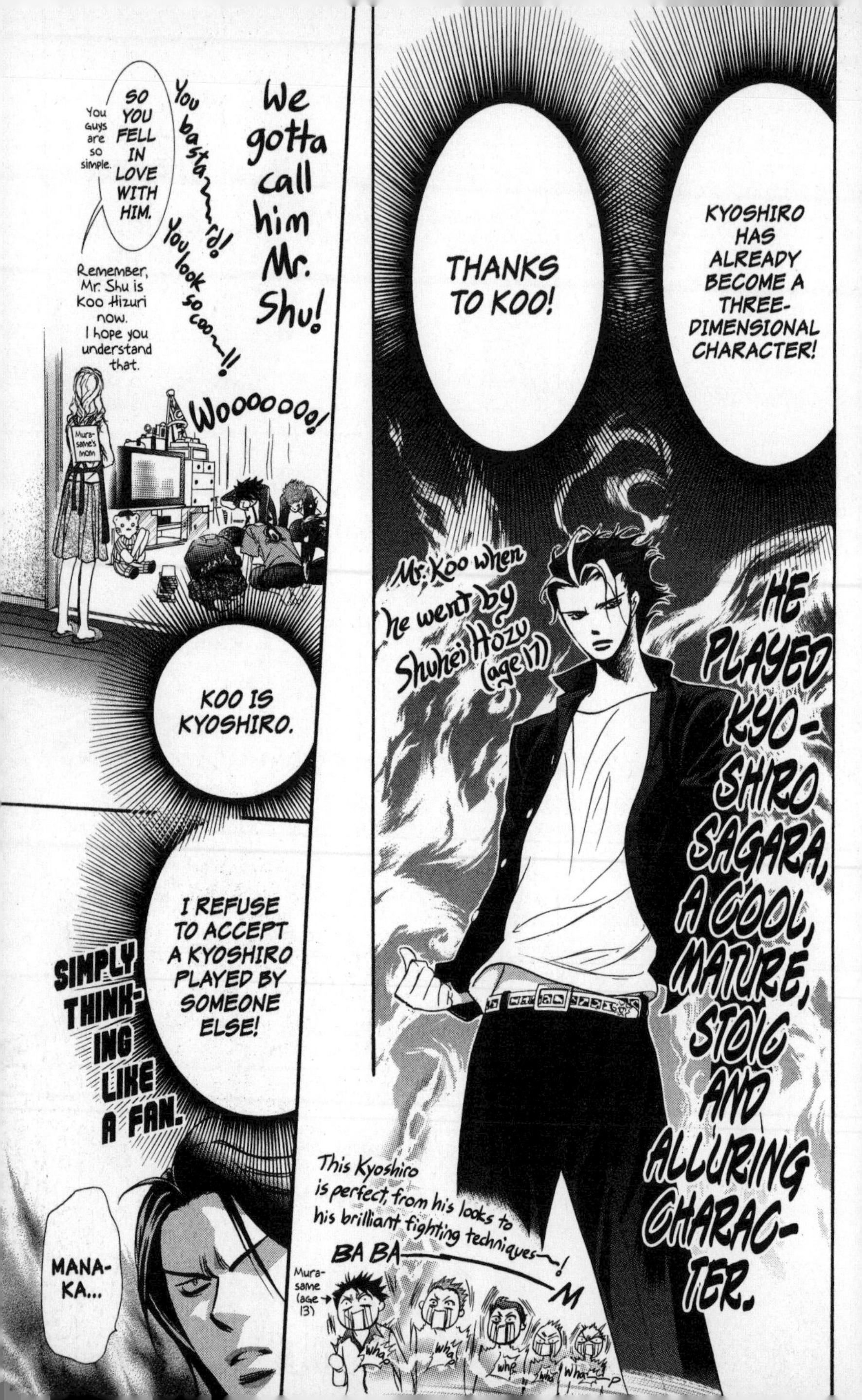
KYOSHIRO HAS ALREADY BECOME A THREE-DIMENSIONAL CHARACTER!
THANKS TO KOO!
HE PLAYED KYO-SHIRO SAGARA, A COOL, MATURE, STOIC AND ALLURING CHARAC-TER.
Mr. Koo when he went by Shuhei Hozu (age 17)
This Kyoshiro is perfect, from his looks to his brilliant fighting techniques~!
BA BA——M
Mura-same (age 13)
Wha
Wha
Wha
Wha
Wha
We gotta call him Mr. Shu!
You basta~~rd! You look so coo~!!
SO YOU FELL IN LOVE WITH HIM.
You guys are so simple.
Remember, Mr. Shu is Koo Hizuri now. I hope you understand that.
Wooooooo!
Mura-same's mom
KOO IS KYOSHIRO.
I REFUSE TO ACCEPT A KYOSHIRO PLAYED BY SOMEONE ELSE!
SIMPLY THINKING LIKE A FAN.
MANAKA...

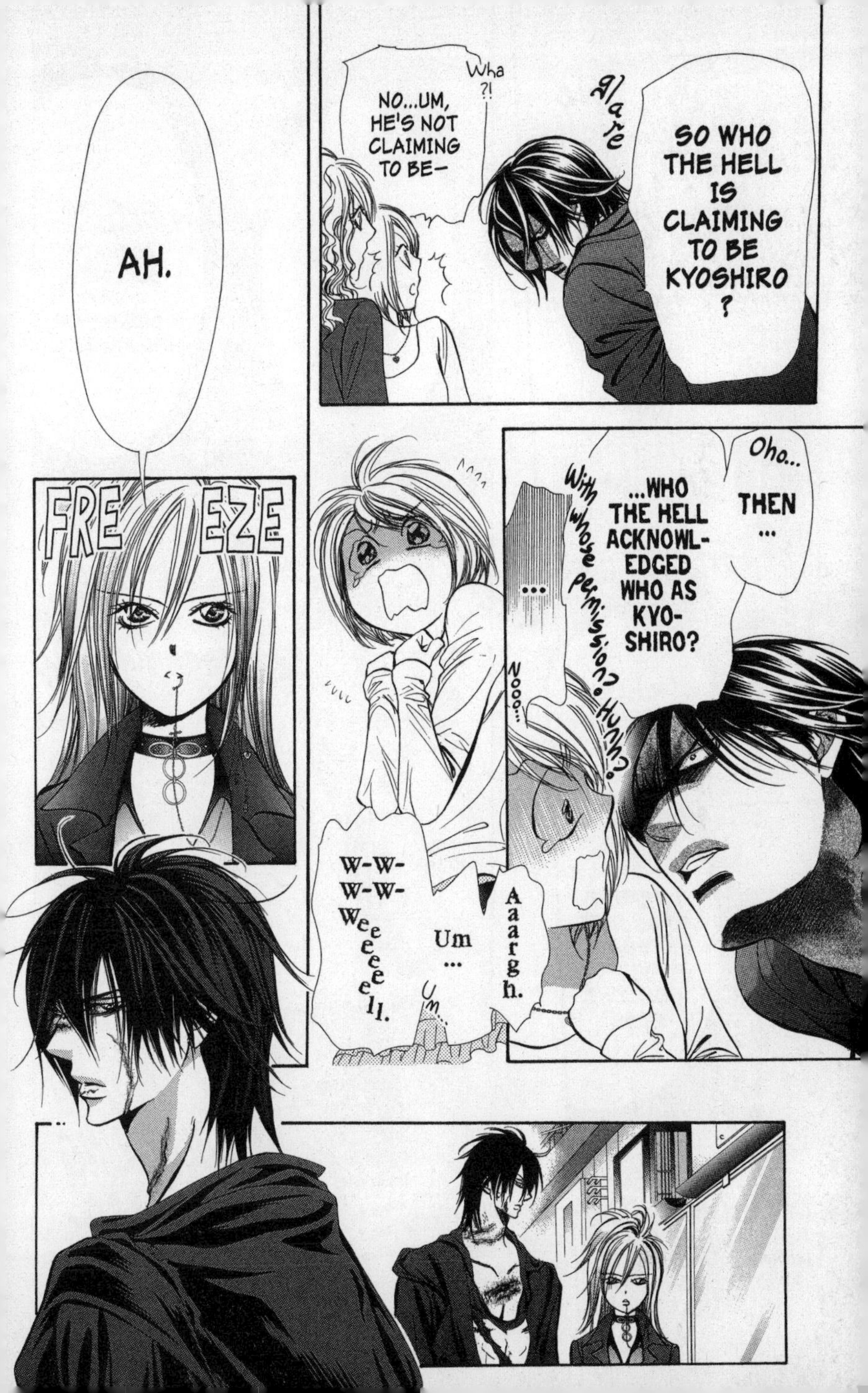
glare
SO WHO THE HELL IS CLAIMING TO BE KYOSHIRO?
Wha ?!
NO...UM, HE'S NOT CLAIMING TO BE—
Oho...
THEN ...
...WHO THE HELL ACKNOWL-EDGED WHO AS KYO-SHIRO?
With whose permission? Huh?
...
Nooo...
Aaargh.
Um ...
Um...
W-W-W-W-Weeeeeell.
AH.
FRE EZE
...

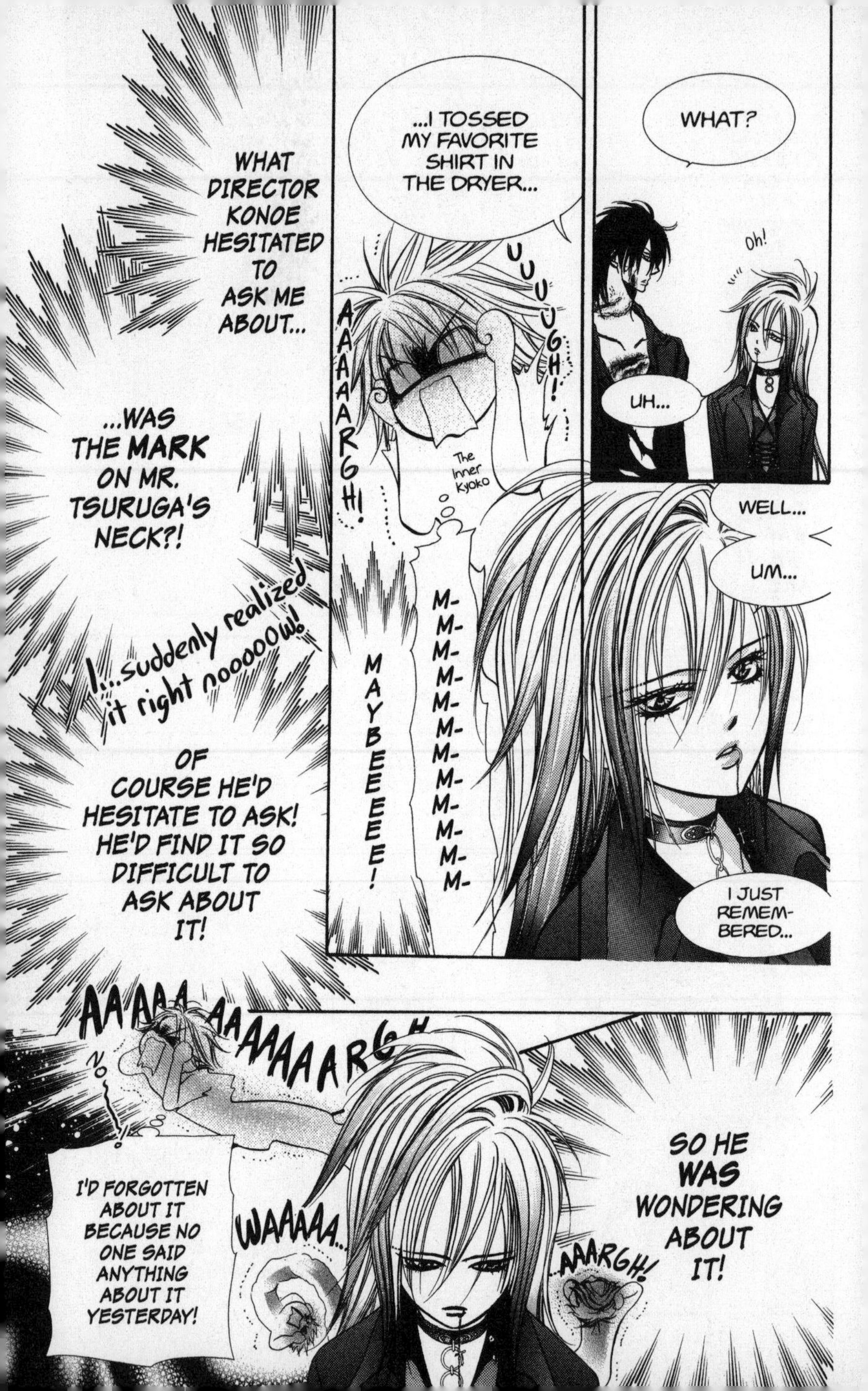

WHAT?
Oh!
UH...
WELL...
UM...
I JUST REMEMBERED...
...I TOSSED MY FAVORITE SHIRT IN THE DRYER...
UUUUUGH!
AAAAAARGH!
The Inner Kyoko
M-MMMM-MMMMMMMMM-M-M-MM-M-M-M-M-M-M-
MAYBEEEEEE!
WHAT DIRECTOR KONOE HESITATED TO ASK ME ABOUT...
...WAS THE MARK ON MR. TSURUGA'S NECK?!
I...suddenly realized it right noooooow!
OF COURSE HE'D HESITATE TO ASK! HE'D FIND IT SO DIFFICULT TO ASK ABOUT IT!
SO HE WAS WONDERING ABOUT IT!
AAARGH!
AAAAA AAAAAAAARGH
NO---!!
WAAAAA...
I'D FORGOTTEN ABOUT IT BECAUSE NO ONE SAID ANYTHING ABOUT IT YESTERDAY!

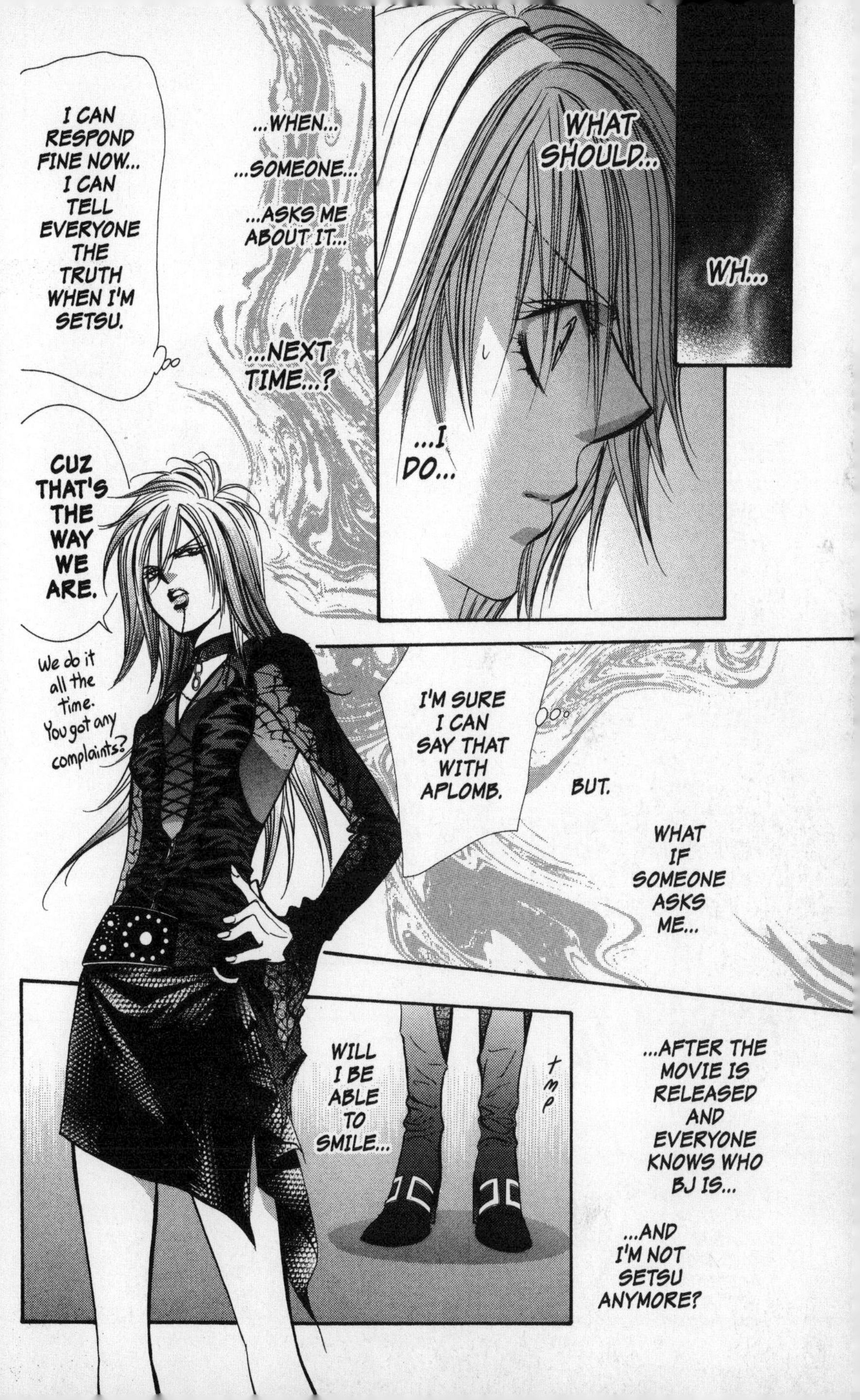
WH...
WHAT SHOULD...
...I DO...
...WHEN...
...SOMEONE...
...ASKS ME ABOUT IT...
...NEXT TIME...?
I CAN RESPOND FINE NOW... I CAN TELL EVERYONE THE TRUTH WHEN I'M SETSU.
CUZ THAT'S THE WAY WE ARE.
We do it all the time. You got any complaints?
I'M SURE I CAN SAY THAT WITH APLOMB.
BUT.
WHAT IF SOMEONE ASKS ME...
...AFTER THE MOVIE IS RELEASED AND EVERYONE KNOWS WHO BJ IS...
...AND I'M NOT SETSU ANYMORE?
TMP
WILL I BE ABLE TO SMILE...

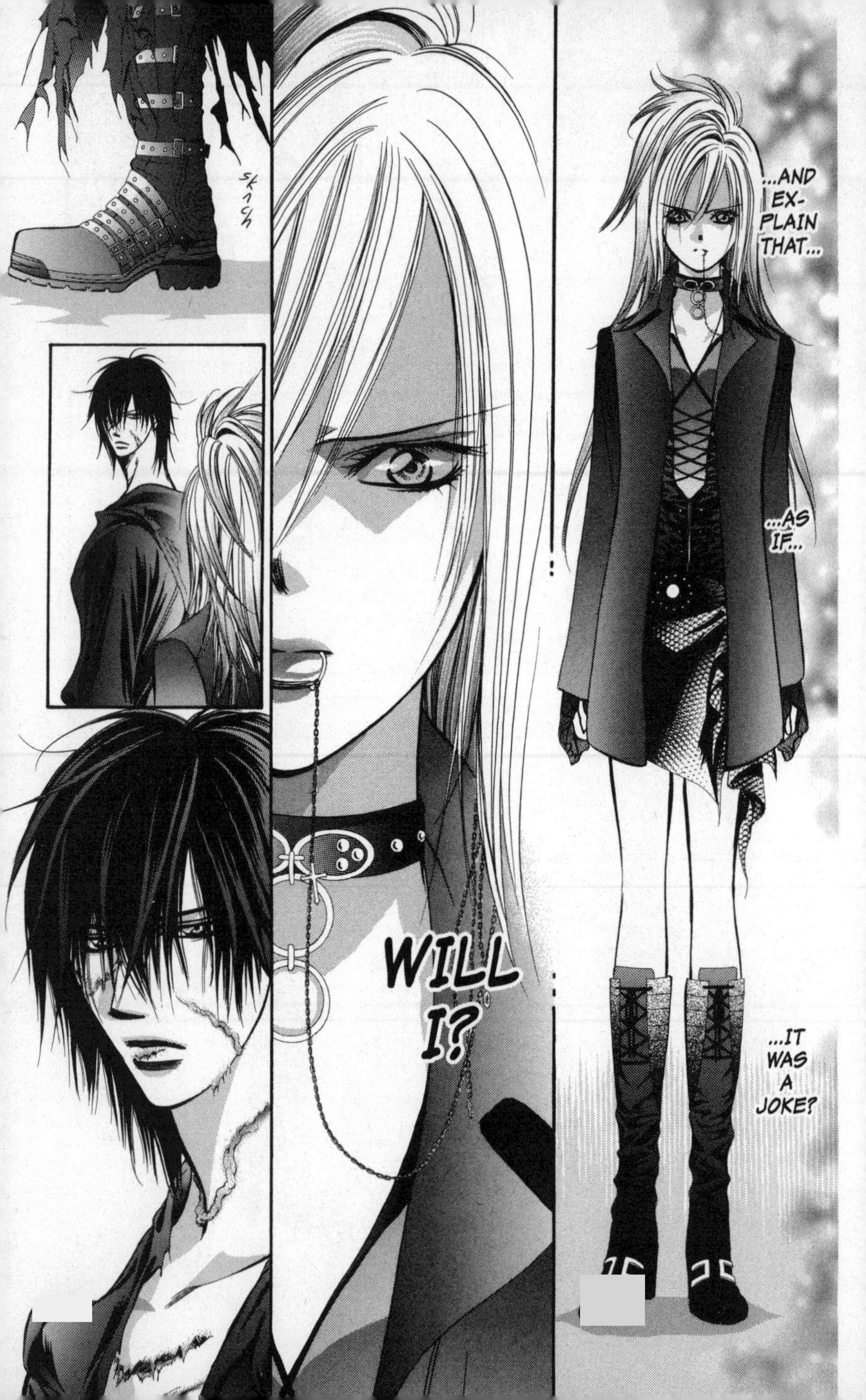
...AND EX-PLAIN THAT...
...AS IF...
...IT WAS A JOKE?
WILL I?
skrch

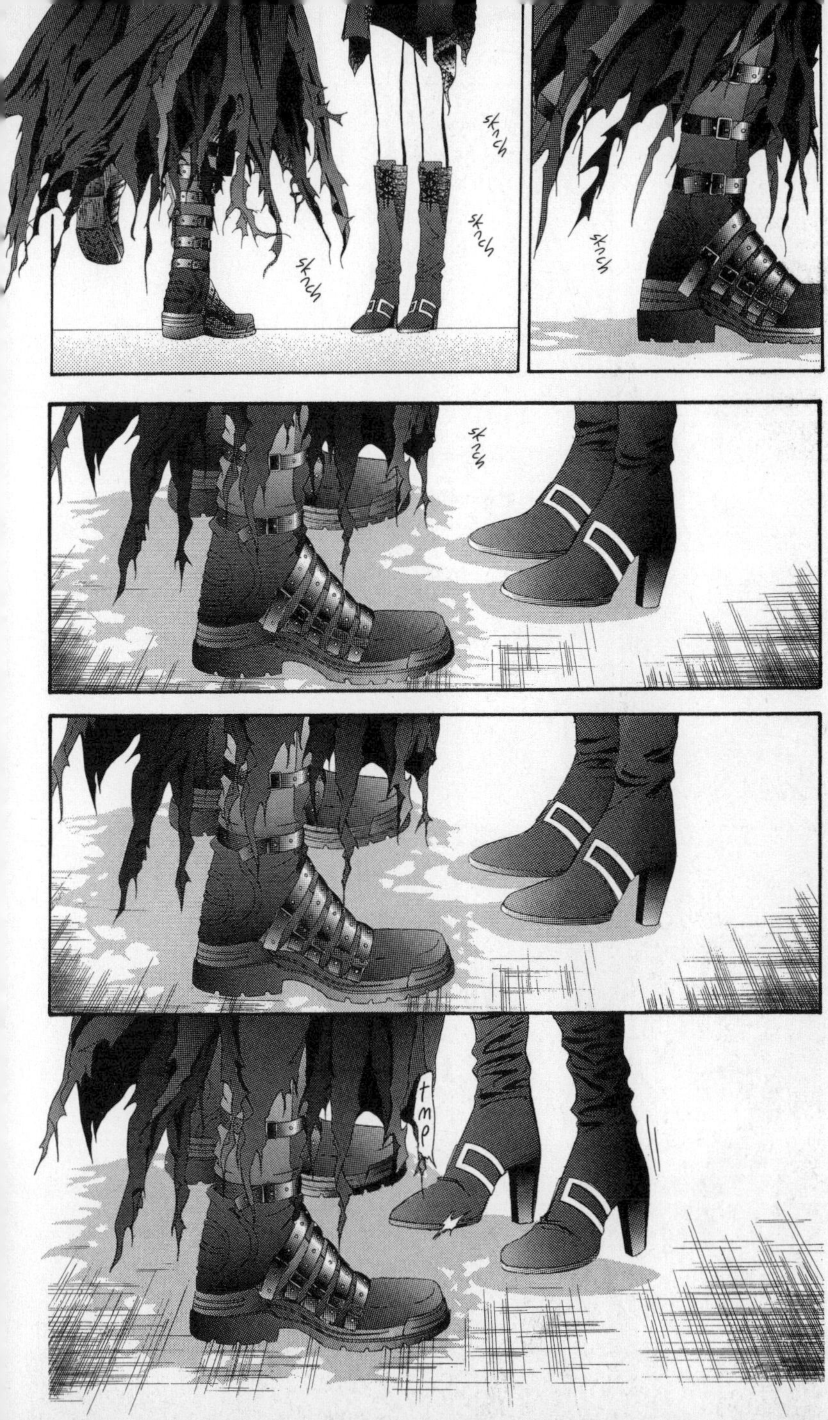
sknch
sknch
sknch
sknch
sknch
tmp

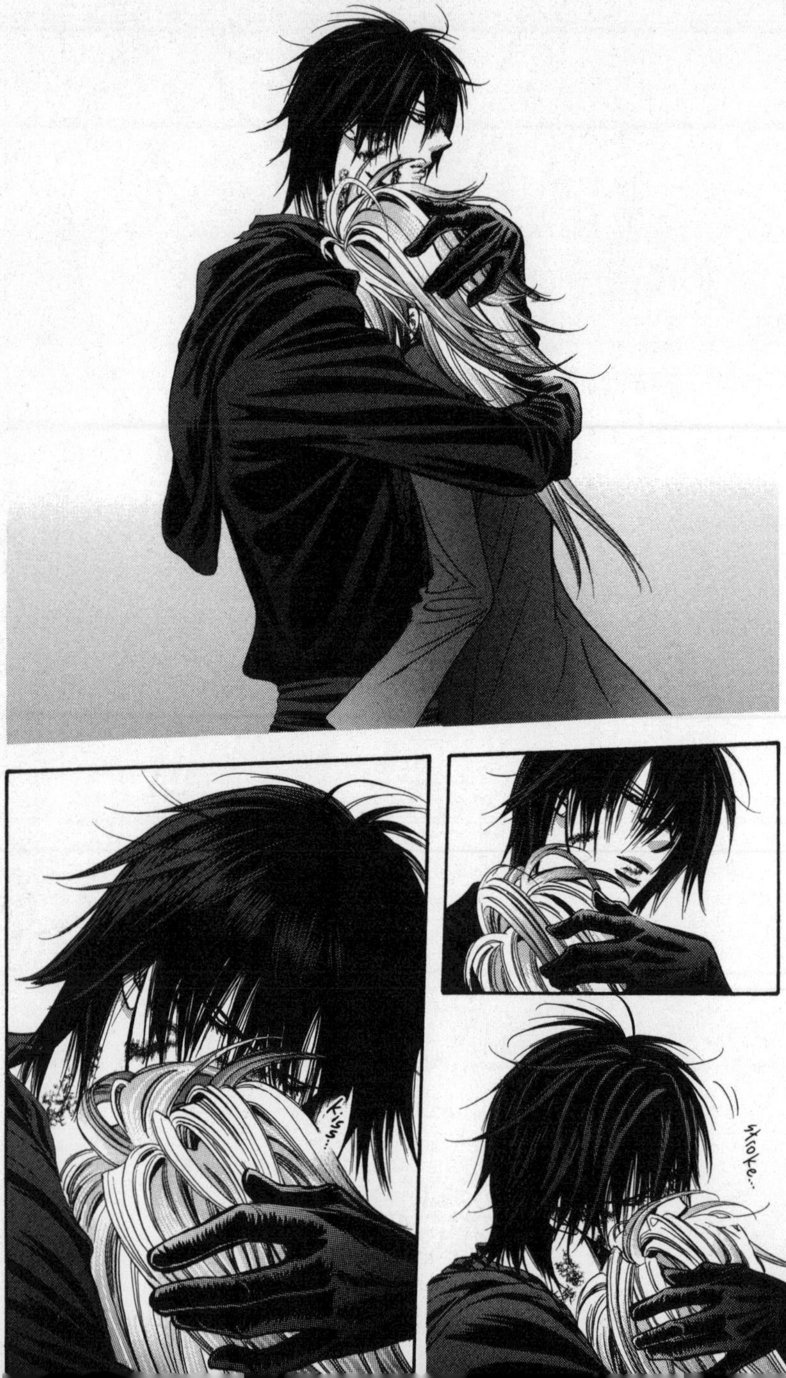
stroke...
kiss...

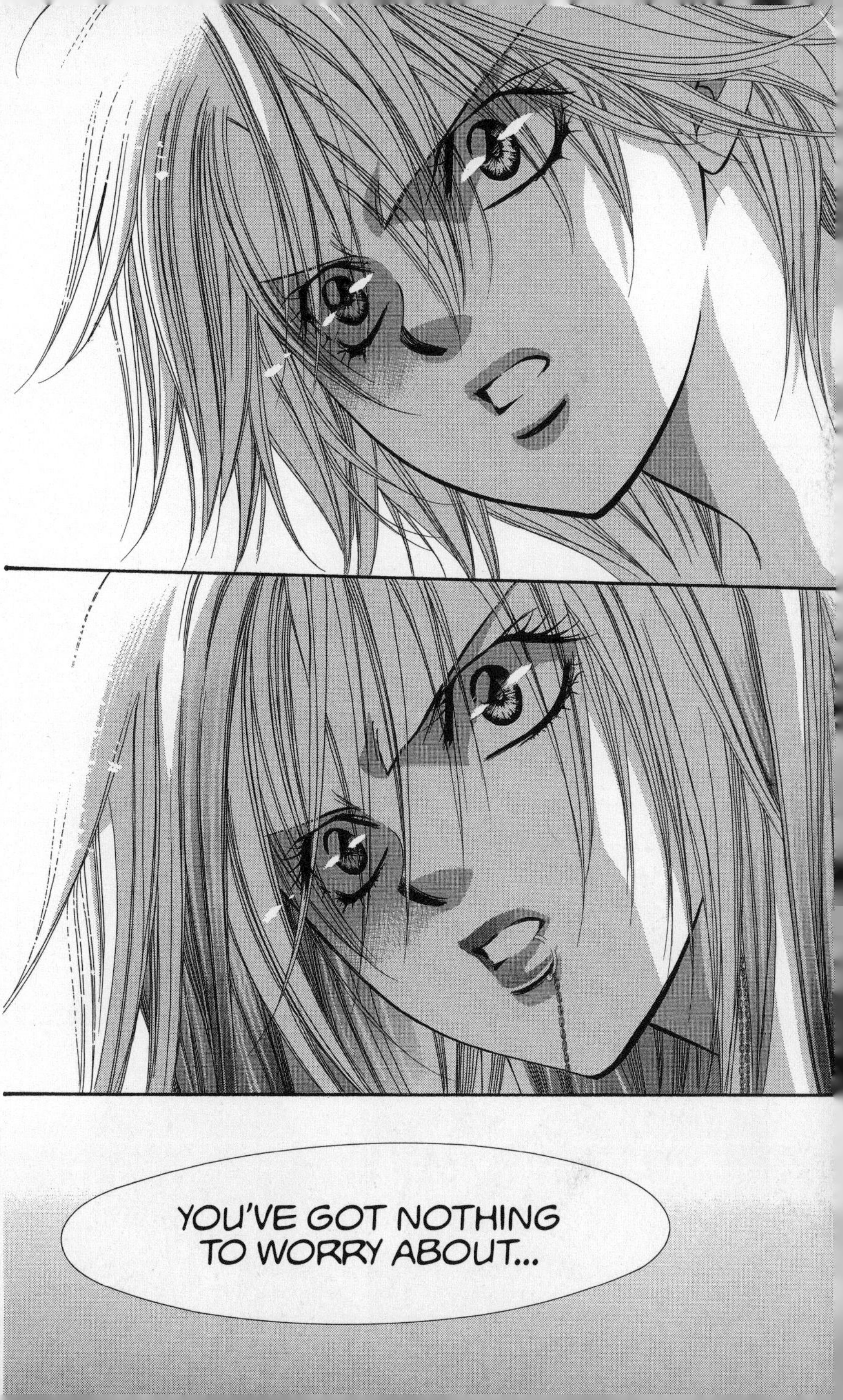
YOU'VE GOT NOTHING TO WORRY ABOUT...

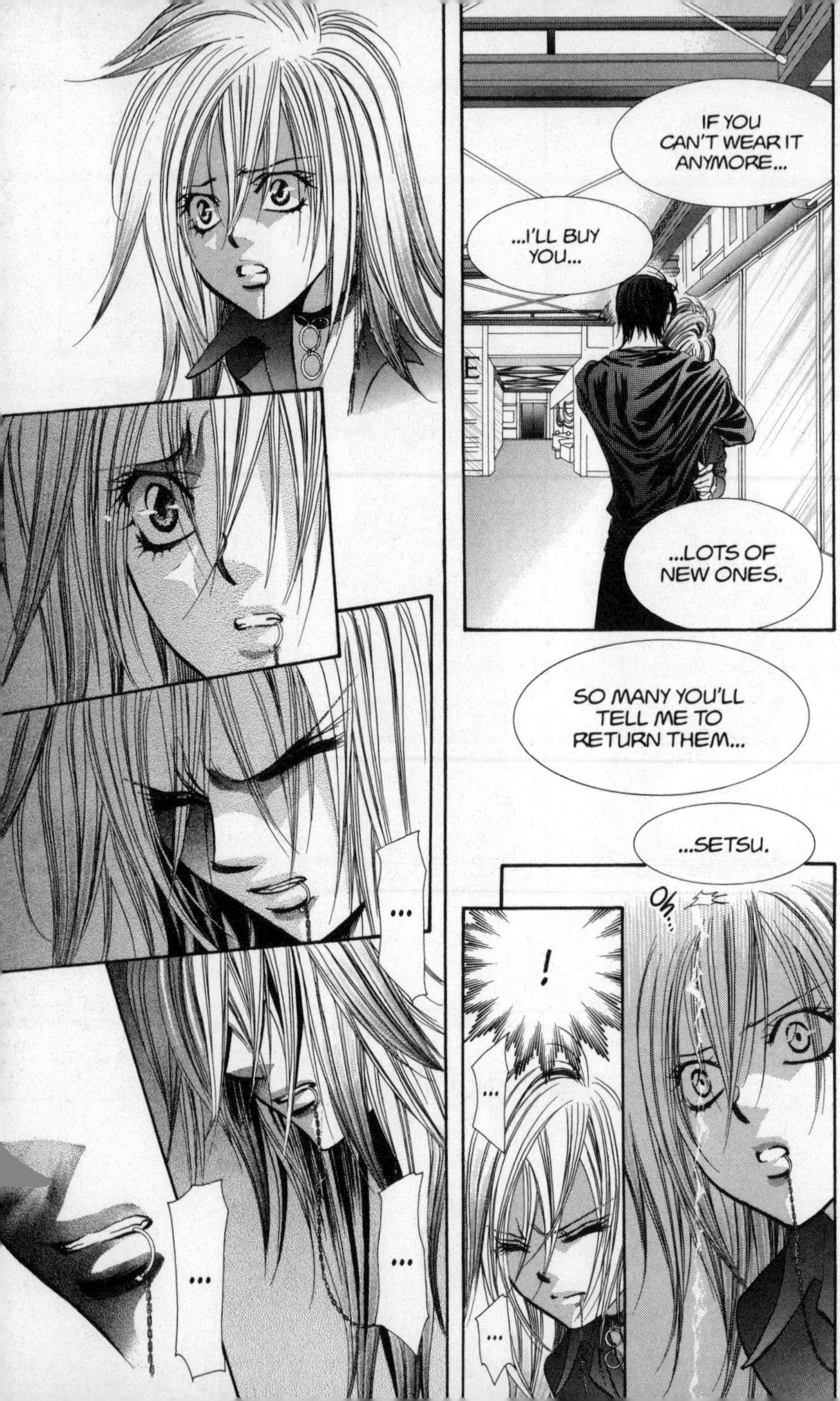
IF YOU CAN'T WEAR IT ANYMORE...
...I'LL BUY YOU...
...LOTS OF NEW ONES.
SO MANY YOU'LL TELL ME TO RETURN THEM...
...SETSU.
Oh...
!
...
...
...
...
...

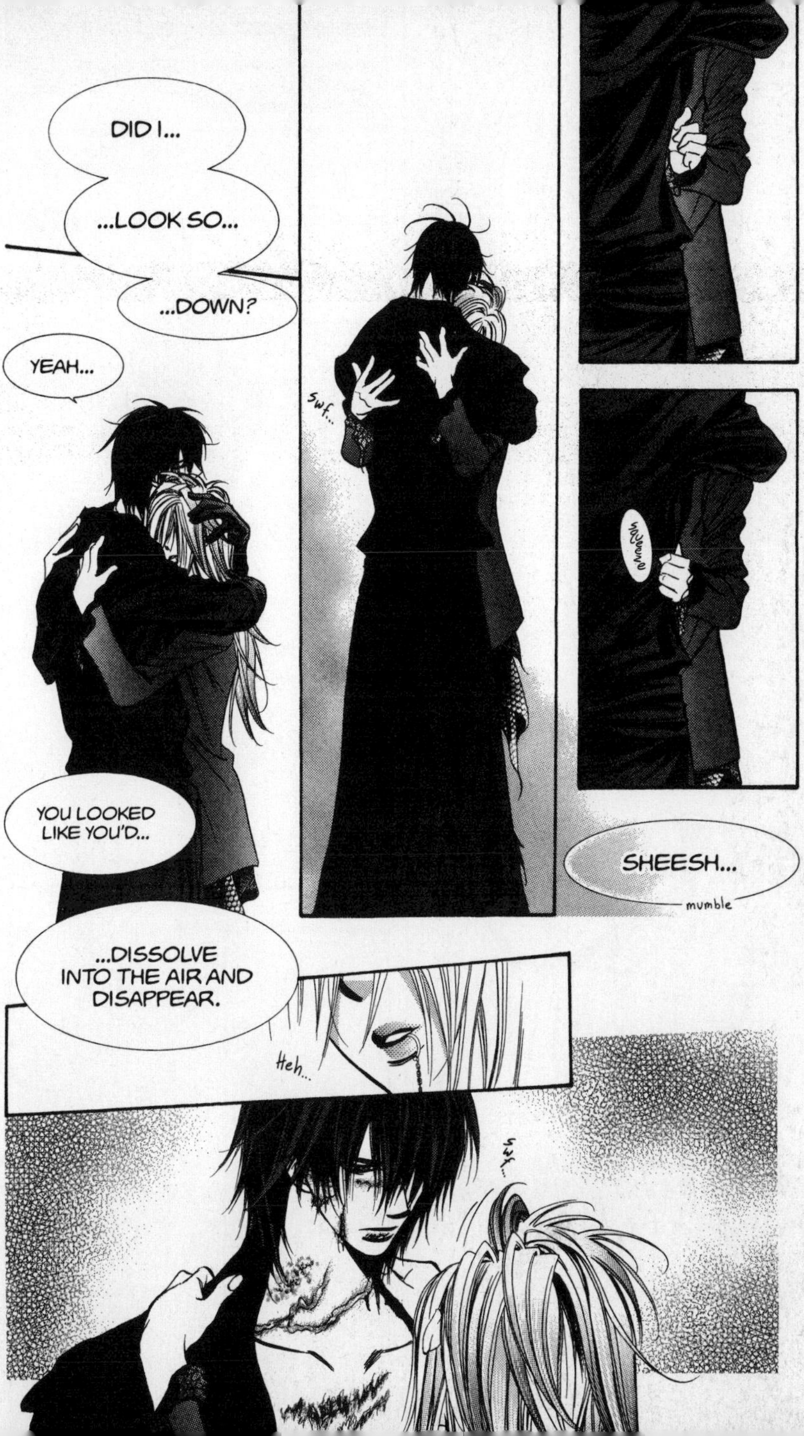
squeeze
SHEESH...
mumble
swf...
DID I...
...LOOK SO...
...DOWN?
YEAH...
YOU LOOKED LIKE YOU'D...
...DISSOLVE INTO THE AIR AND DISAPPEAR.
Heh...
swf...

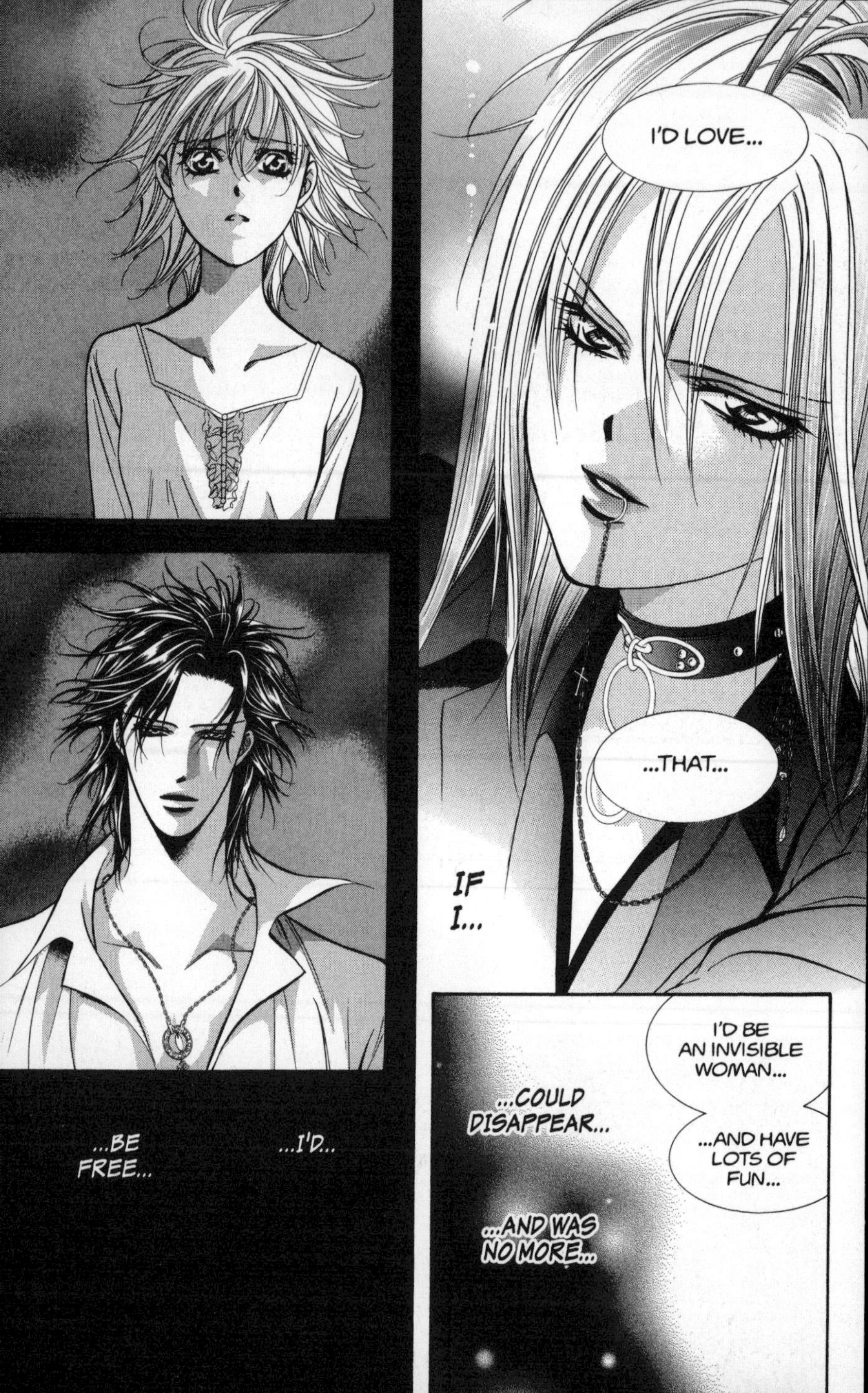
I'D LOVE...
...THAT...
IF I...
I'D BE AN INVISIBLE WOMAN...
...AND HAVE LOTS OF FUN...
...COULD DISAPPEAR...
...AND WAS NO MORE...
...I'D...
...BE FREE...

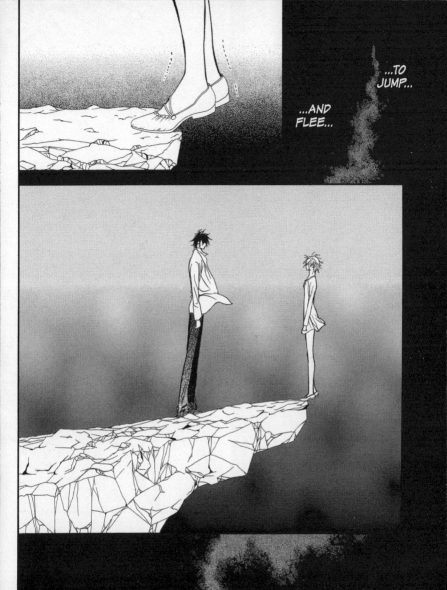

...TO
JUMP...

...AND
FLEE...

...FROM THIS REALITY.

End of Act 198

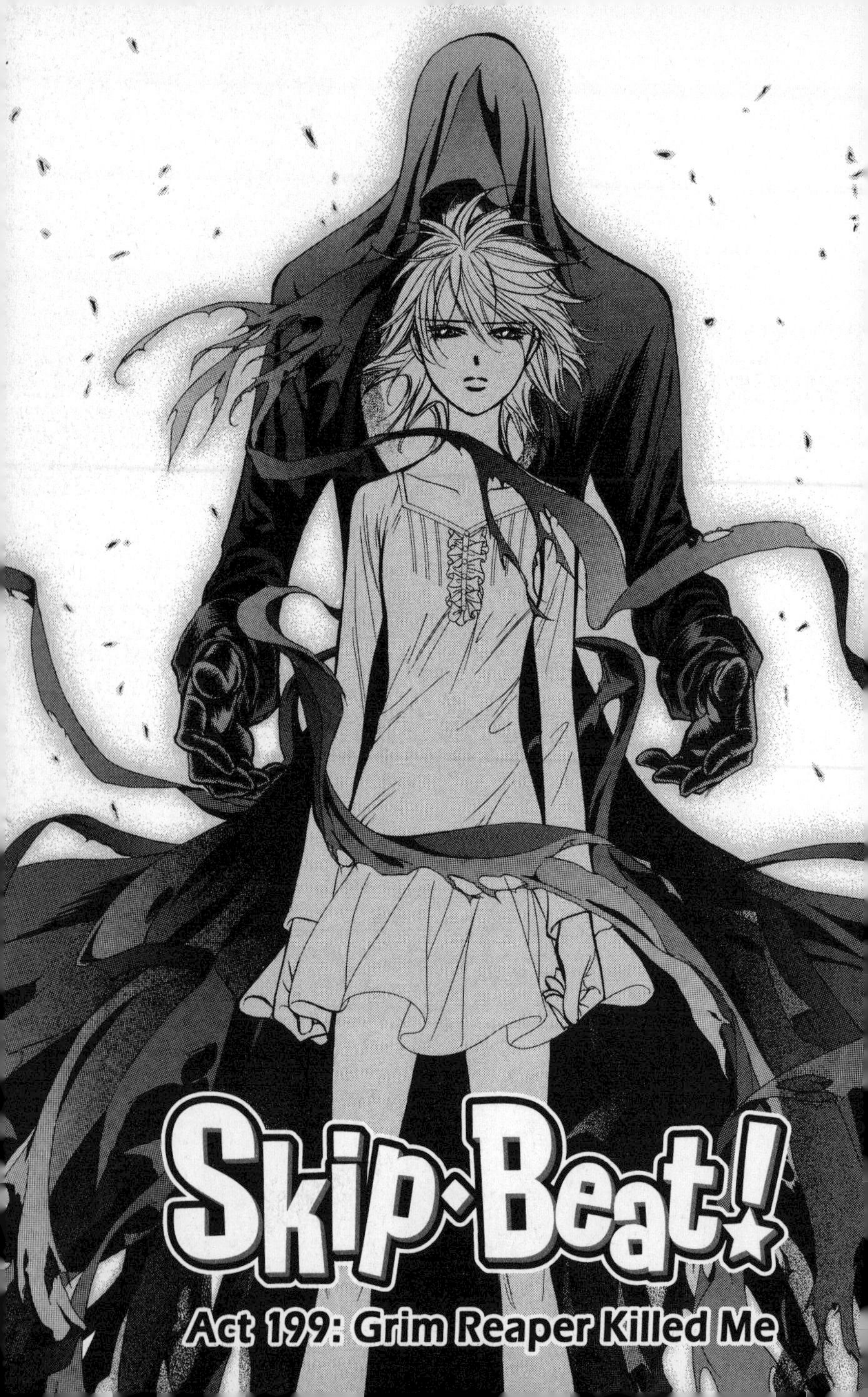
Skip·Beat!
Act 199: Grim Reaper Killed Me

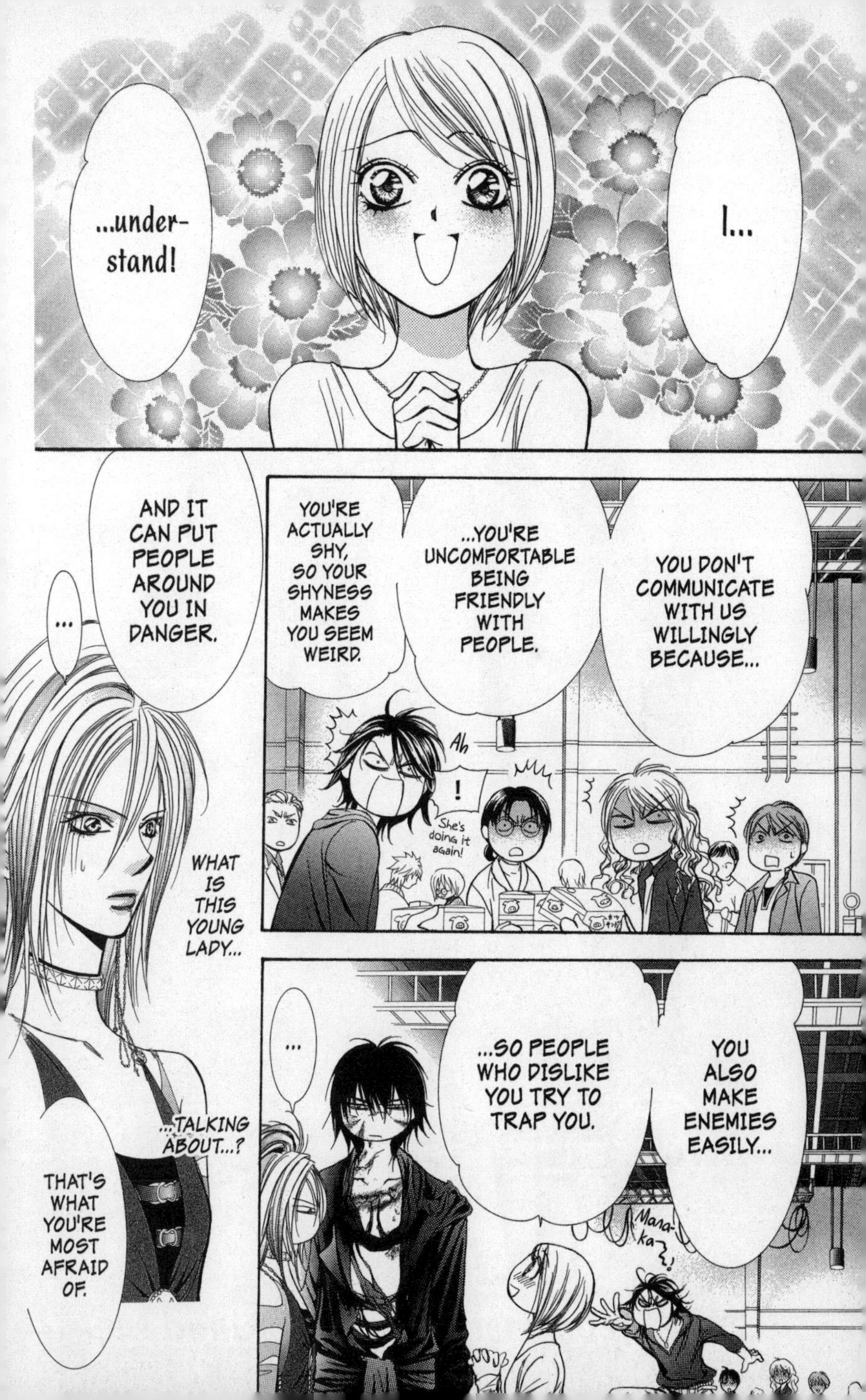
I...
...under-stand!
YOU DON'T COMMUNICATE WITH US WILLINGLY BECAUSE...
...YOU'RE UNCOMFORTABLE BEING FRIENDLY WITH PEOPLE.
YOU'RE ACTUALLY SHY, SO YOUR SHYNESS MAKES YOU SEEM WEIRD.
Ah
!
She's doing it again!
YOU ALSO MAKE ENEMIES EASILY...
...SO PEOPLE WHO DISLIKE YOU TRY TO TRAP YOU.
...
Mana-ka~!
AND IT CAN PUT PEOPLE AROUND YOU IN DANGER.
...
WHAT IS THIS YOUNG LADY...
...TALKING ABOUT...?
THAT'S WHAT YOU'RE MOST AFRAID OF.

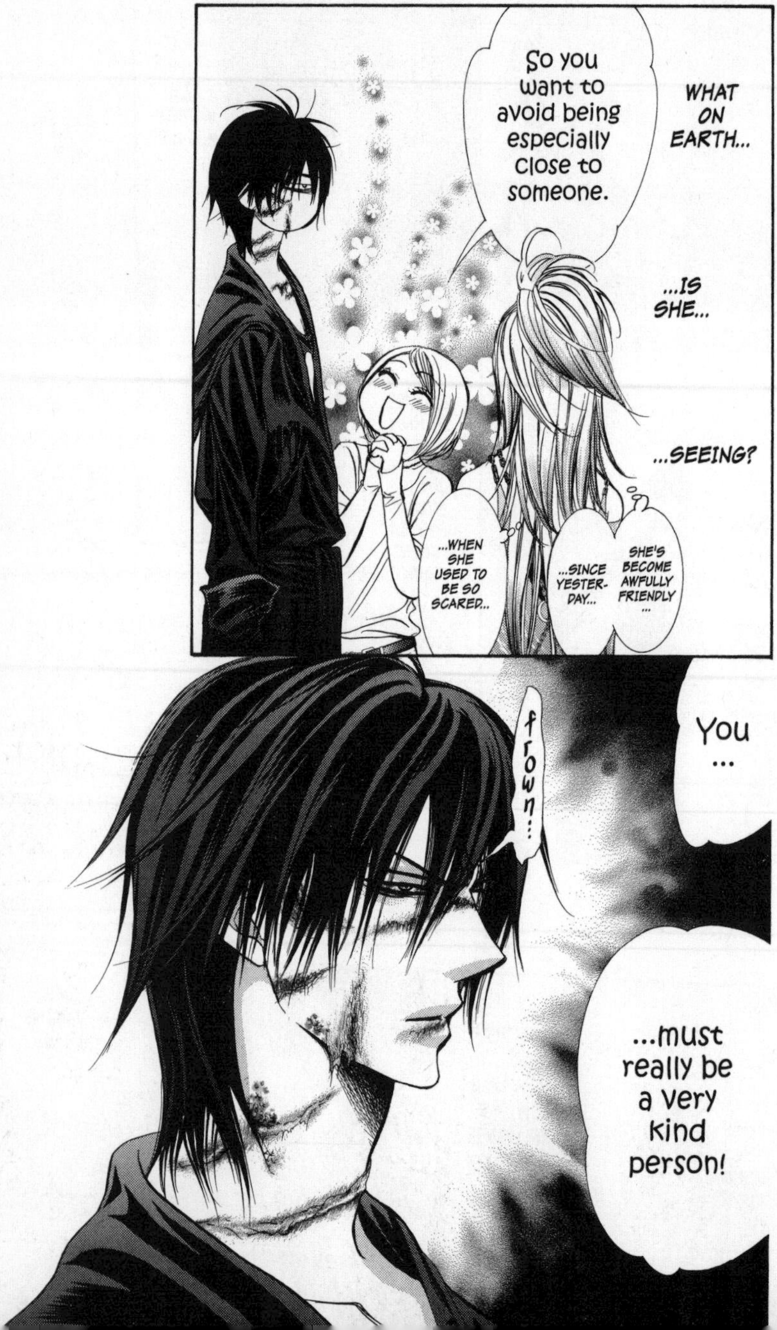

So you want to avoid being especially close to someone.
WHAT ON EARTH...
...IS SHE...
...SEEING?
SHE'S BECOME AWFULLY FRIENDLY...
...SINCE YESTER-DAY...
...WHEN SHE USED TO BE SO SCARED...
You...
frown...
...must really be a very kind person!

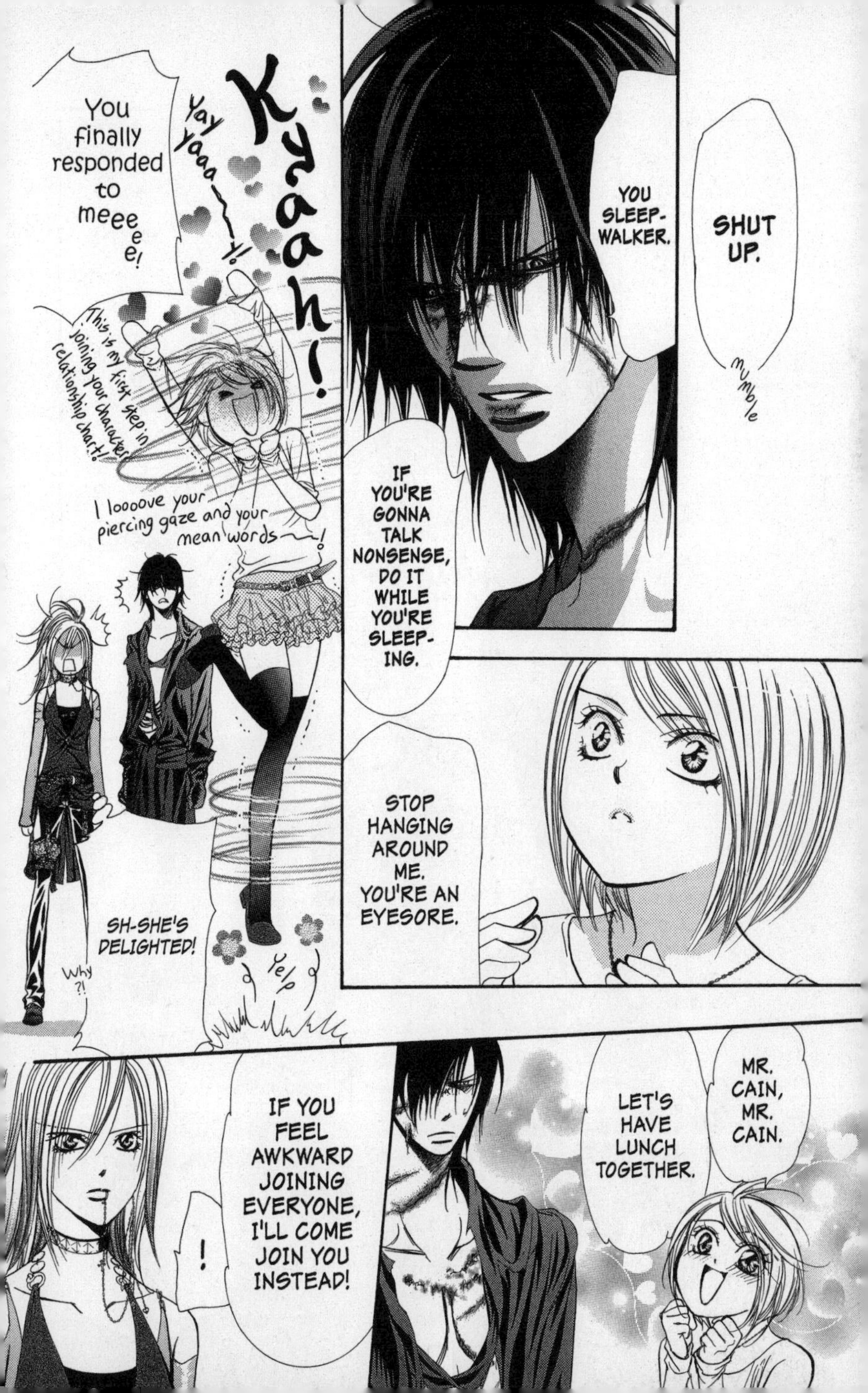
SHUT UP.
mumble
YOU SLEEP-WALKER.
IF YOU'RE GONNA TALK NONSENSE, DO IT WHILE YOU'RE SLEEP-ING.
STOP HANGING AROUND ME. YOU'RE AN EYESORE.
Kyaah!
Yay yaaa~y!
You finally responded to meeeee!
This is my first step in joining your character relationship chart!
I looooove your piercing gaze and your mean words~!
SH-SHE'S DELIGHTED!
Why?!
Yelp
MR. CAIN, MR. CAIN.
LET'S HAVE LUNCH TOGETHER.
IF YOU FEEL AWKWARD JOINING EVERYONE, I'LL COME JOIN YOU INSTEAD!
!

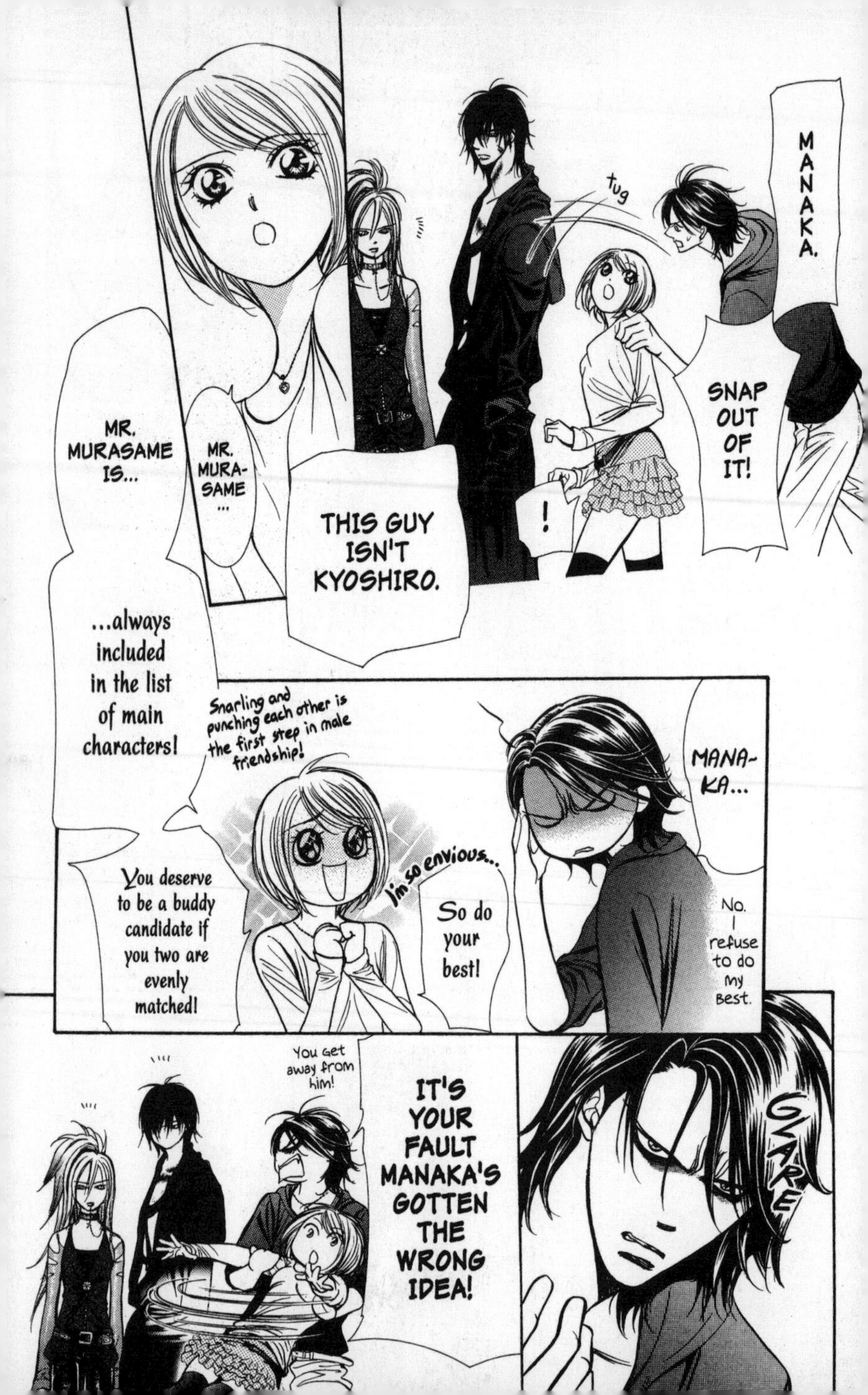
MANAKA.
tug
SNAP OUT OF IT!
!
THIS GUY ISN'T KYOSHIRO.
MR. MURA-SAME...
MR. MURASAME IS...
...always included in the list of main characters!
MANA-KA...
No. I refuse to do my best.
Snarling and punching each other is the first step in male friendship!
You deserve to be a buddy candidate if you two are evenly matched!
I'm so envious...
So do your best!
GLARE
IT'S YOUR FAULT MANAKA'S GOTTEN THE WRONG IDEA!
You get away from him!

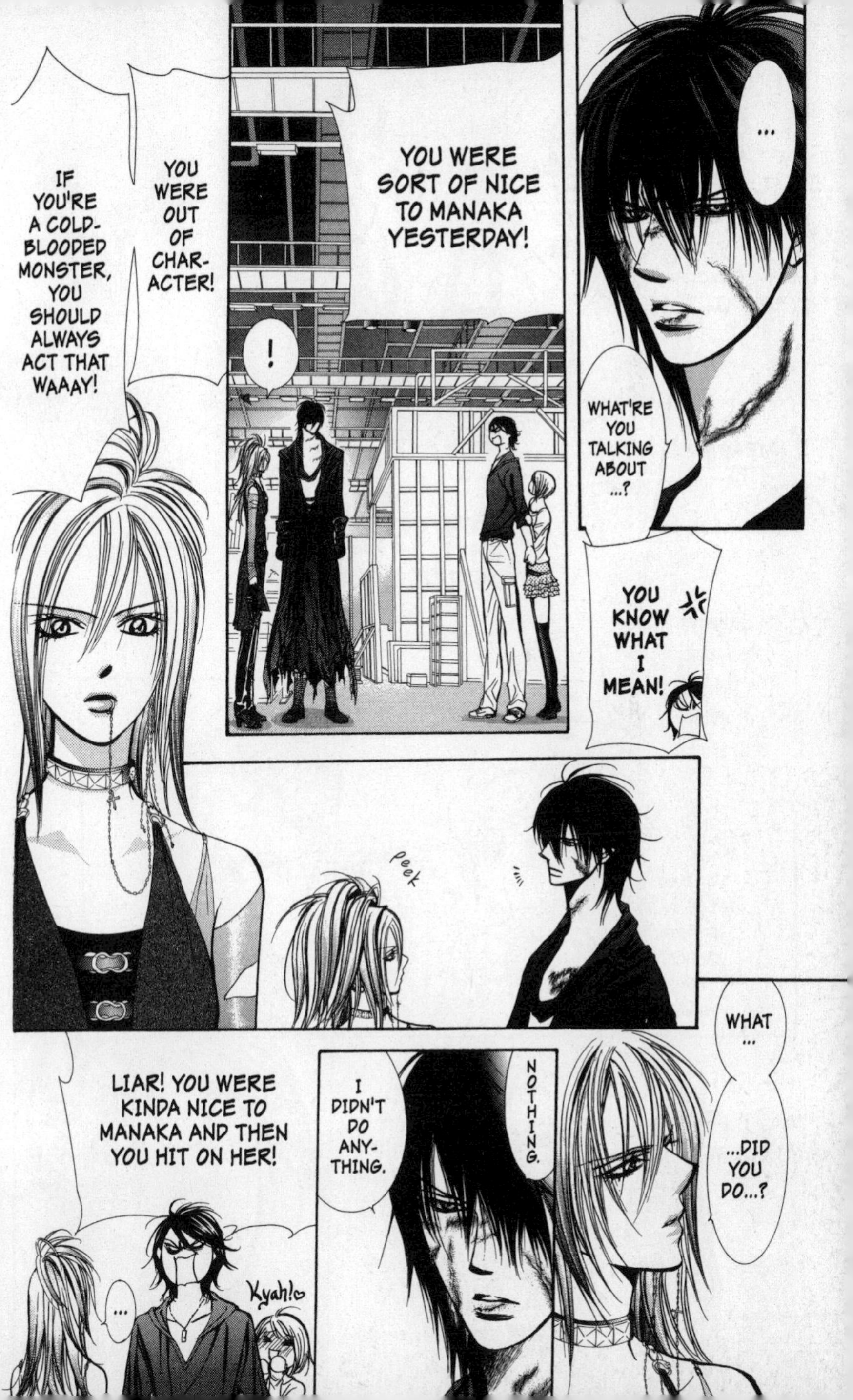
...
WHAT'RE YOU TALKING ABOUT ...?
YOU KNOW WHAT I MEAN!
YOU WERE SORT OF NICE TO MANAKA YESTERDAY!
!
YOU WERE OUT OF CHARACTER!
IF YOU'RE A COLD-BLOODED MONSTER, YOU SHOULD ALWAYS ACT THAT WAAAY!
Peek
WHAT ... ...DID YOU DO...?
NOTHING.
I DIDN'T DO ANYTHING.
LIAR! YOU WERE KINDA NICE TO MANAKA AND THEN YOU HIT ON HER!
...
Kyah!♡

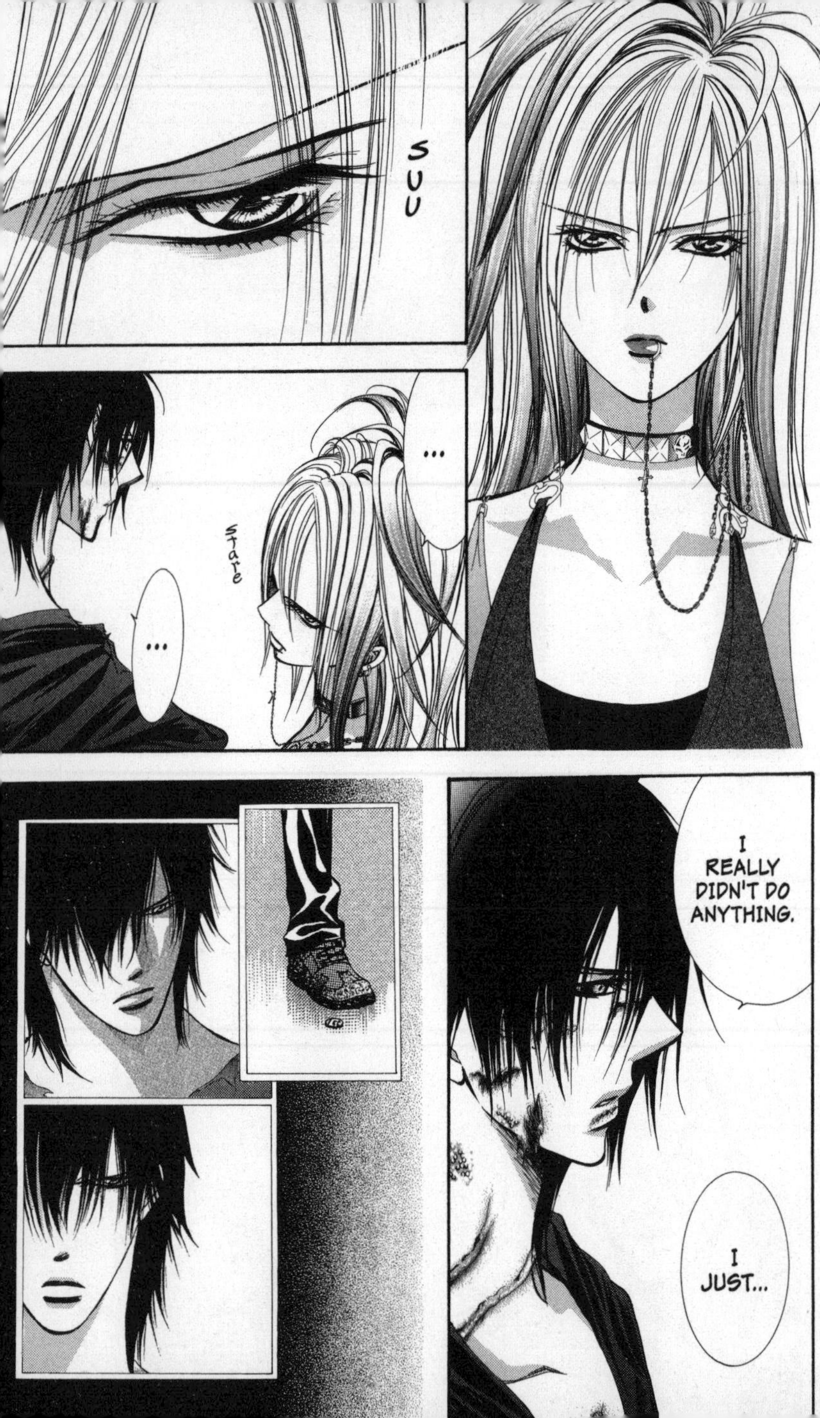
SUU
...
stare
...
I REALLY DIDN'T DO ANYTHING.
I JUST...

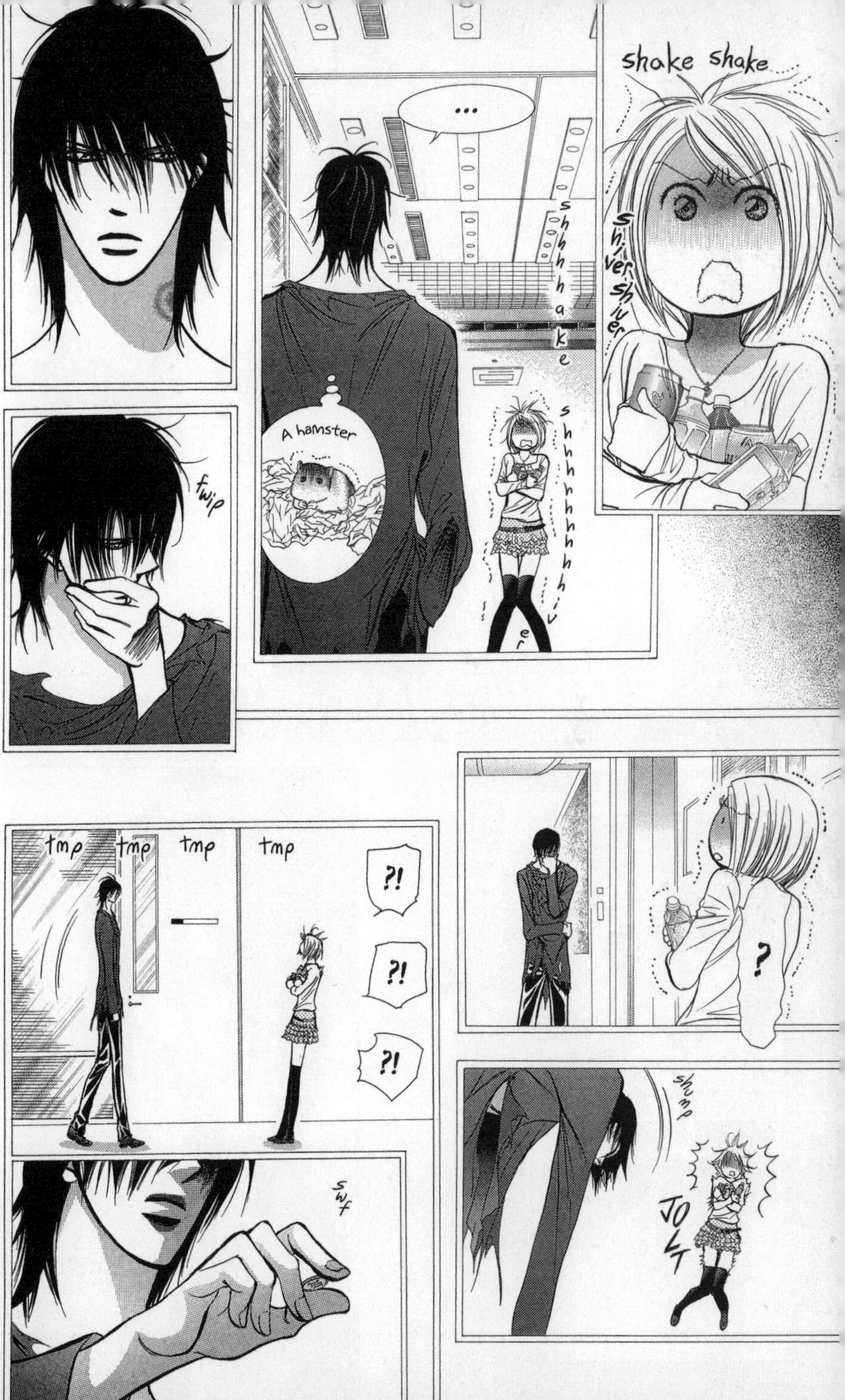
shake shake
shiver shiver
...
shhhhake
shhhhhhhhhiver
A hamster
fwip
?
shump
JOLT
tmp tmp tmp tmp
?!
?!
?!
swf

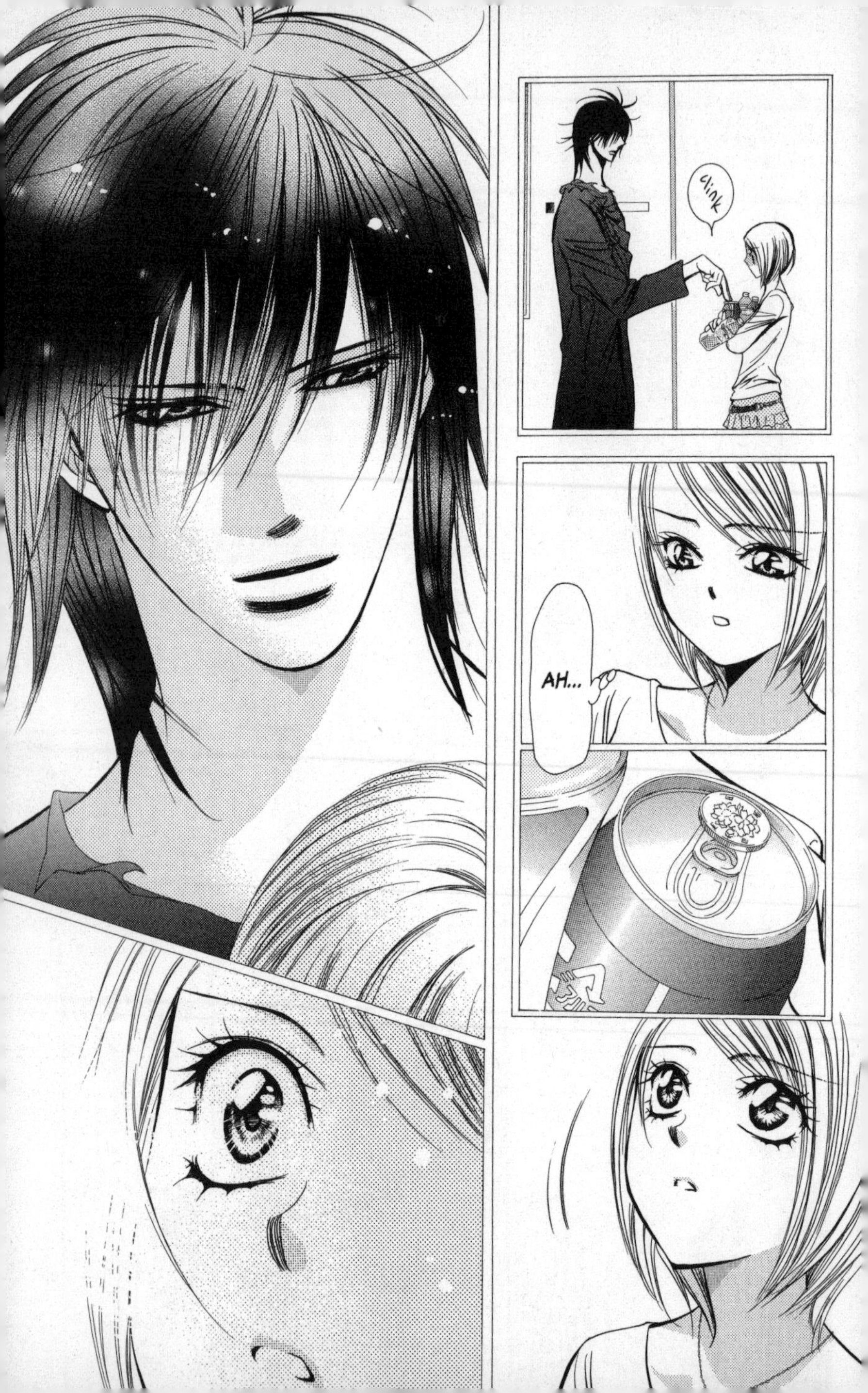
clink
AH...

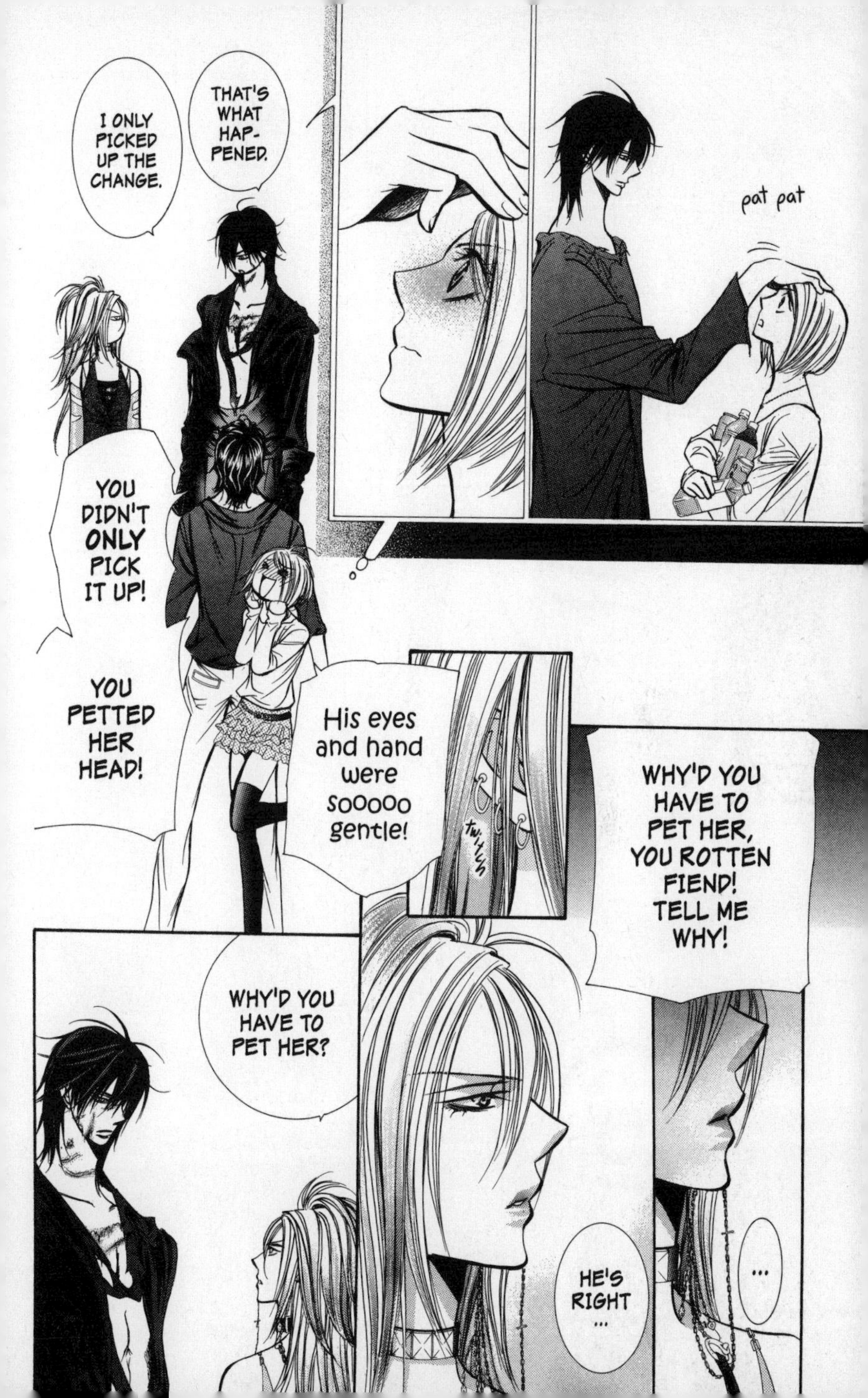
pat pat
THAT'S WHAT HAP-PENED.
I ONLY PICKED UP THE CHANGE.
YOU DIDN'T ONLY PICK IT UP!
YOU PETTED HER HEAD!
His eyes and hand were sooooo gentle!
twitch
WHY'D YOU HAVE TO PET HER, YOU ROTTEN FIEND! TELL ME WHY!
...
HE'S RIGHT ...
WHY'D YOU HAVE TO PET HER?

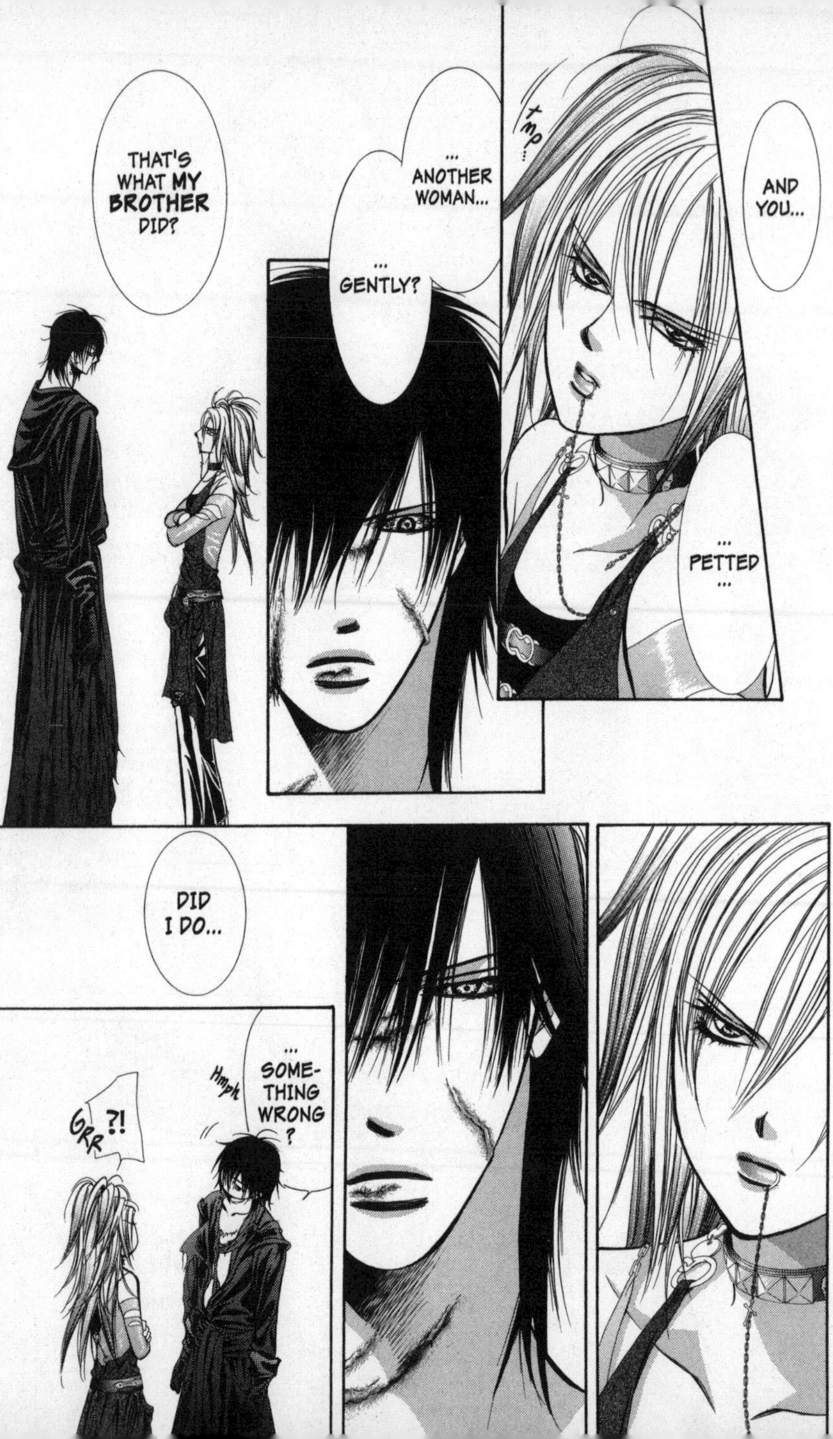
tmp...
AND YOU...
... PETTED ...
... ANOTHER WOMAN...
... GENTLY?
THAT'S WHAT MY BROTHER DID?
DID I DO...
... SOME-THING WRONG ?
Hmph
GRR ?!

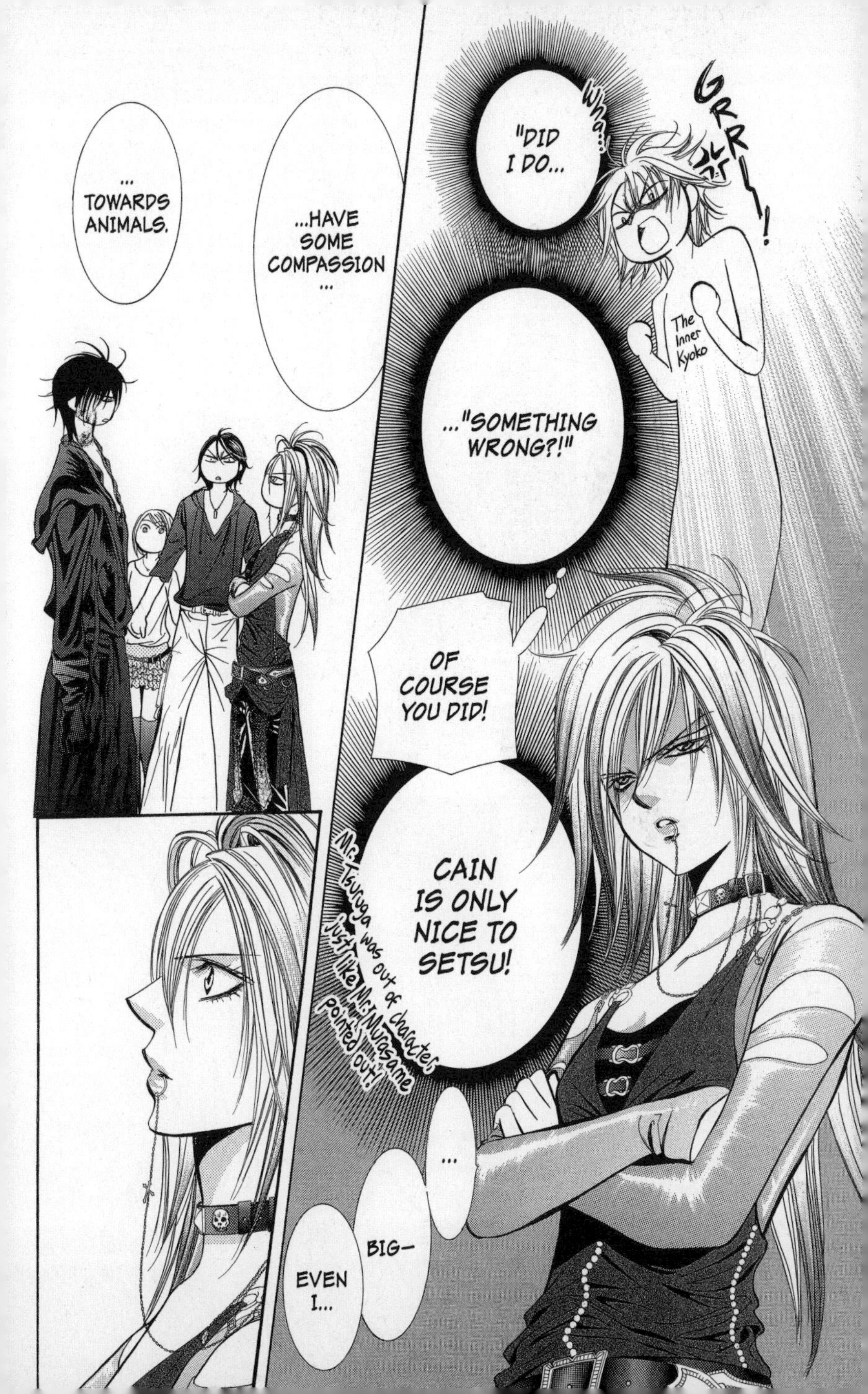
Wha...
"DID I DO...
GRRRL!
The Inner Kyoko
..."SOMETHING WRONG?!"
OF COURSE YOU DID!
CAIN IS ONLY NICE TO SETSU!
Mr. Tsuruga was out of character, just like Mr. Murasame pointed out!
...
BIG-
EVEN I...
...HAVE SOME COMPASSION ...
... TOWARDS ANIMALS.

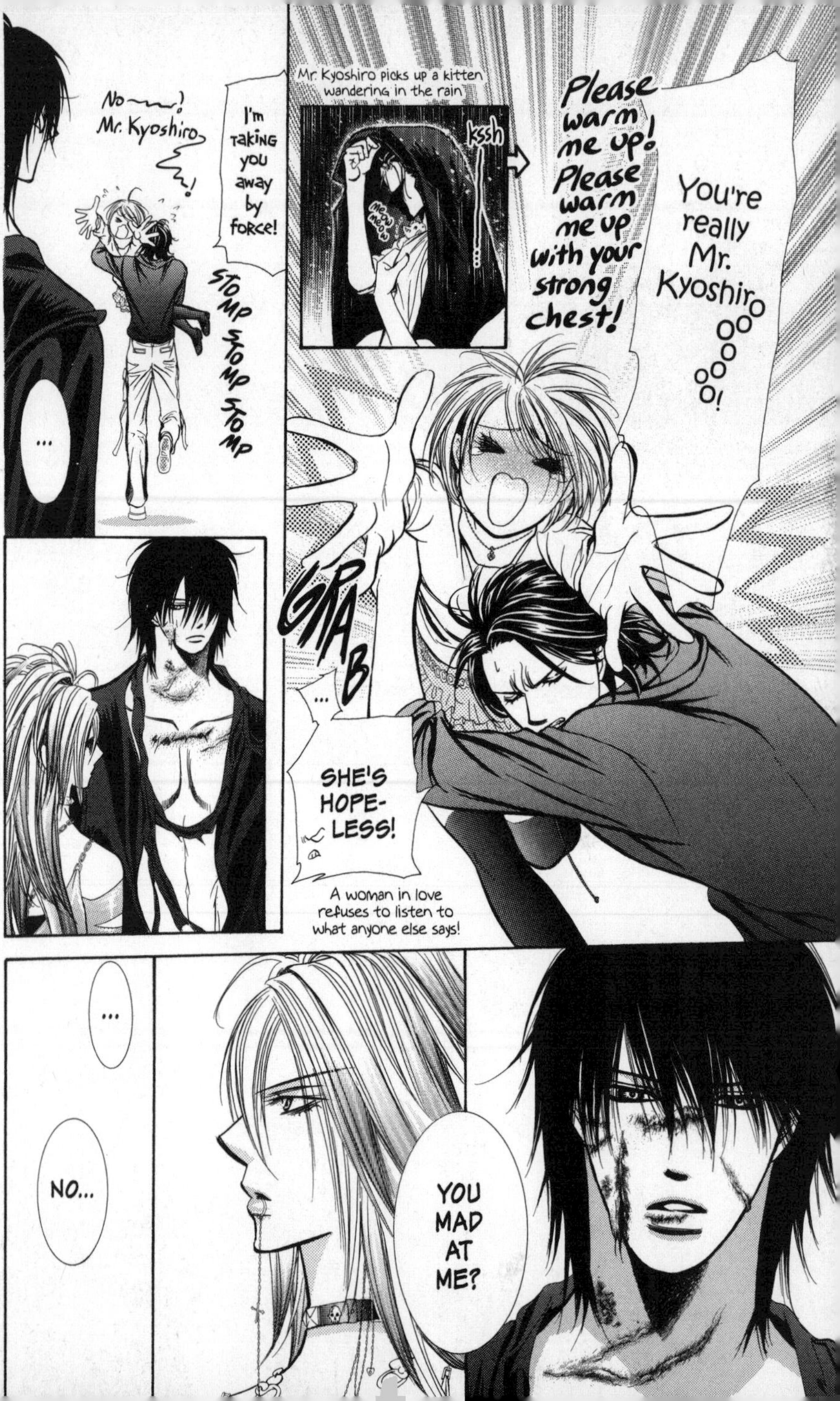

You're really Mr. Kyoshiroooooooo!
Please warm me up! Please warm me up with your strong chest!
Mr. Kyoshiro picks up a kitten wandering in the rain
kssh
meow meow
GRAB
...
SHE'S HOPE-LESS!
A woman in love refuses to listen to what anyone else says!
I'm taking you away by force!
No~~! Mr. Kyoshiro~!
STOMP STOMP STOMP
...
YOU MAD AT ME?
...
NO...

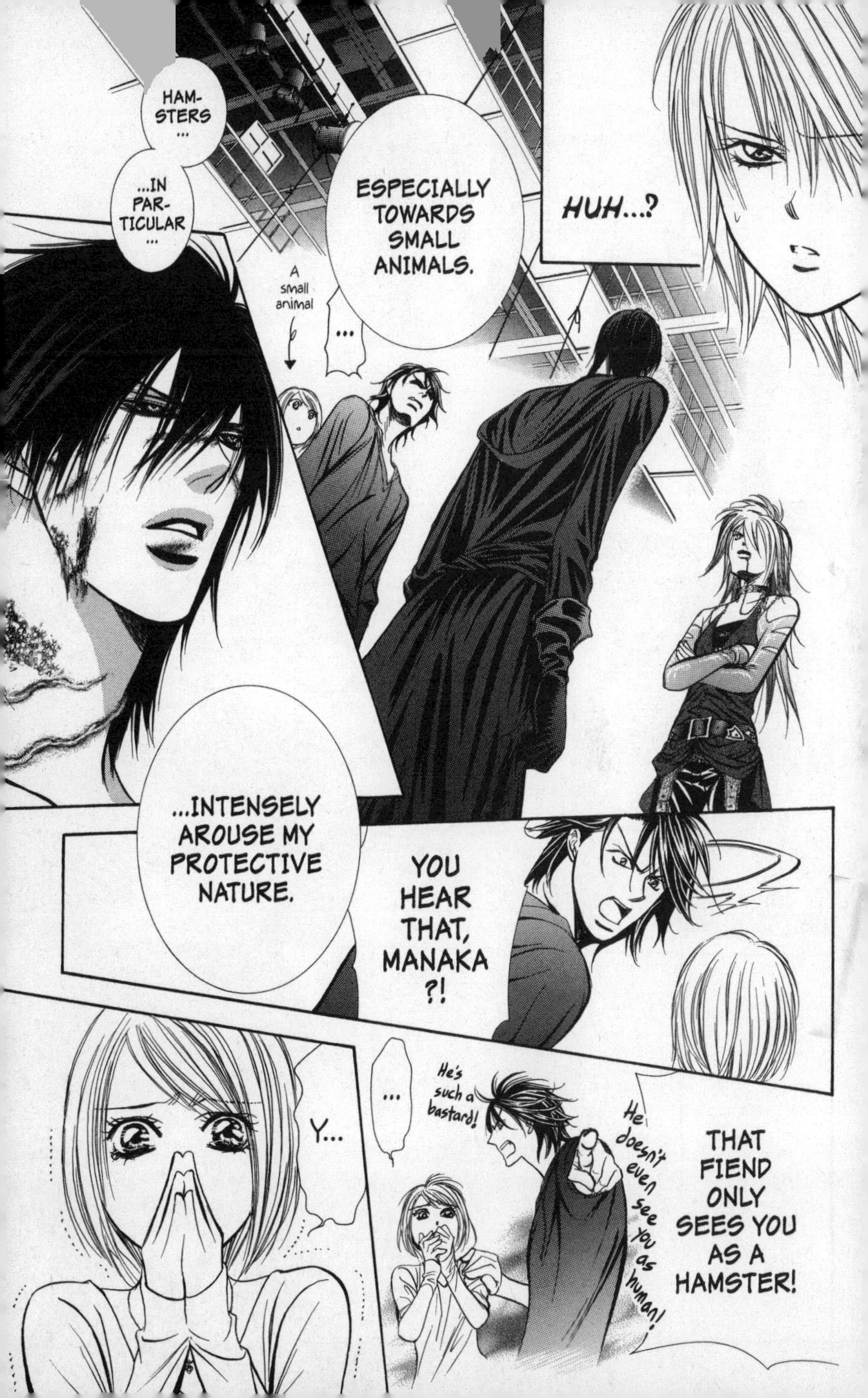
HUH...?
ESPECIALLY TOWARDS SMALL ANIMALS.
...
A small animal
HAMSTERS...
...IN PARTICULAR...
...INTENSELY AROUSE MY PROTECTIVE NATURE.
YOU HEAR THAT, MANAKA?!
THAT FIEND ONLY SEES YOU AS A HAMSTER!
He doesn't even see you as human!
He's such a bastard!
...
Y...

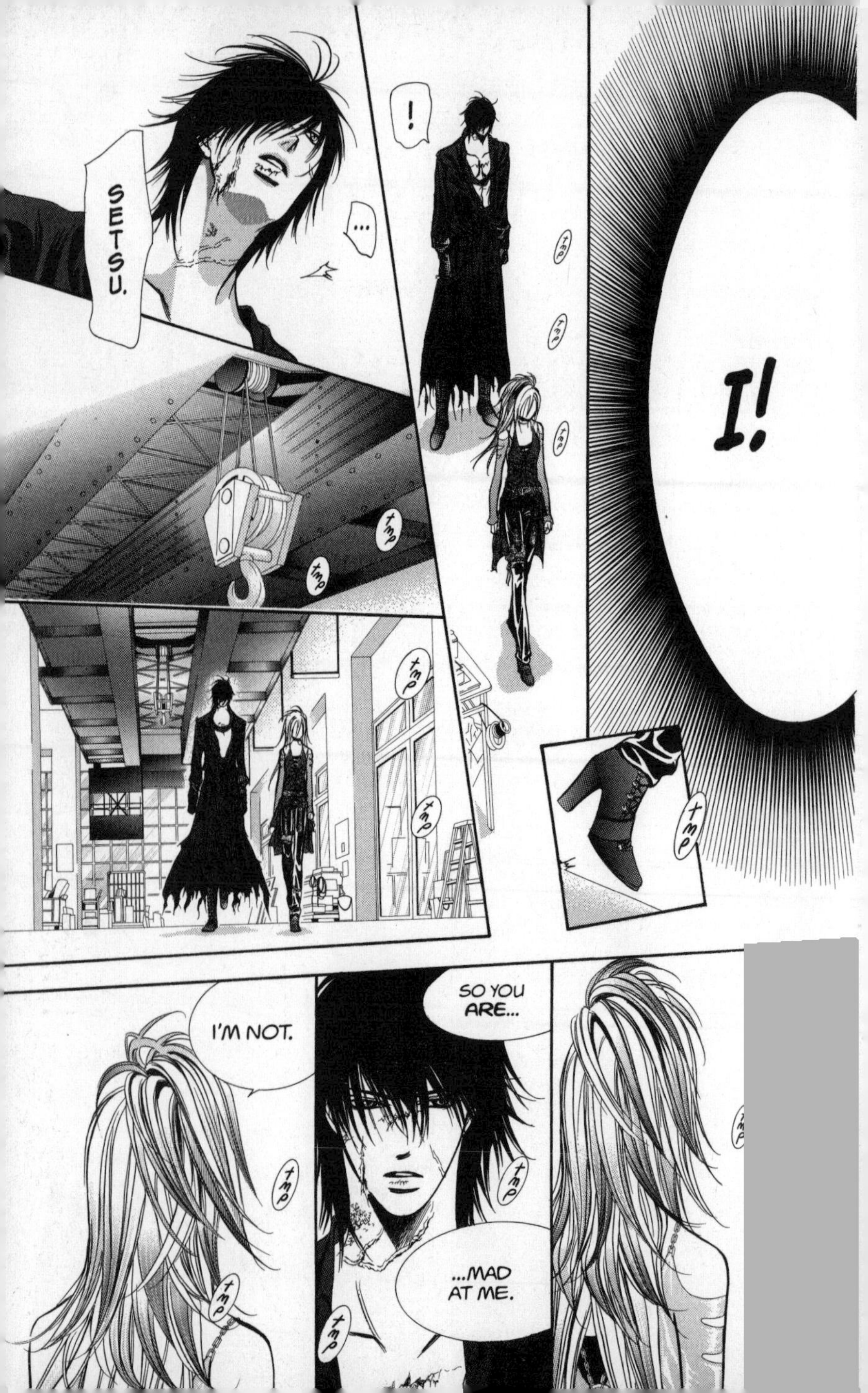
I!
tmp
!
tmp
tmp
tmp
...
SETSU.
tmp
tmp
tmp
tmp
tmp
SO YOU ARE...
tmp
...MAD AT ME.
tmp
I'M NOT.
tmp
tmp

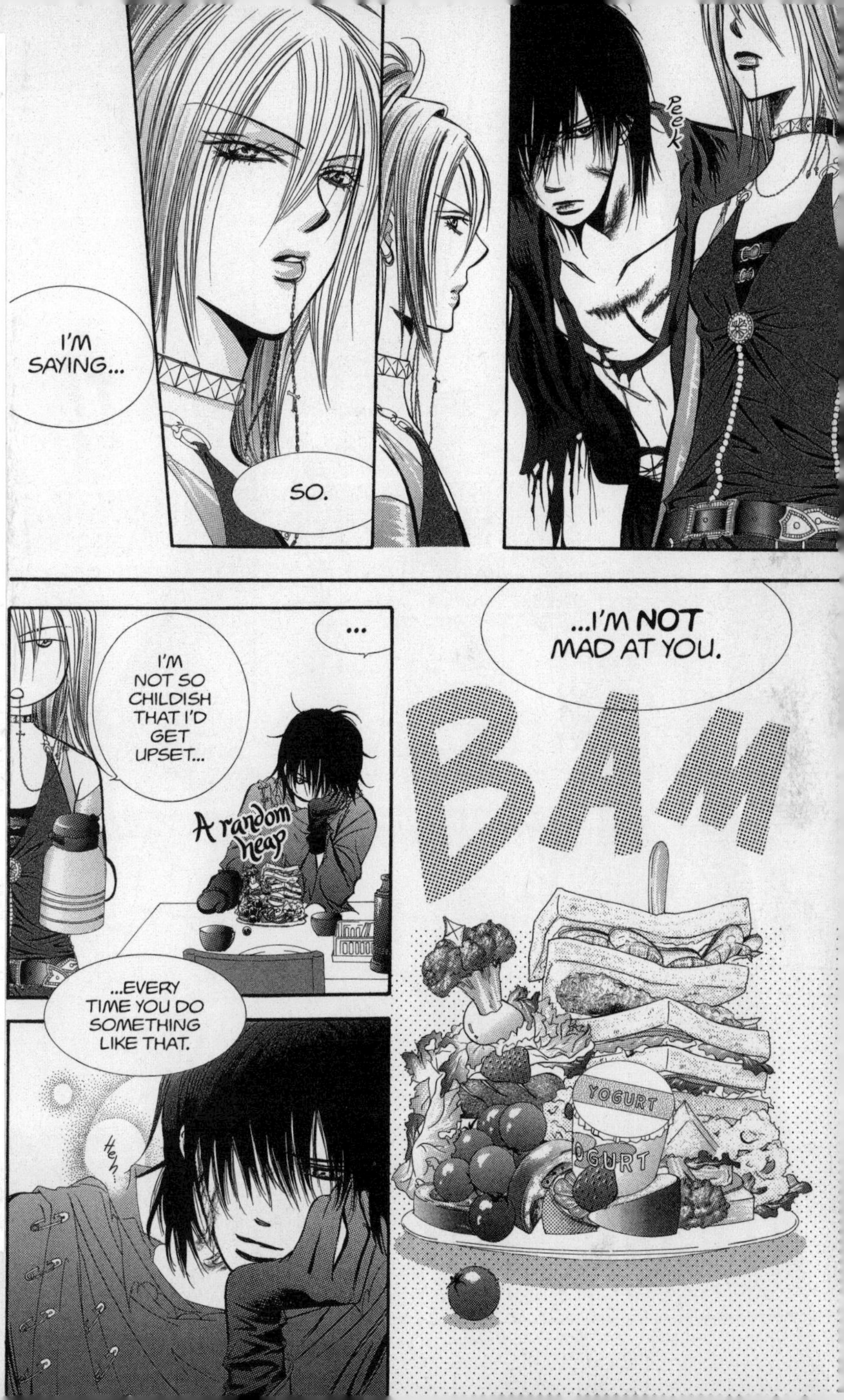
Peek
I'M SAYING...
SO.
...I'M NOT MAD AT YOU.
BAM
YOGURT
...
I'M NOT SO CHILDISH THAT I'D GET UPSET...
A random heap
...EVERY TIME YOU DO SOMETHING LIKE THAT.
Heh...

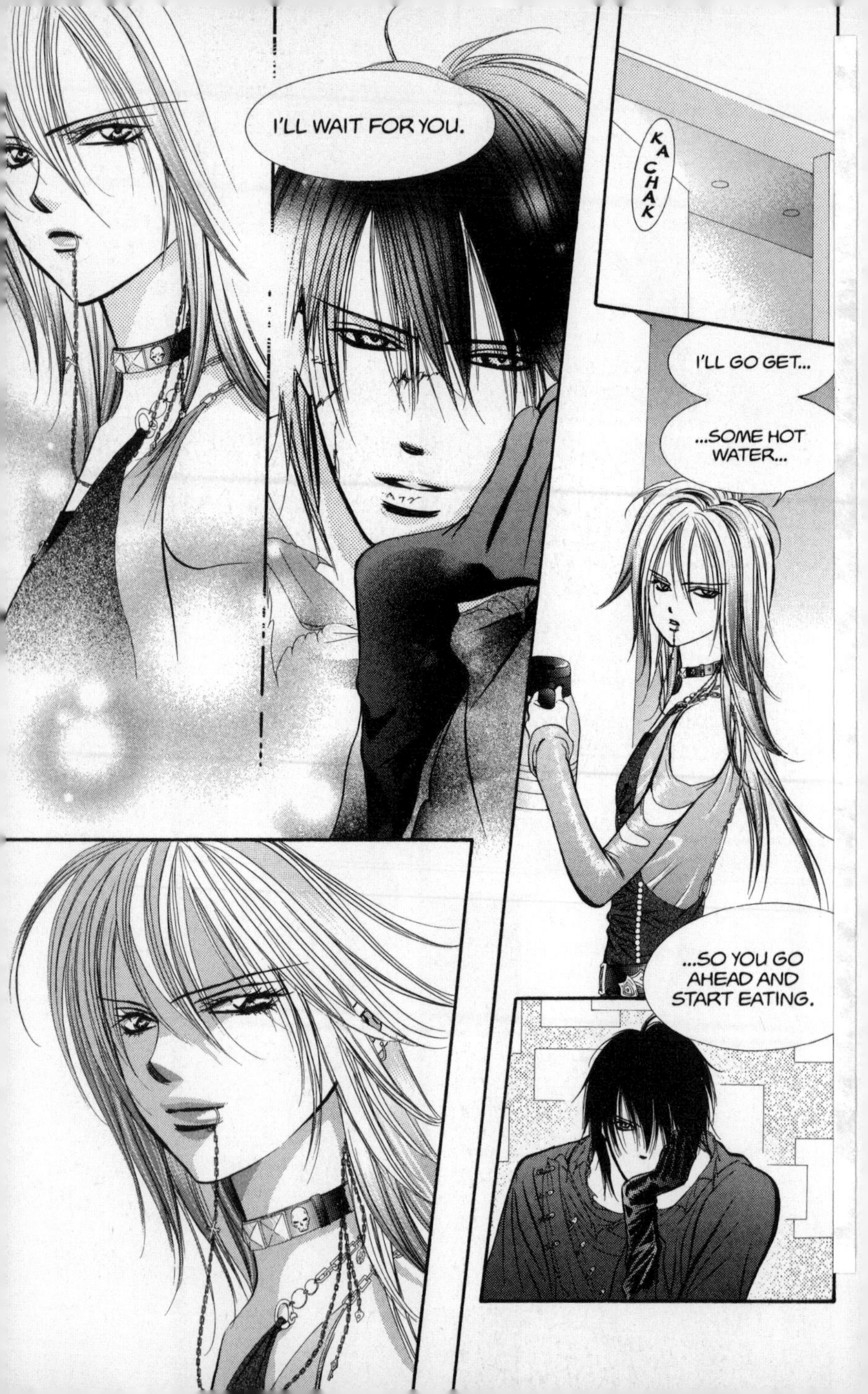
KA CHAK
I'LL GO GET...
...SOME HOT WATER...
...SO YOU GO AHEAD AND START EATING.
I'LL WAIT FOR YOU.

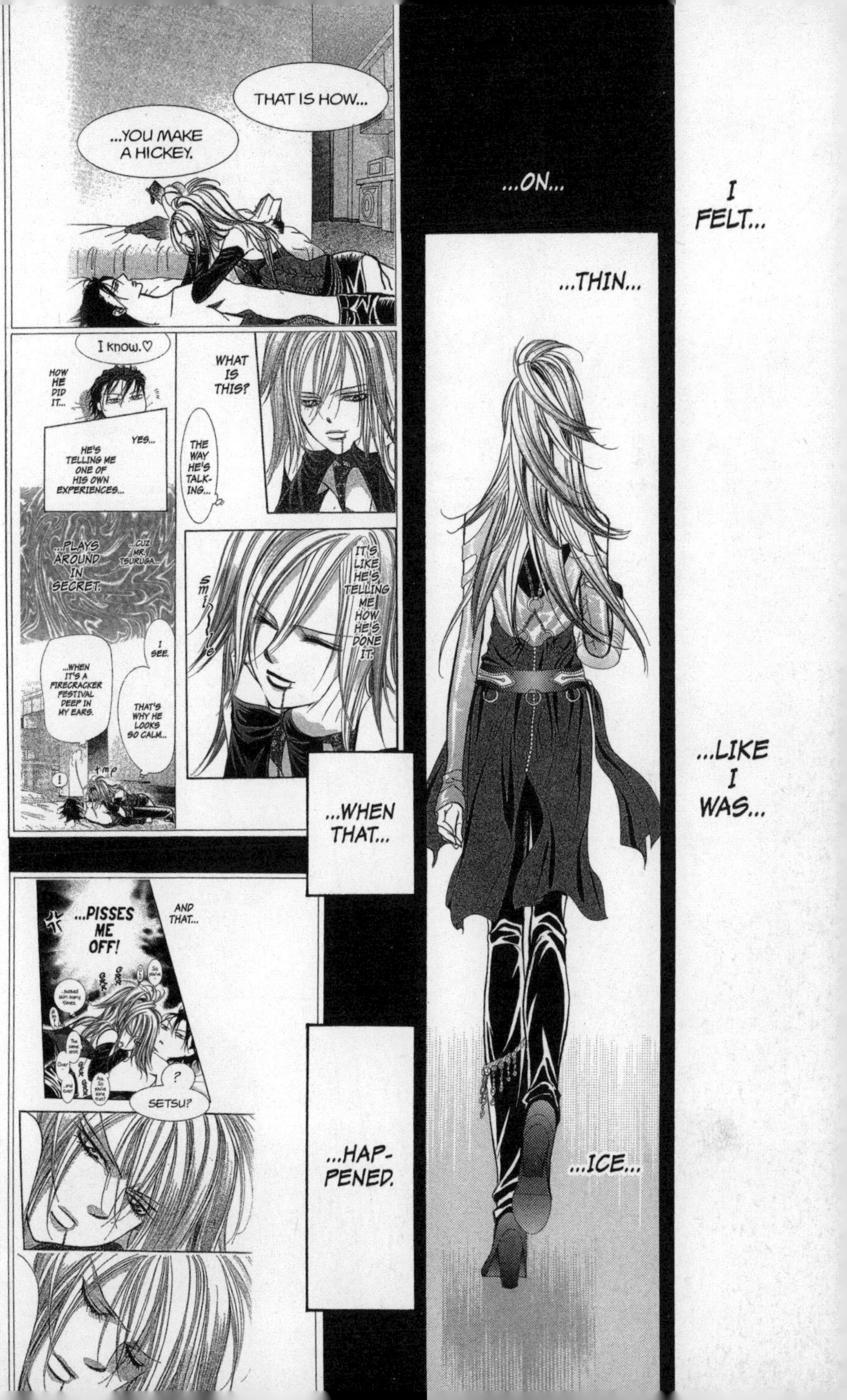
I FELT...
...LIKE I WAS...
...ON...
...THIN...
...ICE...
...WHEN THAT...
...HAP-PENED.
THAT IS HOW...
...YOU MAKE A HICKEY.
WHAT IS THIS?
THE WAY HE'S TALKING...
I know.♡
HOW HE DID IT...
YES...
HE'S TELLING ME ONE OF HIS OWN EXPERIENCES...
IT'S LIKE HE'S TELLING ME HOW HE'S DONE IT.
smile
...CUZ MR. TSURUGA...
...PLAYS AROUND IN SECRET.
I SEE.
THAT'S WHY HE LOOKS SO CALM...
...WHEN IT'S A FIRECRACKER FESTIVAL DEEP IN MY EARS.
tmp
!
AND THAT...
...PISSES ME OFF!
?
SETSU?

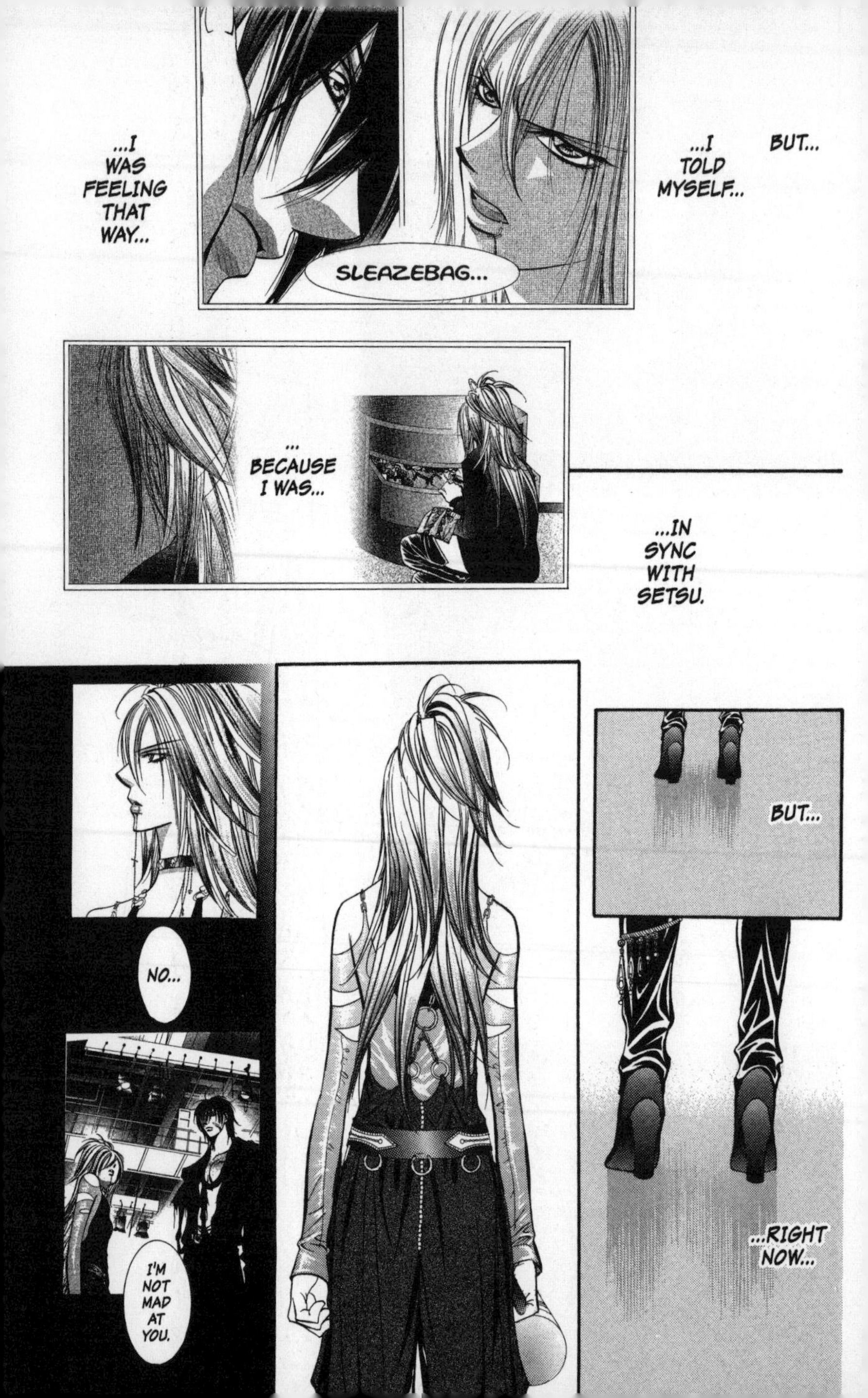
BUT...
...I TOLD MYSELF...
SLEAZEBAG...
...I WAS FEELING THAT WAY...
... BECAUSE I WAS...
...IN SYNC WITH SETSU.
BUT...
...RIGHT NOW...
NO...
I'M NOT MAD AT YOU.

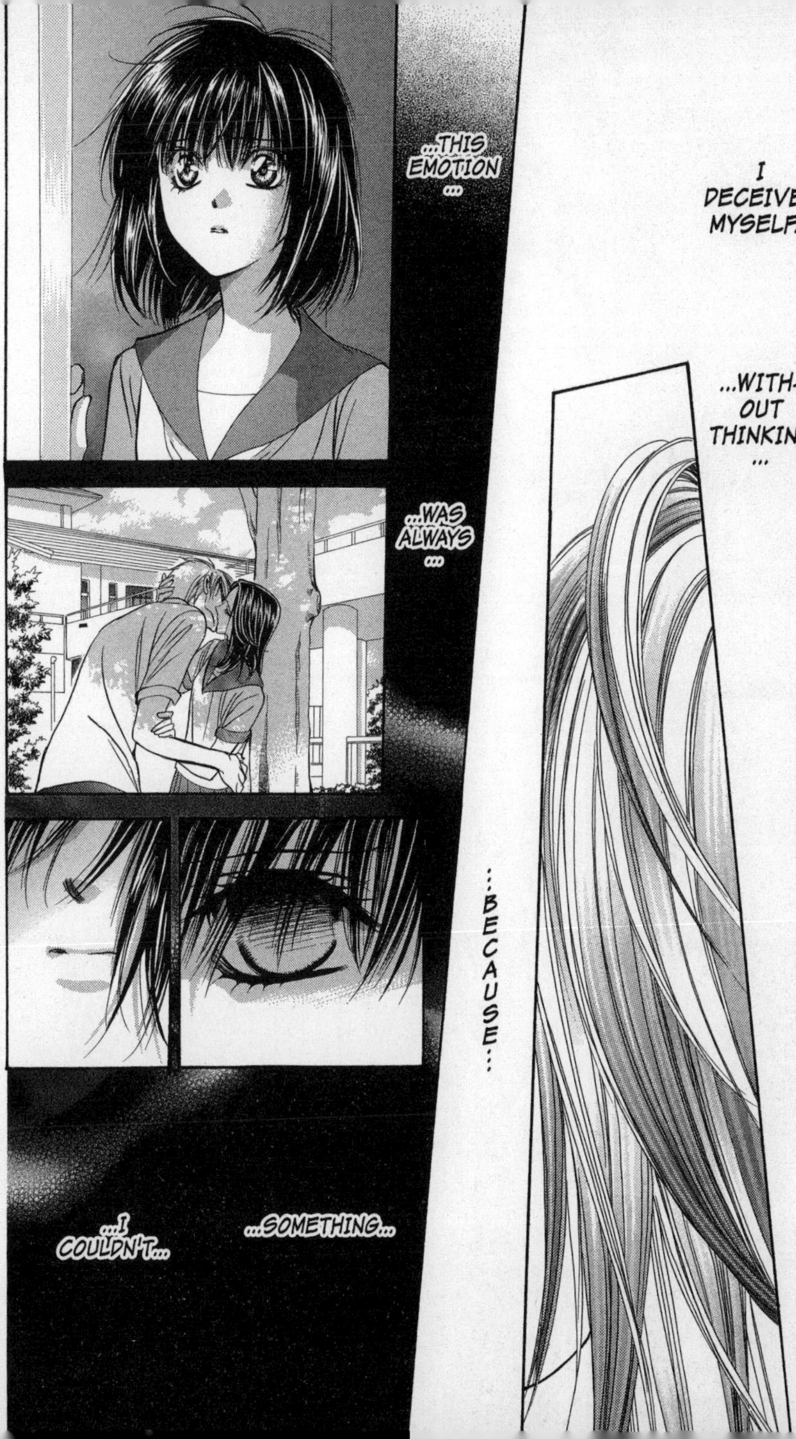
I DECEIVED MYSELF...
...WITH-OUT THINKING ...
...BECAUSE...
...THIS EMOTION ...
...WAS ALWAYS ...
...SOMETHING...
...I COULDN'T...

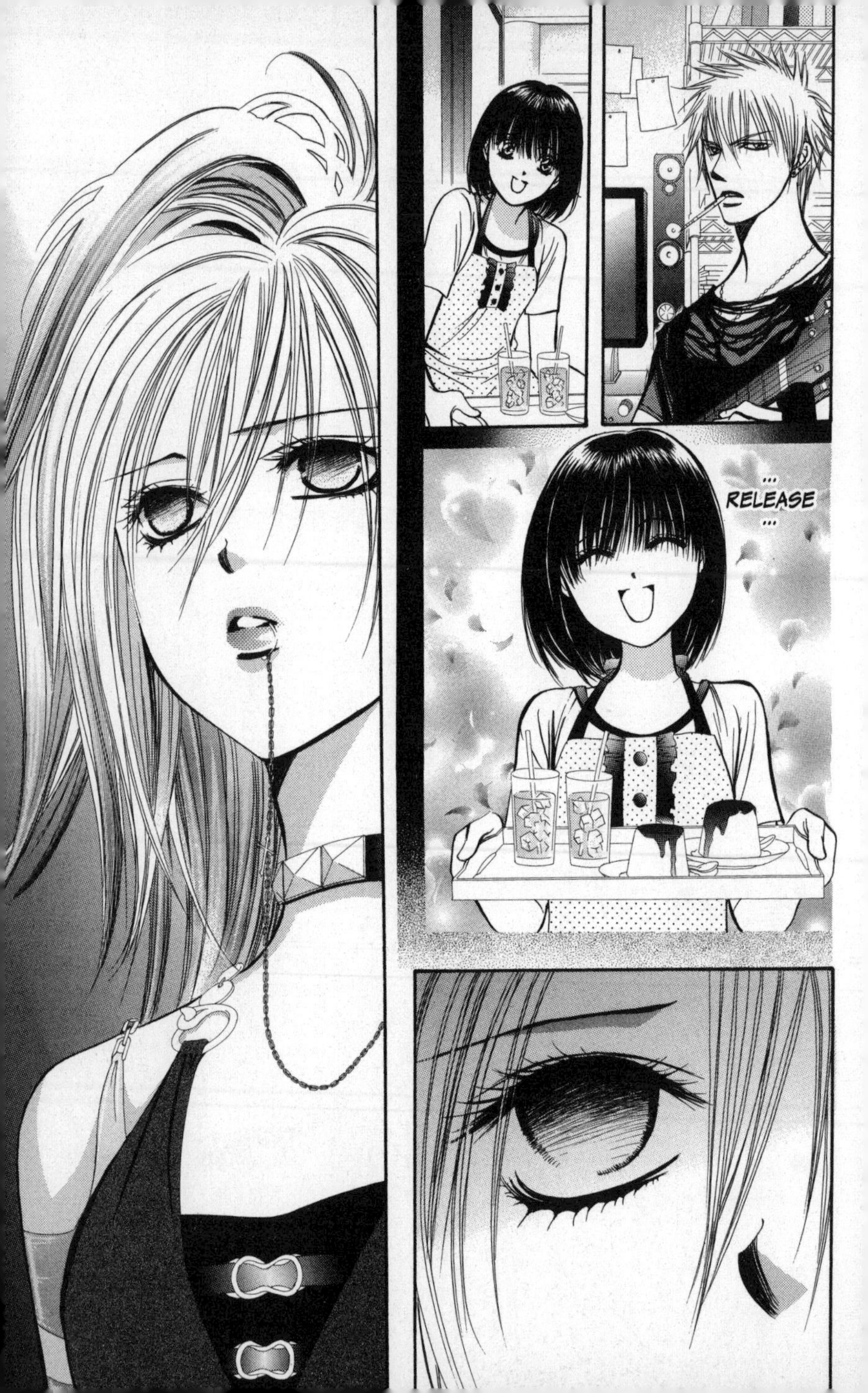
... RELEASE ...

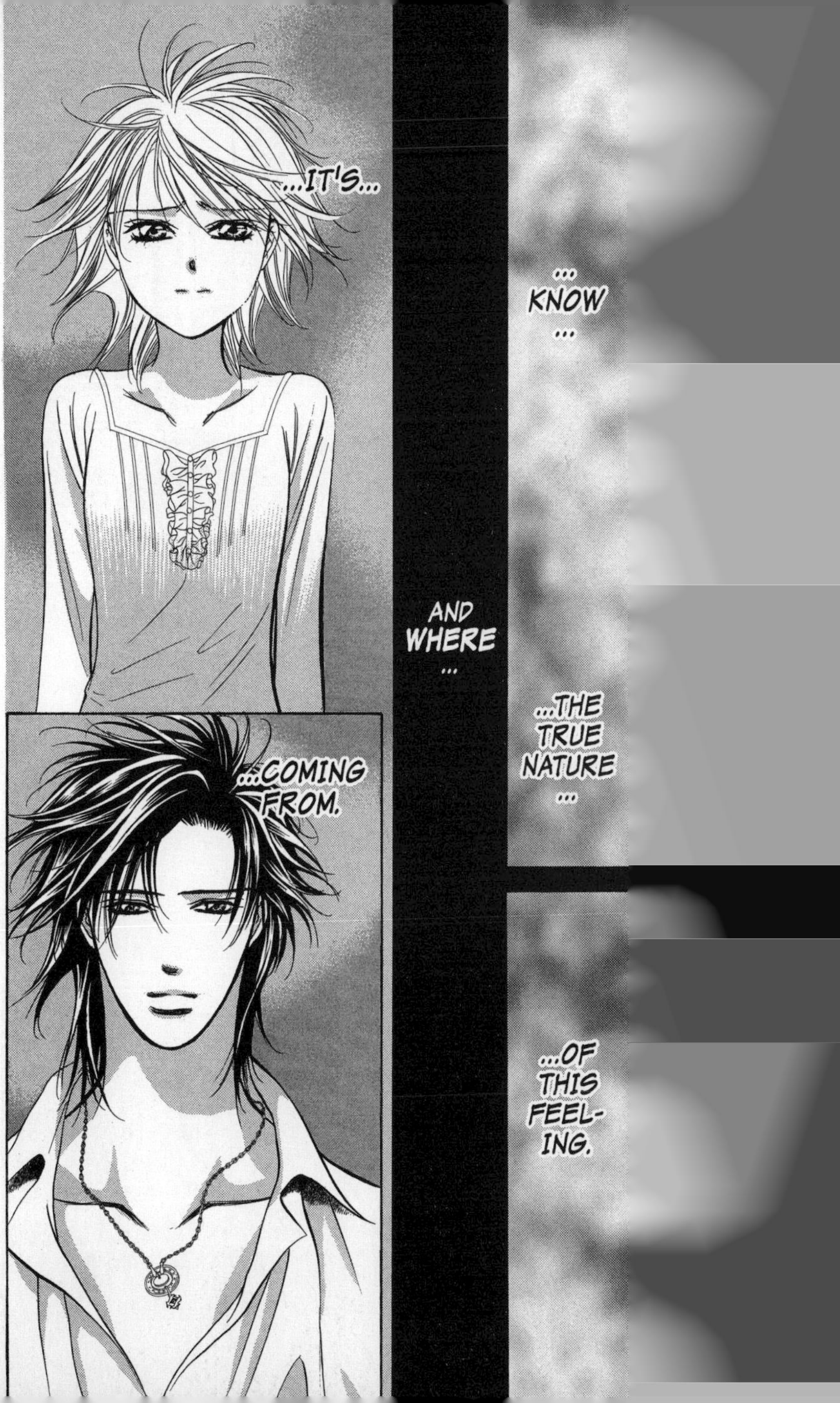
... KNOW ...
...THE TRUE NATURE ...
...OF THIS FEEL-ING.
AND WHERE ...
...IT'S...
...COMING FROM.

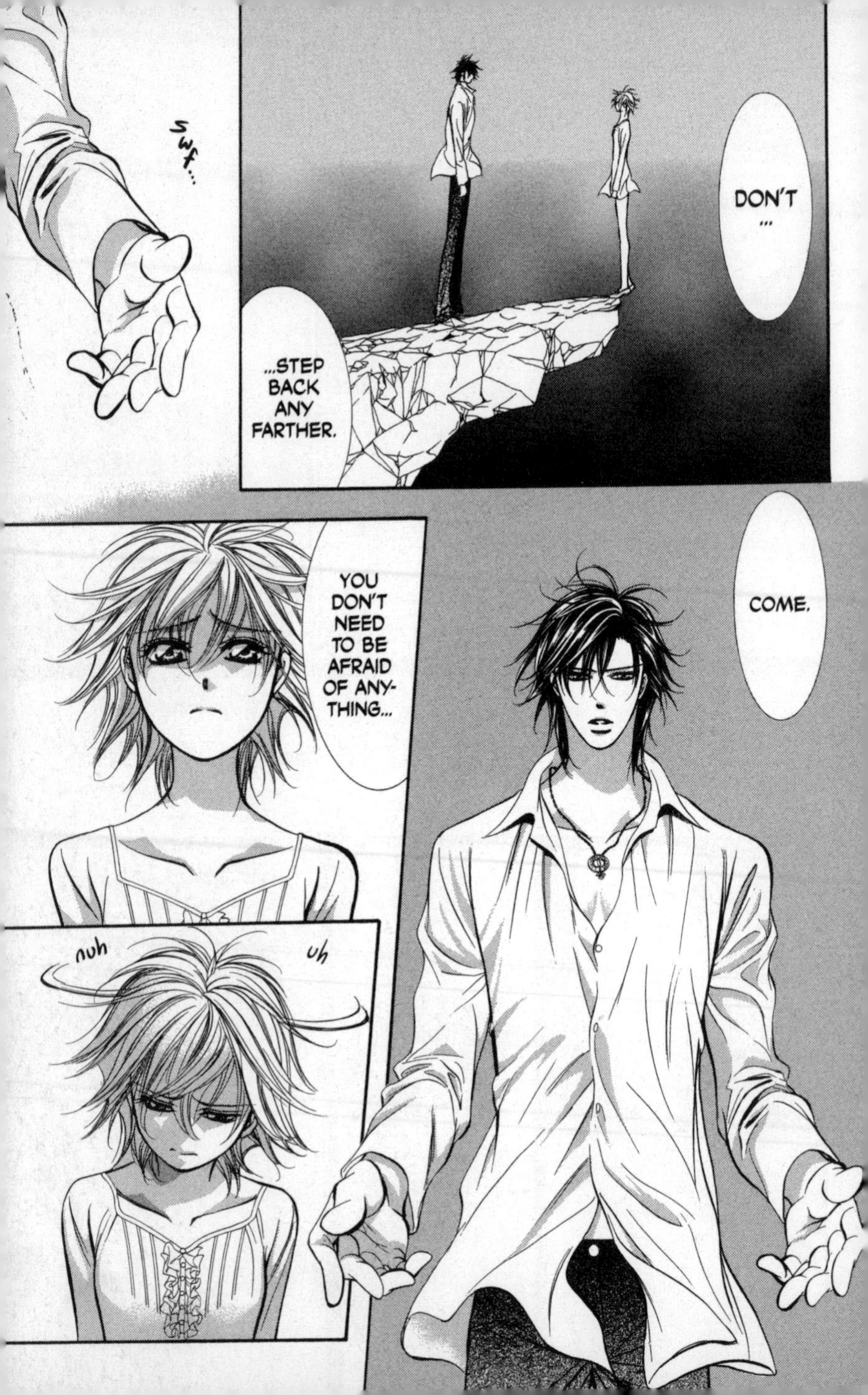
DON'T ...
...STEP BACK ANY FARTHER.
swf...
COME.
YOU DON'T NEED TO BE AFRAID OF ANYTHING...
nuh uh

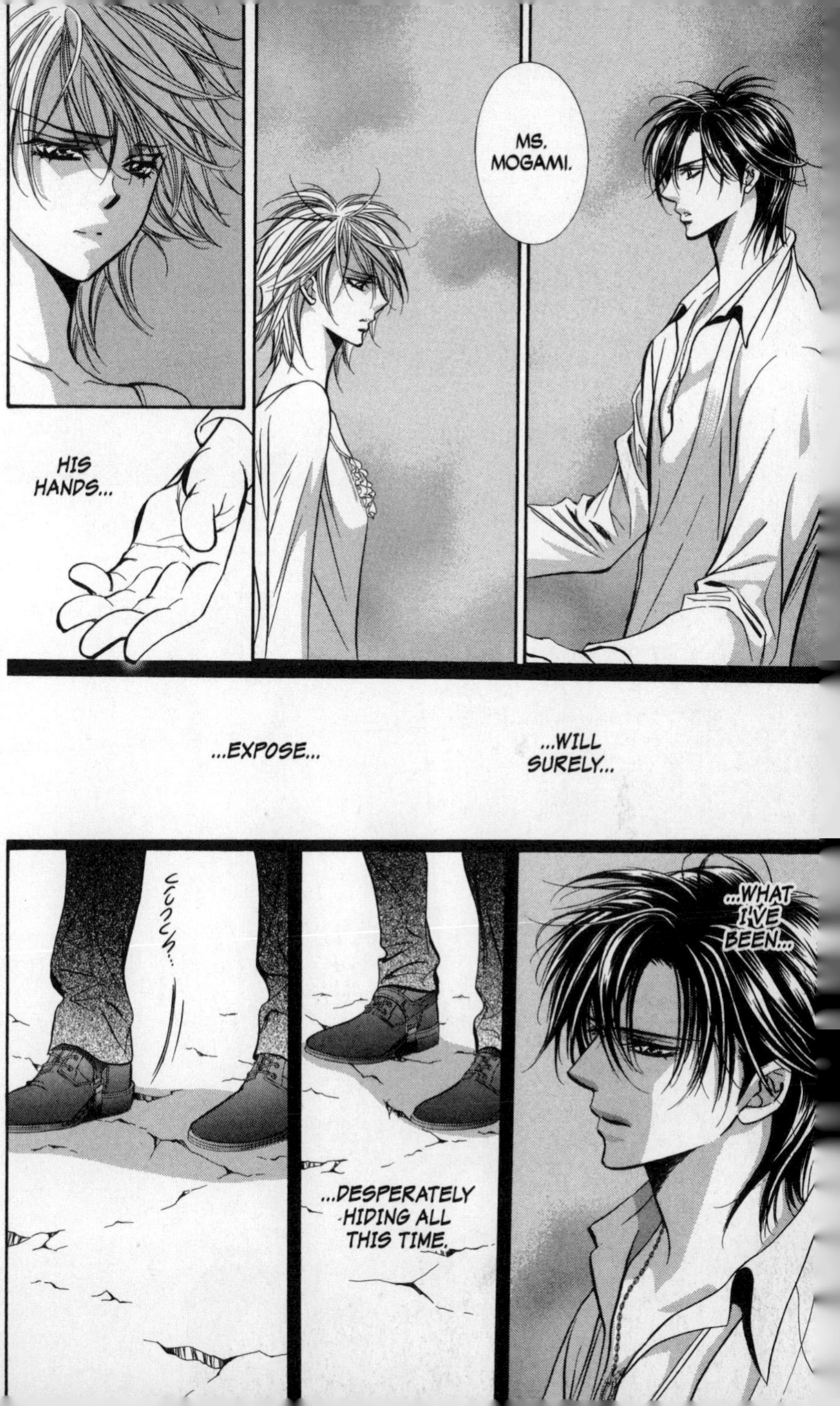
MS. MOGAMI.
HIS HANDS...
...WILL SURELY...
...EXPOSE...
...WHAT I'VE BEEN...
...DESPERATELY HIDING ALL THIS TIME.

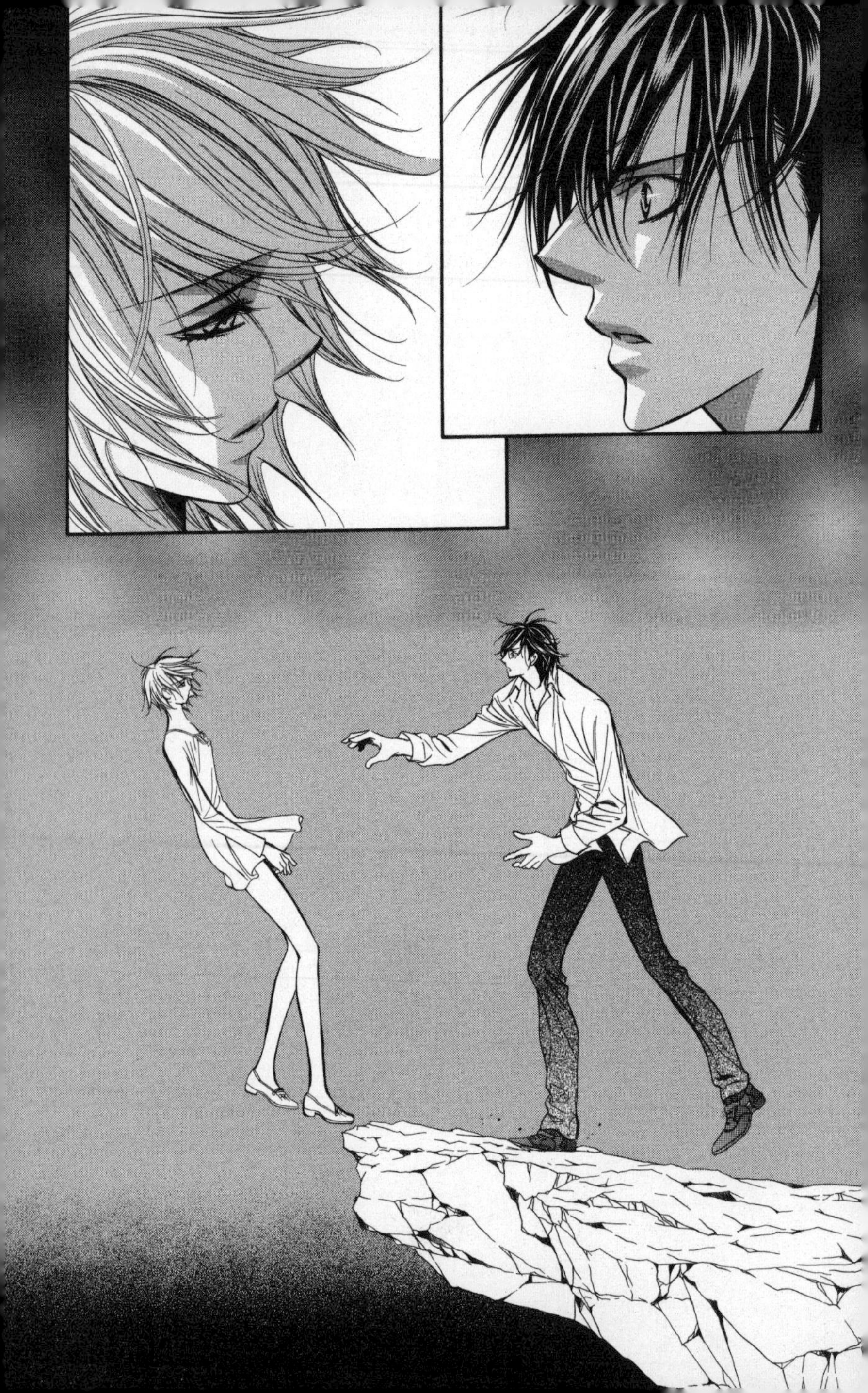

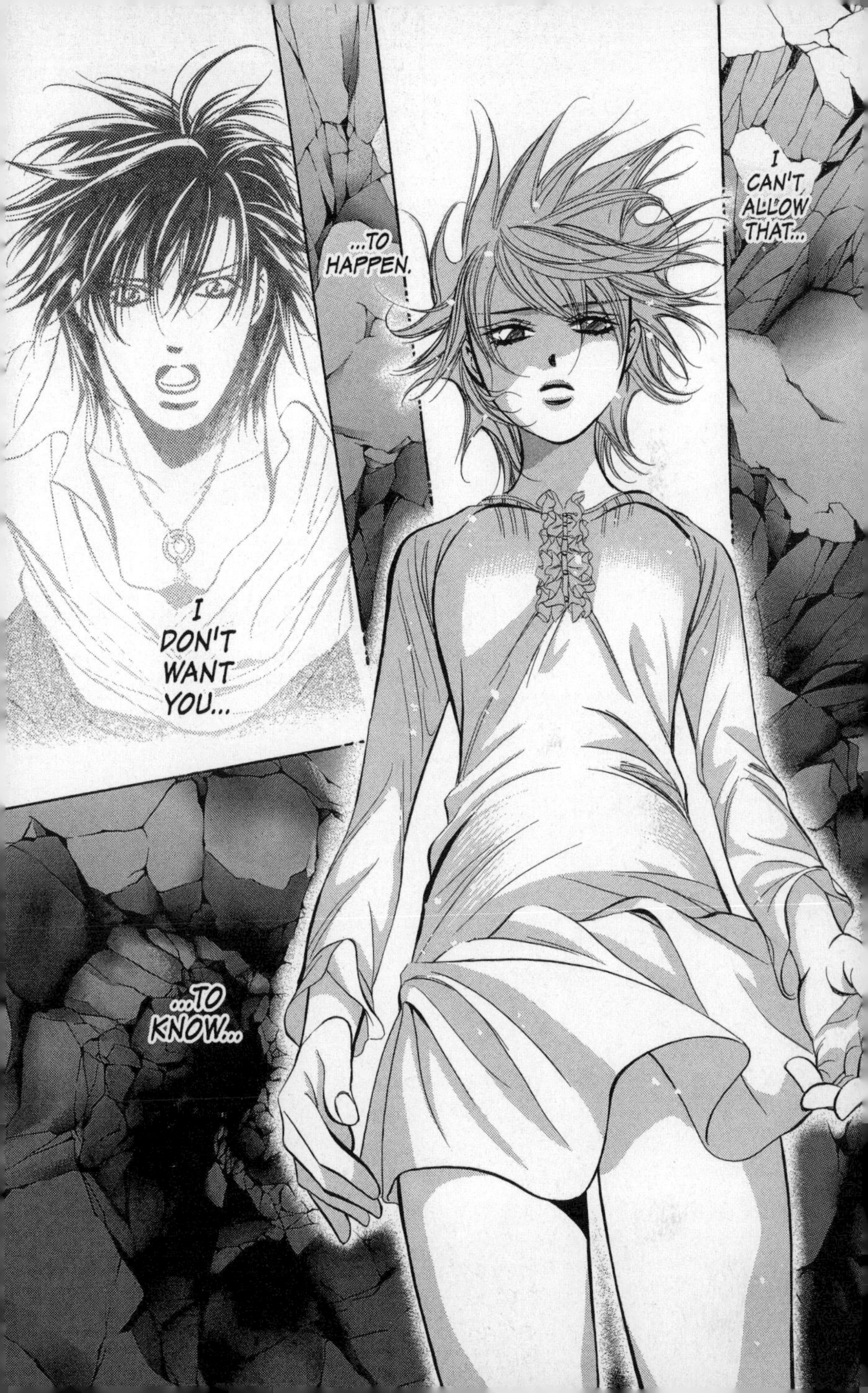
I CAN'T ALLOW THAT...
...TO HAPPEN.
I DON'T WANT YOU...
...TO KNOW...

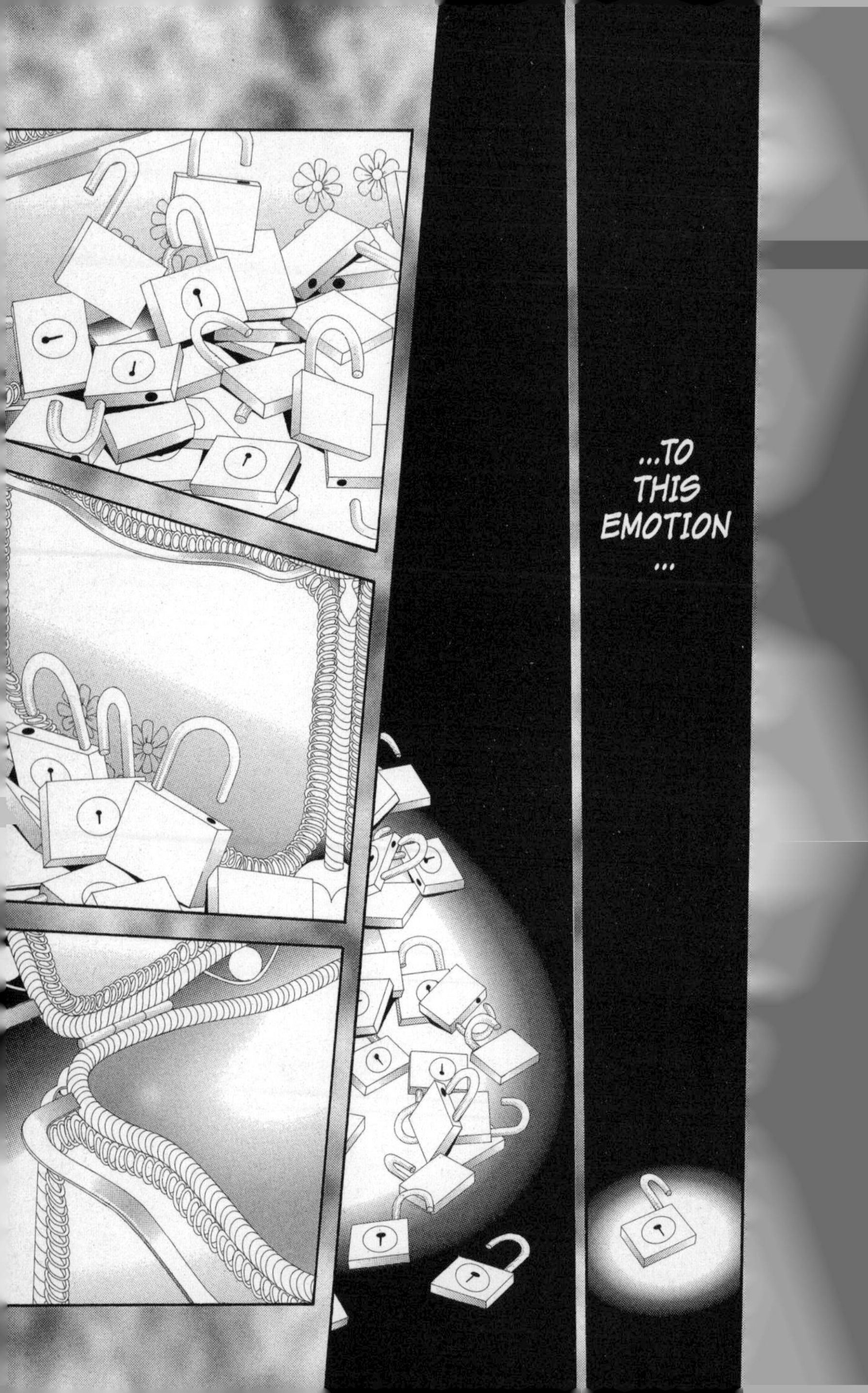
...TO THIS EMOTION ...

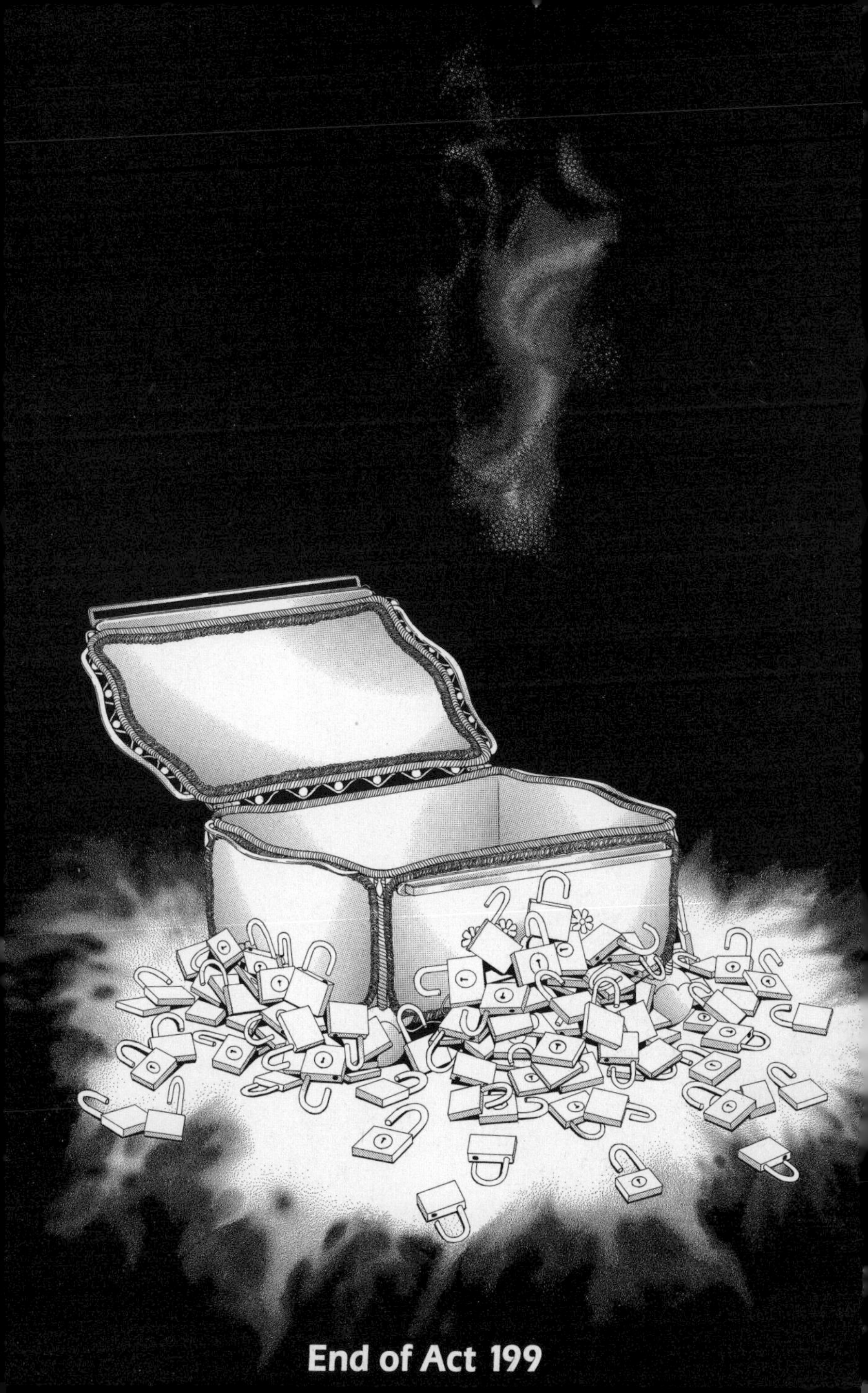
End of Act 199

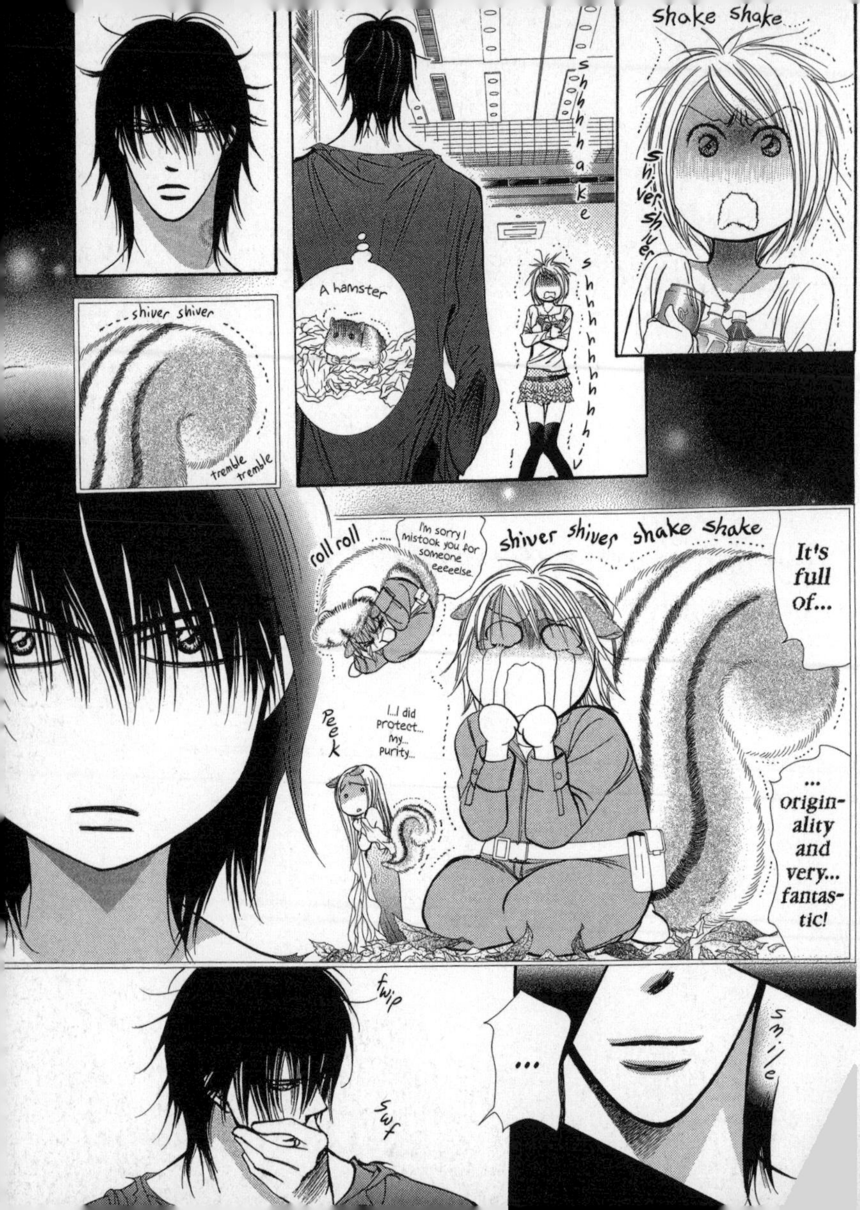
shake shake
shiver shiver
shhhhake
A hamster
shhhhhhhhhhiv
shiver shiver
tremble tremble
It's full of...
shiver shiver shake shake
I'm sorry I mistook you for someone eeeeelse.
roll roll
...originality and very... fantastic!
I...I did protect... my... purity...
Peek
smile
...
fwip
swf

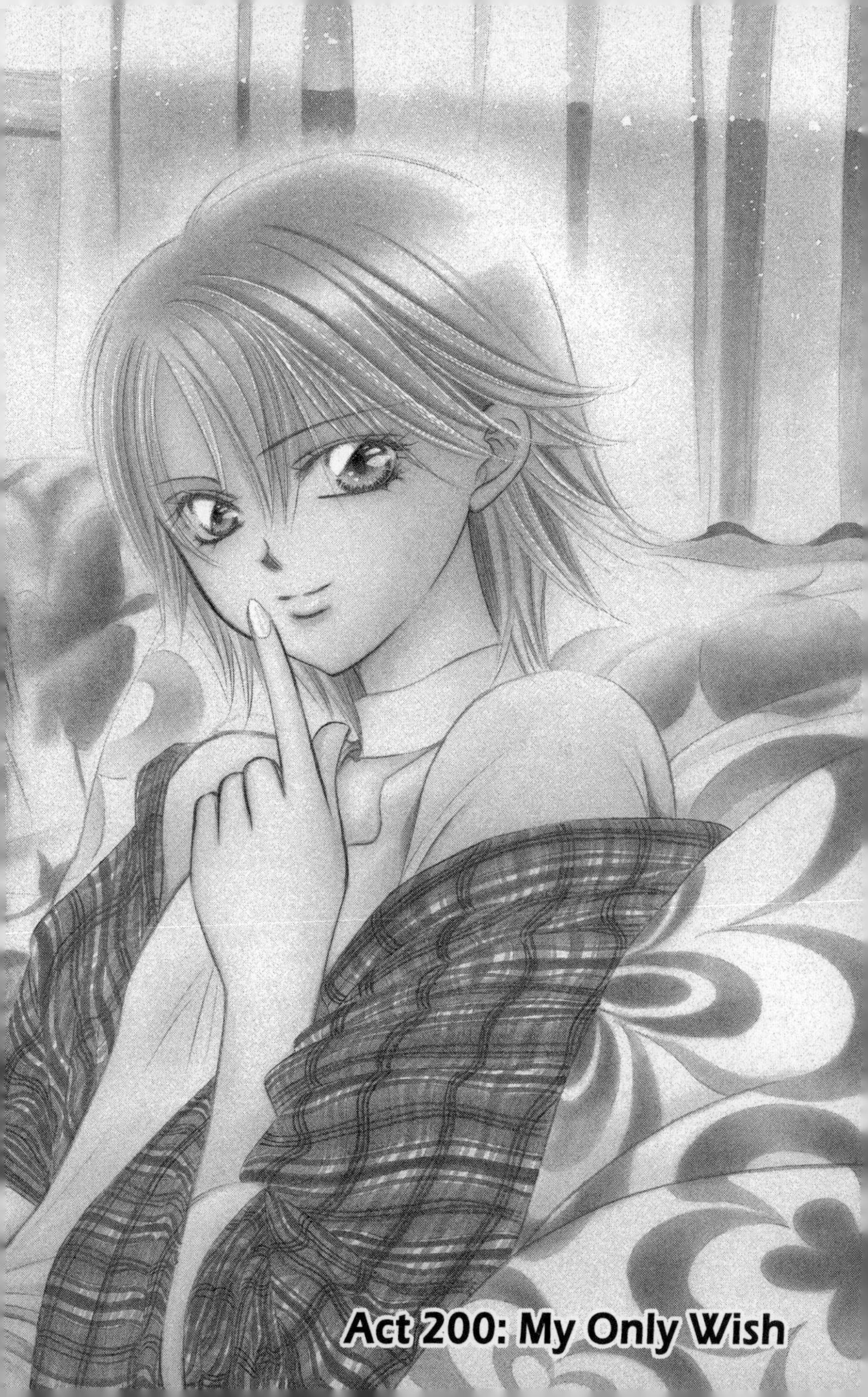
Act 200: My Only Wish

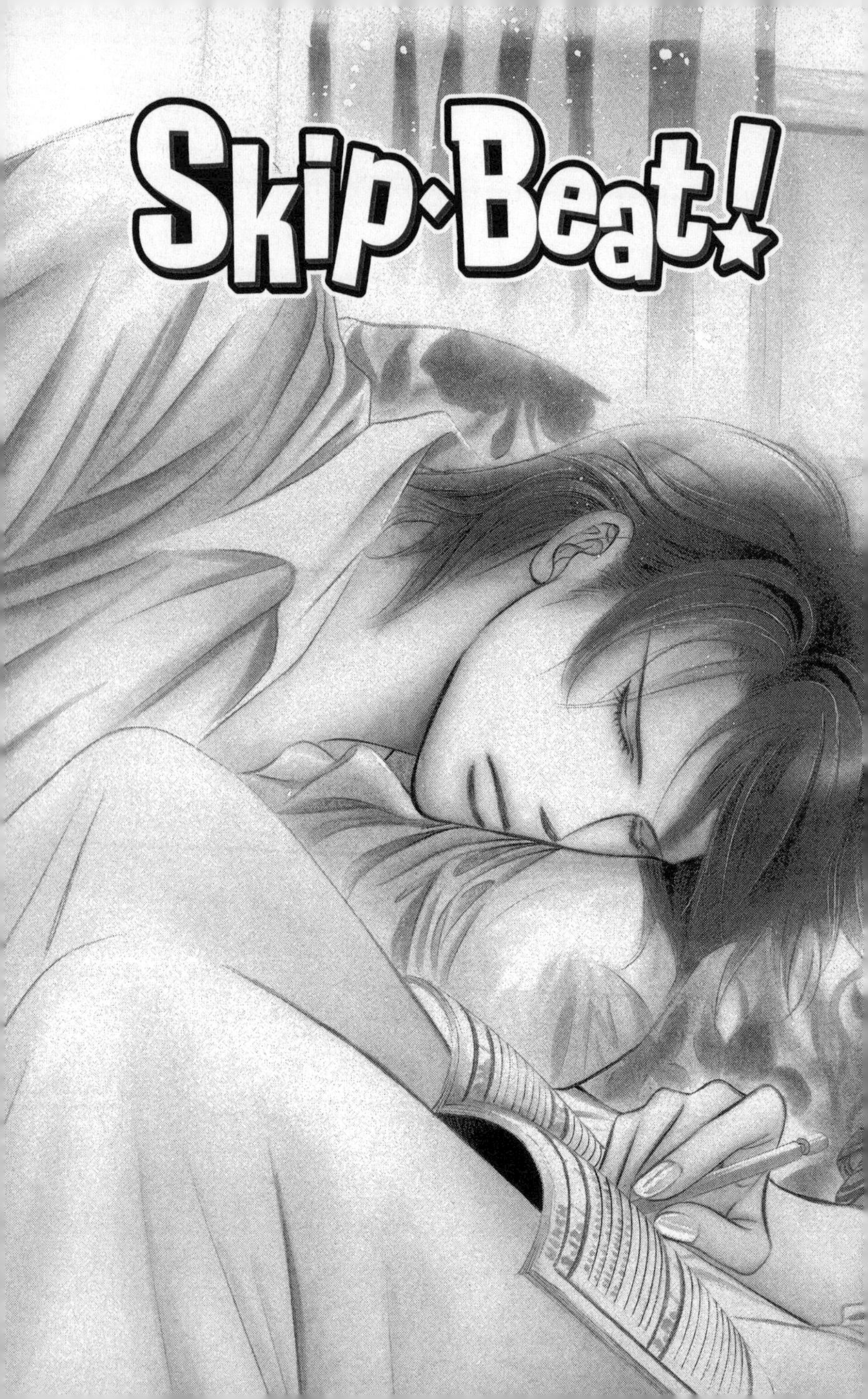
Skip・Beat!

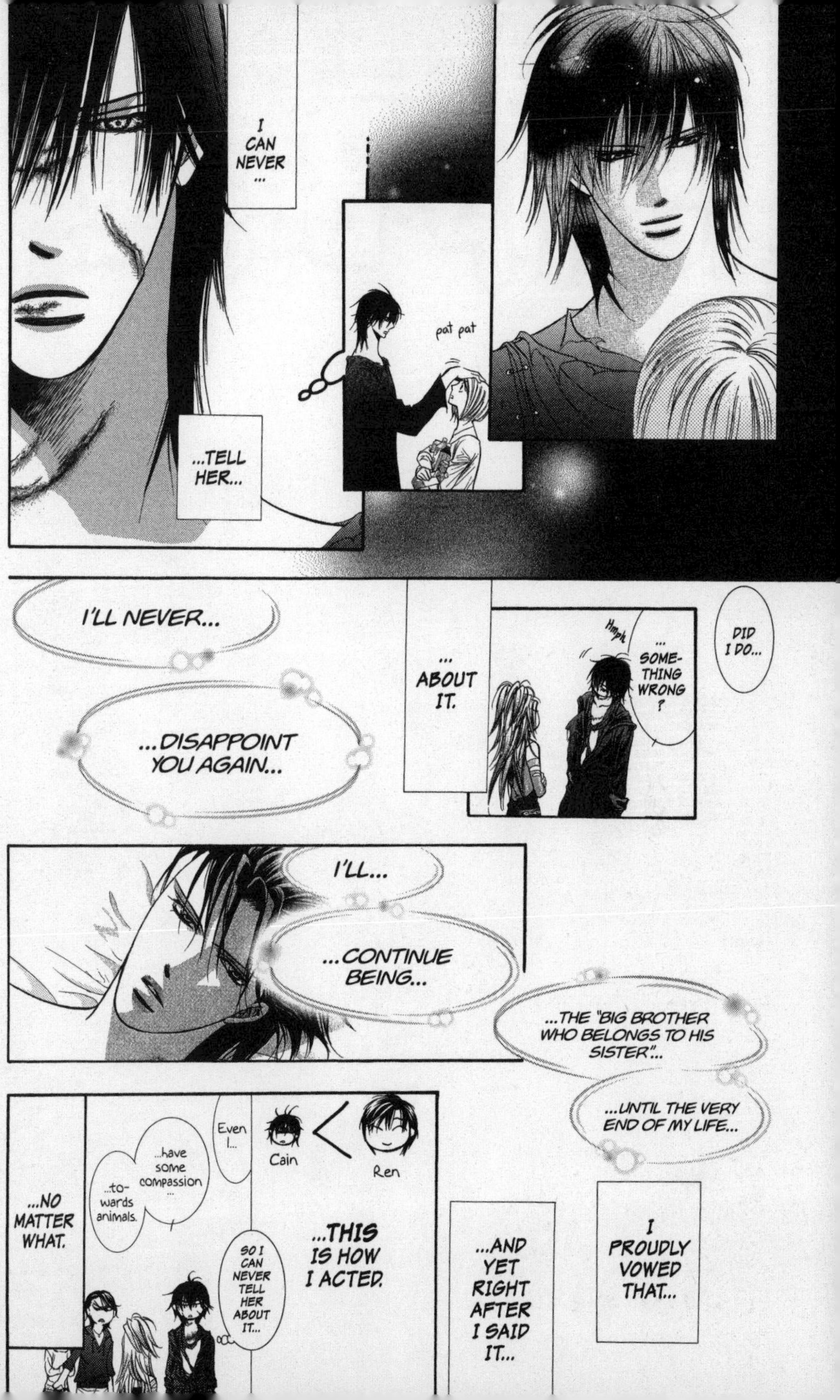
pat pat
I CAN NEVER...
...TELL HER...
DID I DO...
Hmph
...SOMETHING WRONG?
...ABOUT IT.
I'LL NEVER...
...DISAPPOINT YOU AGAIN...
I'LL...
...CONTINUE BEING...
...THE "BIG BROTHER WHO BELONGS TO HIS SISTER"...
...UNTIL THE VERY END OF MY LIFE...
I PROUDLY VOWED THAT...
...AND YET RIGHT AFTER I SAID IT...
...THIS IS HOW I ACTED.
Cain
Ren
SO I CAN NEVER TELL HER ABOUT IT...
Even I...
...have some compassion...
...towards animals.
...NO MATTER WHAT.

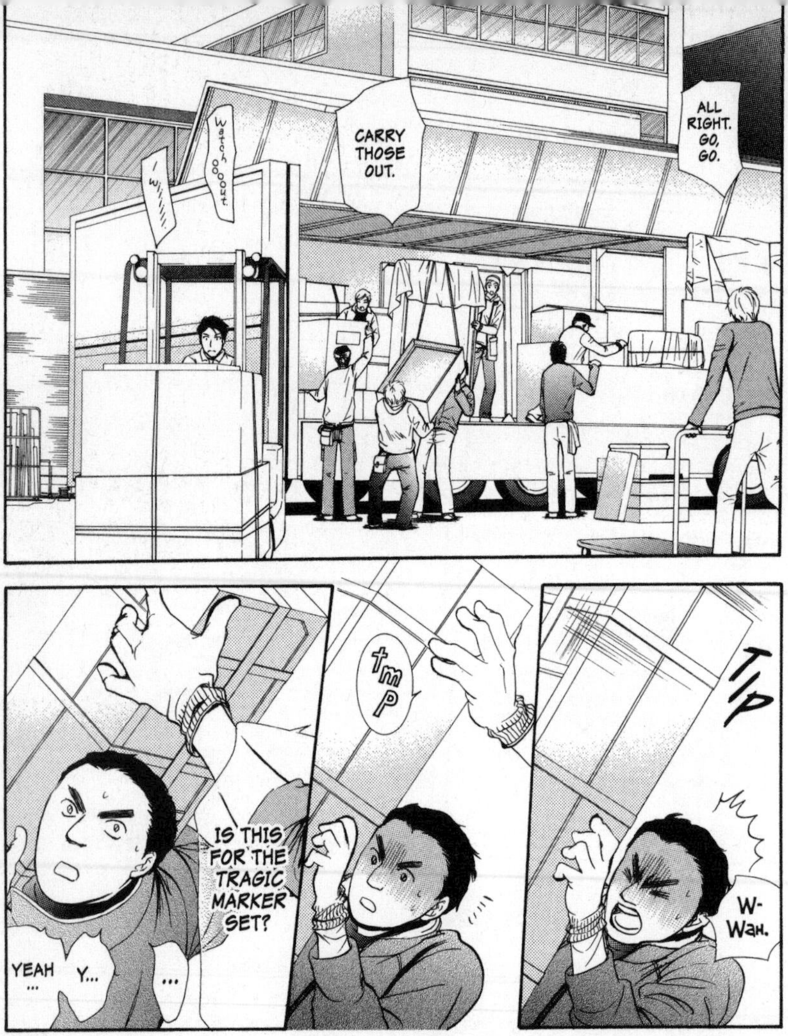
ALL RIGHT. GO, GO.
CARRY THOSE OUT.
Watch ooooout.
I wiiiiiii.
Tip
W-Wah.
tmp
IS THIS FOR THE TRAGIC MARKER SET?
...
Y...
YEAH...

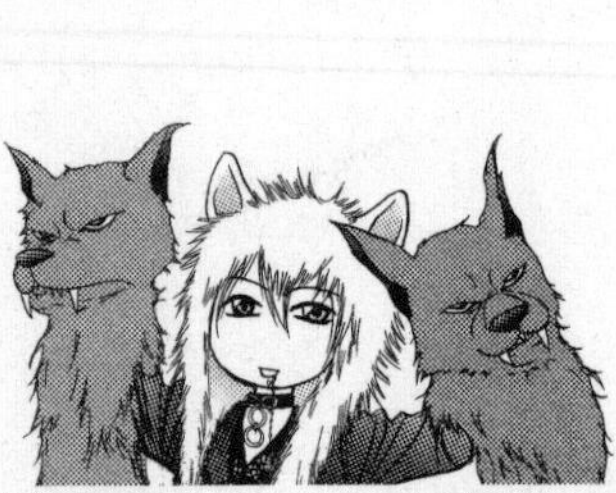

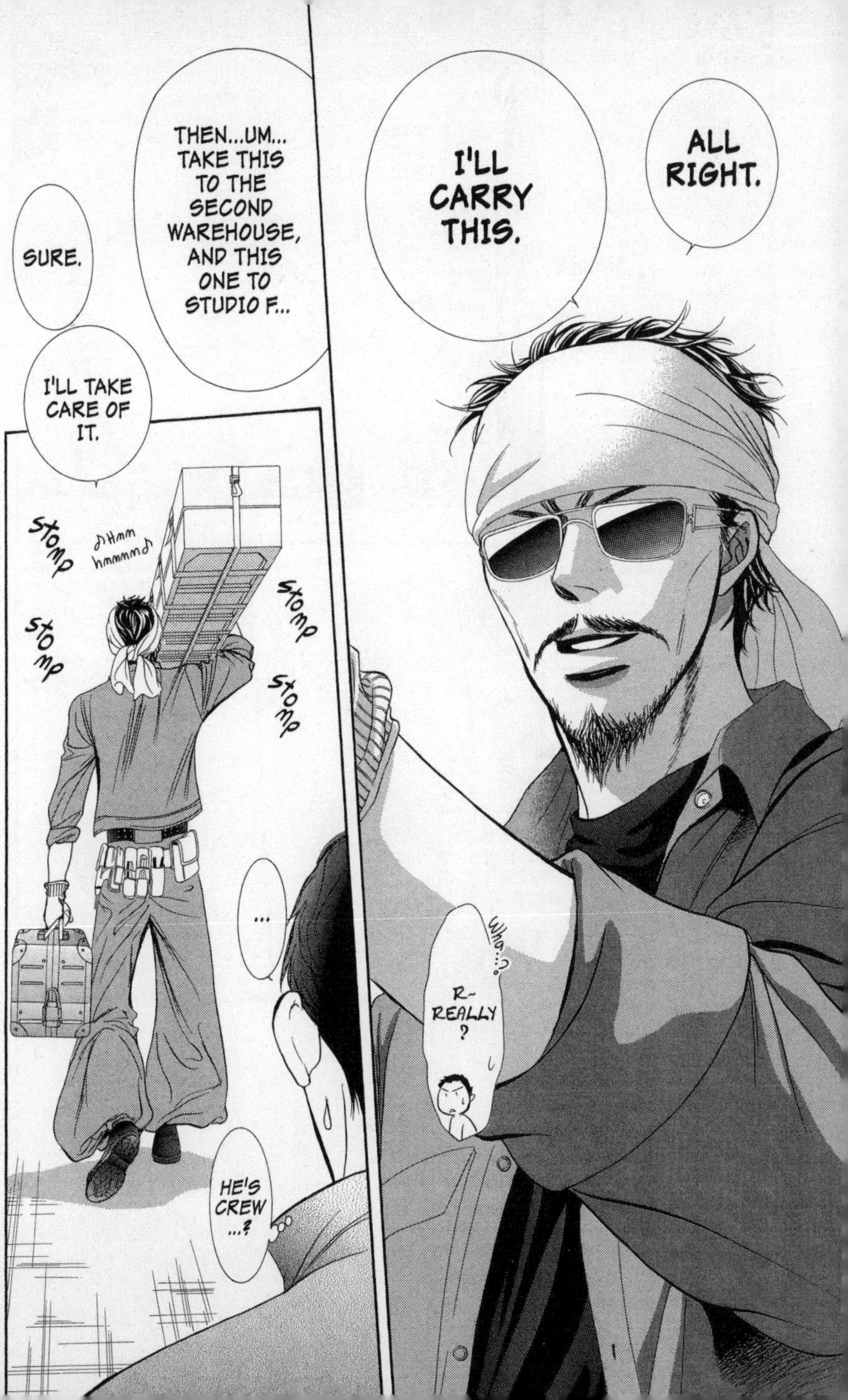
ALL RIGHT.
I'LL CARRY THIS.
Wha...?
R-REALLY?
THEN...UM... TAKE THIS TO THE SECOND WAREHOUSE, AND THIS ONE TO STUDIO F...
SURE.
I'LL TAKE CARE OF IT.
stomp
stomp
♪Hmm hmmmm♪
stomp
stomp
...
HE'S CREW...?

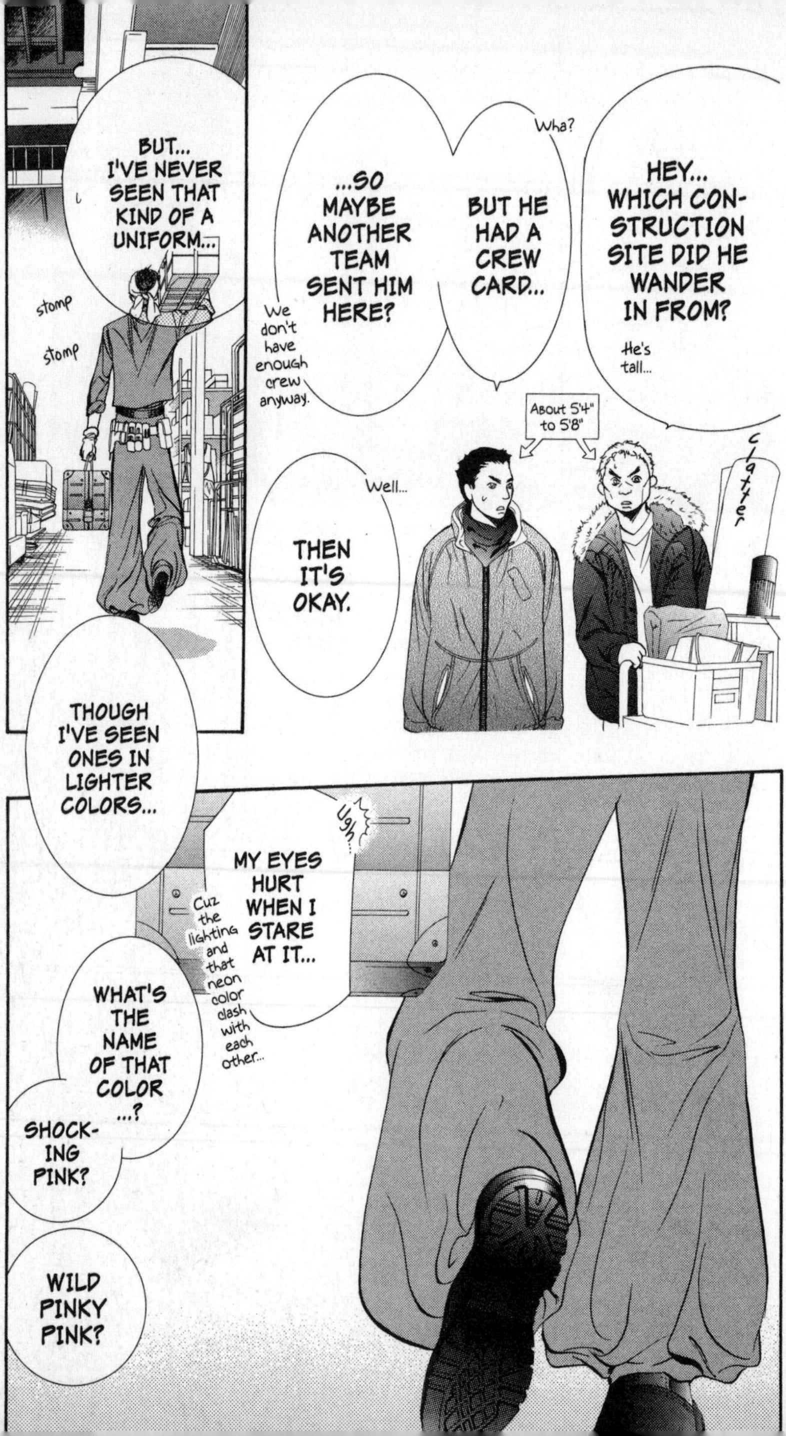
HEY... WHICH CONSTRUCTION SITE DID HE WANDER IN FROM?
He's tall...
clatter
About 5'4" to 5'8"
Wha?
BUT HE HAD A CREW CARD...
...SO MAYBE ANOTHER TEAM SENT HIM HERE?
We don't have enough crew anyway.
Well...
THEN IT'S OKAY.
BUT... I'VE NEVER SEEN THAT KIND OF A UNIFORM...
stomp
stomp
THOUGH I'VE SEEN ONES IN LIGHTER COLORS...
Ugh...
MY EYES HURT WHEN I STARE AT IT...
Cuz the lighting and that neon color clash with each other...
WHAT'S THE NAME OF THAT COLOR...?
SHOCKING-ING PINK?
WILD PINKY PINK?

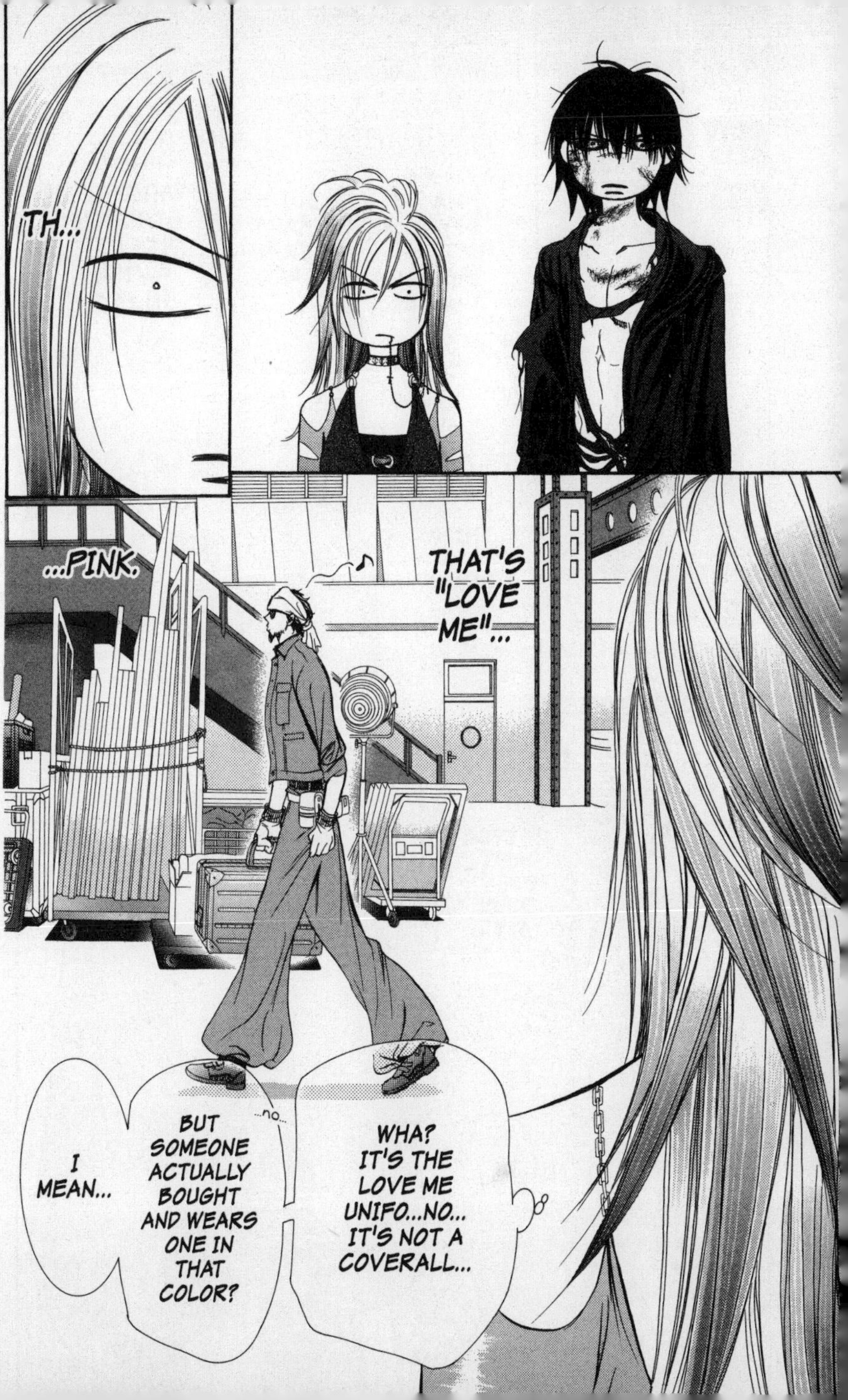
TH...
THAT'S "LOVE ME"...
...PINK.
WHA? IT'S THE LOVE ME UNIFO...NO... IT'S NOT A COVERALL...
...no...
BUT SOMEONE ACTUALLY BOUGHT AND WEARS ONE IN THAT COLOR?
I MEAN...

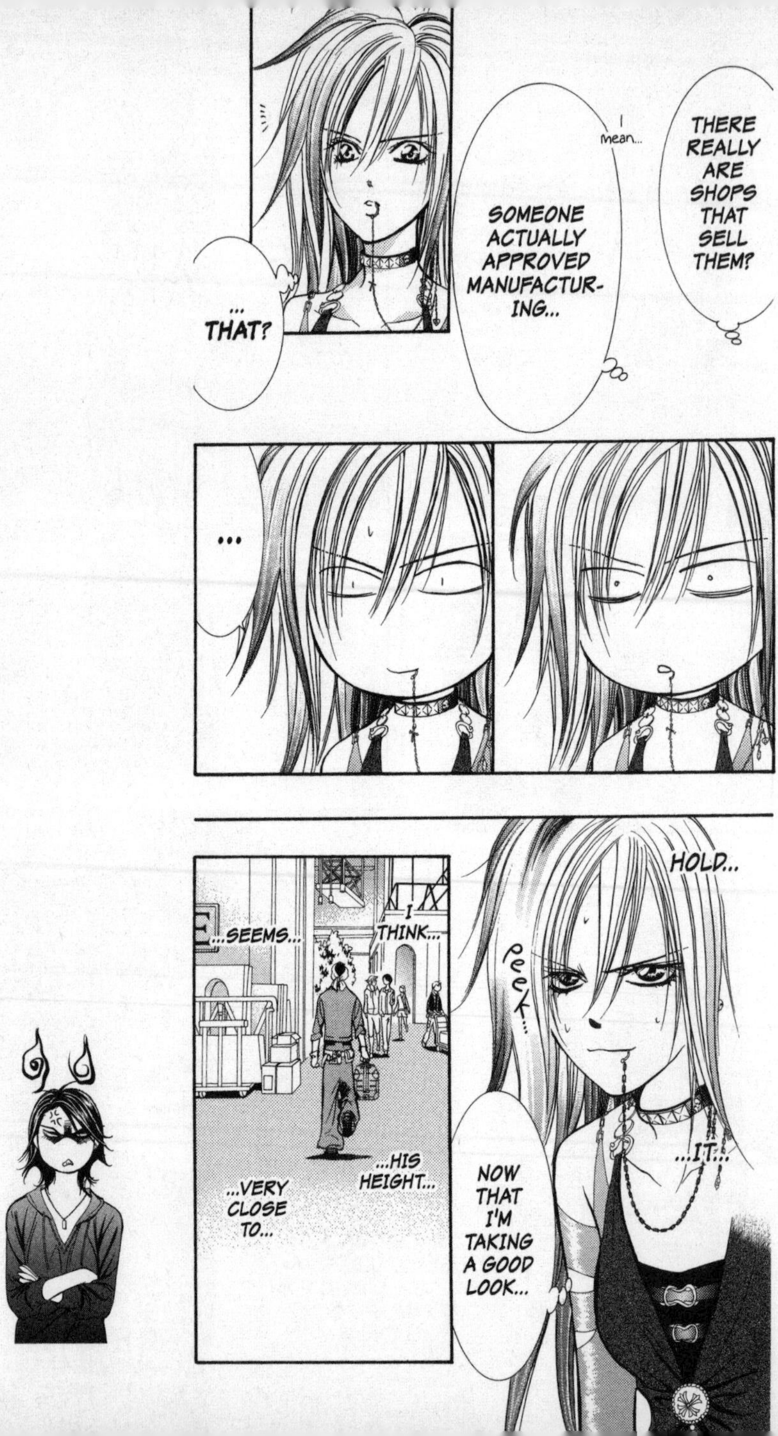
THERE REALLY ARE SHOPS THAT SELL THEM?
I mean...
SOMEONE ACTUALLY APPROVED MANUFACTURING...
...THAT?
...
HOLD...
Peek...
...IT...
NOW THAT I'M TAKING A GOOD LOOK...
I THINK...
...SEEMS...
...HIS HEIGHT...
...VERY CLOSE TO...

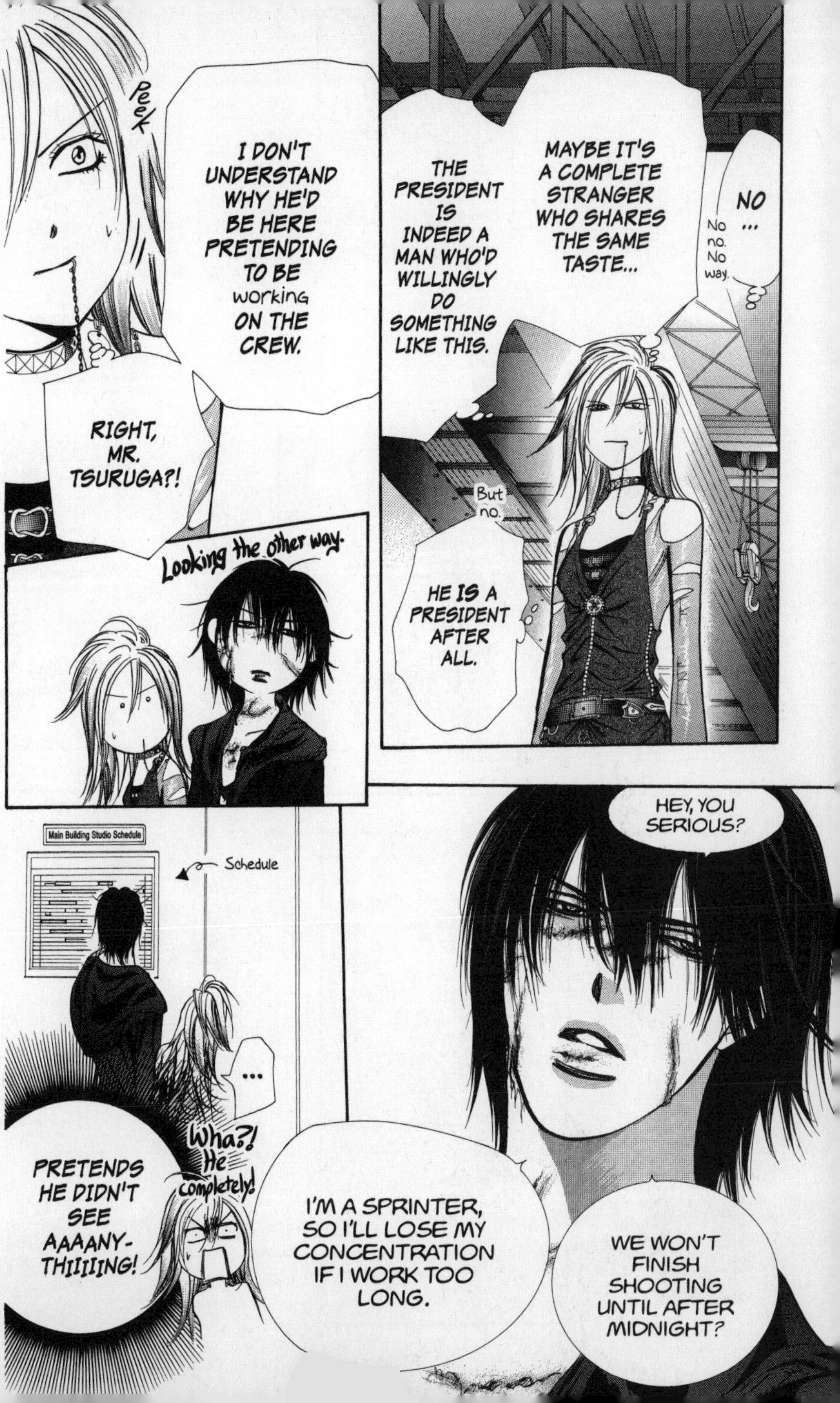
NO ...
No no. No way.
MAYBE IT'S A COMPLETE STRANGER WHO SHARES THE SAME TASTE...
THE PRESIDENT IS INDEED A MAN WHO'D WILLINGLY DO SOMETHING LIKE THIS.
But no.
HE IS A PRESIDENT AFTER ALL.
Peek
I DON'T UNDERSTAND WHY HE'D BE HERE PRETENDING TO BE working ON THE CREW.
RIGHT, MR. TSURUGA?!
Looking the other way.
HEY, YOU SERIOUS?
WE WON'T FINISH SHOOTING UNTIL AFTER MIDNIGHT?
I'M A SPRINTER, SO I'LL LOSE MY CONCENTRATION IF I WORK TOO LONG.
Main Building Studio Schedule
Schedule
...
Wha?! He completely
PRETENDS HE DIDN'T SEE AAAANY-THIIIIING!

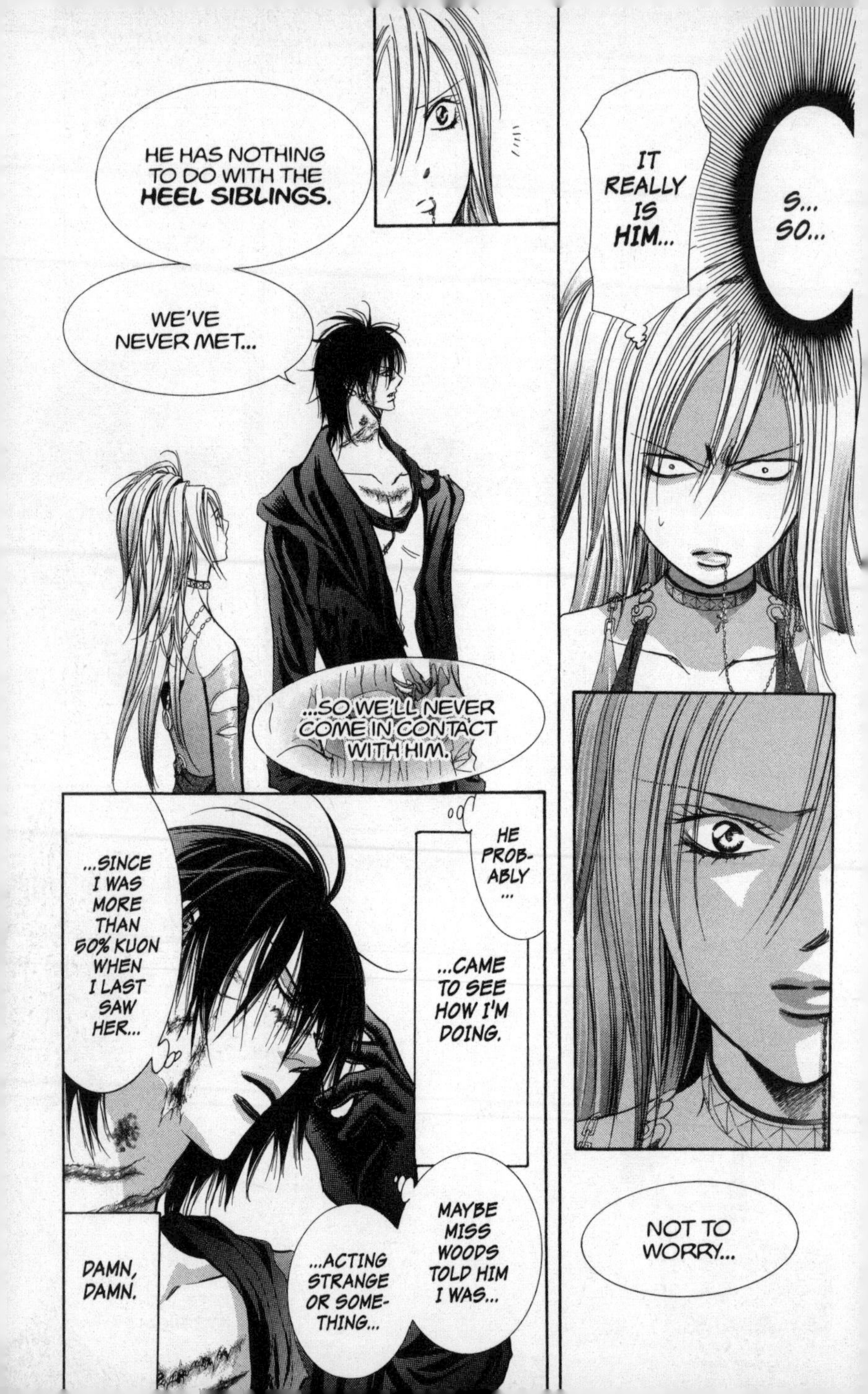

S... SO...
IT REALLY IS HIM...
NOT TO WORRY...
HE HAS NOTHING TO DO WITH THE **HEEL SIBLINGS.**
WE'VE NEVER MET...
...SO WE'LL NEVER COME IN CONTACT WITH HIM.
HE PROBABLY...
...CAME TO SEE HOW I'M DOING.
...SINCE I WAS MORE THAN 50% KUON WHEN I LAST SAW HER...
MAYBE MISS WOODS TOLD HIM I WAS...
...ACTING STRANGE OR SOMETHING...
DAMN, DAMN.

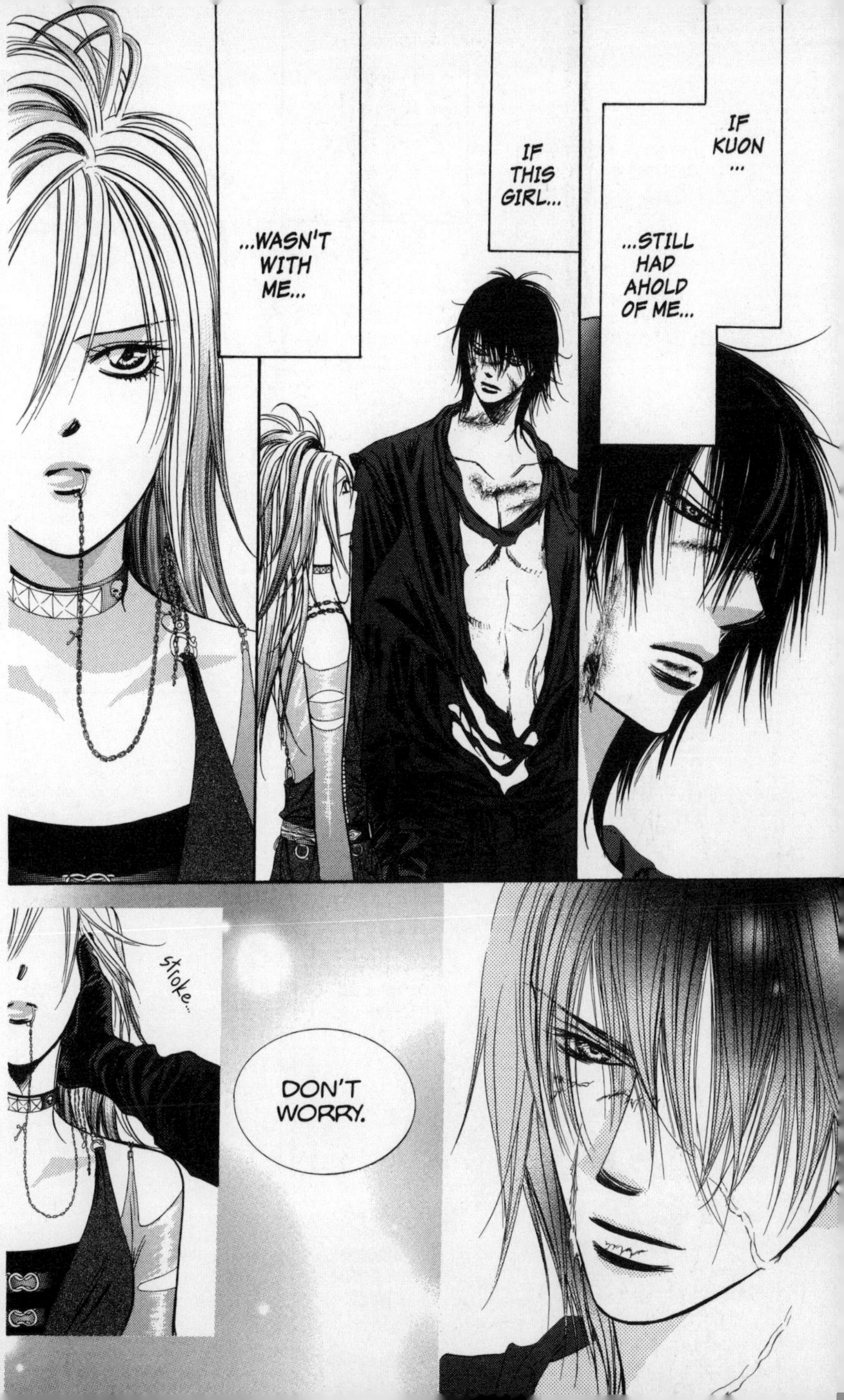
IF KUON ...
...STILL HAD AHOLD OF ME...
IF THIS GIRL...
...WASN'T WITH ME...
DON'T WORRY.
stroke...

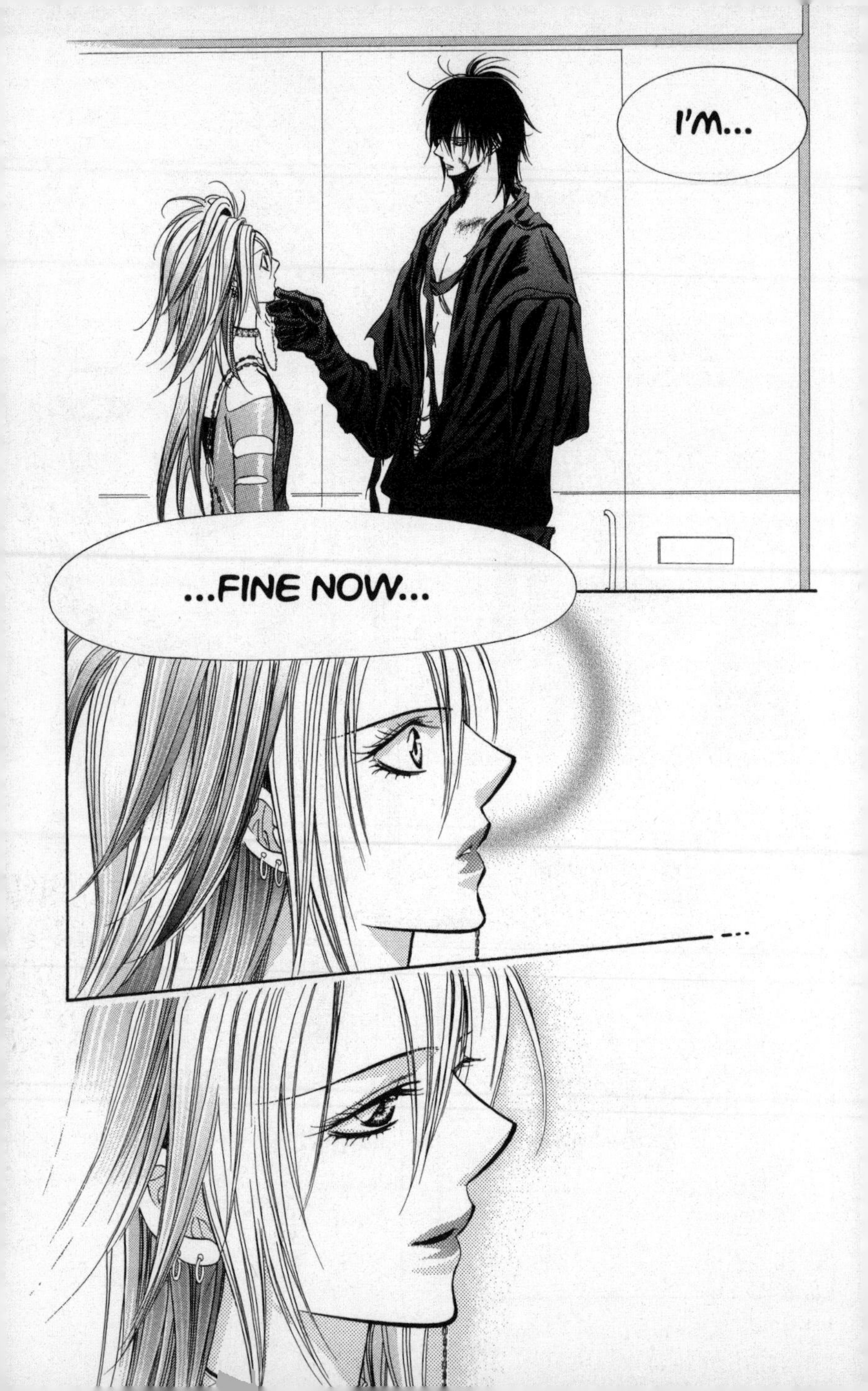
I'M...
...FINE NOW...
...

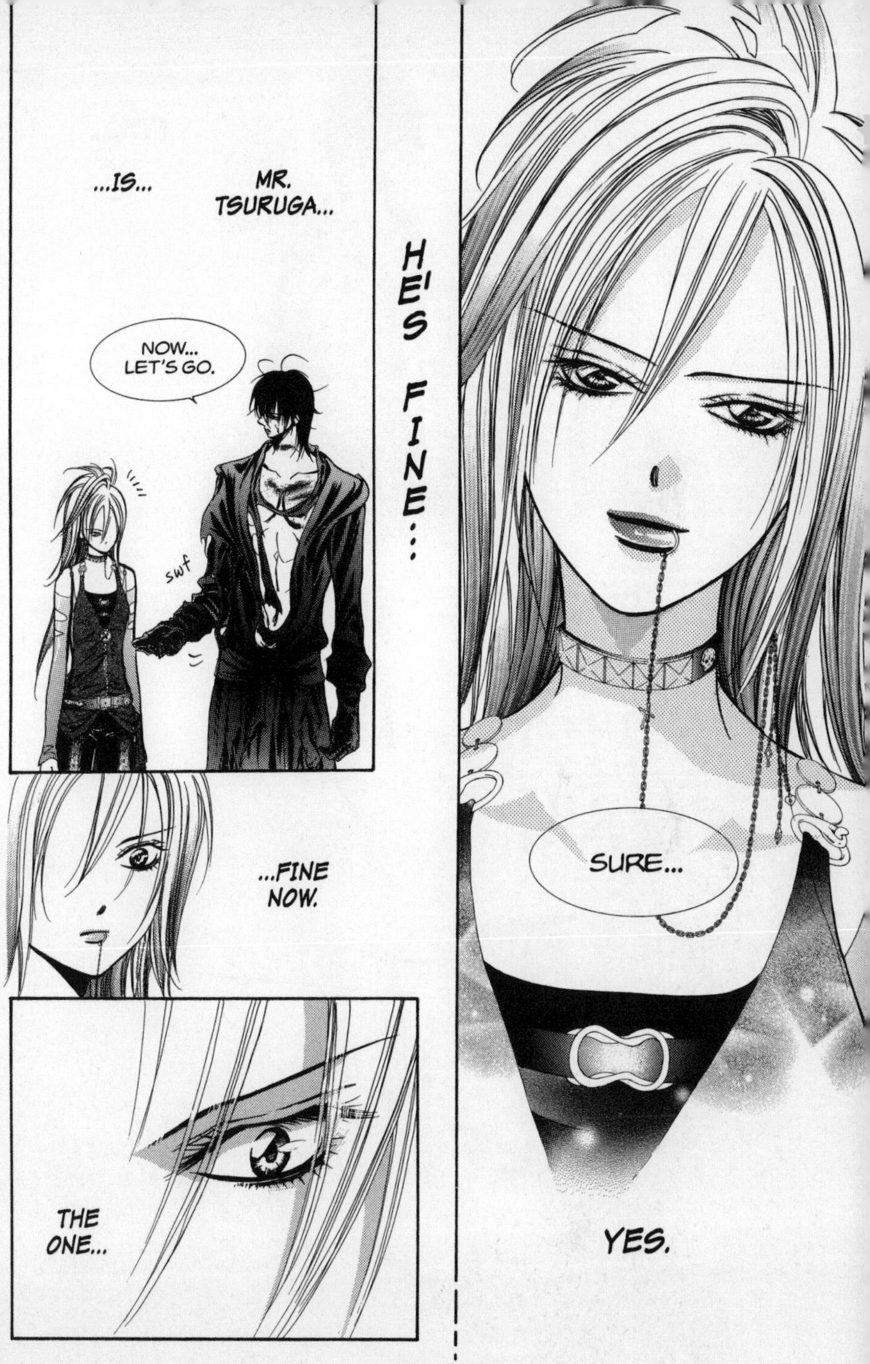
HE'S FINE...
SURE...
YES.
MR. TSURUGA...
...IS...
NOW... LET'S GO.
swf
...FINE NOW.
THE ONE...

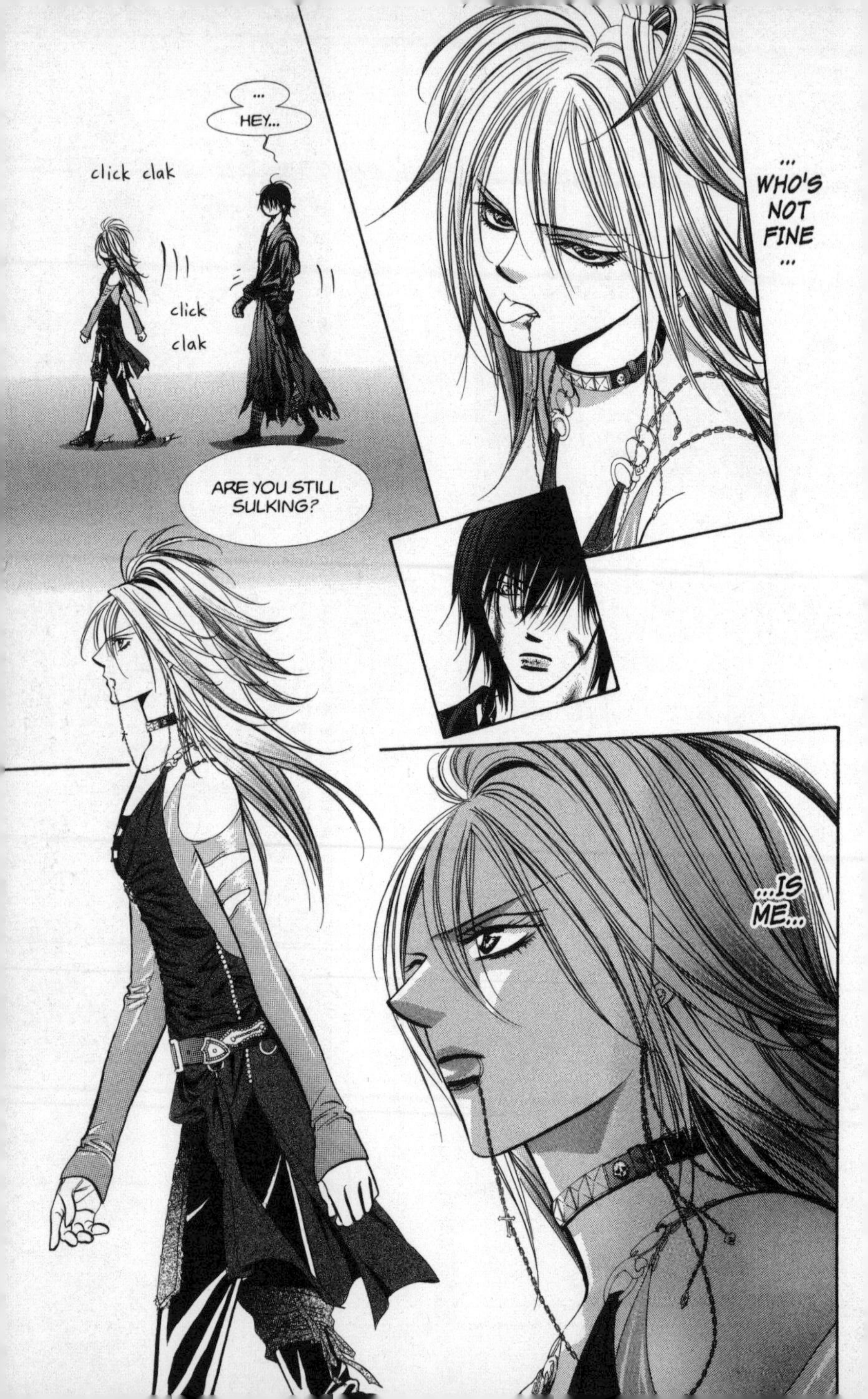

... WHO'S NOT FINE ...
...
HEY...
click clak
click clak
ARE YOU STILL SULKING?
...IS ME...

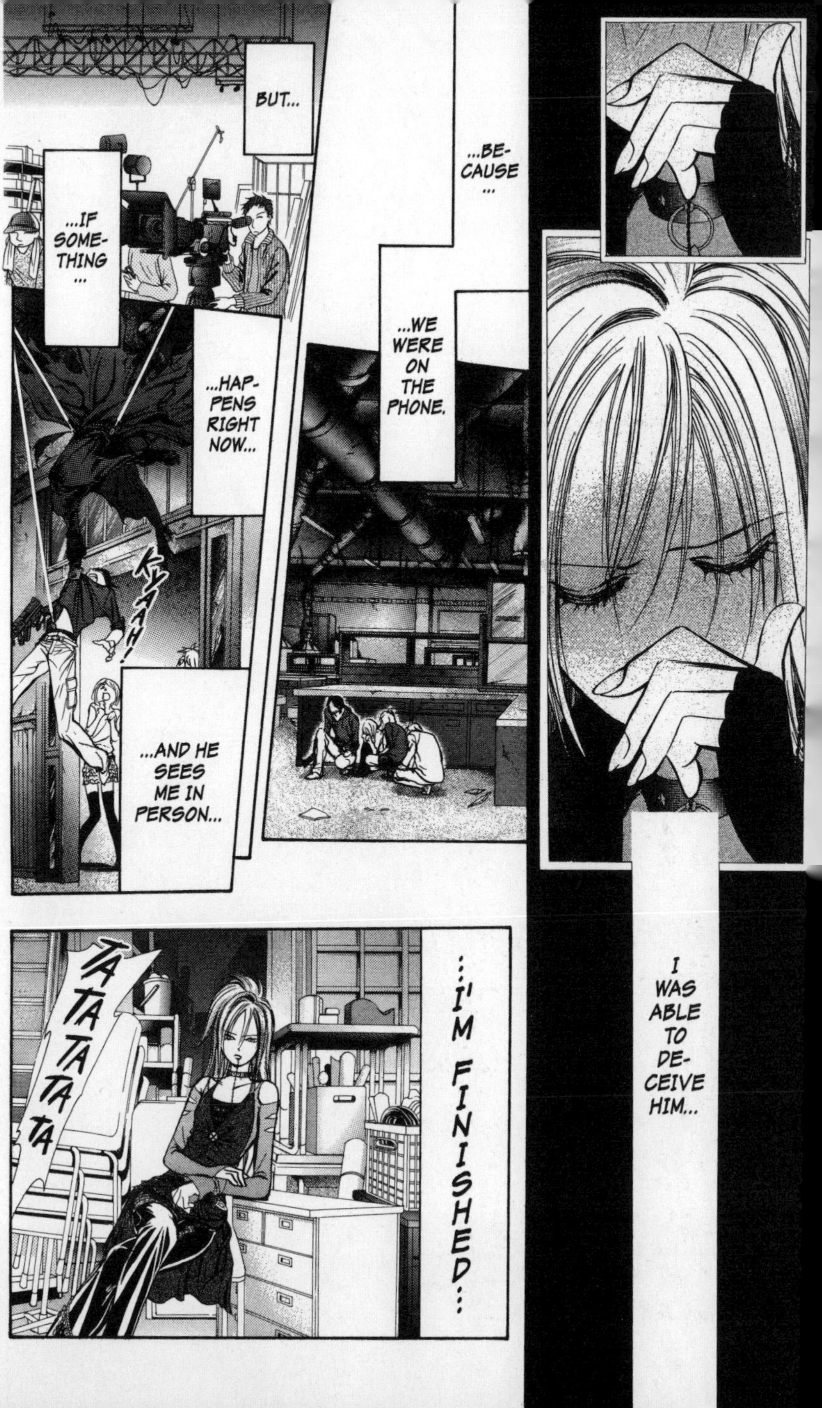
I WAS ABLE TO DE-CEIVE HIM...
...BE-CAUSE...
...WE WERE ON THE PHONE.
BUT...
...IF SOME-THING...
...HAP-PENS RIGHT NOW...
KYAAH!
...AND HE SEES ME IN PERSON...
...I'M FINISHED...
TA TA TA TA TA

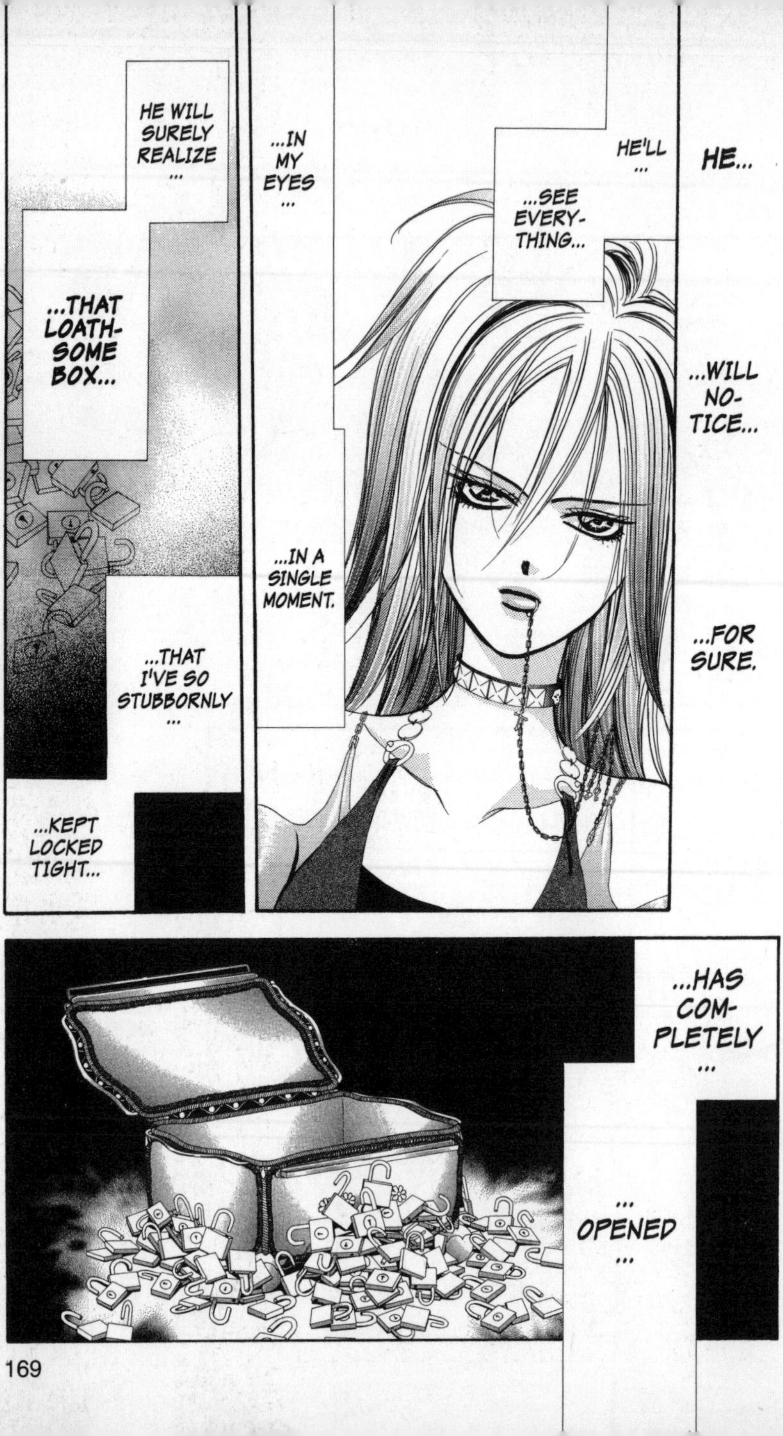
HE...
...WILL NO-TICE...
...FOR SURE.
HE'LL ...
...SEE EVERY-THING...
...IN MY EYES ...
...IN A SINGLE MOMENT.
HE WILL SURELY REALIZE ...
...THAT LOATH-SOME BOX...
...THAT I'VE SO STUBBORNLY ...
...KEPT LOCKED TIGHT...
...HAS COM-PLETELY ...
... OPENED ...

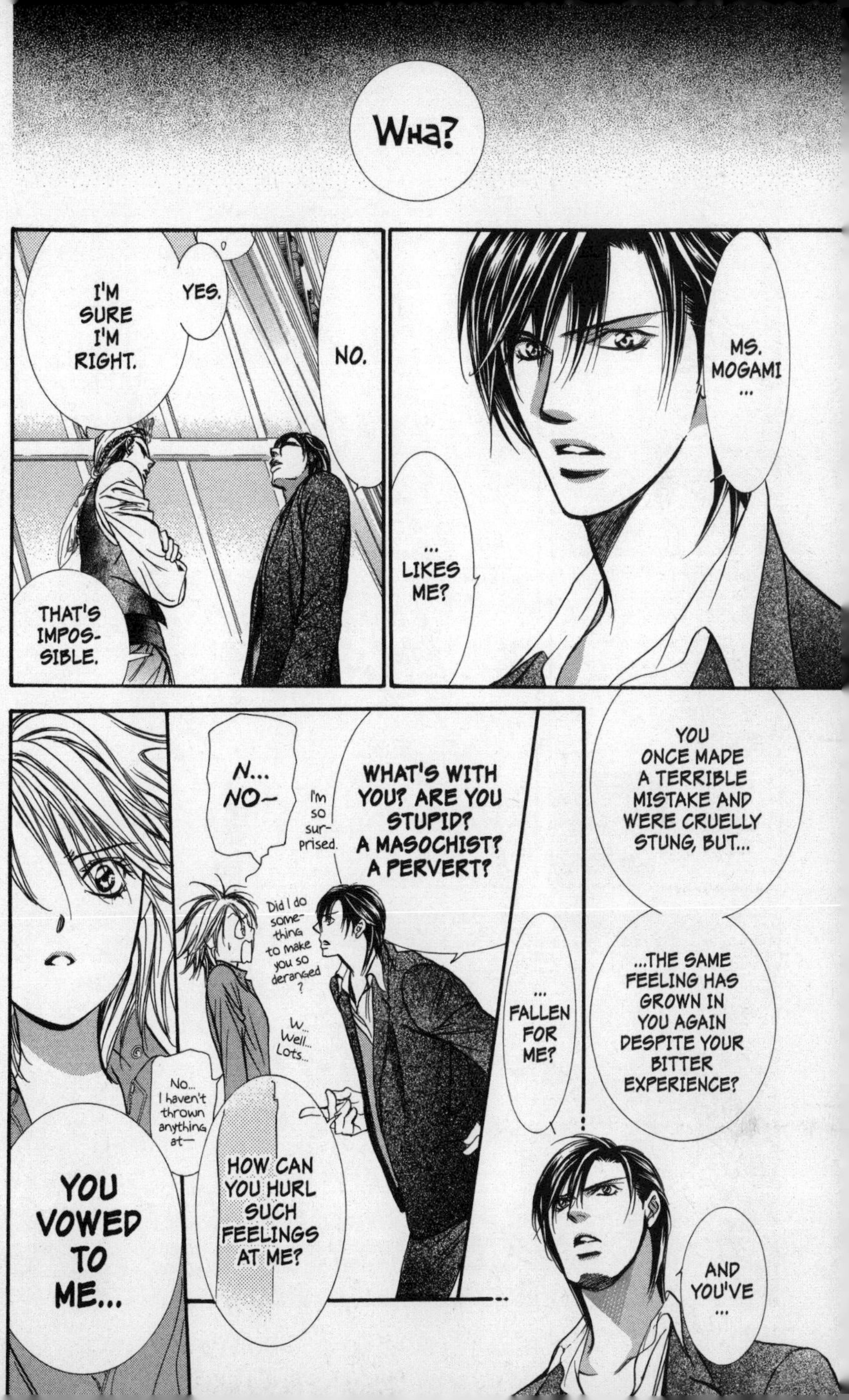
WHA?
MS. MOGAMI ...
... LIKES ME?
NO.
YES.
I'M SURE I'M RIGHT.
THAT'S IMPOS-SIBLE.
YOU ONCE MADE A TERRIBLE MISTAKE AND WERE CRUELLY STUNG, BUT...
...THE SAME FEELING HAS GROWN IN YOU AGAIN DESPITE YOUR BITTER EXPERIENCE?
AND YOU'VE ...
... FALLEN FOR ME?
WHAT'S WITH YOU? ARE YOU STUPID? A MASOCHIST? A PERVERT?
I'm so sur-prised.
N... NO—
Did I do some-thing to make you so deranged?
W... Well... Lots...
HOW CAN YOU HURL SUCH FEELINGS AT ME?
No... I haven't thrown anything at—
YOU VOWED TO ME...

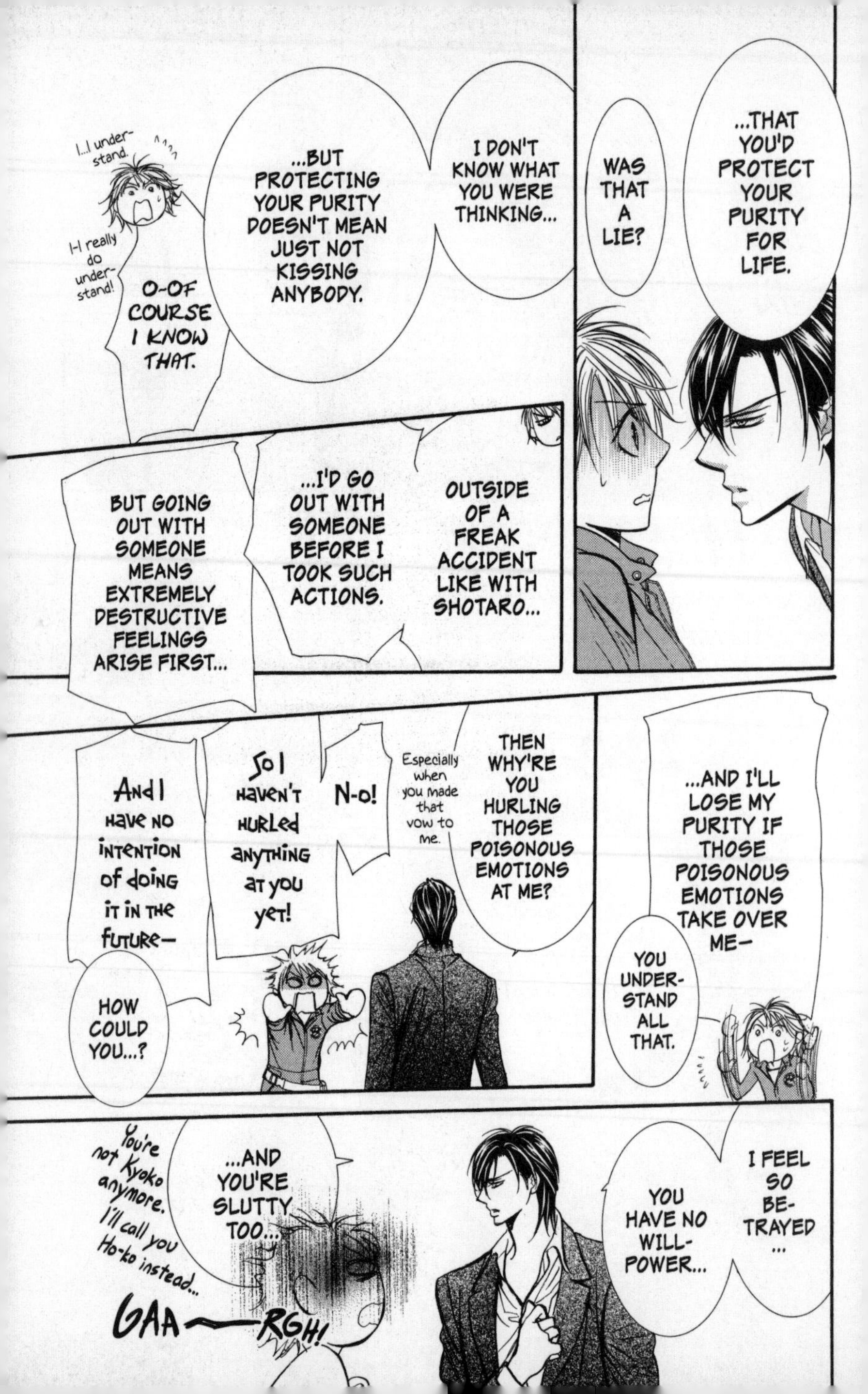
...THAT YOU'D PROTECT YOUR PURITY FOR LIFE.
WAS THAT A LIE?
I DON'T KNOW WHAT YOU WERE THINKING...
...BUT PROTECTING YOUR PURITY DOESN'T MEAN JUST NOT KISSING ANYBODY.
O-OF COURSE I KNOW THAT.
I...I under-stand.
I-I really do under-stand!
OUTSIDE OF A FREAK ACCIDENT LIKE WITH SHOTARO...
...I'D GO OUT WITH SOMEONE BEFORE I TOOK SUCH ACTIONS.
BUT GOING OUT WITH SOMEONE MEANS EXTREMELY DESTRUCTIVE FEELINGS ARISE FIRST...
...AND I'LL LOSE MY PURITY IF THOSE POISONOUS EMOTIONS TAKE OVER ME—
YOU UNDER-STAND ALL THAT.
THEN WHY'RE YOU HURLING THOSE POISONOUS EMOTIONS AT ME?
Especially when you made that vow to me.
N-o!
So I haven't hurled anything at you yet!
And I have no intention of doing it in the future—
HOW COULD YOU...?
I FEEL SO BE-TRAYED...
YOU HAVE NO WILL-POWER...
...AND YOU'RE SLUTTY TOO...
You're not Kyoko anymore. I'll call you Ho-ko instead...
GAA—RGH!

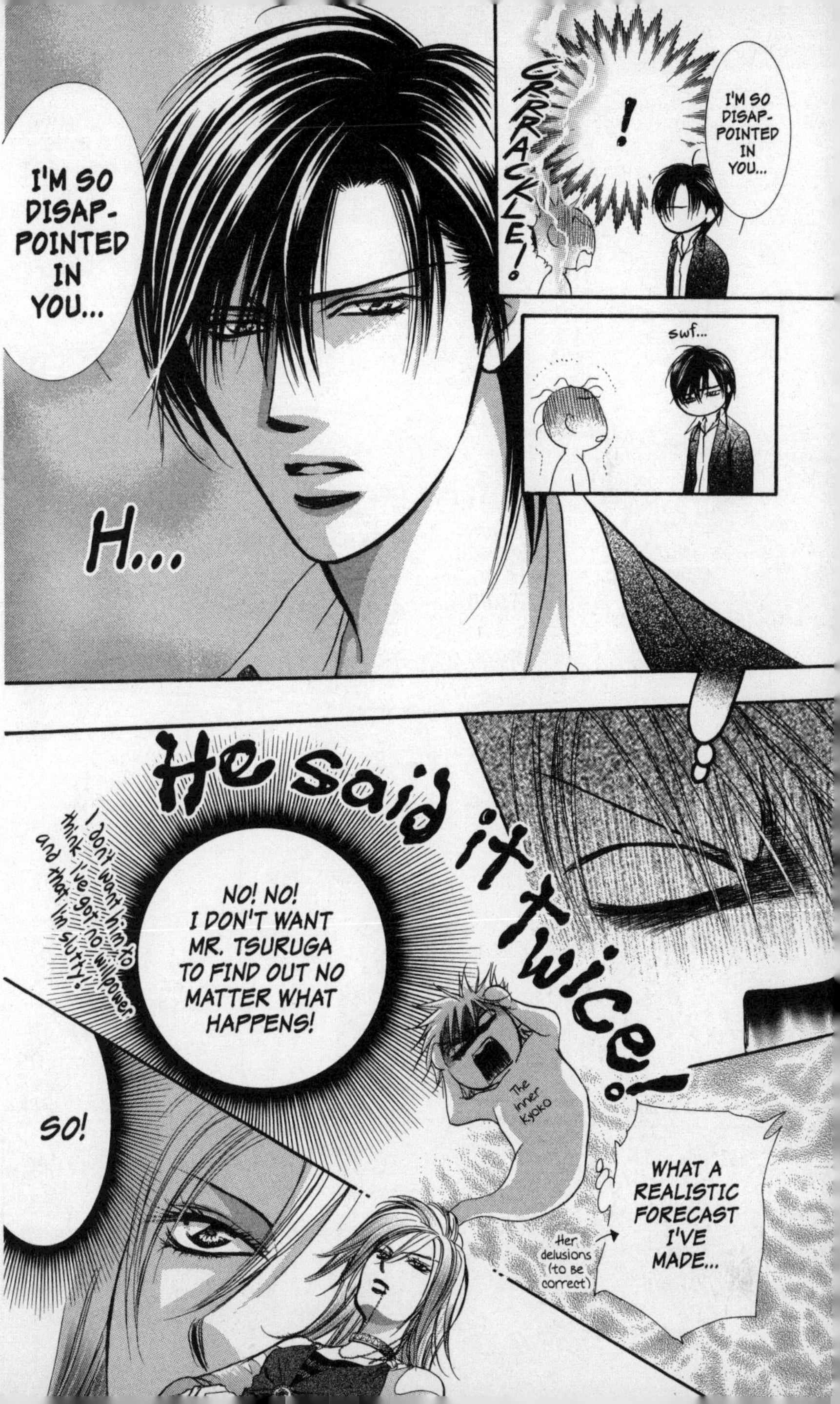
I'M SO DISAP-POINTED IN YOU...
!
CRRRACKLE!
swf...
I'M SO DISAP-POINTED IN YOU...
H...
He said it twice!
NO! NO! I DON'T WANT MR. TSURUGA TO FIND OUT NO MATTER WHAT HAPPENS!
I don't want him to think I've got no willpower and that I'm slutty!
The inner Kyoko
WHAT A REALISTIC FORECAST I'VE MADE...
Her delusions (to be correct)
SO!

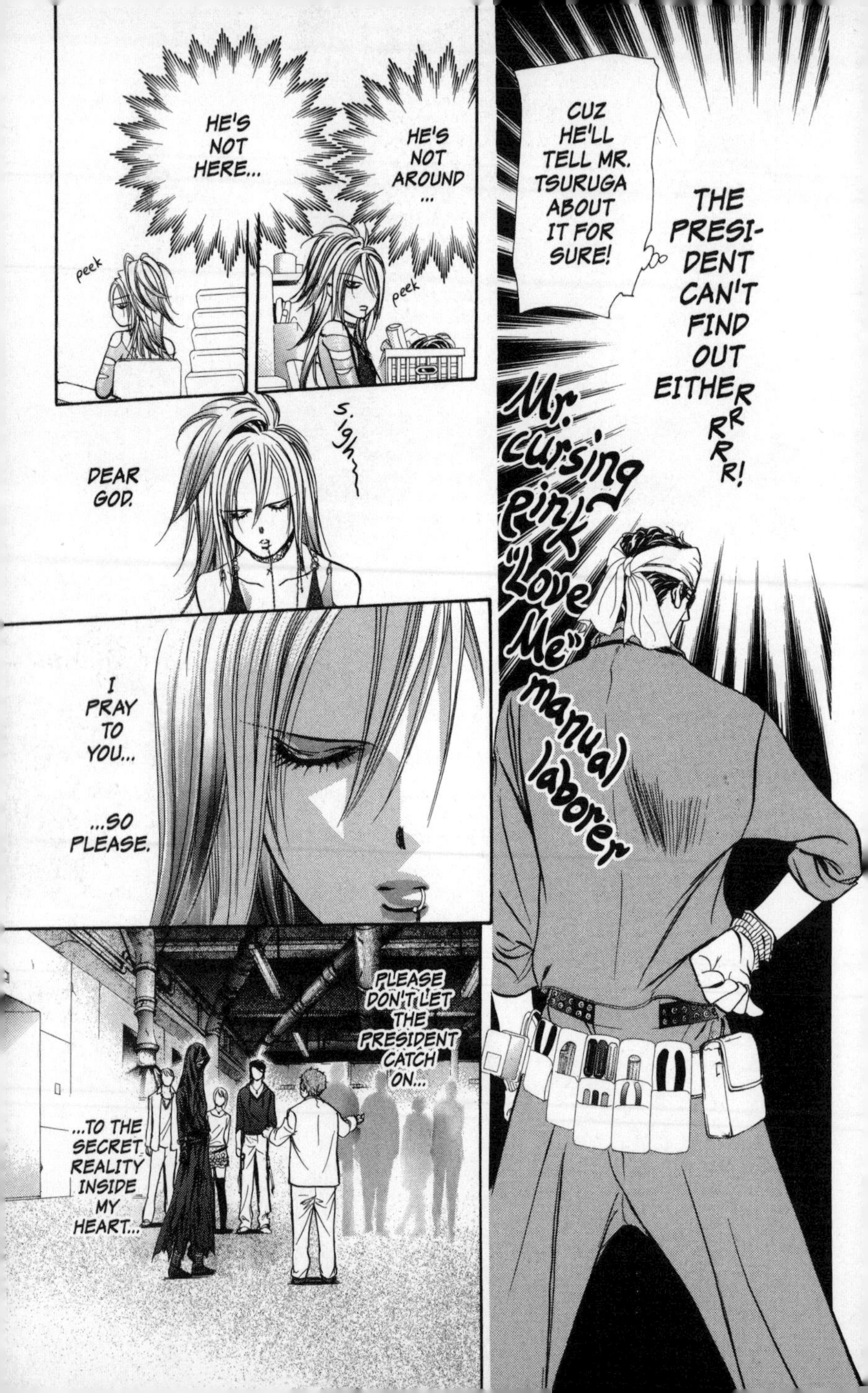
THE PRESIDENT CAN'T FIND OUT EITHERRRRR!
CUZ HE'LL TELL MR. TSURUGA ABOUT IT FOR SURE!
Mr. Cursing Pink "Love Me" manual laborer
HE'S NOT AROUND ...
peek
HE'S NOT HERE...
peek
sigh
DEAR GOD.
I PRAY TO YOU...
...SO PLEASE.
PLEASE DON'T LET THE PRESIDENT CATCH ON...
...TO THE SECRET REALITY INSIDE MY HEART...

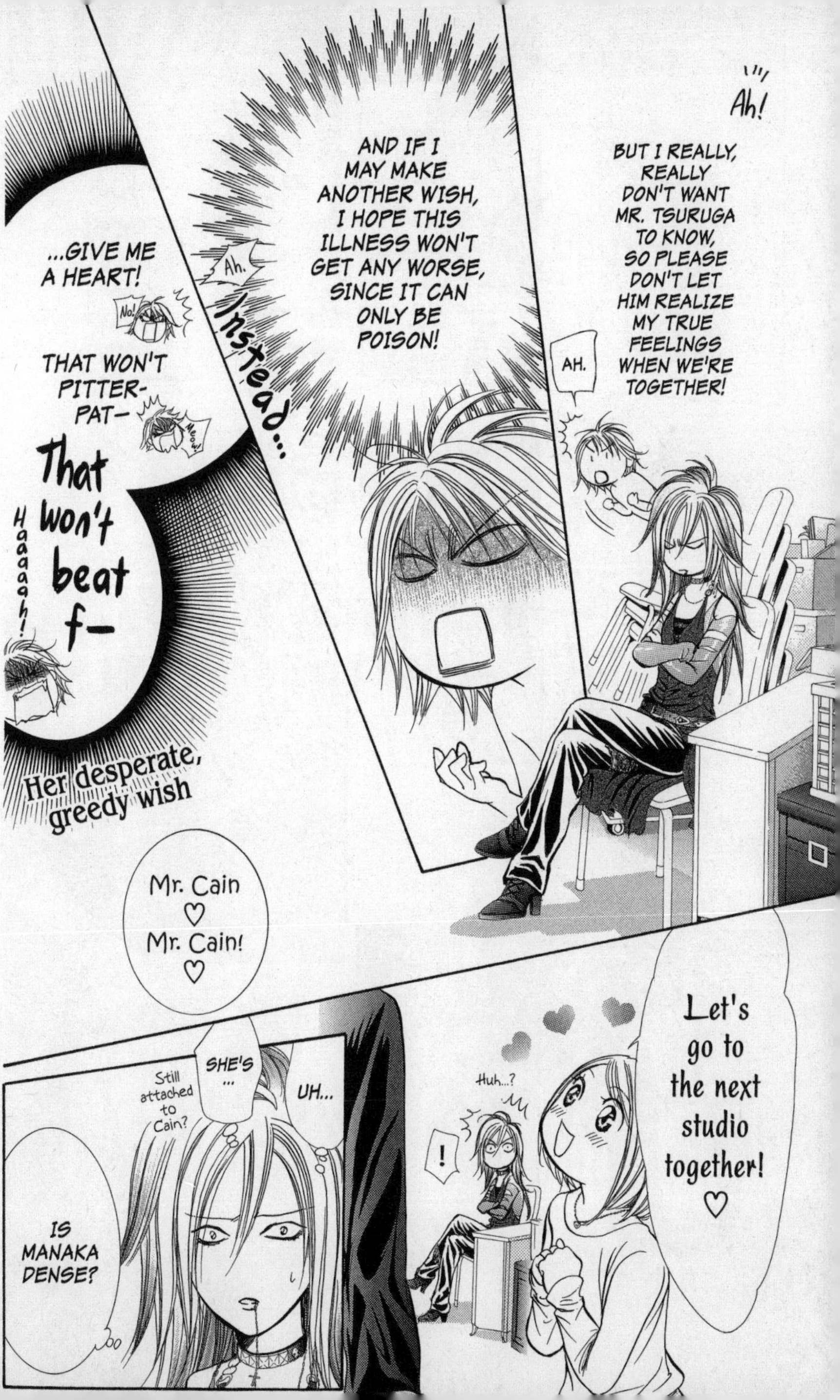
Ah!
BUT I REALLY, REALLY DON'T WANT MR. TSURUGA TO KNOW, SO PLEASE DON'T LET HIM REALIZE MY TRUE FEELINGS WHEN WE'RE TOGETHER!
AH.
AND IF I MAY MAKE ANOTHER WISH, I HOPE THIS ILLNESS WON'T GET ANY WORSE, SINCE IT CAN ONLY BE POISON!
Ah.
Instead...
...GIVE ME A HEART!
No!
THAT WON'T PITTER-PAT—
Meow!
That won't beat f—
Haaaagh!
Her desperate, greedy wish
Let's go to the next studio together! ♡
Huh...?
!
Mr. Cain ♡ Mr. Cain! ♡
UH...
SHE'S...
Still attached to Cain?
IS MANAKA DENSE?

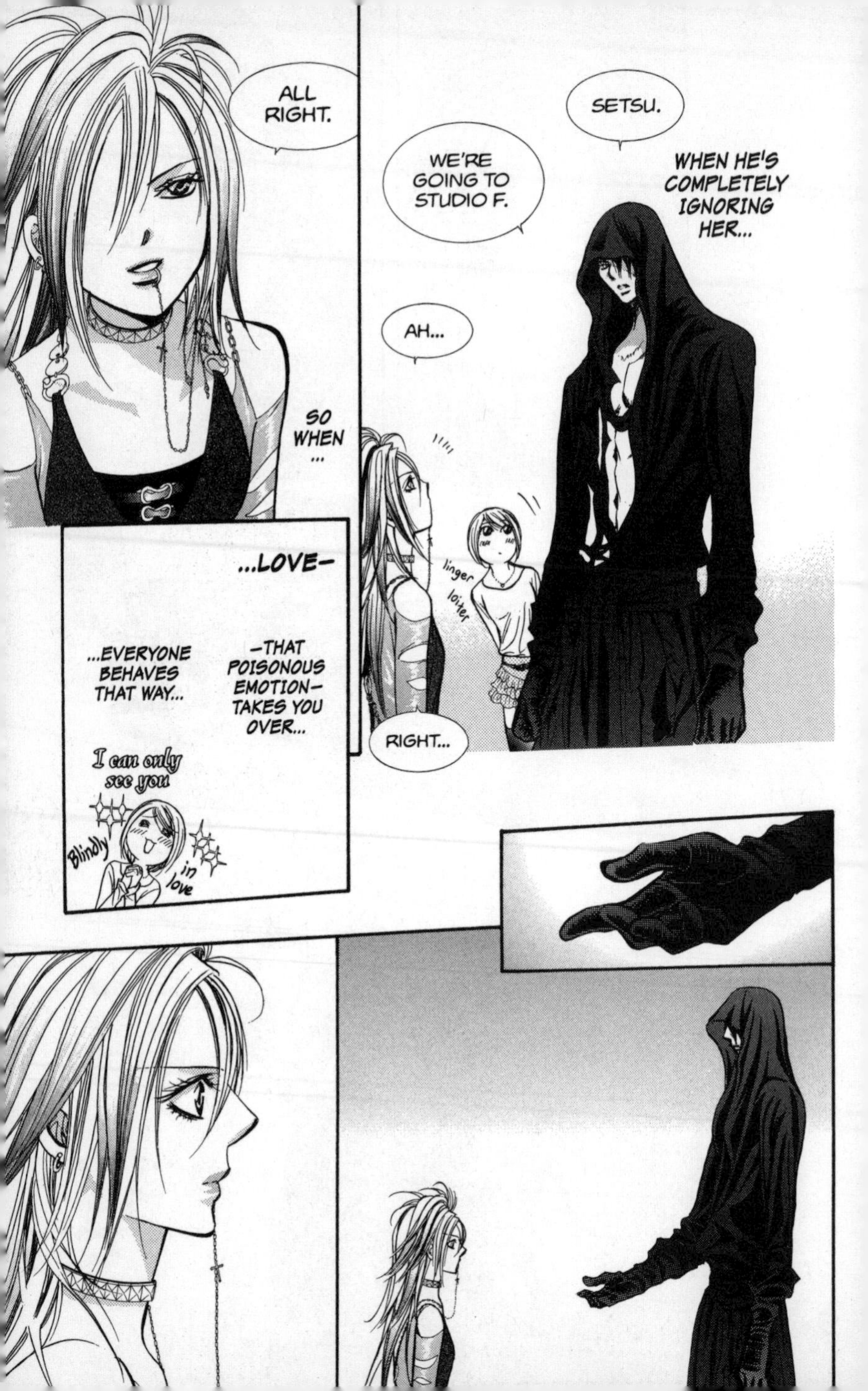

SETSU.
WE'RE GOING TO STUDIO F.
WHEN HE'S COMPLETELY IGNORING HER...
AH...
linger
loiter
RIGHT...
ALL RIGHT.
SO WHEN ...
...LOVE—
—THAT POISONOUS EMOTION— TAKES YOU OVER...
...EVERYONE BEHAVES THAT WAY...
I can only see you
Blindly
in love

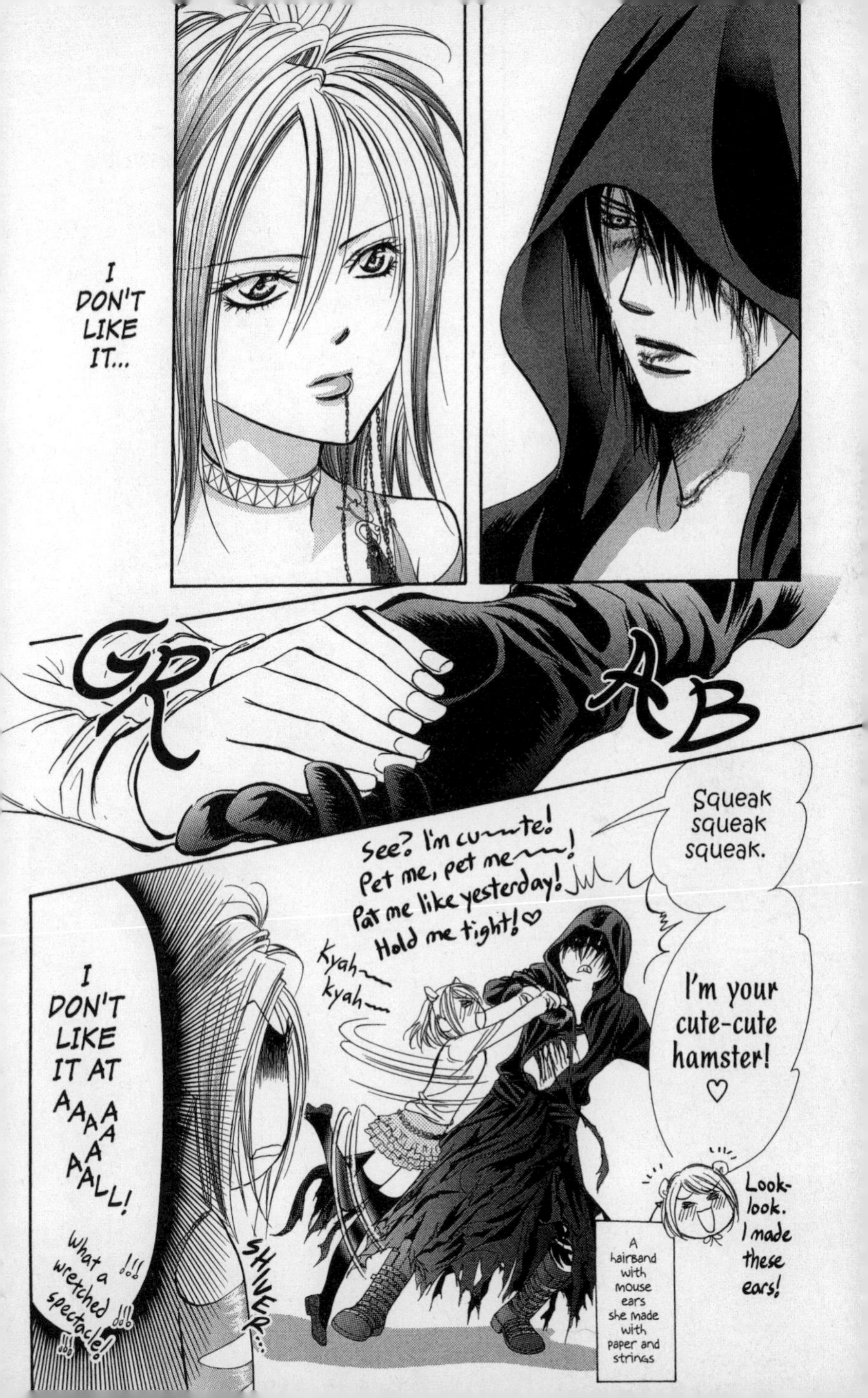
I DON'T LIKE IT...
GRAB
Squeak squeak squeak.
I'm your cute-cute hamster! ♡
See? I'm cu~~te! Pet me, pet me~~! Pat me like yesterday! Hold me tight! ♡
Kyah~ kyah~
Look-look. I made these ears!
A hairband with mouse ears she made with paper and strings
SHIVER...
I DON'T LIKE IT AT AAAAAAALL!
What a wretched spectacle!

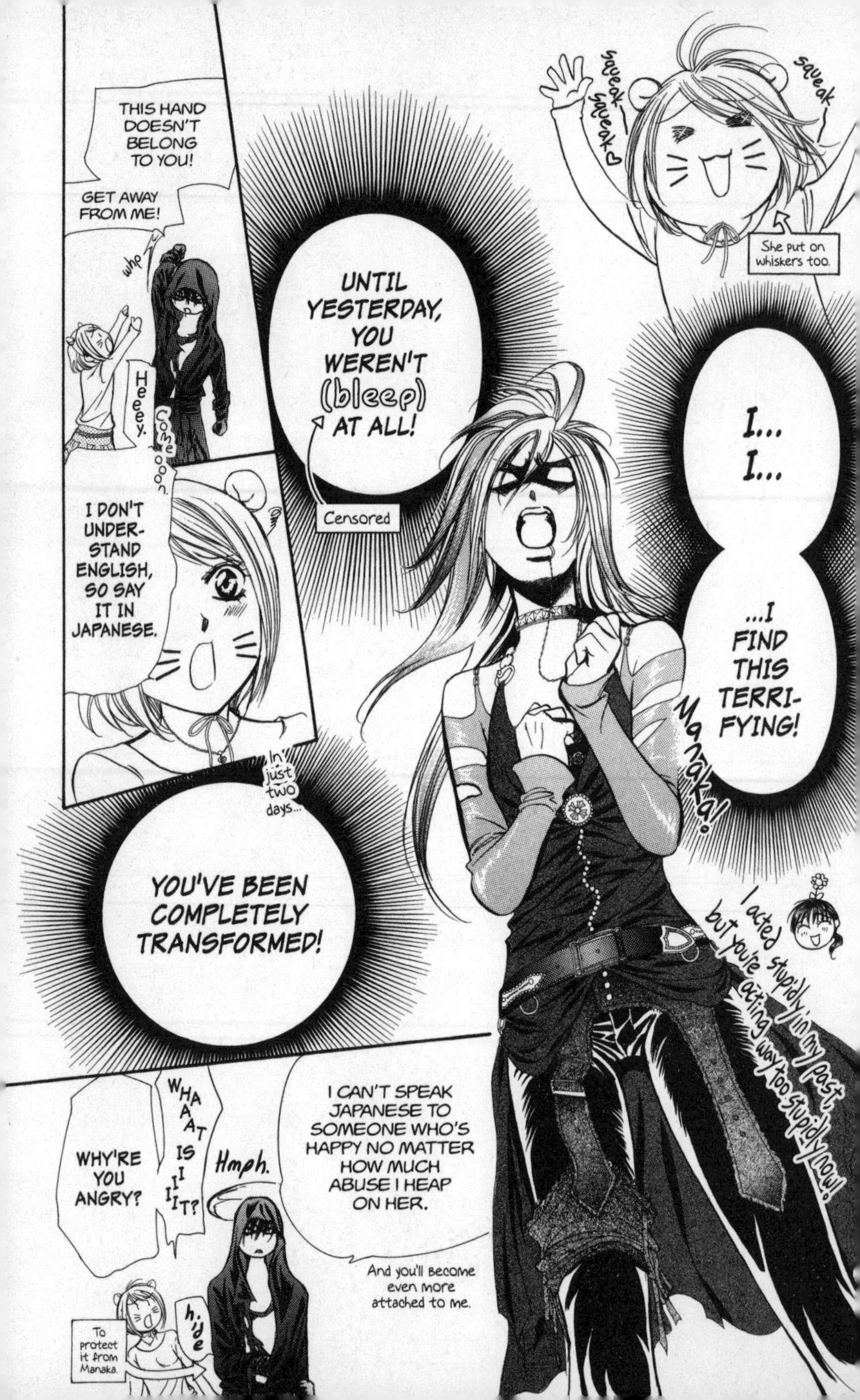
squeak
squeak squeak squeak♥
She put on whiskers too.
THIS HAND DOESN'T BELONG TO YOU!
GET AWAY FROM ME!
whp
Heeey.
Come ooon.
I DON'T UNDERSTAND ENGLISH, SO SAY IT IN JAPANESE.
I... I...
...I FIND THIS TERRIFYING!
Manaka!
UNTIL YESTERDAY, YOU WEREN'T (bleep) AT ALL!
Censored
In just two days...
YOU'VE BEEN COMPLETELY TRANSFORMED!
I acted stupidly in my past, but you're acting way too stupidly now!
I CAN'T SPEAK JAPANESE TO SOMEONE WHO'S HAPPY NO MATTER HOW MUCH ABUSE I HEAP ON HER.
And you'll become even more attached to me.
Hmph.
WHAAAT IS IIIIT?
WHY'RE YOU ANGRY?
hide
To protect it from Manaka.

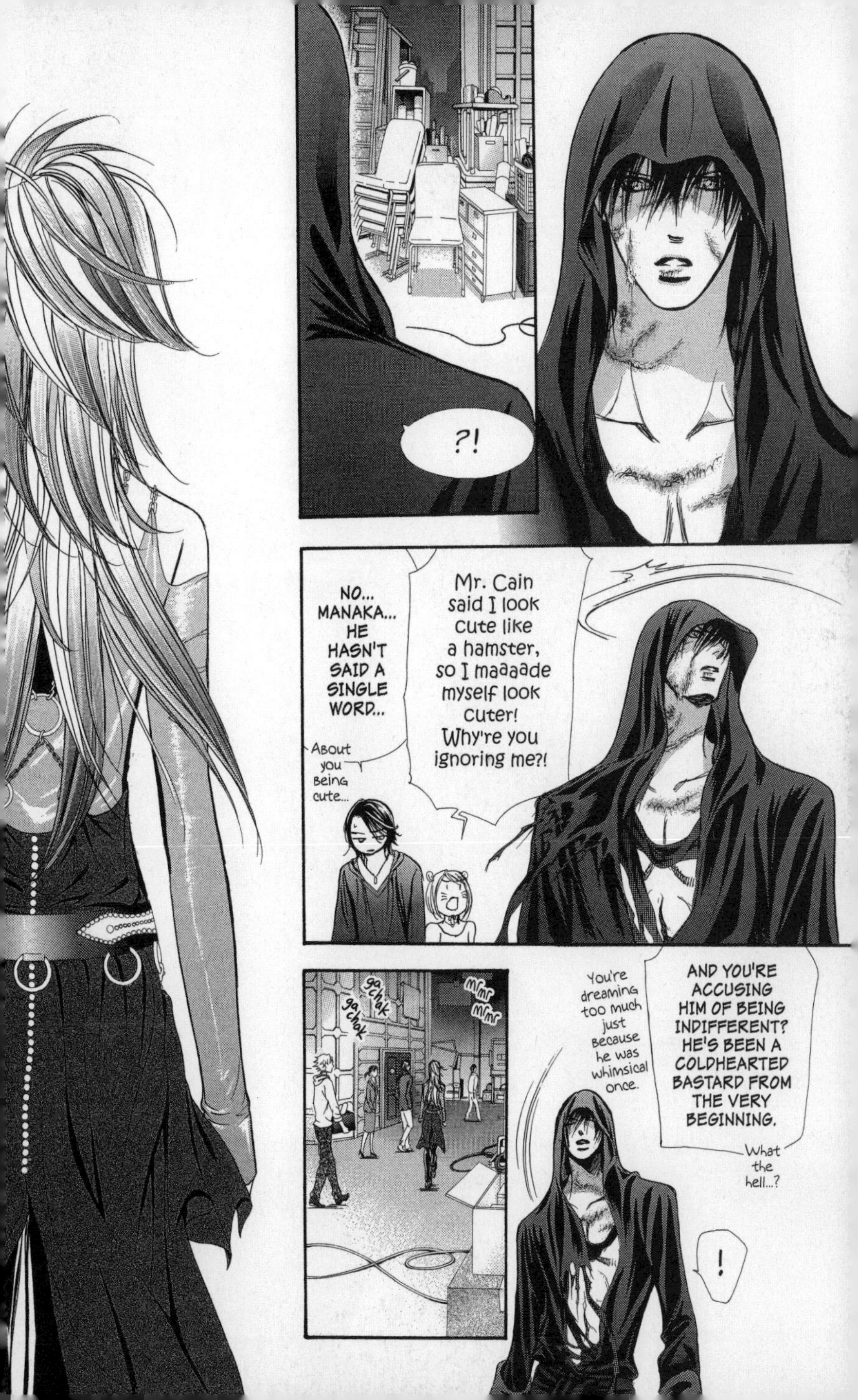
?!
Mr. Cain said I look cute like a hamster, so I maaaade myself look cuter! Why're you ignoring me?!
NO... MANAKA... HE HASN'T SAID A SINGLE WORD...
About you being cute...
AND YOU'RE ACCUSING HIM OF BEING INDIFFERENT? HE'S BEEN A COLDHEARTED BASTARD FROM THE VERY BEGINNING.
You're dreaming too much just because he was whimsical once.
mr mr mr mr
ga chak ga chak
What the hell...?
!

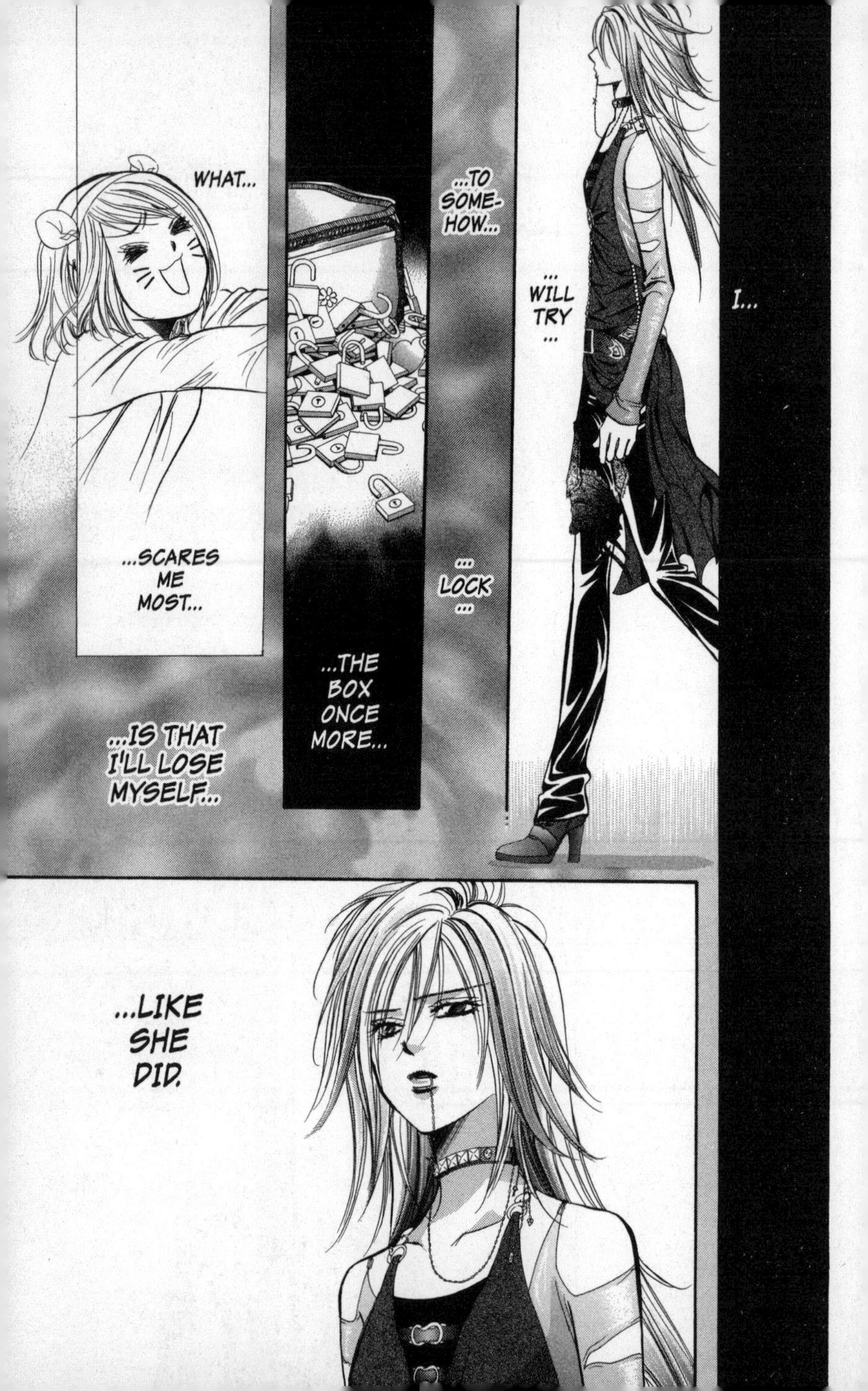
I...
...WILL TRY...
...TO SOME-HOW...
...LOCK...
...THE BOX ONCE MORE...
WHAT...
...SCARES ME MOST...
...IS THAT I'LL LOSE MYSELF...
...LIKE SHE DID.

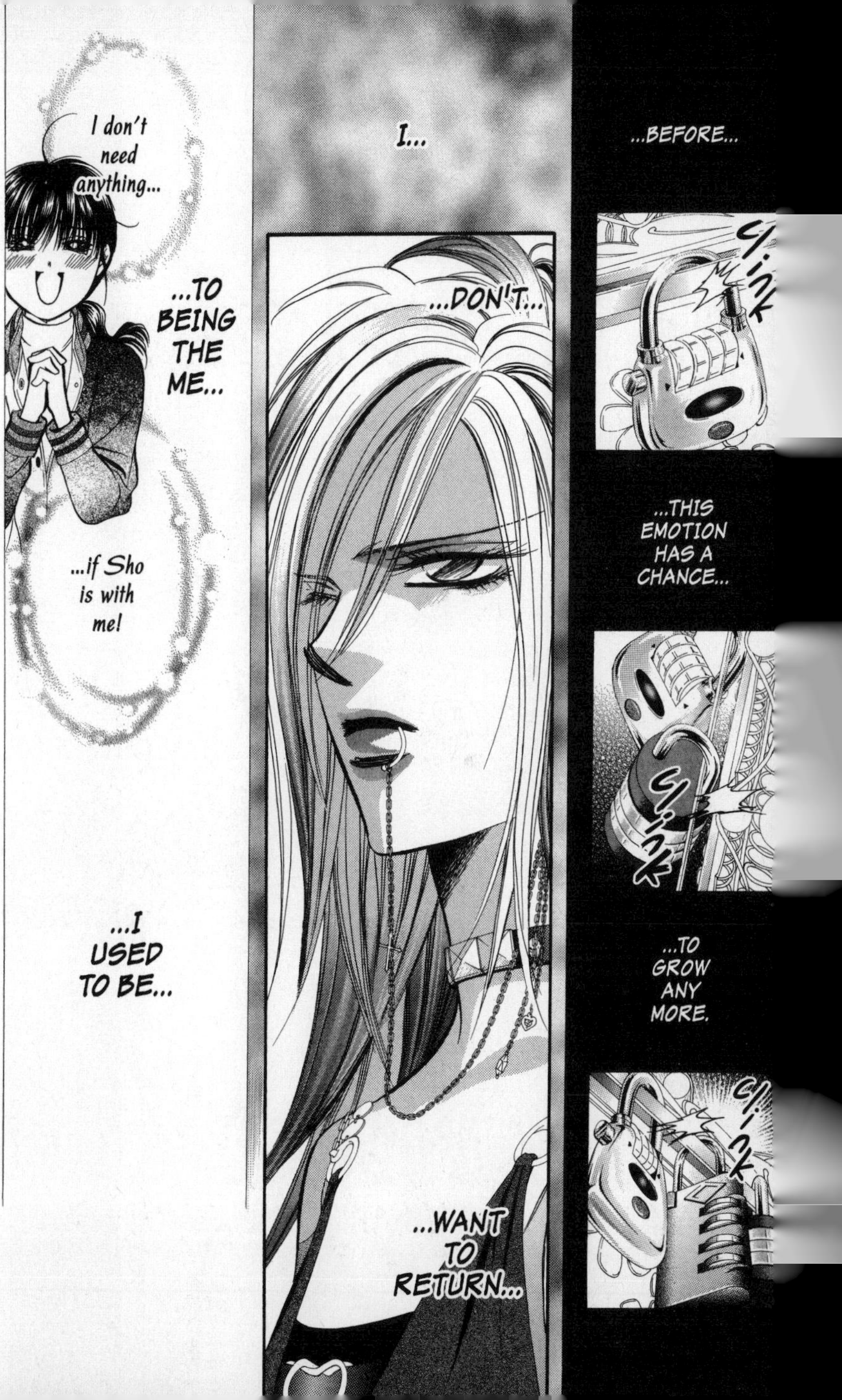
...BEFORE...
clink
...THIS EMOTION HAS A CHANCE...
clink
...TO GROW ANY MORE.
clink
I...
...DON'T...
...WANT TO RETURN...
I don't need anything...
...TO BEING THE ME...
...if Sho is with me!
...I USED TO BE...

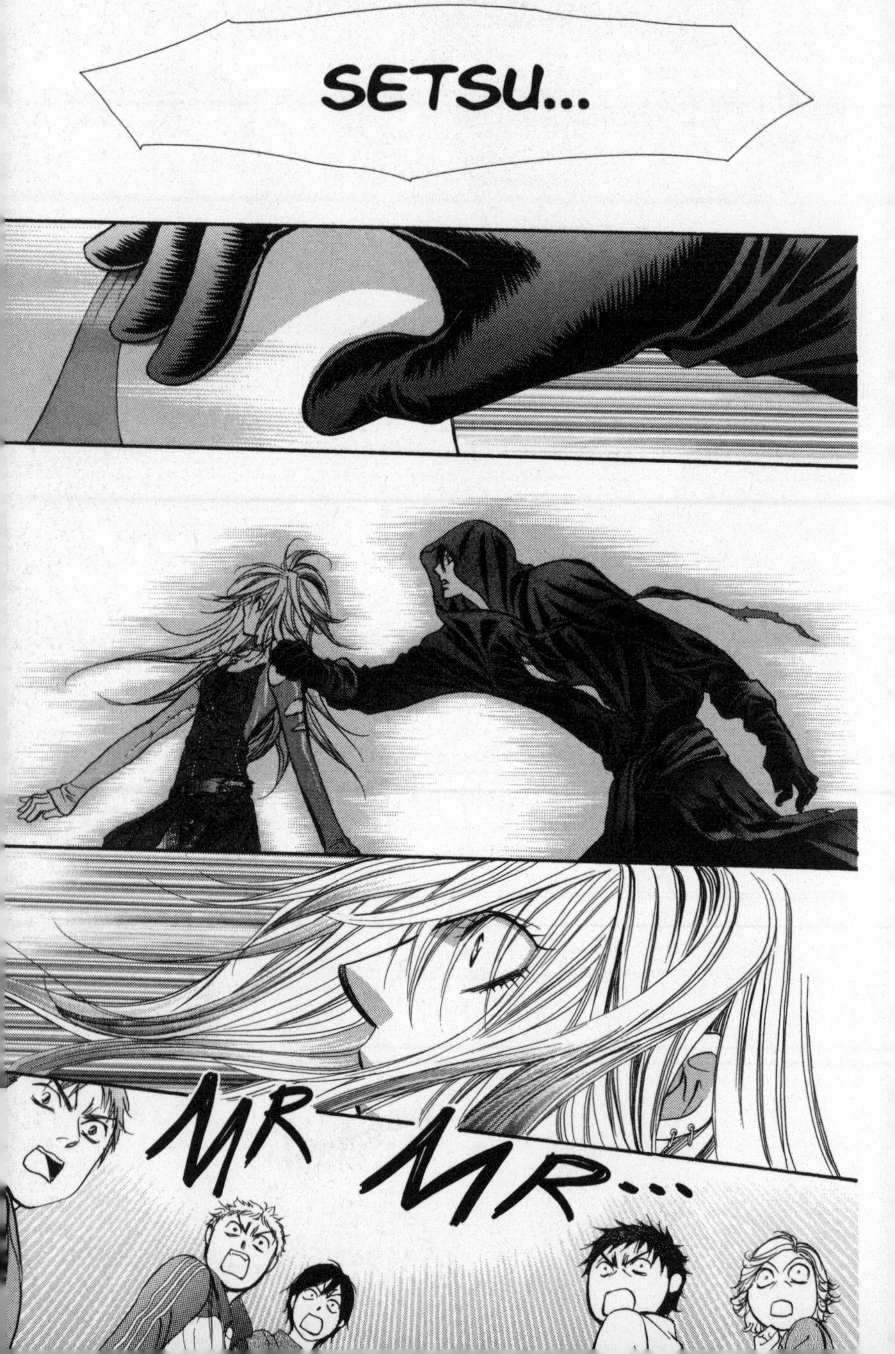
SETSU...
MR MR...

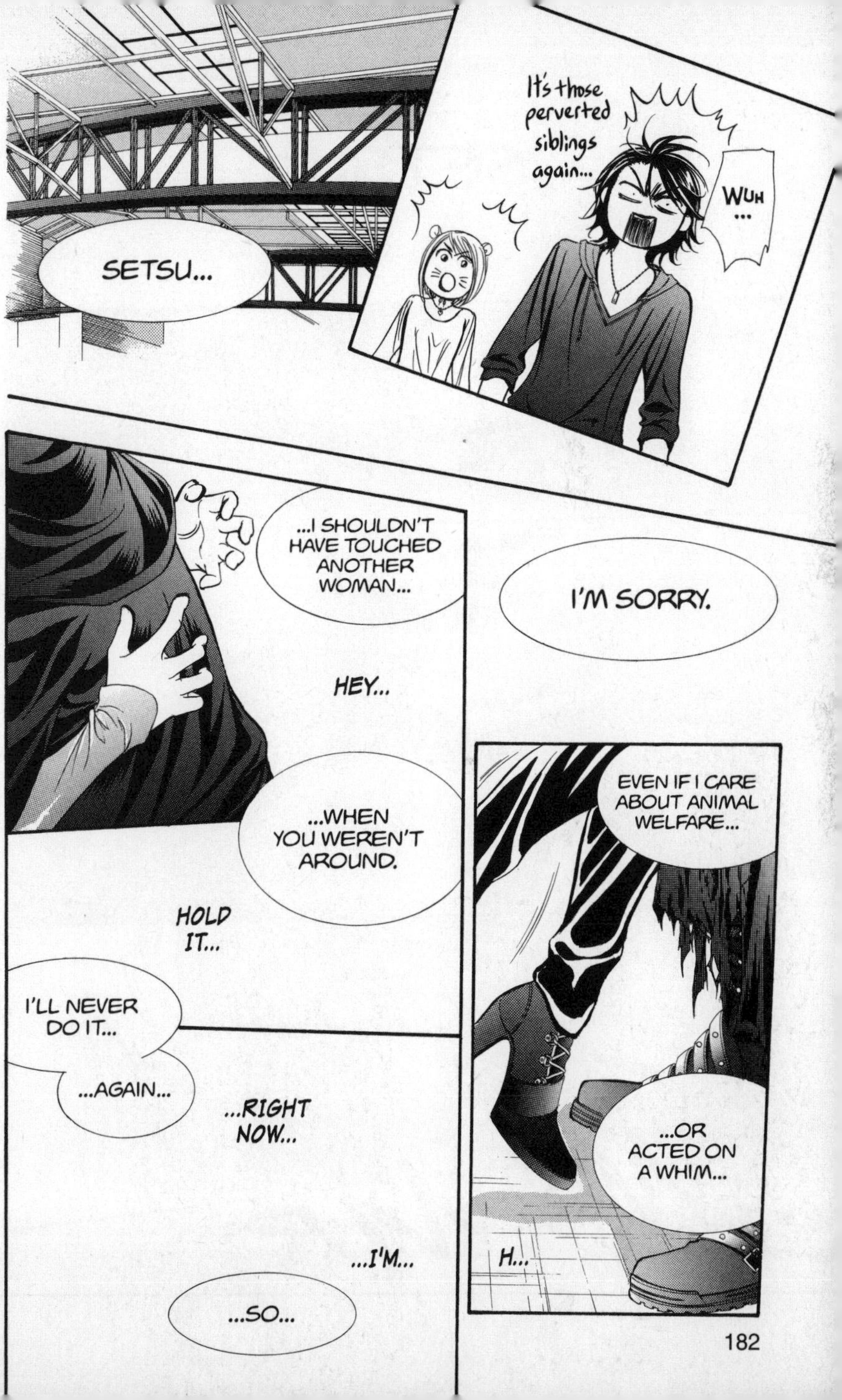
It's those perverted siblings again...
WUH...
SETSU...
I'M SORRY.
EVEN IF I CARE ABOUT ANIMAL WELFARE...
...OR ACTED ON A WHIM...
H...
...I SHOULDN'T HAVE TOUCHED ANOTHER WOMAN...
HEY...
...WHEN YOU WEREN'T AROUND.
HOLD IT...
I'LL NEVER DO IT...
...AGAIN...
...RIGHT NOW...
...I'M...
...SO...

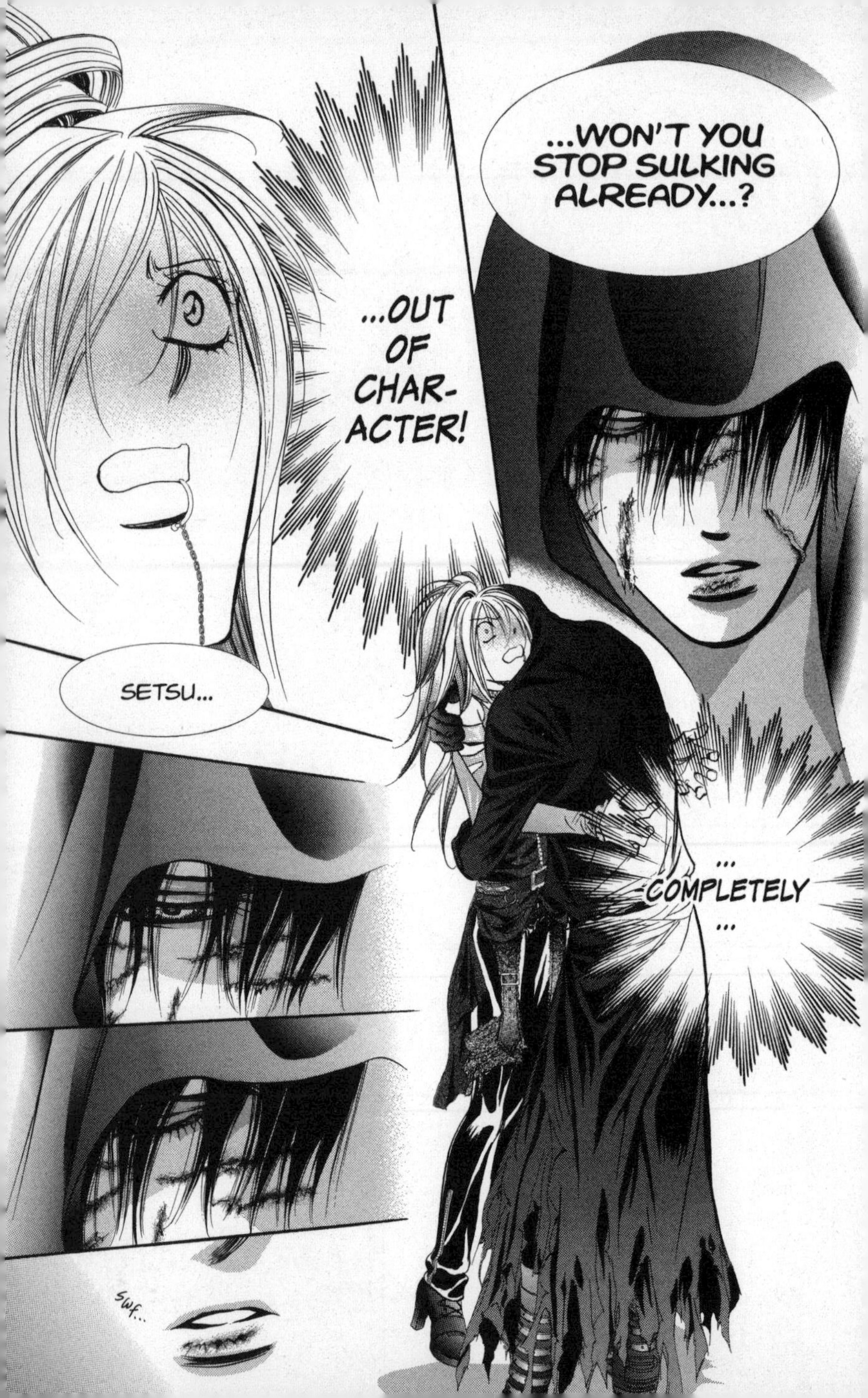
...WON'T YOU STOP SULKING ALREADY...?
...OUT OF CHAR-ACTER!
SETSU...
... COMPLETELY ...
SWF...

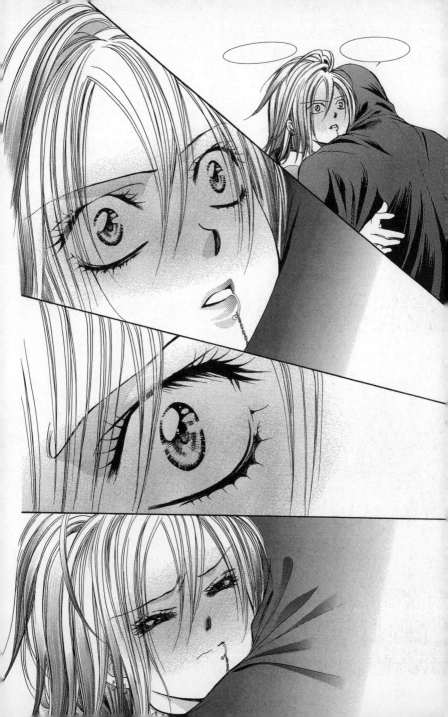

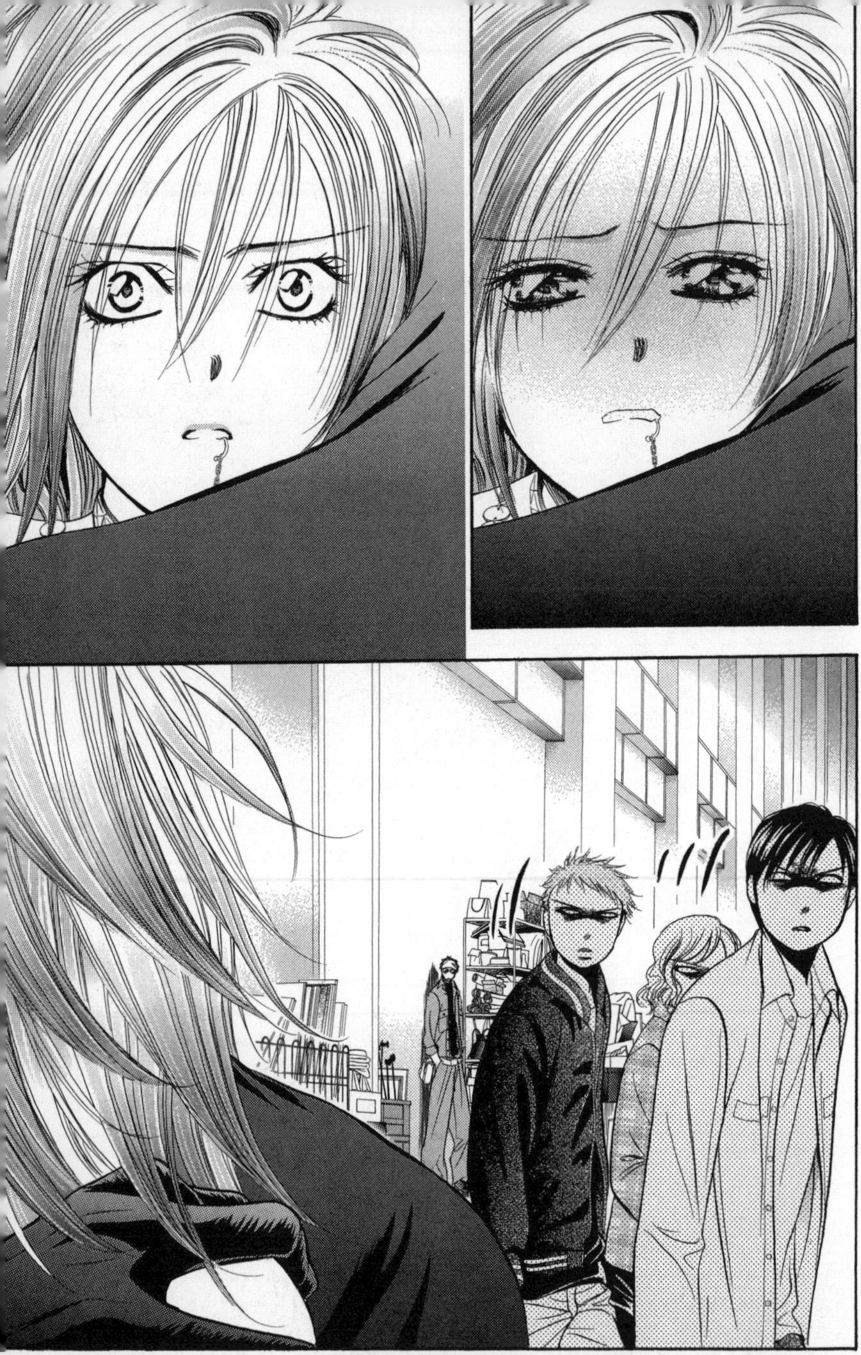

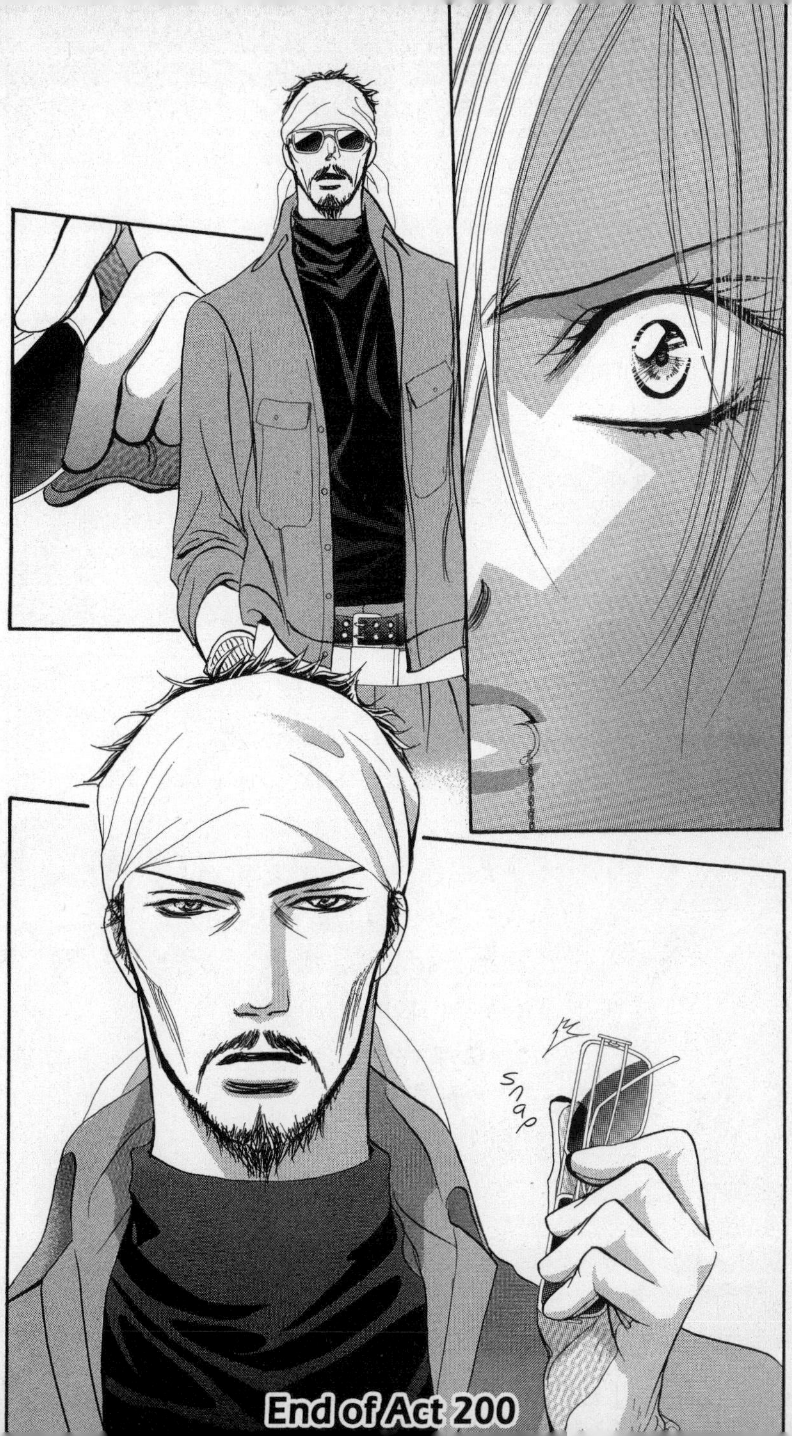
snap
End of Act 200

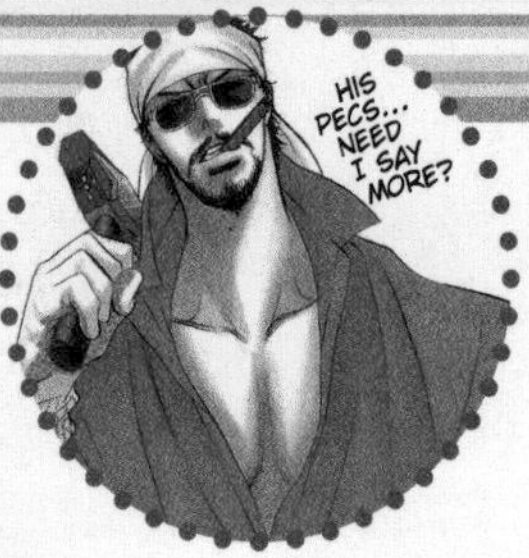
HIS PECS... NEED I SAY MORE?

Yoshiki Nakamura is originally from Tokushima Prefecture. She started drawing manga in elementary school, which eventually led to her 1993 debut of *Yume de Au yori Suteki* (Better than Seeing in a Dream) in *Hana to Yume* magazine. Her other works include the basketball series *Saint Love, MVP wa Yuzurenai* (Can't Give Up MVP), *Blue Wars* and *Tokyo Crazy Paradise*, a series about a female bodyguard in 2020 Tokyo.

Shojo Beat

SKIP·BEAT!

Vol. 33
Shojo Beat Edition

STORY AND ART BY YOSHIKI NAKAMURA

English Translation & Adaptation/Tomo Kimura
Touch-up Art & Lettering/Sabrina Heep
Design/Ronnie Casson
Editor/Pancha Diaz

Printed in the U.S.A.

Published by VIZ Media, LLC
P.O. Box 77010
San Francisco, CA 94107

www.viz.com www.shojobeat.com

10 9 8 7 6 5 4 3 2 1
First printing, September 2014

RATED T FOR TEEN

PARENTAL ADVISORY
SKIP·BEAT! is rated T for Teen and is recommended for ages 13 and up. This volume contains a grudge.

ratings.viz.com

SURPRISE!

You may be reading the wrong way!

It's true: In keeping with the original Japanese comic format, this book reads from right to left—so action, sound effects, and word balloons are completely reversed. This preserves the orientation of the original artwork—plus, it's fun! Check out the diagram shown here to get the hang of things, and then turn to the other side of the book to get started!

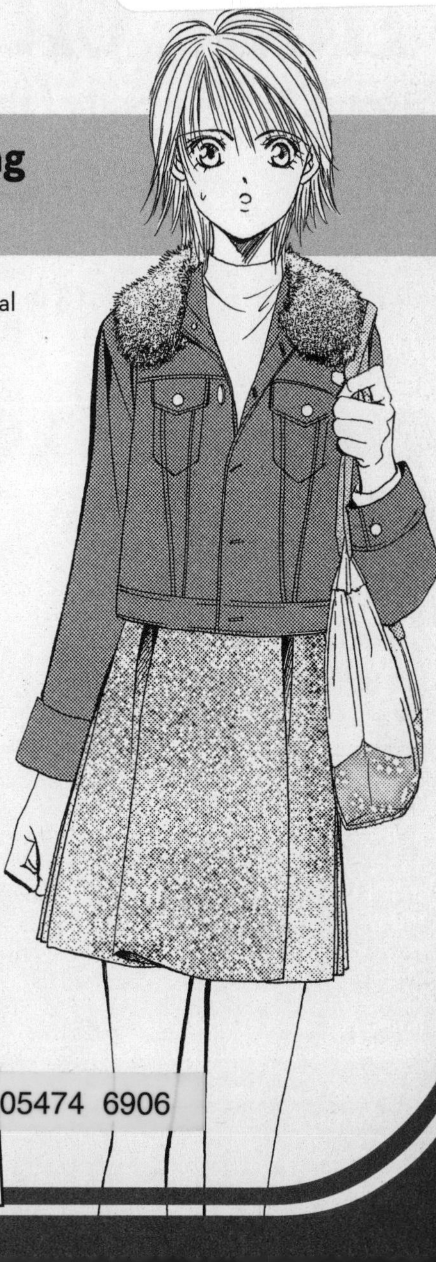

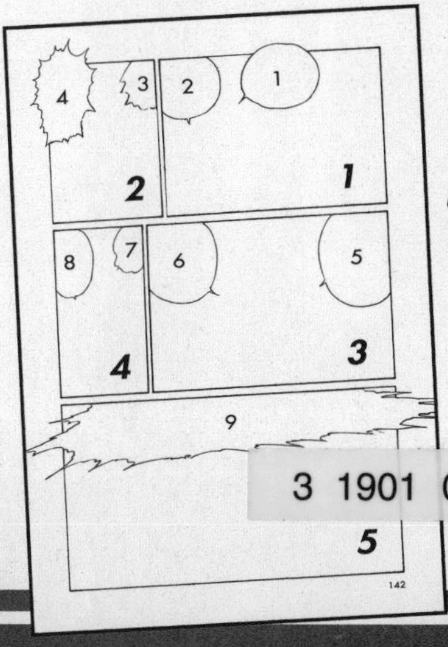
1
2
3
4
1
2
5
6
7
8
3
4
9
5
142